The Politics of Massacre

The Politics
of Massacre

Political Processes in
South Vietnam

Charles A. Joiner

TEMPLE UNIVERSITY PRESS
Philadelphia

Temple University Press, Philadelphia 19122
© 1974 by Temple University. All rights reserved
Published 1974
Printed in the United States of America

International Standard Book Number: 0-87722-060-3
Library of Congress Catalog Card Number: 72-95882

FOR DORIS, who has provided continual inspiration for my study of a nation whose citizens we both regard as intimate members of our extended family

Contents

Preface

THIS work is highly critical. There is no other word to describe more succinctly the theme running through all of the essays. It is critical of American foreign policy as that policy affects Vietnam and indeed all of Indochina. It is critical of the several governments of South Vietnam, whose behavior has often epitomized authoritarianism, inefficiency, corruption and lack of sympathy with their numerous constituencies. It is critical of the government of North Vietnam for its attempts to gain its objectives regardless of the sacrifices which Vietnamese must endure. Naturally, I hope that polemics do not dominate, yet the fact remains that such polemics are difficult to avoid. Although I have not focused upon the United States or North Vietnam, those two nations are involved up to their ears in the story of South Vietnam and inevitably enter into a discussion of political processes in South Vietnam. Polemics are also difficult to avoid when discussing the government of South Vietnam. A high proportion of the problems faced by residents of that embattled country must be attributed to governmental failures.

Regardless of whether a reader interprets a statement or a given thesis as being polemical, I have presented, in various guises, a definite personal position concerning a set of political issues. Perhaps it is often implicit when an explicit statement would be more appropriate. Explicitly, *each essay is an appeal for sympathy for the legitimate desires of the millions of residents of South Vietnam to be left alone to pursue their individual and national destinies. Each essay supports the right of South Vietnamese to determine the nature of their own political system through their own political behavior within their own political processes.* Nothing is more irrelevant to those processes than the views of any and all external sources of opinion and pressure. *Only the struggles among residents of South Vietnam over the nature of their own government and over the division of the products and services of their government are relevant.*

Despite the recurrently critical and polemical nature of the following statements, I have scored few villains in the classic sense. Most of the cast of characters have been foolish, but foolishness is not the standard characteristic of villainy. More accurately, most of the cast are in the classic tragic mold; they actually believed (or at least persuaded themselves that they believed) that their actions and decisions were undertaken for noble causes, for what they considered "right" reasons and "right" goals. The tragedy of Vietnam has been that every stage has had consequences enormously compounding the mistakes stemming from previous steps that were assumed to be correct. Each year's increment has expanded and deepened the errors. Immediate objectives and even stated long-range goals have changed as a given tactic has been discarded to the mounting garbage heap of failures. Succeeding goals have been rationalized in a framework of pretense that new objectives are consistent with prior ones.

The repercussions of those goals and the consequent actions have been felt by all participants in the struggle. But the brunt has been borne by residents of South Vietnam. This group of human beings has suffered first and foremost because they happened to stand in the way of what Hanoi and Washington considered an appropriate destiny. It has also been subjected to the atrocities of persons who qualify as villains in any sense—war profiteers, adventurers and the outlandishly corrupt. Suffering at the hands of the true believers has combined with suffering at the hands of the variously self-interested to produce fearful results. None of the parties involved can hope to escape the guilt that his role has brought upon him.

These essays are directly concerned with the internal political behavior of South Vietnam. Attempts to exert power by other nations are naturally considered, but only as they have affected South Vietnamese political processes. Analysis of the Indochina War is also included only to the extent that it relates to political processes. Unfortunately, external powers and the continuing war have directly influenced nearly all actions of the government of South Vietnam and in turn have at least indirectly been major factors in most political behavior. Despite the inevitability of discussing the policies of Washington and Hanoi, as well as revolutionary warfare and conventional warfare conducted on South Vietnam's soil, my central thesis is that those indeed are and always have been secondary to the major theater in South Vietnam. Of foremost importance to residents of South Vietnam is the subject of South Vietnamese politics.

It would be almost axiomatic to say that a nation's residents are concerned more about their own government and politics than they are about other topics—except the topic of their own survival. At least, most political observers would so assume for any other nation in the world. Residents of South Vietnam are not inhabitants of another planet somehow transplanted to a tiny nation in Southeast Asia, bringing with them types of behavior and a system of values which are unique among the world's nations. Residents of South Vietnam want to survive physically and psychologically. Like everyone else they have social and economic, personal and family goals. But they also have an intense interest in the questions of who is to receive what forms and quantities of goods and services from governmental actions, of who is to have political power over which objects and persons, and of who is to make decisions affecting their own lives. In South Vietnam, as in every other nation, the earthmen consider their own politics of considerable importance.

Decisions of local political power, while certainly often affected by or determined by the nature of revolutionary warfare, are more often than not determined by political processes that do not involve any warmaking machine. Devastating as the actual war was and continues to be, the image of warfare each and every day and night in every hamlet in South Vietnam is false. Not only are human beings incapable of psychologically surviving the presence of total war in their midst every waking hour, but there is no force on earth capable of sustaining such warfare hourly and simultaneously in thousands of hamlets over thousands of square miles. While no living individual may have escaped the effects of a war without front lines, the vast majority of residents have been mercifully spared the plight of unending physical encounter with the horrors of war.

For a majority of that majority, this is relatively small consolation for continued suffering, but respites from the actual presence of warfare meant that residents of South Vietnam, like all human beings, devoted a portion of attention and energy to things other than sheer survival. Questions of education, health, welfare, land distribution, economics, religion, social affairs, etc., are as important to them as to residents of other lands. To a great extent these are political questions, and their resolution is contingent upon political processes. Directly political questions such as representation in councils of government, a voice in determining local leadership, taxation, inflation, autonomy or semi-autonomy and protection for ethnic-religious-cultural group interests are also vital issues to nearly all residents of South Vietnam. Increasingly, primarily due to rural warfare, problems of urban congestion (housing, streets, water, etc.) became predominant subjects of political controversies. It is these political questions, involving allocation of resources, of structures of government, of who shall control public power, and of self-interest, which are paramount.

Who gets what, when, where and how are questions central to all political systems; South Vietnam's earthmen cannot escape this inevitable trait of social relationships even if they are so inclined. The important point is that they are not so inclined. It has always been folly to attempt to understand South Vietnam as though it were a quasi-vacuum, an apolitical set of human beings whose "politics" are a function of western or communist ideologies. It is the political processes of residents of South Vietnam and of those residents only that explain the failures or successes of external forces and ideologies struggling on South Vietnam's soil. The Indochina War has always been a political war. So-called revolutionary warfare made it inevitable that the war would be a political one, but revolutionary warfare is but one aspect of the political processes of South Vietnam.

Rather than being apolitical, South Vietnam is in fact one of the world's most politicized nations. The standard joke that two Vietnamese on a street corner constitute a political party, while three constitute a party and at least one faction, is more accurately descriptive than it is humorous. And what happens in a foreign state is at most of secondary importance to such a party or any of its factions. Who attains social, economic and political power is the topic of primary concern. The goals of external nations or groups are relevant only to the extent they may aid or hinder movement toward that primary ambition.

Each essay in this work stresses this one underlying principle, this one underlying explanation of the contemporary history of South Vietnam. As must any nation, South Vietnam must be considered on its own terms and from the perspective of its own residents and of its local and national leaders. Those residents have natural aspirations that can be met only through indigenous political processes. Comprehension of those political processes is the only avenue for understanding South Vietnam or the operational aspects predominant during the Indochina War.

Permission to reproduce eleven slightly revised essays included in Chapters 2, 4 and 5 was extended by the *Administrative Science Quarterly, Asian Survey, Current History,* the *Journal of Southeast Asian*

Studies, and *Vietnam Perspectives.* I wish to thank the editors of those journals and also my excellent co-authors for three of the essays, Guy H. Fox, John C. Donnell, and Roy Jumper, each of whom has made significant contributions to a better understanding of South Vietnam and of all of Indochina.

Abbreviations

ARVN	Army of the Republic of Vietnam
DRVN	Democratic Republic of Vietnam (North Vietnam)
GVN	Government of the Republic of Vietnam (South Vietnam)
NLF	National Liberation Front (South Vietnam)
PAVN	People's Army of Vietnam (North Vietnam)
PNM	Progressive Nationalist Movement
PRG	Provisional Revolutionary Government (South Vietnam)
PRP	People's Revolutionary Party
VC	Viet Cong, Viet Nam Cong San, Vietnamese Communist
VNQDD	Vietnam Quoc Dan Dang (Nationalist or Kuomintang Party)

The Politics of Massacre

1

South Vietnam's Political Actors and Political Constituencies

THE parameters of Vietnamese politics have never been clear, but the Vietnamese pattern of political behavior historically and currently is not inconsistent with similar patterns that characterize politics in much of the world. Many individuals have always contended for power. Certain interest groups (religious, regional, ethnic, economic) have always vied to protect themselves against encroachments upon their prerogatives initiated by other groups. Both Vietnams as well as Cambodia and Laos have, and have always had, political processes. This natural, inevitable phenomenon continues to exist.

Yet for various reasons the great powers of the earth and most of the giant audience of "Vietnam observers" have refused to accept this fact. Internal political behavior has been deemed either less than relevant or hypocritical. It has been as though a fish were belittled because it tries to swim. Indigenous political behavior is made an object of scorn in the press of the world, on the ubiquitous posters at rallies, and in erudite war or polemical journalism. Vietnamese politicians, political parties, interest groups and public policy makers are depicted as cartoon characters. The roles, goals and elements of constituencies of Vietnamese political forces are captured on television and in news photos and clever news items as the minor characters in a lesser Gilbert and Sullivan opera.

The Vietnamese have every intention of retaining their own scale of priorities even if those priorities may be considered backward by some, inconsistent with world trends as perceived by others, or secondary roadblocks to obscure aims of momentary social justice by still others. They would very much like to be left alone to make their own mistakes. As a community they are tough (they could not have survived

otherwise), highly cynical, and very human. Suddenly the entire world
has cast an eye upon them. It is difficult for most Vietnamese to at-
tribute their inexplicable notoriety to anything but an evil eye.

Asia, Africa, South America—the world is filled with nations whose
populations crave "modernization" (however they perceive that ambiguous concept) and political independence, but whose governments
have stumbled before the overwhelming loads they have assumed. Such
nations typically are unstable, their national boundaries are artificial,
their "citizenry" is heterogeneous and particularist, and their post-independence political-administrative systems are miles apart from their political history and from the internal divisions of true day-to-day influences. Patterns approaching universality cannot be dismissed as
peculiarly characteristic of a given nation simply because they are observed in that nation. But the many nations for which these patterns
hold are hardly household words throughout the world.

"Vietnam" is such an international word. Bad as many of the phe-
nomena associated with Vietnam are, judged by almost any objective
or subjective standard, most are hardly atypical. Corruption is a characteristic of most governments. Torture, indiscriminate slaughter of
innocent and guilty alike, rampant terrorism, political imprisonment, all
the evils of man toward man, are found in superabundance in Vietnam.
One night a Viet Cong troop might disembowel a victim at random, or an
especially popular public health worker, hanging a decapitated, castrated
corpse on a poisoned stake with the unrecognizable mutilated head of
the victim, testicles stuck in its mouth, beside the crucified object. The
following day government troops may return the favor in kind, picking
up a few chickens in the bargain. The unhappy "constituents" can vote,
realistically, only for a choice of horrors.

These are grotesque truisms, but still not unusual enough in man's
history to make a small nation an international word. The corruption,
kangaroo court justice, inhumanity and contempt for "world sensitivity"
are no more or less gross than innumerable examples around the globe.
Hundreds of thousands of persons can be eliminated in Indonesia without much attention in even the great international newspapers. Hangings
of political opponents en masse can occur in Iraq or Guinea without
those nations becoming symbols of iniquity for school children. Poland,
Hungary and Czechoslovakia can be brutally brought to heel by force
of imperialist arms, and their cause can be soon forgotten. A world can
turn its back while a solution is found to the "Jewish problem," or while
Palestinians in the hundreds of thousands are rendered homeless or are
subject to the whims of suppressive rulers in "brother" states. Through-

out the world governments are incompetent and cruel, populations are backward, politicians are corrupt, and the antithesis of statesmanlike, groups discriminate against other groups, and states accept outside help while as often as not playing one gargantuan sugar daddy off against one or more of his sugar daddy opponents.

Few "underdeveloped" nations have escaped insurgencies. Few have not witnessed the intrusion into local political feuds of materials donated by a generous "other side" for making insurgency possible. Few have not had military encounters—on however small a scale—with their neighbors over artificial, ill-defined boundaries or suzerainty over a minority group that may be akin to the majority group of the neighboring state. It is as easy for an external power to aid the forces of insurgency as it is to aid the forces of counterinsurgency. But only Vietnam has gained the distinction of being brought before the tribunal of world censure.

American military forces were assigned there on an ill-defined, ambiguous mission brought about by the miscalculations of the most sophisticated war machine in history. A war was fought, a brutal war with no splendid, defined battlefields. Many, many died, the innocent particularly feeling the brunt of impersonal, "modern" warfare. Sophisticated sociopsychological weapons faced sophisticated technological weapons. It was a televised war. And the great powers might have escalated the encounter into World War III. It attracted the reporters in droves.

Where were the Vietnamese in this mélange of terror? They suffered, first, last and most. Their political figures were portrayed as clowns. Their demands were considered as dysfunctional to the war experts' notions of saving them from "communism" or from the "imperialists and their lackeys." All sides destroyed them in order to save them—not just an obscure, much-quoted, junior American officer. Needless to say, most Vietnamese are tired of being saved. They are exhausted from being saved from communism and from imperialism. In South Vietnam they are quite prepared not to be saved by colonialism, neocolonialism, assistance from "fraternal brother nations," or assistance from the "free world." They would much prefer not to have fighting men from Hanoi, Cleveland, Bangkok or Seoul disputing over their real estate.

Paramount in the tragedy is that the views of residents of South Vietnam were never solicited on the world's major political issue. Critics of the Vietnamese or Indochina War have placed emphasis upon American foreign policy and military policy follies. Often these critics have also stressed the popularity of North Vietnamese appeals to all Vietnamese, assuming that residents of the South are being forced to accept an alternative to the Hanoi government against their will. Supporters of the militarization programs have stressed the threat of international communism to the freedom-loving residents of the South, assuming that those residents would rather be dead than red. Both explanations sound plausible to advocates of particular policies. It would be unfair to assume that they have motives other than to interpolate legitimate personal values into the political process of a small state in Southeast Asia; and, of course, to reinterpolate to the politics of domestic public policies in Washington, Bangkok, Paris, London, Moscow, Peking. But whatever the rationale for the Vietnamese war was, it definitely was not, *as far as residents of South Vietnam were concerned,* an excuse for any foreign government or its domestic opponents or supporters to advance domestic policies.

The only legitimate question that can be raised in this connection is whether or not the Democratic Republic of Vietnam (North Vietnam) is truly a foreign government. Extremely penetrating analyses of the Geneva Conference of 1954 terminating the First Indochina War have raised more questions than they have answered pertaining to the status of the two Vietnams in international law. On the one hand, elections were not held in 1956. The question to have been voted upon in such a referendum is not clear; presumably it would have related to whether there should be one or two Vietnams. Whether there would have been a second or even a third election on questions of a national constitution and of national officers is even less clear. On the other hand, did the French indeed have the legal right to negotiate a political settlement without the approval of the government of Bao Dai, a government recognized as the lawful regime for all of Vietnam by numerous nations? There is presumably no doubt that the French could entertain negotiations for a resolution of hostilities between French forces and Viet Minh forces.

The leaders of the Republic of Vietnam (South Vietnam) have always claimed that their government was deprived of its northern half without its consent. The leaders of the Democratic Republic of Vietnam (DRVN) have claimed with equal consistency that they had represented the lawful government since 1945 and that the political settlement which they signed was understood to involve only a temporary division of the entire country. Regardless of one's interpretation of the Geneva Agreement, the political issue remains one of direct concern only to Vietnamese. Realpolitik in Washington, Paris, Peking or Moscow notwithstanding, from a Vietnamese perspective the only valid topic at issue is a question of Vietnamese political processes. Any active role by any capital other than Hanoi and Saigon can be regarded by them only as a flagrant violation of the sovereignty and independence of their nation or nations.

Of course, this perspective does not resolve the question of whether Hanoi represents a foreign power infringing upon the rights of residents of South Vietnam. This is a much more complex problem, even when omitting discussion of implications of international law vis-à-vis the Geneva Agreement. There have been no referenda on this question. In fact, there has never been a real referendum on the question of what is Vietnam. The highlands and much of the now heavily populated far south had not been historically under the true control of any Vietnamese precolonial government. Many of the residents of both Vietnams are not Vietnamese. The territory of what is now Vietnam was long divided between rival powers along coastal lines not too dissimilar from the 1954 partition lines. Central and southern Vietnam were never prepared to accept rule by northerners.

In fact, one of the inherent political weaknesses of the various governments of South Vietnam has been the presence of native-born northerners in positions of authority. Yet something under one million current residents of South Vietnam are northerners, refugees fleeing DRVN jurisdiction prior to partition. Now this is the real stuff of politics: divergent claims to power affected by perceived regional interests. Naturally, regional claims are but one fabric of the political processes of South Vietnam. Also to be considered are diverse religious differences, ethnic demands for increased autonomy or at least elimination of varied forms of discrimination, village and city demands for material resources and the authority to administer usage of those resources, standard economic struggles between commercial interests and organized labor as well as agriculturalist-distributor-consumer demands, landlord-tenant claims, political demands of the intelligentsia, and the pressures of civil service and military personnel.

Above all there are political personalities, claiming to represent the interests of well- or ill-defined constituencies, through virtue of their positions in the legislative system, in organized interest groups, in political parties, in secret societies, or simply on their own. Many of these personalities can make legitimate claims to representing their constituencies while others cannot. What is important is that these are political personalities, practicing the art of politics within the political system of South Vietnam. They may or may not be affiliated with a given regime at a given point in time. They may be acting politically within the legal framework for political processes under the Constitution of the Republic of Vietnam. Or they may be performing their political role outside that framework, either simply in a clandestine fashion or from the maquis. Whatever their actual role is, they are not clowns.

Whether their persons or programs are applauded or condemned in Hanoi, Washington or Peking is irrelevant. Almost without exception these political personalities, political parties and interests do not want South Vietnam to come under the control of North Vietnam. For some this would represent regional enslavement. For others it would preclude them from ever attaining their political objectives. For still others it would represent the Götterdämmerung: those who fled the North would feel they had done so in vain; those who fought against the opponents of the Saigon regime feel they would be in physical and other danger. Many fear, rightly or wrongly, that a policy of genocide would deplete their numbers.

The possibility of a unification of the two Vietnams resulting in other than northern domination is not one seriously considered by the South's political personalities, interests and parties. There is, of course, one interest group in the South whose leadership and rank and file do not dismiss such a possibility. The National Liberation Front (NLF), Provisional Government of South Vietnam, Peoples' Revolutionary Party, i.e., the so-called Viet Cong, make certain political assumptions. First, the government of the Republic of Vietnam, presumably regardless of its composition unless there are NLF representatives in that government, must be superseded. Second, the unification of the two Vietnams probably will come about in time through appropriate procedures. Third, whether there is or is not a unification, there will not be complete domination of all Vietnam by northerners or by representatives sent from Hanoi.

One of the most debated subjects of the Vietnam conflict has been the independence exercised by the Viet Cong (presumably a southern force) vis-à-vis Hanoi. Although Hanoi has claimed rightful authority over both Vietnams, it has always claimed that the Viet Cong was a completely indigenous southern movement. Regardless of the way this claim increasingly became a fiction after full-fledged American intervention in 1965 and especially after the 1968 Tet offensive, the origin of the NLF and the exact nature of the role of the DRVN throughout the insurgency apparatus to date remain shrouded in a certain mystery despite the efforts of numerous very keen observers. The DRVN's stated position in effect has been that it is formally a foreign power, however provisional that status might be, and that its goal is for a particular coalition (the NLF), which represents the "legitimate aspirations" of the residents of the South, to gain effective control of the Saigon government. Afterwards, as in the NLF platform, there would be appropriate discussions about possible unification procedures. Neither the stated position of the NLF nor that of Hanoi proclaims that there definitely must be a reunification of the two Vietnams.

To the extent that the NLF is a grouping of residents of South Vietnam, an organization of political personalities, interests and parties (it does consist of several announced political parties) competing in the political processes of the South over public positions, policies, and power, it must be considered a political movement pursuing power goals within an indigenous political milieu in the same sense as the so-called nationalist parties and personalities. The NLF political personalities are also certainly not clowns.

Obviously, the operational definition, that the indigenous forces competing over political goals within the South include only residents of South Vietnam, has inherent ambiguities. Just as there are many adherents of the Republic (GVN) and of various "legal" political parties who were born in the North, there are adherents of the NLF who have long been resident in the South but were originally from the North. A person normally resident in Hanoi, who is employed on the payroll of the DRVN, cannot be considered a resident of the South, any more than a person normally resident in St. Louis who is employed on the payroll of the United States can be so considered. But the Hanoi resident will be as Vietnamese as a resident of Saigon is, just as residents of East and West Germany are Germans and residents of North and South Korea are Koreans.

However, race or even "nationality" are not the relevant criteria. The genuine resident of the DRVN, the northerner, is an "outsider." He would be so considered in the South even if the two Vietnams were united formally and legally. To a southerner the presence of large numbers of northerners who have volunteered to reside in the South, with or without persuasion by the Catholic bishops of Tonkin or by other interest groups, presents a perceived threat to his presumptions to influence a political system with a division of power he deems proper. When large numbers of northerners have been sent by the legitimate government of the North with the explicit goal of effecting a change in the political system in the South, the danger sensed by the southerner is augmented by geometric proportions. By no definition is such an action by an "outside" (if not necessarily "foreign") power an aspect of truly indigenous political processes. It is inconceivable that the bona fide southern residents who are adherents of the NLF are not consciously perturbed by the phenomenon of "outside" interference in all phases of their political strategies and military tactics directed toward assuming control over the southern political system. Whatever goals southerners within the NLF have, domination by northerners can hardly be among them.

Indeed, somewhere along the line everything did become confused. South Vietnam at the very least must be considered as having a de facto government. As such it has its own political system. The Republic of Vietnam has a constitution, a legislature, a president and vice president, a national cabinet and a prime minister, a judiciary, a national administrative apparatus, a series of provincial-district-village-hamlet governments, and a national military force. It would be as difficult to find a definition of "government" that would deny such a political system de jure status, as to exclude the Democratic Republic of Vietnam from such a legal status.

South Vietnam has held national, provincial, village and hamlet elections, an undeniable form of political process regardless of valid criticisms that might be made concerning the procedures of this particular aspect of South Vietnamese political behavior. South Vietnam's legislators unquestionably are political personalities who do represent certain constituencies and who have served as supporters or critics of political system variables. The judiciary is weak, but it does represent a force in public policy implementation. South Vietnam has political parties, numerous and constantly involved in what can only be termed political processes.

There also are numerous organized interest groups—unions, chambers of commerce, farmers' associations, retired officers' associations, youth groups, Confucianist studies associations, et al.—that compete in a political arena in an attempt to influence public policies affecting their constituencies. Religious groups are adamantly active political (sometimes even administrative and military) forces. The civil service, the elected local councils, and the military bureaucracy represent potent interests involved in political processes at different levels of the system. Many of these forces may be ineffectively organized, many represent very small constituencies, and many are based upon one or a few political personalities rather than on carefully articulated policy platforms. But all of them are party to an intricate, often sophisticated and subtle, and seemingly omnipresent political process.

Finally, the NLF, while remaining beyond the pale of the formal political system of the Republic of Vietnam, is a political force of vast significance operating as part of the total political process of South Vietnam. Unlike most other political forces its primary goal is not simply to replace current power holders (or obviously preserve power positions) or to influence public policies. The goal of the NLF is to replace the formal political system with another political system more to its liking. But, again, to the extent that the NLF is an indigenous force it is but one of many political interest groups whose focus of attention is South Vietnam. As such, the NLF, just as the Dai Viet Party or the Vietnam Nationalist Party, for example, is an element of the southern political process.

Why and how did everything become confused? A small nation in Southeast Asia has numerous groups that are competing over political power. Most of those groups want to gain power by obtaining national and local executive, legislative, judicial and administrative positions which are structural levels of the formal political system. Most of these groups function and compete within the framework established by the political system. Some have quasi-military forces to bolster their group position; most do not. Some have actually served as at least de facto governments in certain villages or larger areas where their constituents are predominant; most have not.

Still others, notably the NLF, have operated outside the framework of the formal political system. These groups have played the revolutionary role. They have followed an historically time-honored tactic of many Vietnamese political opposition groups. They have occupied the maquis. They have militarily attacked the formal political system whenever it appeared vulnerable. They have attempted to disrupt the operations of the administrative system, to eliminate supporters of the government whenever possible, and to destroy both governmental effectiveness and the legitimacy (as perceived by the population) of the government's claim to govern.

None of this represents something unique in a political force's attempts to assume political power. Few revolutionary parties can pretend to emulate the efficiency of the NLF (and the Viet Minh) as a revolutionary force. The tactic of the "organizational weapon," the expertise in population control, the training, tactics and strategy adopted for its war-making machine, and its constant priority for political over military objectives—these have made the NLF a most formidable opponent for its foe, the formal political system. Still, the NLF is only *more efficient* than its peer organizations in other nations. It is not different in kind from elements present in the political processes in those nations. In brief, NLF efficiency, appeal and prowess are not the reason for Vietnam's notoriety.

Thus, the confusion over South Vietnam has not been a function of legal conflict over provisions of the Geneva Agreement, or over the absence of a political system for the South, or over the existence of a strong revolutionary party. Nor has this nation been singled out because of the nature of its governmental operations. Dictatorships, military or otherwise, are hardly new. Corruption, inefficiency and incompetence are not unique state characteristics. The horrors of war, including the reversion to savage disrespect for the worth of human life, have always been unstated aspects of military struggle. Even the horrors of systematic terrorism or systematic application of overkill gadgetry have ample parallel.

Every ingredient of military and governmental folly can be witnessed in the long Vietnam-Indochina war. There are no excuses permissible in the court of natural or human justice for the atrocities committed by all formal sides to the conflict. It is baseless to claim that another side committed the atrocity first. It is false egoism to cry that the ends of a political philosophy or utopian system, whichever it be, are in any shape or form a justification for the human misery, social upheaval and profound devastation forced upon one small nation.

Those who believe that mankind remains brutish and self-serving, a cosmic joke, unquestionably find in Vietnam their prime example. But this is not enough to explain the attention. It is the first televised war. Indonesia and Biafra hardly received universal attention, although their dramas were staged during the television era. The horrors have been compounded during the Second Indochina War, but they were devastating enough during the First Indochina War, when outside of France the encounter was basically ignored by the world's populations.

Of course, the answer is the American presence. Suddenly everything was blown up to Texas-style proportions. More, bigger, better war-making machinery. Every over-sin was good press. Lavish amounts of money intensified corruption. Bigger bombs killed more people (innocent and targets alike). Bullyism, racism, "neocolonialism"—each added to the insult. An American army did not travel light, but with massive machinery, giant logistical organizations, offshore hospitals, and volumes of money. Each successive year, the previous year's appraisals and budgets were increased. Money, ingenuity, hard work could resolve anything. For once, the combination failed.

From the failure and from the internal inconsistencies permeating the entire futile endeavor, an alienated generation and a newly articulate, deprived socioeconomic sector found the Achilles heel of the world's most materially advanced nation. These groups struck; simultaneously and almost spontaneously significant numbers in nearly every nation spoke out. The giant had misinterpreted; he learnt that he who can afford to wear the coat of many colors should not expect to be loved. The potential for big power rivalry also set off widespread fear, some feigned but much real. All sides intervened directly or indirectly. All of Indochina watched while their historic northern neighbor took steps to attain long-range objectives by proxy. And to much of the world the theme of the war was clearcut. America had geopolitical interests. It had a puppet in Saigon. The puppet had to be a sham. The system had to be one imposed by the new neocolonialism against the will of the oppressed population. To many it appeared that the South Vietnamese were being blocked in their attempts to welcome northern domination.

The thesis, of course, was not completely invalid. Examples of American king-making attempts were numerous enough. Boors from across the Pacific had obviously lorded it over their oriental compatriots, and clearly viewed Vietnamese life as of little importance. Still, if there has ever been a case study of a tail wagging a dog, it has been the Saigon-Washington relationship. Beginning with Ngo Dinh Diem, the politicians of South Vietnam outfoxed, blackmailed and cajoled the Americans into an increasingly untenable domestic political posture. If there are clowns in the tragic scenario, they are more likely to be found in Washington than in Saigon or in the provinces of South Vietnam.

Throughout the succeeding acts political process in South Vietnam has continued relatively unabated. Political personalities, interest groups and parties have continued without stopping to catch their breath to struggle over who gets what, when and how. Most groups have had setbacks. The NLF has never lost sight of the fact that their only real opposition lies in the interest groups of South Vietnam. Nor has any Saigon regime overlooked the potential clout of the constituencies those interest groups represent. Their sheer variety and their continued incapacity to form even temporary coalitions while momentarily compromising even a few of their immediate objectives has had a devastating effect upon Vietnamese politics. It has been this incapacity that has permitted the Viet Minh, the NLF, and also the regimes governing the Republic of Vietnam to gain the victories they have attained over their opposition. To ignore these political factors is to misread what South Vietnam is all about.

It is a mistake that has been common in American foreign policy.

Underestimation of those factors led Hanoi to undertake the 1968 Tet offensive—an order of the day resulting in devastation to a previously brilliant plan of replacing the South Vietnamese political system. It was this underestimation, and not allied firepower, that led to destruction of much of the NLF's formidable infrastructure. The residents of South Vietnam survived the holocaust to support their parochial, chauvinistic interest groups for the forthcoming decade. Neither the Washington nor the Hanoi strategists had foreseen the obvious. The sea of the people of South Vietnam is no sea at all, but many separate bodies of water, too many to acquiesce readily even in their own political processes—let alone to the interests that ignore those processes.

2

Political Behavior
Vietnamese Style

Introduction

Primary among the characteristics of political behavior in South Vietnam is the impact of centrifugal forces. The diversity of interest groups, their sheer number, their relationship to cultural and economic variables, their significance in political socialization and even in personality development, and the unending effect which they have in reinforcing differences among Vietnamese—these factors have been of considerably more influence in determining the style and content of political behavior than have such important topics as war, peace and colonialism. Religious, regional and ethnic interests have permeated all social, political, economic and governmental activities. They have penetrated even the military of both North and South Vietnam. Public administration, elections, national legislatures and local councils, courts, education, formal pressure groups and political parties—each has been intricately a part of the political processes of South Vietnam and each has been enmeshed in the politics of centrifugal interest groups.

These groups have remained the same over the years. Catholic–Mahayana and Theravada Buddhist–Confucianist–Hoa Hao–Cao Dai: each religious group claims the right to represent and at least somewhat control the political interests of its constituents. Each also demands a prominent part in local and national administration and public policy formulation. But each religious group is invariably less than autonomous in any sphere of influence it might claim due to a series of further interest group overlays which augment even further the diversity of claimants to political power in South Vietnam. Confucianist–Taoist–Animist overlays permeate and divide all major religions. The result is that there is no majority religion; in effect, no group, not even a religious one, can justifiably ever pretend to be more than an influential minority. Regional overlays (northern, centrist, southern) and the issue of lay vs. clerical leaderships divide even the major Buddhist and Catholic religions into relatively small minorities. Ethnic groups, also severely divided by regional and cultural factors—Chinese, Cambodians, Indians, Chams and the large variety of highland tribes—represent still additional interests which preclude the building of any majority bloc.

The essays in Chapter 2 describe the political behavior of these numerous minorities in South Vietnam. Their struggles over public positions (elective and appointive), over general public policies, over policies providing special treatment for given interest groups, and over relationships with North Vietnam and with the National Liberation Front comprise the framework for much of the nation's political conflict. The NLF, also subject to regional and other schisms, is yet another relevant overlay. Individual political personalities and formal pressure groups also are identifiable at least partially in terms of their roles within the matrix of competing religious, regional and ethnic groups.

Since the fall of Ngo Dinh Diem in 1963, numerous new personalities have come to the political forefront. Many of the newer figures have been associated with the military. Probably most of the individuals who have been active in politics are, however, persons who were also active prior to 1963. Among the prominent figures who have had a pronounced impact upon political processes there is a significant percentage who were important in the politics of the 1950's and even the 1940's. In fact, one of the intriguing aspects of Vietnamese politics is the political biographies of its leaders, often persons who have fought or were associated with the French, the Japanese, the Viet Minh, and the Diem government and all subsequent governments. Many of these leaders have life histories much more exciting than even the most romantic novels.

What has been eternal about their personal stories has also been a characteristic that has undermined the viability of South Vietnam's political system. They have never closed ranks for any cause. Individualistic, suspicious and cynical, they have not joined forces against any common adversary. They have carried this attitude over into public administration, national assemblies, local governments, the national executive office and the military. It has been pervasive among the leaders of all religious groups and of nearly all political parties. Diem came closest to establishing a set of national policies implemented by a national government. But in the process he so alienated the diverse interest groups and political personalities as to make his position untenable long before 1963.

Since 1963 all interest groups and political personalities in South Vietnam have operated in a milieu that lacked strong central leadership. President Nguyen Van Thieu has attained a certain stature as first among equals and has been more clearly in charge of the national administration than any leader since Diem. But despite his autocratic tendencies, Thieu has neither brought contending forces together nor has he established a political structure to rise above the host of competing minority structures. Diem did try to create political institutions which would bring about the integration of the numerous elites, and he failed dismally to establish anything but a Potemkin facade. Thieu has used the government and the military to extend his political control, to assist in his first campaign for the presidency and to guarantee his reelection. These attempts by Thieu have maintained him in power but have had even less effect than Diem's measures in bringing about central political control.

Thieu has also been unsuccessful in furthering political integration. This has occurred more through National Assembly elections and operations and through village council elections than through Thieu's efforts. These elections, assemblies and councils have certainly not lessened the influence of centrifugal forces, and in many ways they have strengthened those forces. Still, the major shift which has occurred since 1963 has been related to broadened electoral processes. Although elections have ratified claims of interest groups to strength among their constituencies, relatively they have also somewhat aided the growth of a political party system and of political linkages between the capital and the villages. In the abstract this development has a potential for dramatically changing the political processes of South Vietnam.

Elections have not eliminated clandestinism but they have forced political party leaders to construct organizations for communications, coordination and visibility to electorates. They have not succeeded in such organization-building attempts, but they have laid the groundwork for combining interest groups at least for the purpose of influencing specific elections. Whether such cooperation actually will occur is doubtful. It is, however, extremely important for future national elections, and would be a matter of vital concern to all nationalist parties if the National Liberation Front should enter the political arena as an electoral competitor. The nationalists still retain the support of an unquestioned majority among residents of South Vietnam. But it is unlikely that any of the political parties or religious political groups (with the possible exception of the militant Buddhists) could obtain a plurality of votes in a multi-party national contest in which the NLF is one of the contestants. In nearly all provinces a given political party could outpoll the NLF, but many different parties would be likely to receive pluralities and even majorities in different provinces.

The most important, purely political problem for South Vietnam thus continues to be what it has always been. Only some coalition of diversified interest groups can constitute any form of national majority. Only some coordinated combination of minorities can provide generally accepted legitimacy for the national political system. In the absence of such a coalition, existing political forces cannot escape subordination to a strong executive and perhaps to the military leadership as well, regardless of formal constitutional provisions for electoral processes, political party development, national government separation of powers, and decentralization of governmental powers and functions to elected provincial and village leaders.

This problem has invariably been a circular one in South Vietnam's politics. Because political factions have been so divided, they have not been able to hold a strong executive in check and to establish a national representative government. Because the executive has been paramount the various political groups have been unable to gain access to public-policy-making positions. Where they have gained such access it has been locally, where one group could claim supremacy over others. Political behavior South Vietnamese style is really the politics of a weak confederation. Perhaps culturally this has thus far been inevitable. Pragmatically it has been near suicidal in times of revolutionary and conventional warfare. The potential for a change has existed for several years, although the possibilities for establishing a majority consisting of minorities were thwarted by Thieu's actions. The groundwork which has been laid through electoral and legislative and council politics may still be enlarged upon and political party activities, especially if combining nationalist-Buddhist-labor interests, could still provide for increased national integration and for political system linkage with the various interest groups. At the most optimistic, however, one would be foolish to assume that even such combinations, leading to development of two or three major parties that might or might not include the NLF, would result in anything more than a shift in South Vietnam from confederation politics to weak federation politics.

Patterns of Political Party Behavior in South Vietnam

■ A number of new political parties have been formed since this essay was written. More accurately, existing parties have splintered into even more subdivisions than listed here. One of the splinter groups, the Progressive Nationalist Movement (PNM), has adopted Dai Viet principles permitting it to encourage responsible democracy and constructive loyal opposition.[1] Or so its advocates perceive their role. The militant Buddhists have entered into electoral processes and have established an important party—though not terming it to be such—which has become particularly significant in central Vietnam. Village elections have to some extent given a few political parties a new lease on life. All major parties have won elections for village council positions, and because of this all can claim a local base rather than simply big city offices. Stronger organizationally, more experienced in campaigning for local, regional and national legislative offices, a number of South Vietnamese parties undoubtedly have gained in maturity during the last several years. Those parties which have won local elections have gained some practical administrative experience. Those which have elected representatives to the Senate and Lower House have practiced a representative and public policy role denied them previously. In all probability, opposition for opposition's sake, so long a standard Vietnamese political practice, has slightly lessened. A few parties, especially factions of the Dai Viet, have even exercised administrative responsibilities at the national level.

None of these developments should be taken to indicate that South Vietnam has established a responsible party system in the classic American presidential or the British parliamentary mold. What changes have occurred have been purely Vietnamese-style developments. Party leadership is still as frequently hidden as it is overt, regardless of a formal party constitution. Party politics are still carried out as much by infiltration into the ranks of public administration and into the military hierarchy as through electoral and legislative activities. The total number of parties continually has increased and includes many organizations consisting of a small number of leaders and fewer followers. Parties oriented toward Catholic, Buddhist, Hoa Hao and Cao Dai constituencies have continued to splinter. Both the Dai Viet and the Vietnam Quoc Dan Dang (VNQDD) parties have not lost their ability to subdivide into factional groups.[2] Even a revitalized Diemist political party has split before it could establish electoral inroads. This perpetual fractionization has frequently been abetted by the Thieu government, which has backed (or at least not opposed) different parties in different electoral districts. And the government itself has ventured several times into the field of party development, only to drop the effort once a minimum groundwork had been completed.

Because of all these factors, South Vietnam remains a multi-party state in which there are no national parties. Differences among existing parties remain often a matter of personality or communal self-protection rather than of differences over public policy. Cynically viewed, each one appears to have the acquisition of power as its major, and perhaps only, objective. While this is not unusual in the politics of many countries, in South Vietnam contending factions have not been able to work together even when such cooperation would assure their obtaining positions of power. The inability of opposition forces to concentrate on a candidate and program to challenge President Thieu in 1971 guaranteed his reelection. Later rationalizations that such an effort would have been useless because the election would not have been fair are accurate enough, but they represent excuses more than position statements. The oppositionists tried to build an anti-Thieu coalition but could not agree on terms. In such an effort there had to be some political personalities who were more equal than others, a contingency unacceptable to the potential allies. Even parties that might have joined such a coalition to be in a position to be bought off by the government did not do so. At the same time, parties that did ally themselves with Thieu found as often as not that government-sponsored candidates opposed their local candidates.

Thus, on balance, the political party system continues to be very weak. Most so-called party activity is primarily that of an interest group trying to obtain gains for a narrow constituency. What has changed is that several parties are relatively more viable than during the Diem era. They are capable of achieving village and also provincial electoral victories. Often they have even defeated government candidates both for village council positions and for seats in the National Assembly. In a period when nongovernment parties have not fared well in most underdeveloped nations, a number of parties in South Vietnam have, ironically, gained in importance. This gain became obvious at the end of the 1960's as the NLF suffered heavily from attrition in many local areas and religious and nationalist political parties frequently moved into the village power vacuum. The Buddhists fared particularly well in gaining official positions in locations where their organization had made its greatest advances. Further, the Buddhists proved capable of obtaining a national plurality in the 1970 Senate election when facing a divided field of opponents. Party building in terms of organization, number of cadres, field offices and increased financing of activities also showed relative improvements in the total party system. All parties continued to be plagued by government road blocks, by difficulties in retaining cadres in wartime, by failure to fulfill promises because of executive attempts to limit legislative initiative in formulating public programs, and by increasing costs for campaigning and for operating party organizations.

But most important, each major party remained incapable of breaking out of the historic confines imposed by Vietnamese pluralism. No one religious party could obtain support from others. No primarily secular party could escape vestiges of a regional orientation. In the Center the Dai Viet and VNQDD made gains, only later to lose many of them to Buddhist-backed candidates. In the South, Dai Viet factions and the PNM frequently had to compete with Cao Dai and Hoa Hao local parties. And all parties had to oppose candidates favored by either the national government or province or district chiefs.

Further, Thieu's emergency decrees late in 1972 affecting village council elections and placing stringent requirements on formal political party formation, as well as his attempts to set up a monolithic Democratic Party under his control, undermined many gains of the political party system during the previous five years. Even the National Liberation Front and its constituent political parties became increasingly fractionated as northern representatives often replaced southern local political leaders, a development which did not necessarily indicate an irreparable split within the NLF's ranks but did force it to become more regional and less national in orientation. Thus the matrix of contending forces served to prevent any one or two or three political parties from making substantial advances. This was a repetition of Vietnamese history, but it was also a sign that political integration was a very distant goal.

FOLLOWING the initialing of the Treaty of Hue in 1884 ceding Tonkin and Annam to France as "protectorates," the Vietnamese Emperor Ham Nghi led a nationalist imperial party against consummation of the colonialists' gains.[3] This Nguyen imperial party, a regional guerrilla and terrorist faction based only in the north central section of the nation and operating from highland fiefs, relied upon violence, the personality of its leader, the mystique of his cause and the mystique of nationalism. This combative "party," while hardly a party in the strictest sense of the term and perhaps not even a movement in the strictest sense of that term, was defeated with the capture of its leader in 1888.[4] Yet this party has continued to serve in miniature as the model for subsequent political party activities in Vietnam. Nearly all of the numerous Vietnamese parties have more or less emulated the patterns of behavior of the first anticolonial party and few in South Vietnam have gone much beyond modifying the tactics of that vanguard group.

Perhaps the outstanding continuing factors influencing Vietnamese parties to retain much of the first Nguyen model have been: (1) the unwillingness or inability of the militant party elites to compromise among themselves for the purposes of presenting a united front and of aggregating support behind an agreed-upon program or behind a select group of leaders; and (2) the considerably less than nationally-oriented objectives and constituencies of these elites. The first factor continues to remain a function of the second. Within the framework superimposed upon Vietnamese internal politics by the perennial presence of these two factors, political competition over interpretation of the role of central government and over the composition of central government ministries has been primarily an exercise of concern to the small group of urban intellectuals. On the other hand, the role of parties as instruments for governing the population typically has been regional and local. Exceptions to this party role are found in occasional attempts by various central government regimes to balance national ministerial portfolios and numerous forms of appointive council positions somewhat. Political party participation in central government operations, possibly because of the erratic nature of such participation, has often ranged from being less than constructive to being suicidal for the regime in power. A consequence has been the development of numerous central regimes with little or no constituency, which rule but rarely govern. In fact, regardless of the composition of South Vietnam's numerous governments, institutionally it has been the civil service vestiges of the mandarinic system which have provided the most visible and viable national presence of central government on a day-to-day basis.[5]

Patterns of Development of South Vietnam's Political Party System

The most striking feature of the major parties in South Vietnam has been their similarity. The current significant parties display not only similar patterns of behavior but they also have displayed characteristics in their operations during the era following the fall of Ngo Dinh Diem quite similar both to parties long defunct and to their own experiences under the French before and during the Indochina War. There is even a rather amazing continuity of political party personalities from the French period who have become overtly active again under the several ruling military tribunals that have succeeded Diem. The longevity of personalities no doubt helps to explain the similarities in political party behavior, but it can serve only as a partial explanation. The important factors reside in the heterogeneity of the South Vietnamese nation, in the norms of acceptable modus operandi which have evolved for party activity over the past several generations, and in the deep psychological and even religious commitments of numerous segments of the South Vietnamese population to their community or locale and to the party which serves as spokesman for such a community.

Despite their many similarities, there has been a continuing proliferation of political parties of one form or another. The proliferation process has been considerable throughout most of this century, particularly during the 1920's and 1930's when the impact of the Russian and Chinese revolutions was most immediate in Asia, during the relatively liberal colonial period of the French popular front, during World War II when both the Chinese Kuomintang and the Japanese sponsored Vietnamese parties, and in South Vietnam after the revolution against Diem in 1963.[6] A standing joke among the traditionally cynical Vietnamese is that the number of "parties" at any time outnumbers the total "membership" of a majority of the formally declared parties.

Many of these organizations have been formed to provide a source of support for personal ambitions or to advance grievances against a specific assumed injustice.[7] A few have articulated grand philosophies for guaranteeing the destiny of the Vietnamese nation-state and an even smaller number has legitimately claimed adherents in the millions. Most, however, have not spelled out a grand program nor have they provided a detailed analysis of the current situation or a programmatic statement of goals and procedure which a government under their direction might follow. Rather, their principal line of argument, with quite few exceptions, has been singularly concerned with criticism of the existing political system, particularly criticism of the leading executives and of specific ministers. Nearly all have augmented their critical approach with a militancy which has often led them to resort to violence as a standard vehicle of political activity. A large number of these organizations can be regarded as parties only in the most liberal sense, but as they are usually attempting to influence particular policies, bring about changes in government personnel, or demand representation in the councils of government, and also attempt to impose the interests of their clientele upon the total Vietnamese population, the fact they label themselves "committees," "councils," "leagues," etc., and often alter such labels, hardly eliminates them from consideration as political parties operating vigorously in the political arena.

Historical Development: The Three Eras of Party Development. The historical development of the numerous parties in what is now South Vietnam can be roughly divided into three stages, i.e., the period

of prepartition colonialism and the First Indochina War, the era of Ngo
Dinh Diem, and the post-Diem phase of executive control by military
tribunals.

Parties of importance in the South before 1954 included three major
types. First, there were a number of independence parties and constitutional revision parties which professed to support nationwide goals but
whose influence was limited largely to Annam and Tonkin. Among the
more important of these parties were the following: (1) the Association
for the Restoration of Vietnam founded by Phan Boi Chau in 1912,
which supported the imperial claim of Prince Cuong De but which also
supported the abortive revolt in 1916 led by the Emperor Duy Tan
and Tran Cao Van;[8] (2) the Progressive Party led by Pham Quynh,
which attempted to persuade France to adopt constitutional reforms including a role for Vietnam in the French Union;[9] (3) the Viet Nam
Quoc Dan Dang (VNQDD), founded in 1927 by Nguyen Thai Khoi
upon the Kuomintang pattern, which led the abortive Yen Bay Revolt
in 1930 and later joined with other exiles (including the Viet Minh)
in a Chinese-sponsored nationalist organization (the Viet Nam Cach
Mang Dong Hoi) and then returned to Tonkin with Chinese forces in
1945, only to be outmaneuvered by the Viet Minh after joining a shaky
coalition and after a violent struggle;[10] (4) the Dai Viet Party, initiated
in the 1930's but founded formally primarily with civil servant support
and Japanese assistance during the 1940's, which was the most important legal party in Tonkin from the point the Viet Minh went to the
maquis until the partition.[11]

The second pre-Diem group were the communist parties. After a
stormy beginning involving three communist parties, a coalition was
agreed upon in 1930 resulting in the formation of the Indochina Communist Party. However, the ICP and its later organization, the Viet
Minh, met with resistance in Cochinchina from the Trotskyite Party,
which successfully competed for elected positions upon both the
Cochinchina and Saigon councils.[12]

The third group of parties of importance to the South during this
period were organizations almost exclusively Cochinchinese, including:
(1) the Constitutionalist Party founded in 1923 by Nguyen Phan Long
and Bui Quang Chieu, which failed in its attempts to obtain constitutional reforms for Cochinchina;[13] (2) the Cochinchina sect parties, i.e.,
the Hoa Hao's Social Democratic Party and the Cao Dai's National
Restoration League, both supported by the Japanese, then joining in
a coalition with the Viet Minh, but finally becoming the backbone of
Bao Dai's support in the south;[14] (3) the Cochinchina separatist organ-

izations (of whom elements of the sects upon occasion were partners) including the Party for an Autonomous Indochina, the Party for Cochinchinese Autonomy and the Democratic Party of Nguyen Van Thinh.[15] A rather clearcut line could be drawn before 1954 between those parties which were in one way or another standard-bearers for either Cochinchinese autonomy or ultimate suzerainty of the South over the North and Center.[16] The remaining parties being Annamite and Tonkinese in origin and in leadership were generally more national, at least in that they believed themselves heirs to the Nguyen kingdom and felt Cochinchina and the southern economic base belonged to the independent nation-state they envisioned.[17]

During the Diem era, political party activity in South Vietnam was greatly restricted.[18] After militarily defeating challenges to his authority by the sects, the Dai Viet, and the VNQDD, by operating through the Bureau of Political and Social Research of Dr. Tran Kim Tuyen and through the manipulations of Ngo Dinh Nhu and Ngo Dinh Can, Diem's government rendered the old parties impotent politically.[19] Leadership of the two sect parties together with the Socialist Party were staffed by personalities favorable to Nhu.[20] The Diem government also created its own "nationalist" parties, the most important being the National Revolutionary Movement (the state's "mass" party), the National Revolutionary Civil Servants League, and the Can Lao Party (see next section). Nhu and Tuyen relied heavily upon the Can Lao Party, which remained a group with a secretive membership list, to maintain surveillance over the bureaucracy, the military, and the nation's nongovernmental interest groups. These political parties were supplemented by a series of sponsored organizations, e.g., the Women's Solidarity League and the Cong Hoa Youth, whose purpose was to provide shows of support for the regime. None of these numerous structures, with the exception of the Can Lao, yielded any appreciable influence upon the processes of government.[21] Even the legislature, selected in two elections, was not formally related to the parties, instead being organized simply along lines of majority and minority blocs.[22]

After the November 1963 coup against Diem the various Nhu structures were eliminated, and the old parties were revived. Many exiles, who were not considered "neutralist," returned, and imprisoned political party leaders were released either to participate in one of the post-Diem governments or to re-form old alliances to oppose the existing central governmental power structure.[23] The Dai Viet gained almost immediately, extending its membership rolls to include many of the nation's elite, particularly among the Catholic elite. Also, the Dai Viet, in addition to the VNQDD and the two sect parties, regained control over several geographical sections of South Vietnam. None of these parties has been able to display complete unity or discipline within its own ranks. Instead elements of these and other parties have joined temporarily to support or oppose a particular central government or specific decisions of the government. Frequently these party factions, on occasion utilizing American assistance provided as part of the general counter-insurgency plan, stress their point of view with the support of their own armed militia and youth organizations.[24] Various groups of both the Catholics and the Buddhists have also developed armed "protection" forces.[25] The results have often been violent.

Temporary alignments for self-protection to thwart any one interest from obtaining complete power have been frequent. The military has managed to maintain formal control, even despite formidable attacks by various Buddhist forces upon the Nguyen Khanh government in 1964 and upon the Nguyen Van Thieu-Nguyen Cao Ky government in 1966, with a brief and somewhat perfunctory interlude of "civilian leadership," because the existing parties fear each other more than they do the relatively uncomplicated and basically impotent military councils. A number of interests, including the military, combined to check the early attempt of elements of the Dai Viet Party, the Catholic forces, and the Hoa Hao to create a Dai Viet directed national government. Catholic coup and demi-coup attempts have been abortive because most of the military leadership and the other interests, except for elements of the Dai Viet Party, feared both control by this interest and reprisals from the other parties. Still, regimes have fallen primarily from the weight of "militant" Buddhist opposition (Nguyen Khanh in 1964) and the pressures of the sects and the Catholics (Dr. Phan Huy Quat in 1965), as well as from the political turmoil within the ranks of South Vietnam's military leaders (Duong Van Minh in 1964, Khanh in 1965).

The so-called "militant" Buddhists, led by Thich (or Venerable) Tri Quang, managed to play the part of alternating oppositionist and coalitionist to the hilt. Having both attacked the Catholics and worked with them, having cooperated with the military tribunals before attacking them, having made agreements with elements of the sects but not lived up to them, having attacked the VNQDD in the center, having attacked not only the Co Son Mon Buddhist sect but the old General Buddhist Association (particularly the influential Southern Buddhist Association under Mai Tho Truyen),[26] and having finally failed in a long standing attempt to deprive Thich Tam Chau of his control of the secular division of the United Buddhist Church—the "militant" Buddhist

Struggle Forces finally managed to block their own room for maneuver. But this development, as most others in Vietnamese politics, was not a permanent development.

The Incidence of South Vietnam's Combative Political Parties

Many explanations can be advanced for the divisive, combative, uncompromising, and often obstructionist nature of the proliferated structures comprising South Vietnam's political party system. These explanations must recognize the historical lack of national unity, the historical development of diverse social-economic-religious groups, and the historical background of parties which have developed with few options except for revolutionary activities against the central powers of the moment. To a great extent, three factors are of particular significance in describing the dilemmas of Vietnam's parties and their subsequent combative nature.

Political Party Inexperience in Governmental Processes. Lack of political party experience in electoral, legislative, and administrative processes is undoubtedly a variable of importance in explaining the uncompromising nature of much of Vietnamese politics. It has denied political parties the opportunity to incorporate into their programs a plea to sentiments on an interregional and national basis. Instead, in general they remain steadfast to regional and communal policies as advocates for their limited constituencies. Absence of elections has also meant that central governments have been organized, reorganized, and succeeded in short order on the basis of such factors as the secondary demands of minority urban interests, foreign pressures, and the demise of patchwork coalitions composed of unrepresentative politicians. Under these circumstances few parties have been willing to assume responsibility unless given assurances that they could govern on a nationwide basis instead of simply rule at the pleasure of another power. This is a concession the French refused to give to any of the governments under Bao Dai just as the Japanese had refused such a concession after their 1945 coup d'etat. It is also a concession the South Vietnamese military leadership has felt unable to make since 1963, although it provided certain leeway to the Huong and Quat governments in 1964 and 1965. Political parties such as the VNQDD and the Dai Viet have had representatives in practically every central "government" of Vietnam (and later of South Vietnam) since the end of World War II. Yet neither party has ever controlled a "government" during this period. The Dai Viet Party under the first Nguyen Khanh government in 1964 was permitted certain vestiges of actual party responsibility for running the national government.[27] This discretion was peremptorily withdrawn once the Dai Viet leadership actually gave operational indication it intended to exercise it.[28]

The elections which have been held were on an irregular basis and were designed for the immediate purposes of the regime in power. Elections set by a regime for the "right" moment have found many parties off guard, frequently with their leadership in exile, in prison, or in intransigent opposition to every act of a regime. Participation in such elections has been viewed by many party leaders as acceptance of the legitimacy of the French, or of Bao Dai's Associated State within the French Union, or of the Diem government, or of the Viet Minh, or of the various post-Diem military council governments.

Diem himself never participated either in governments or in elections during the First Indochina War.[29] As rules prescribing organizational activity restricted party operations, and as manipulation of voting precluded any possible victory at the polls for any party he might create, Diem protested by abstaining. Knowing also that any government he might form, even if he had led a party to electoral victory, would not be a governing party, meant to him that participation in elections would be particularly futile. The Paris exile community and Saigon both are well staffed by personalities who attempted to win elections, or to participate in various administrations or councils according to the rules laid down by the French, by the Viet Minh, by Diem, and by the military juntas. However, the Diem *attentiste* psychology has always been the most prevalent psychology for Vietnamese parties and for their leaders in dealings with the central government. This psychology to a great extent explains the politics of Vietnam both before and since 1954, only after this date it was Diem and his successors rather than the French whose claims to legitimacy was opposed.

The limited electoral experiences which the Vietnamese population has enjoyed testify that it is far from politically apathetic. In 1953 and again in 1965 under conditions where a choice was permitted—despite the fact that the electorate recognized that their impact upon government policy would be a façade—the election turnouts were impressive.[30] Local issues played an important role in both elections as did the importance of local personalities. Although party labels were not used, the 1965 elections did help to legitimize the claims of party leaders to regional leadership.

Nearly all of South Vietnam's political parties in the summer of 1966 looked forward to the possibility of elections to provide for repre-

sentation of their varied interests.[31] Questions of procedure and of timing as always were divisive. Obstructionist and opportunistic tactics of
first the Military Directorate and then the militant element of the United
Buddhist Church under the leadership of Tri Quang clouded considerably the significance of any election either for a Constitutional Assembly
or a Legislative Assembly. Tactical obstructionism by shifting coalitions
among elements of the sects, the Catholics, the Dai Viet Party, the
VNQDD, the Democratic Party, and the various Buddhist groups not
under control of the centrist Struggle Forces was gauged for optimization
of their own position in any elections. The government, ignoring the
recommendations of its own Electoral Commission, took steps to force
a coalition, at least on a regional basis, of the numerous parties by declaring that slates rather than individual candidatures would be voted
upon under convenient symbols. Such a procedure was a greater pragmatic force to persuade party leaders to form into a few major parties
than was the skilful needling of the ill-fated Colonel Pham Ngoc Thao
who attempted to obtain the same objective earlier. Central-govern-
ment-dictated procedures also assisted manipulation for election of preferred candidates.[32]

Regionalism as a Variable in Party Behavior. The perennial Vietnamese dilemma of nationalism vs. regionalism, of centralization of governmental authority vs. decentralization permitting local autonomy, has
always had a significant bearing upon political party operations. Given
the intrinsic regional nature of the interests supporting most parties, the
frequent opting for some form of regional autonomy in Vietnamese history has added to the perplexity of forming nationally oriented parties.
During the Le Dynasty autonomy was provided for the northern (House
of Trinh) and the southern (House of Nguyen) regions. This formula
was followed through the regional governor system under Gia Long and
Tu Duc, through the French "Ky" scheme, and through regional governors again under Bao Dai.[33] Despite Diem's attempt to centralize administration, the regional program was, in fact, in effect in the person
of the "political advisor for central Vietnam," Ngo Dinh Can. It has
also been significant under the military council system, which has appointed corps commanders as regional delegates. This practice has
proved to be a matter of some embarrassment to Saigon especially when
General Nguyen Chanh Thi used his position in the northern five
provinces to cooperate with Thich Tri Quang in appointing local officials of questionable loyalty to the central government. The regional
system, providing appointive, fiscal and even military powers to regional

governors, has always supplemented more than created the regional orientations of Vietnamese parties.

Regionalism as a variable in Vietnamese political life is a composite of social, economic, and cultural factors. Historically the North and the South were opponents. The Vietnamese march southward alienated Chams, Khmers, and Chinese who preceded the Annamite expansion. Once the Annamites had conquered the South, dynastic rivalries brought a separation of ties still significant in the perceptions of inhabitants and former inhabitants (refugees) of North, Center, and South. When the French arrived they created a system of government aimed at perpetuation of this division. Early pro-Nguyen parties were always centrist and Tonkinese, and nearly all subsequent nationalist parties retained a regional bias.

Diem's "party" before 1954 was Annamese, but his potential strength was reinforced by the Catholic interests in the North, by the labor union and other activities of Ngo Dinh Nhu in Saigon, and the general importance of Ngo Dinh Thuc within the Catholic community. But it was in Hue that demonstrations favoring Diem in 1945 influenced Bao Dai in sending Diem a never delivered invitation to form the new government following the Japanese coup d'etat. Throughout his tenure in power the major opposition to Diem remained regional. Military operations against the southern sects and the centrist Dai Viets were not undertaken against a national opposition. The continued sect opposition and the later National Liberation Front insurgency can be traced as a southern movement blown larger through an evolutionary policy.[34] When the "Buddhist Crisis" exploded in 1963 it was really an Annamese revolt carried to Saigon but having minimal direct impact upon the remainder of South Vietnam. The military era in South Vietnam has witnessed a repetition of past patterns of regionally oriented politics, including a growing restiveness in the Central Vietnamese Highlands under the direction of the *Forces Unifées de Lutte pour la Race Opprimée* (FULRO).[35]

Each active interest in the Vietnamese political scene has continued to make demands upon the central government from these localized points of strength. In fact, the role of political parties as de facto local governments, i.e., as states-within-the-state, has been extremely important in Vietnam since the end of World War II, particularly prior to 1955 and after 1963. This role in turn has been a significant factor in determining the relationship which the parties have maintained with the central government. The impact of the National Restoration League of the Cao Dai[36] and of the Social Democratic Party of the Hoa Hao in west South Vietnam,[37] the VNQDD and the Dai Viet Party in central Vietnam, and the refugee Tonkinese bishoprics and committees representing Catholic interests in several areas of South Vietnam, has been considerable. Acting on occasion as local agents of the central regime and on other occasions as the only visible government to provide services and protection for their constituents, these parties have maintained a much closer relationship with those constituencies than has any other government.

Traditionally, the party-controlled areas have been characterized by a commitment of the population to its party leadership, a popular involvement in attempts of the dominant party to obtain its goals, and a willingness to identify with the party and its movement even in times of crisis. On the other hand, parties themselves in these areas have been characterized by a number of features, including: (1) their tendency to serve as instrumentalities to administer all local public services; (2) their propensity to provide and control a total community framework for religious, economic, and social activites; (3) their attempts to provide the symbolism in the form of uniforms, rituals, rallies, etc., to intensify identification with this "functionally diffuse" community framework; and (4) their militancy and generally combative nature when faced with outside pressures from either the central government or from other parties.

The picture of local party states-within-the-state is too analogous to many of the operations of the Viet Minh and later of the National Liberation Front to escape notice. The Viet Minh operated as a party government initially in the Tonkinese highlands and expanded its area of operations until the partition of Vietnam in 1954.[38] Since the partition, the Viet Minh–National Liberation Front complex has expanded its party government role in South Vietnam, beginning in Zone D north of Saigon, in Zone C in Tay Ninh Province, in the Cau Mau Peninsula, and in a number of locales in the southern highlands.

Like the religious and nationalist parties, the Viet Minh–NLF complex has always maintained its own governing structure, has always received fervent support from determined adherents (as opposed simply to acceptance from a constituency), has always retained militant protective-proselytizing shock forces, and has always attempted to provide first for indigenous needs while subordinating specific local policies to the requirements accompanying survival of its general cause and its organization.[39] The Viet Minh, associated with a movement and an ideology of international dimensions, and operating under the direction of a strongly disciplined and sophisticated organization has remained without peer vis-à-vis its competitors in retaining and expanding areas of operational control. Neither the NLF nor its formal communist party affiliate in South Vietnam, the People's Revolutionary Party, have managed to emulate the extent or organization and discipline perfected by the Viet Minh in the North, although their efforts in this regard have proved more than adequate to cope with the counter-efforts of the Saigon government.

Role of the Urban Elite in Party Activity. Interestingly enough the demands made upon the central administration by the regionally-oriented political parties usually have been dramatized through demonstrations of massed adherents, particularly of the youth groups and "militia" attached to each of the major parties, in and around Saigon, Da Nang, Hue, Da Lat and a few provincial capitals. Tactically such urban displays provide by far the greatest visiblity for party claims and claimants. This is particularly true of Saigon, for it is here that the large majority of the Vietnamese elite resides and that this elite and the numerous associations it controls maintain constant contact with ministerial and other higher-level national government officials.

The economic and intellectual elite of Vietnam remains a fairly small group whose influence still is much more extensive than its numbers might indicate. University groups, study associations, employers' associations, labor unions, and commercial groups under the guidance of the urban elite historically have been catered to by the various parties. The universities in particular have always provided sources of support for different political parties.[40] Most of the other groups, often having fairly direct access to national regimes, have attempted to maintain a relatively aloof status vis-à-vis the party organizations, either remaining *atientiste* in struggles for power or shifting allegiances once a succession in central executive personnel occurs.

In most instances the university student groups have not provided leadership to nationalist movements as they have in the past in other Southeast Asian nations. The French attack upon the mandarinic system, including particularly the classical basis of education, was geared toward producing assimilated adherents. Despite the difficulties they faced, the French were far from unsuccessful in this enterprise. Student groups supported Phan Boi Chau and gave romantic glances toward Prince Cuong De and each nationalist movement as it came along, yet this support was typically mixed. The rewards offered by the French were frustrating but tangible. Significant numbers of the intellectuals, including university students as well as the broader intellectual community, adopted dual citizenship and dual manners, while civil servants donned white suits, and a new privileged class assumed dominance within the Vietnamese community. This class has not been altered appreciably since 1954, and from it nearly all of the leadership for those secular organizations with pretenses toward being "nationalist" parties has developed. This group is mostly from mandarin stock, frequently professionals (particularly medical doctors and professors), economically well situated, and in general is perceived as representing the modern-day version of the traditional "notables" system of communal leadership.

Economic power has also remained under the control of this limited elite class. Both unions and employers' associations, led usually by representatives of this elite, have remained among the most cohesive organizations in South Vietnam. Each type of organization has found it more expedient to retain only casual relationships with the parties while dealing at considerable length with the civil service, the most permanent institution in the Vietnamese political system, and with specific relevant ministerial or local government functionaries. In a nation where national public policies are primarily the product of urban-oriented decision makers, where political parties rarely offer economic programs except in the most general terms, where the Socialist Party has remained a very minor factor in politics, where the practice of *ung ho* (bribery) has always been a normal way of doing business, and where governmental procedures affecting commercial interests outside of Saigon are under the control of local officials and civil servants, it is not surprising that neither business nor labor officials have deemed it necessary or even ideologically pressing to participate actively in political party politics.[41] In regions of the countryside where political parties are the de facto government, e.g., in An Giang Province where the Social Democratic Party of the Hoa Hao is a significant force, naturally it is expedient for Chinese and other business interests to cooperate with the local party.[42] But even this type of cooperation typically has little relevance to interest group involvement in the partisan politics surrounding decisions concerning the central government, because such politics almost always concern the question of executive leadership succession rather than significant changes in public policies.

Conclusion

It is not possible for any observer of the political party system in South Vietnam to escape being quite critical. In a number of instances since World War II there were possibilities, however slight, for the creation of an effective central government if only the parties had compromised their minor policy differences and worked together. Instead they permitted personal ambitions and individual party demands for total power to interfere. Since the fall of Diem in particular a number of opportunities have been lost. The military leadership has naturally little respect for the politicians but remains too weak in its position to continue as the focus of power without support of some coalition of parties. The fact that many of the military leaders have close party connections and commitments has even further compromised the military tribunals. But the division and mutual distrust among party leaders preclude their uniting to take advantage of a situation which intrinsically has the potential of working in their favor. The objective conditions of South Vietnam's current governmental process readily lend themselves to a coalition of parties assuming control of the central government. This has often been quite likely to occur, but it is quite unlikely that any such coalition would maintain an extended tenure of office.

Considering the odds against South Vietnam's parties serving as a source for stable leadership of the central government, a plea in June, 1966, by Dr. Phan Quang Dan that the parties be assigned additional administrative duties and responsibilities appeared paradoxical. However, Dr. Dan, one of the nation's best known and most respected politicians, was describing something much more important than the utility of the parties holding a few ministerial positions or even being represented in a National Assembly. He tied his request to what he perceived as the inevitable failure of the Saigon government's program of civic action and counterinsurgency. Dr. Dan was advocating that the parties assume responsibility for those programs. This concept has broad implications. The VNQDD, the Dai Viet Party, the Hoa Hao, and a number of tribal groups indeed have supervised the most successful civic action programs within specific locales. In their element, the parties have served as the most continuing challengers to the NLF. This success has always been a function of local support for a party rather than because of local support for the national government.

The potential of utilizing party regional and local support has rarely been realized. In fact, what would probably be the most expeditious method for effectively using this prestige will never be tried. This method involves a federal rather than a unitary system of government wherein the varied interests would receive representation, responsibility, and obligations on a regional basis. This remains one of the few possibilities for most parties to participate effectively in the governmental process.

Organizing Bureaucrats: South Vietnam's National Revolutionary Civil Servants' League

■ The Ngo Dinh Diem regime actually did attempt to build secondary organizations which could serve as agents for political mobilization and as instruments of linkage between the political system and the host of fractionated interest groups in South Vietnam. This attempt was a combination of certain Viet Minh organization-building tactics and of an esoteric Catholic socialist labor philosophy too complicated even for its most ardent adherents to comprehend fully. As noted in this essay, the strategy proved to be a failure. It was an artificial exercise recognized as such by most persons who participated in the National Revolutionary Civil Servants' League, the National Revolutionary Movement and even in the Can Lao. At the same time it is an interesting example of the type of activities and procedures that have been typical of much of Vietnamese politics. Clandestinism or semi-clandestinism, a network of cells (some overt, others covert), a nationalistic orientation, and educational *cum* propaganda sessions were characteristic attributes of such parties as the Viet Minh, the VNQDD, and the Dai Viet.

The difference between the organizations established primarily under the tutelage of Ngo Dinh Nhu and numerous other political groups was that the Nhu-inspired institutions had government support and the National Revolutionary Movement at least was supposed to be a mass organization. Most political parties since 1963 have retained many of the characteristics of the groups which formally evaporated after the anti-Diem coup. Even Nguyen Van Thieu generally followed the Nhu precedents when he initiated steps to create progovernment parties, although Thieu invariably backed away from establishing such parties because he feared they could eventually compete with the executive power. Only when a ceasefire appeared imminent in 1972 did Thieu make a concerted attempt to establish a strong political party he considered capable of competing with the National Liberation Front and potential nationalist coalitions in possible future elections.

There are numerous reasons why the secondary organizations established by Nhu failed. Primarily they did not have the iron discipline of the Viet Minh nor did they have the competency for socialization of members in which the Viet Minh excelled. Their objectives were vague, their procedures were mechanically rather than religiously followed by party cadres, and their philosophy was more appropriate for Left Bank philosophers than for mass consumption. In a word, they were not structurally or ideologically adequate for the type of indoctrination they were supposed to provide. Despite these weaknesses,

residues of the organizations prominent before 1963 have continued
to be active forces in South Vietnamese politics. A Diem "cult" has
developed and former Can Lao officials and members have increasingly
influenced the civilian and military bureaucracies and have experienced
various electoral successes. This has partly been a function of political
power among segments of the Catholic community. Also, nearly all
of the elite were somehow involved in one or another of Nhu's secondary structures, and many if not most of that elite continue to
occupy positions of at least some influence in South Vietnam.

Undoubtedly the existence of such a residue is more complicated
than this. Ngo Dinh Diem was almost everything his critics claimed,
but he also was a uniquely Vietnamese political personality. In retrospect, he is often enough romanticized now even by those critics and
most certainly by those who supported him or blamed all faults of
his regime upon Nhu. In all probability he had much more support
than even he recognized—or certainly this was true until the early
1960's. Diem was perceived as the scholar-patriot, a nonhero who,
at least from a western perspective, personified almost every conceivable
weakness of a leader except for one quality. He was the nationalist
par excellence. Despite the fact most Vietnamese believed he should
have entered the priesthood rather than politics, despite his tendency
to act as a semi-recluse, despite his stubborn insistence upon making
an incredible number of petty decisions himself while permitting members of his family to act as semi-autonomous viceroys (usually to
his detriment), Diem was never conceived as the epitome of government evil by most Vietnamese. His patriotism was never at question
nor was his personal incorruptibility. By Vietnamese standards to many
he appeared to be the recipient of the Mandate of Heaven, regardless
of how strange a choice they may have felt Heaven and the cosmic
energies had made.

Diem possessed the two qualities all Vietnamese consider essential
for retaining power, virtue and ability. In the eyes of most Vietnamese
he lost the latter by his performance in later years, particularly during
the Buddhist crisis but also in dealing both with nationalist opposition
and with the NLF. Still, few denied him the respect traditionally offered
to the man of virtue even in his last hectic days and after his death.
While there was much rejoicing once his era ended, there was
also a great deal of regret that his assassination had been the culminating act of an otherwise broadly welcomed coup. "A great deal" is
not a quantifiable sum, but the sentiment was at least extensive enough
to warrant official rationalizations and actual lies concerning the cause
of his demise. Whether an expanding Diem "cult" will itself be of
significance in the future is doubtful. However, underground quasi-
Diemists are present in nearly all institutions in South Vietnam. They
will be of importance in any conceivable future government, even

one dominated by the NLF. The upsurge of former Can Lao members in recent years may also have been at least partially a consequence of a greater success in indoctrinating members than I have recognized, either in this essay or later, but the sentimentality (an almost love-hate or more accurately respect-disbelief) of so many Vietnamese toward Diem himself surely has not been completely irrelevant.

CONSOLIDATION of Vietnam south of the seventeenth parallel seemed an impossible task in 1954 when Ngo Dinh Diem returned to assume the reins of government.[43] The Geneva partition presupposed a temporary division and did not envision the rise of a government in Saigon which could establish a viable nation. Setting up the Republic of Vietnam required considerable housecleaning due to the chaotic state of affairs which were the remnant of colonialism, rebellion, terrorism and economic underdevelopment.[44] The fall of the Binh Xuyen gangster sect, the temporary subjugation of the military-religious Hoa Hao and Cao Dai sects, and the discrediting of the Emperor Bao Dai are part of the folklore of President Diem's widely heralded rise to absolute power south of Tonkin. These victories, combined with American assistance, permitted a consolidation of government, which meant that South Vietnam became a nation rather than a matrix of miniscule territories under the direction of locally omnipotent warlords.

But a second, more penetrating and farreaching step was required in order to achieve a consolidation which would preserve the Republic as a viable political system promulgating and implementing public policies throughout all of Cochinchina, southern Annam and the *pays montagnards du sud* (PMS). The regime had to obtain effective control over the various strata of the Vietnamese population and over the diverse interests represented at each stratum. During 1954 and 1955 it was even necessary to pursue a course which could insure gaining the loyalty and overseeing the reliability of governmental employees. Diem and his immediate entourage devised a program of pacification to secure the acquiescence of minimum numbers, although bona fide support remained lacking. This program has evolved around attempts to place the numerous interests of the nation under the guidance and surveillance of groups of manageable size.

When Diem first occupied the Palace Norodom, few organized groups in South Vietnam were capable of serving as unifying agents or of providing controls over the various interests in either the urban

This essay was co-authored with Dr. Roy Jumper.

or rural sections of the new nation. The few groups which were part of the post-Geneva scene pulled against national unity, promoted individual, parochial and sectional interests, and were of questionable loyalty to the Republic. This problem was magnified many-fold because the administrative bureaucracy initially maintained an *attentiste* posture. Even a strong national movement under the leadership of a universally acclaimed and respected personality such as Ho Chi Minh would have encountered tremendous difficulties consolidating government, town and country in such a way as to build a strong new nation. Neither the Republic nor Ngo Dinh Diem possessed those qualifications.

Many techniques were adopted to harness the energies of the diverse interests in South Vietnam, but none has received such systematic and perpetual attention as the creation of intermediate social structures to provide control over specific segments of the population. Under the tight leadership of Ngo Dinh Nhu, the President's brother and official political advisor to the presidency, a concerted attempt has been made to integrate and consolidate interests by establishing government subsidized or semisubsidized "voluntary" associations and "private" organizations.[45] And each was established to fill a vacuum and to inculcate the principles of Diem's "personalism" concept into the code of all group interests in South Vietnam.[46] Government-sponsored associations have aided the regime to bring together and guide aggregates of individuals with specific common interests, activities and bonds, at the same time providing points of access wherein government propaganda and indoctrination cannot be avoided.

The National Revolutionary Civil Servants' League has played an important role in the efforts to consolidate and control the interests represented in South Vietnam's administrative bureaucracy. This association in turn has been an important instrumentality for maintaining Diem in power. It proved its usefulness initially by helping bring government employees in line, particularly the mandarins of the South, and later as an instrument for supervision of the civil servants. Today nearly all government employees are members of the League, and it operates as a potent source of control over the entire administrative bureaucracy.

Civil servants' associational activities were not Nhu innovations. However, such activities under the French had an undistinguished history. As all attempts at organizational political innovation and activity were suppressed if possible, the colonialists did not emphasize the role of front groups to control Vietnamese special interests. The French concentrated on sponsoring the creation of "nonpolitical" organizations, usually benevolent associations. A few of the associations established during the period of French rule, including the Civil Servants' Union, did serve to articulate membership interests and demands. The civil servants' group solicited privileges for its membership (increased wages, fringe benefits) and attempted to intervene on behalf of members harmed by governmental statutes. In some respects the Civil Servants' Union served as a legitimate labor union in terms of organizational goals and operations.[47] However, its membership was small and its impact almost insignificant.

The civil servants' associational activities became more political following World War II but at no time provided a powerful force during the war of resistance. One of its few significant political acts was its adherence to the United National Front in August of 1945. The Front, an ill-fated and short-lived organization composed of nationalist groups, the sects, Trotskyists and others, was beguiled by the Viet Minh League into accepting the Viet Minh government established for a brief period prior to the reoccupation of Indochina, and promptly went out of existence.[48]

Once Diem attained power in Saigon, the organization of functionary representation underwent drastic alterations in line with the Nhu policy of promoting and controlling interest-group activity throughout South Vietnam. Ngo Dinh Nhu's experiences both prior to and during the resistance era provided him with empirical evidence that associations could make valuable contributions in an over-all governmental program.[49]

Preliminary Stages in the Creation of the National Revolutionary Civil Servants' League. Steps leading to the creation of the National Revolutionary Civil Servants' League began in mid-1954. An association, first called the "Committee of Employees in Government and Private Agencies for Assistance to Refugees" and later the "Democratic Revolutionary Force," was formed under the leadership of Nguyen Huu Khai. The Khai group officially aimed at the promotion of "revolutionary activities" among employees. In addition to assistance for refugees from the North, it supported Diem during the Binh Xuyen fight, proclaimed its complete support to Diem in April 1955, and assembled its members on May 5, 1955, to participate in the National Revolutionary Movement's mass proregime demonstration in Saigon. The actions of the Khai group were particularly significant, since many governmental employees maintained a neutral stance during most of this historic period.

On June 25, 1955, a provisional executive committee working with the Khai group announced plans to establish a new civil servants' orgainzation. The members of the committee were hailed by *Tu Do,* an influential Saigon newspaper, as men with "advanced ideas." Five points were listed by the provisional executive committee as goals of the new association: (1) bring down the old regime and replace it by a democratic and free regime; (2) carry out principles tending to strengthen the independence and unity of the country; (3) serve the people according to the motto "The civil servant is the people's servant"; (4) bring forth the revolutionary spirit in the administration which is to be a strong and democratic organ; (5) arouse the civil servant's consciousness of his duty and usefulness to pave the way for a union of civil servants.[50]

The projected League was to be a mutual association dedicated to obtaining solidarity among all governmental employees, stimulated by a "national spirit," and pledged to the goal of action as a revolutionary force working in cooperation with other national groups. As a consequence of this cooperation, the provisional committee hoped there would be a consummation of the national personalist revolution envisioned by Diem.

As a preliminary to the first national congress of the League, in June of 1955 the association launched a campaign against all vestiges of the *"régime d'esclavage."* All civil servants were requested to participate actively in this campaign by (1) removing pictures of Bao Dai from public buildings; (2) using Vietnamese rather than French in all public service operations and speaking Vietnamese in all conversations; and (3) publicly denouncing any civil servant who refused to obey the League's request.[51] The role of the new association began to take form with this campaign. Civil servants were to act as agents for personalist nationalization. In this capacity the League has served to aid both in implementation of regime policies and in policing the conformity of its membership to those policies.

Double Seven Day, July 7, 1955, the anniversary of Diem's accession to office, was chosen as the opening date for the first national congress of the League. Over four hundred representatives approved the five points subscribed to by the provisional committee, and a pledge was made that all civil servants would support the regime "without reservation." The congress pledged that the League would display a "combative spirit" in the struggle for personalism and against communism, feudalism and colonialism. Support also was promised for the causes of national independence, unification of national territory, construction of a democratic and powerful Vietnam, and achievement of durable world peace.[52]

The Interlocking Directorate and the League's Electoral Role. From its inception the new civil servants' association was tied to and under the control of an interlocking directorate composed of government officials who have been leaders of South Vietnam's two major political parties, the National Revolutionary Movement (NRM) and the Revolutionary Personalist Labor Party (Can Lao). Most of the actions of the League in the summer and fall of 1955 were part of the regime-NRM buildup preceding the October referendum. Although the League, NRM and Can Lao have no legal organizational bonds, membership of the three frequently is overlapping. Further, they cannot be separated in terms of policy commitments or of operational goals.

To a great extent the League and the NRM are instrumentalities for implementing policies promulgated by the Can Lao. This latter group not only strongly influences the policies and leadership of the other two groups but also plays a direct or indirect role in the leadership selection of almost all private organizations in the nation. The Can Lao itself is principally an instrument for carrying out Nhu's programs. It attempts to implement his dictates both throughout the bureaucracy and throughout all structures within Vietnamese society. An organization with a selective and supposedly secret membership, the Can Lao is composed mostly of civil servants and military personnel who have Ngo Dinh Nhu's confidence. Members are expected to display unswerving loyalty to the political advisor, including spying upon colleagues to determine the intensity of their loyalty.

Because membership in the higher echelon of the Can Lao ostensibly signifies that one is in the inner circle of national policy makers, it is the most significant group to which a civil servant may belong. Little is known concerning the actual decision-making processes of the Can Lao, especially at the highest levels. But it is known that a cabal of three to five at most has surrounded Nhu since the beginning of the Republic. It also is known that this inner core has had a fluid composition through the years. The increasing mistrust and loss of confidence in all nonfamily members displayed by the Ngo family has made a tenure of the Can Lao's top elite extremely insecure.

The third link, the NRM, is the regime's mass political party. At the national level the NRM has always had a majority of the membership of the National Assembly and has operated at this level under the direct control of the Nhus. It has established branch offices in each province, district and village, as well as *Ap Bo* units of 20–40 members at the hamlet level, in most of the pacified regions of South Vietnam. Local party activities usually are carried out by civil servants who utilize government facilities. NRM members pay two piasters a month dues and attend weekly political training sessions dealing with the latest manifestations of personalism. In return, local members can anticipate certain rewards for loyalty.[53] The NRM has been eminently more influential in central Vietnam, which remains under the feudalistic control of Ngo Dinh Can, another of President Diem's brothers, than in the remainder of the nation. In Saigon the NRM's attempts have been so unsuccessful that the regime actually fared poorly in the 1959 controlled elections.

Although the connection of the National Revolutionary Civil Servants' League with the Can Lao and the NRM is usually expressed in somewhat more subtle ways, the League organized civil servants to support its two partners during the election campaigns of 1956, 1959 and 1961, as well as during the 1955 referendum.[54] League chapters held special meetings to study techniques for supporting Diem and legislative candidatures. As most Can Lao members and many NRM candidates chose not to run under party labels, the League provided its members with lists of persons worthy of receiving their votes. Some League chapters also organized campaigns for local candidates, including campaign financing from League funds. In other instances special subsidies were allocated by the Can Lao to cover League branch office campaign expenses.

Formal Organization of the League

According to the regime-approved bylaws of the League, all civil servants are eligible to become members if they display a genuine "nationalist spirit."[55] In theory, party affiliation, race, religion and sex are not criteria for membership, the interests of all members are represented, and all members participate on an equal basis. In practice, membership is obligatory for nearly all employees of government agencies and semi-autonomous government agencies. A scattered few do not belong; but this group is mainly composed of intellectuals who feel they can afford a small amount of discretion and who are occasionally permitted a minor heresy.

Proselytizing for the League is carried out by government officers acting in their official capacity. Several high officials, usually four to six in each department of the central government and in each provincial office are assigned as organizers. Usually working directly for the

NRM—although some specialize in obtaining League members—they use government office time, and facilities and resources provided by the government. Accountability for use of these funds, resources and facilities is based primarily upon personal confidence in the officials involved.

Formally, the rights of membership include freedom to make propositions to the League and to participate in discussions, debates and deliberations during association meetings. These rights are quite restricted in practice because the government, the Can Lao and the NRM, as well as the national office of the League, determine topics to be discussed, principles to be approved, and actions to be taken. Failure to observe League regulations or to execute orders of the leadership results in "critical observation," warnings, interruption of assignment and either temporary or permanent expulsion from the association. Such disciplinary action would usually be followed by dismissal from the public service. As failures leading to expulsion may involve what are viewed as antiregime actions, political and legal sanctions also may be anticipated.

The formal structure of the League is patterned after the French style of unitary government found in South Vietnam and after the formal structure of the NRM. Central offices are located in Saigon, and organizationally the association is divided into "working agencies," i.e., groups and subgroups whose composition is determined along geographical and functional lines. League working agencies are located at the central, provincial and district levels of government. A special group also has been created for the Saigon Prefecture. Each department of the central government has its own group, and separate groups may be established for each independent agency. Each group (*Chi Doan*) is divided into subgroups (*Phan Doan*), and the number of subgroups is unlimited. In addition, there are special provincial groups for retired civil servants.

At the provincial and district level the League's organization follows closely that of the NRM. Usually the same facilities are used by both groups. Association attention is paid primarily to the province employees because regular cadres are present only at this level, although some regular cadres are found in district offices. In the district offices League members operate through the *Quan Bo* NRM offices.[56]

Each level (central agency, groups, subgroups) is governed by an executive committee which typically includes the following officers elected for one-year terms: chairman; vice chairman; secretary; treasurer; propaganda, research and training officer; planning officer; fine arts officer; welfare officer; youth, physical training officer; financial officer; social welfare officer; women's officer; retired civil servants' officer and organizing officer. These titles indicate the many functions of the League itself and encompass the various techniques stressed for ensuring civil-servant conformity both in official and nonofficial activities. If the officers listed actually were efficient in carrying out their assignments, all South Vietnamese civil servants would soon find their social, political and professional energies channeled along the lines dictated by the regime. Rank and file apathy, however, has precluded such efficacy. Executive committees do have advisors, and often the expertise for propaganda functions, etc., comes from this source. In the provinces such expertise usually is provided by the NRM.

At the national level the governing body includes the chairman and the secretary general, who belong to an 18-member executive committee. For the central agency, the executive committee is divided into three major groups each headed by a League vice chairman: the committee for propaganda, research, and training; the committee for planning; and the committee for social welfare. These three groups are further divided into ten subcommittees performing functions similar to those of officers at lower levels, e.g., the subcommittee for women. Top leadership of the association has consistently come from highest-level *fonctionnaires* who are close to or even part of the leadership of the Can Lao and the NRM. The present national chairman of the League, for example, is the secretary of state for finance. At all levels, although leadership selection is by election, in practice selection is made by the League hierarchy and its governmental and political party affiliates.

League Finances

Financing of the League illustrates an important phase of Vietnamese governmental and associational operations. Regular revenues come from the sources typical to groups around the world, including entrance fees, monthly contributions collected from members, fund drives and sale of tickets to theatrical and athletic events. The three League levels share fees and contributions: 35 per cent to the group, 35 per cent to the subgroup and 30 per cent to the central agency. Also the League bylaws permit ownership, management, purchase and sale of real estate. These property relationships, which must be approved by the central agency, in practice serve as an elastic clause in the organization charter and permit the League to address itself to practically any form of entrepreneurship.

League business endeavors in turn permit the government to sub-
sidize associational operations officially. Subsidization takes the form
of using governmental facilities, of free civil servants' time and, in certain instances, of actual financial assistance to business operations. Perhaps most important, the government aids League financing through
condoning a time-honored Vietnamese practice known as *ung ho*. This
almost institutionalized practice permits the League as well as several
other Vietnamese nongovernment structures to operate somewhat as protective associations. Private donations can be accepted both by the
NRM and the League. It is unofficially expected that businessmen, particularly Chinese businessmen whom the Vietnamese term "fat cats,"
will give monetary contributions to "patriotic organizations" such as the
League and the NRM. The leaders of these two organizations who
solicit *ung ho* contributions are officials in the government agencies
which regulate the operations of the firms of the donors. Businessmen,
when solicited, almost unanimously make contributions. Refusals could
arouse governmental disfavor and sanctions, such as unusually strict interpretation and implementation of statutes relating to business operations and to tax payments.

Ung ho donations and other revenues are deposited in a special secret account by both the League and the NRM. Money from this account is invested in entrepreneurial ventures. Usually 50 per cent of
the profits go to the League or NRM for their respective business, although the percentage varies for different ventures. Import-export firms
are favorites for obtaining organization revenues. The chief NRM business venture once involved salt transportation, but a scandal resulted
in a withdrawal from this lucrative trade. Today perhaps the most
profitable NRM business is the sale of fertilizer. Bird refuse for fertilizer
is found in abundance on the Paracel Island off the coast of central
Vietnam, transported to the mainland to be sacked and then shipped
to Japan, the Philippines and other Asian countries.

Restaurant management is one of the most important League enterprises. "Social restaurants" throughout the Saigon metropolitan area
cater to lower occupation levels, e.g., day laborers and *cyclo* (bicycle
cab) drivers. These restaurants charge only five piasters per meal, a
price with which no other restaurants can compete. The government
supports this cheap meal program as a service to the large number of
extremely low income laborers who work in the capital vicinity. Heavy
governmental subsidies are provided in the form of free rice. Because
the major staple of the meals is obtained free of charge, the restaurants
make large profits. Managerial positions in these profitable food shops

are considered quite lucrative, are highly coveted and are reserved for League, NRM and Can Lao members.

For two years, 1960–61, the League also operated a restaurant for civil servants. Meager offerings made this unpopular with its intended clientele despite the low cost of twelve to fifteen piasters a meal. Facilities were converted into a social club for League members. Other League clubs today are business ventures on a small scale, renting a limited number of beds for approximately 30 piasters per day and serving meals at ten piasters.

Current League Functions

Relationships both among individual civil servants and between civil servants and the Diem regime are encompassed in the functions currently performed by the League. Its educational functions include training programs, centering upon professional topics, and study groups providing self-education in current public policies. The discussions at meetings provide interpretation and interpolation of governmental programs affecting members professionally and privately.

In addition, personal and professional ethics are stressed. Operations and Youth Director General Cao Xuan Vy, secretary general of the League's national executive committee, stated that League actions "center on turning civil servants into good elements, physically and morally, in order to bind them all together into a hard-core force for effective service to the nation and people."[57] Diem has constantly proclaimed moralistic goals in his demands upon civil servants. Speaking to a delegation on March 19, 1962, representing the seventh national League convention, Diem outlined five goals to be sought by the League, all with heavy moralistic overtones:

1. Civil servants must prove to be deserving of their duty, must overcome difficulties with courage.
2. Civil servants have greater prestige in more advanced countries, where they deserve the noble title "public servants."
3. Observe basic principles governing national policy which must comply with universal values and with national tradition.
4. Condemnation of (i) easy-going attitude of the Vietnamese civil servants, (ii) bad behavior, (iii) absence of respect towards moral and intellectual criteria—laziness, dishonesty, loose living.
5. Civil servants must try to improve themselves both morally and intellectually and must prove to be exemplary citizens in both their private life and in exercising their public functions.[58]

Following this interview, several Vietnamese newspapers reported that Diem had attacked the bureaucracy because it had previously failed to live up to his five points. *Tieng Dan* even commented that it deplored "the fact that a number of leading cadres in our regimes still show an authoritarian attitude toward their subordinates, lack initiative and a sense of responsibility, waste public funds and property, are not active in their work, and are therefore unable to make the people confident in the future of our revolution."[59] The League formally denied the announcements concerning presidential criticism and pledged to work diligently toward attainment of all points in Diem's program.

Several other League functions are almost exclusively related to services to members. Clubhouses are operated for leisure-hour activities and for social gatherings. Attendance at these social clubs is quite poor. However, club facilities do not go idle, because they are frequently used for regular League meetings and also are lent to the NRM for regular or special meetings.

Scholarships for children of civil servants is one service to members which is quite popular, although the amounts available for scholarships are too meager to have had any real impact. Recipients of grants receive about 150 piasters a month, which in most cases is just enough to pay tuition to secondary schools. Finally, a new variety of this second function has just gotten underway, and could in time be a very important League activity, i.e., establishment of consumer cooperatives.

The most important functions of the League, however, relate to what the membership—individually and collectively—can do for the regime. These functions center upon two themes: (1) League actions attempting to influence the general population as well as civil servants to act as the government decrees; and (2) actions providing a display of loyalty and support for Diem personally and for his policies. In practice it is not possible to differentiate between these two types of action, both of which according to Finance Secretary Nguyen Luong, chairman of the National League executive committee, are expressions of unanimous civil servant "absolute faith" in Diem and his "enlightened leadership."[60]

Organized demonstrations, which were so prevalent in the early days of the Republic, remain an important phase of the third type of League activity. These demonstrations take the form of large-scale parades, rallies and even mass prayer for the success of personalism and of the president, usually carried out in cooperation with the NRM. Frequent fund drives are more subtle attempts to display organized support for governmental programs. Donations are solicited from League members,

Chinese merchants and others. Many contributions are further examples of the *ung ho* principle. Some fund drives are part of charitable movements such as the relief drives for flood and fire victims and the Anti-Communist War Chest. Recently, the League has devoted considerable attention to fund raising for the NRM-sponsored Public Movement for Renovation of Independence Palace. All major associations in South Vietnam have participated in this drive to obtain funds for rebuilding the presidential home destroyed during the February, 1962, assassination bombing attempt by two pilots of Diem's air force.

League members also have been called upon to support the strategic hamlet program. This has been termed by the League's national chairman the "positive mission" of Vietnamese civil servants.[61] The entire hamlet construction program, including its supposedly important implications for the successful implementation of personalist principles, has been the topic of numerous study sessions in all League chapters throughout the country. Members "volunteer" to perform manual labor in building pilot hamlets to set an example for local communities, although frequently individual volunteers hire others to do this work for them.[62] The construction of four model strategic hamlets was one of the primary goals of the 1962 association activities. The League also provides financial assistance to a number of new hamlets and aids in the program established during 1962 for training cadres in the techniques of administering strategic hamlets. Civil servants employed in various provinces have even donated a month's salary to the hamlet program.

Finally, all civil servants participate in the various paramilitary programs which receive such constant emphasis by the regime. For most persons the paramilitary groups tend more to provide additional opportunity for further indoctrination rather than to develop skilled and properly equipped cadres to defeat the Viet Cong. At the same time, paramilitary training undoubtedly is of importance to many civil servants in the provinces who are, as Finance Secretary Nguyen Luong has stated, "living and serving in an atmosphere of war, crossing mine and trap-studded areas, and working day and night together with gallant soldiers."[63] Nearly all governmental employees of all ages are members of the Cong Hoa Youth, and in Saigon many (both male and female) have completed special paramilitary courses for civil servants designed to teach them how to aid in the defense of the capital if the need should arise.[64] Many civil servants in Saigon also serve obligatory guard duty at night at various buildings throughout the city. While performing this function they usually wear their blue Cong Hoa Youth uniforms and sometimes are armed. This rather wide deviation from what in most countries is normally considered as the duty of a public servant has been criticized periodically in the Vietnamese press because of alleged discrimination in guard duty assignments.

Conclusion

In some respects, it is impossible to measure the impact of the government's unofficial arms. The unreal nature of their claims to autonomy and spontaneity are recognized both by their membership and by the community at large. Yet such bodies as the NRM have had more than a negligible effect since the partition of Vietnam. A vast majority of the population within the pacified sections of the nation does belong to one or more of the nongovernmental intermediate structures. Meetings are held regularly, propaganda is heard, and donations of time and money are made. Constant checks are kept on potentially "dangerous" members. Hatred of communism is widespread, although such sentiments were no doubt inculcated through firsthand experiences rather than through indoctrination sessions. Membership rolls are large and the proportion of members marching in parades or contributing to such programs as strategic hamlet construction is always impressive.

A use has been found for the elite of South Vietnam. Political, educational, professional, business, labor leaders have been absorbed into the regime's propaganda network through their almost mandatory associational activities. Their role as natural leaders of specific community interests has been channeled along lines insisted upon by Ngo Dinh Nhu. They are subject to constant scrutiny in the performance of their leadership roles. Potential deviationism is usually found early and eradicated immediately. In practice this attempt to enforce conformity has been so successful that all constructive opposition is silenced, apathy among the elite is almost universal, and deviationist forces are completely unorganized. Further, positions of leadership in the associations have been filled principally by elitist elements that came to the fore during the period of French rule. Their reputation for opportunism is so widely agreed upon that they could not possibly lead deviationist elements even if they might manifest delusions of grandeur during one of the Republic's recurrent crisis periods.

In retrospect, although the associations have failed completely to develop "true believers" through socialization of their membership, the presence of such governmentally sponsored and controlled nongovernmental structures has been of significant benefit to the regime. Energies have been harnessed, physical and financial assistance for governmental programs has been obtained and the membership has not only been the constant recipient of government indoctrination but has frequently provided enough acquiescence and actual support for government pro- grams to insure their implementation.

The vacuum which existed in 1954 has been partially filled. Yet groups representing and articulating the interests of specific segments have not developed. At the same time, however, groups have been cre- ated which can represent and articulate the interests of the government to those segments. The strategy of instituting intermediate structures to serve as support agents was a most promising move, in that it permitted personalism to emulate forms used successfully by the communists. These structures combined with the intricate Vietnamese governmental matrix of official structures through the level of the *lien gia* (inter-family groups) and the individual household head might possibly have resulted in a control network even more effective than those of the communist nations. Failure can be attributed to a consistent inability to obtain even minimum overt support beyond innocuous public display. The Republic has given little and demanded all. It has required sacrifices in exchange for emoluments which were of no value to affected interests. At the same time it has so alienated a vast proportion of the population that association members in good standing simply have accepted the down- fall of the regime as a foregone conclusion. Under such circumstances it is not surprising that association membership is almost universally accepted solely as a perfunctory chore.

Perceptions of the Vietnamese Public Administration System

■ Public administration is a very important part of South Vietnam's political processes. This is partly because national ministries and pro- vincial-district-village administrations to a great extent determine how resources are allocated by these governments. Recruitment, per- formance and jurisdiction of administrators are vital political topics. Extremely weak before 1963, the administrative system became victim of nearly all national problems after that point. As warfare increased, responsibilities of the civil service and of public administration generally also increased. Performance became more difficult as security lessened, frequent shifts in persons holding ministerial portfolios caused confusion, and frequent structural reorganizations added to this confusion, as did the proliferation of new agencies within both the government and the military to administer crisis projects. The expanding military influence affected all levels of administration. Graduates of the National Institute of Administration (NIA) became part of a military-civil provincial and district administrative structure. Many administrators were called into the military, often performing functions similar to those they performed while working for civilian agencies. The entire administrative system came to be an integral cog in the overall program for dealing with problems associated with the war.

Most of the procedural and personnel problems of public administration described in this article have been intensified. Personality traits such as those implied by mandarinism have not been changed. The one new factor has been a debilitating one. American funds flowed so freely and were administered by so many organizations, which were led by persons frequently at odds as to the purpose of their distribution, that corruption was inevitable. Although regular civil service employees were less involved in siphoning off funds into their pockets than those associated with programs administered by military and ad hoc civil units, graft became commonplace. Temptations were enormous, public employees' pay was so low in an inflationary economy, and financial audits were so flimsy that corruption did become rampant. In addition, owing to the excessive increases in cost of living a high percentage of the civil servants of necessity began moonlighting.

Each of these factors weakened the administrative system. On the other hand, this system proved to be more capable than the following essay implies. Problems of public services in South Vietnam have been gigantic. Vietnamese public administration has not been able to resolve those problems, but it has coped with them more effectively than anyone assumed it could. By the end of 1971, prior to intensification of warfare once again, the rebuilding program which had occurred was impressive. It is easy to be cynical about the accomplishments of providing at least minimal public services, but considering the handicaps presented to the administrative system this was no small achievement. Credit is due the National Institute of Administration, particularly for the period when Nguyen Van Bong served as rector before his assassination in 1971, for much of such accomplishments. Throughout the war it has provided graduates with both academic and field experience to staff some of the nation's most difficult positions. Many of these graduates replaced prior graduates who had been victims of terrorist attacks. While there is no way to measure the total impact of the NIA, I definitely subscribe to Bernard B. Fall's statement that the NIA has represented the most effective and enlightened use of American aid to South Vietnam.

Of course, the NIA is but part of the story. The public administration system often stood nearly alone while warfare was waged around its normal activities. During the 1968 Tet offensive it frequently carried on when the political system appeared to be crumbling. For the long era when governments and ministries were being changed with great frequency, only the public administrators represented any government at all. To a certain extent this was possible because so many had mastered routine. Some plodded along while letting others attend to more ceremonial functions. Others undoubtedly were always much more dedicated and proficient in handling their own little slice of public services than I, or most persons, have ever given them credit for being. Usually unarmed, they faced reprisals and received small protection. Many were massacred in Hue in 1968 during the period of NLF occupation. Countless others have suffered a similar fate over the years.

The basic fact is that the Vietnamese administrative system has remained rather inefficient, has parochial habits, follows red tape and routine religiously, is very weak at the middle management level, and is extremely class and status conscious. A corollary to this fact is that it also is less inefficient, less parochial, less subject to routinization, and less particularistic than are similar institutions found in most underdeveloped nations. The administrators in South Vietnam, almost invariably closely tied to specific religions, ethnic and regional communities, are an extension and somewhat of a microcosm of the broader society. Often they are more nationalistic than the norm, and usually they are more politically aware than is the general population. They represent an elite whose numbers are skewed out of proportion, although less so today, to the urban centers. At the same time public service personnel may be more broadly representative of the total population than is the military leadership and much of the purely political leadership. This is partly because of the variety of functions they perform. It is also partly because the civil service remains a higher status profession in South Vietnam and competition for available positions is keen.

The civil servants discussed in this article are higher public officials, often ones who had at least indirect roles in political party activity. Partly because of connections with the NIA and with the Progressive Nationalist Movement founded by Rector Bong, the political-party activities of administrative-class members of the civil service have actually increased. While this has not been without its disadvantages, it has had positive implications as well. Public administrators have frequently stimulated village electoral activity and have aided the more autonomous village governments in adopting practices consistent with their enlarged responsibilities.

In retrospect the administrative system, with all of its continued weaknesses, has been the foundation which has permitted South Vietnam to survive. Not only on occasion has it been the only government of the nation, but it has been the only institution which has consistently assumed its tasks regardless of the pressures of the moment. There have been numerous examples of public service personnel retreating before advancing DRVN and NLF armies, as occurred frequently during the 1972 Easter offensive. Still they have been a significant factor when the government's military has held its ground. In the final analysis, the public administration system is one main hope South Vietnam possibly has of becoming a viable state. This may be a thin reed, but it certainly far outdistanced my own previous projections.

PUBLIC administration, as practiced in formerly colonial and underdeveloped nations, displays numerous common transitional characteristics.[65] Their administrative apparatus is strongly influenced by features of the political systems concerned, such as (1) precolonial and historic cultural norms, invariably traditionalistic and frequently highly romanticized, but supposedly indigenous, (2) an aura of rectitude, not infrequently Messianic, attached to the political elite who opposed colonial rule and assumed power after independence, and (3) an "ideology" consisting of nationalism, frequently an interpreted Marxism, and a hybrid form of socialism adapted to Asian or African circumstances. These basically endogenous influences have combined with primarily exogenous pressures to force change in administrative structures and functions, presumably because existing administrative practices were considered inadequate to cope with the inherent problems and ambitious goals of developmental administration. Formally this transition has been toward a "westernization" of traditional administrative systems, including a tendency to bureaucratize operations in line with impersonal "public"-oriented formulae.[66] Colonial practices provided an initial impetus to change, but the process received its principal legitimation following independence. This occurred chiefly because of (1) a desire, real or formal, for "modernization," (2) an impatience with irrational techniques deemed unsuitable for developmental administration, (3) the practical needs of implementing developmental goals, and (4) pressures for "reform" stemming directly or indirectly from foreign aid, assistance, and even threats.

Inevitably resistance has arisen to bureaucratization of public administration operations and orientations. Frequently endogenous and ex-

This essay was co-authored with Guy H. Fox.

ogenous influences have been mutually incompatible. The implications of "rationalized" administration are potentially destructive to the social, economic, and political vested interests of most of the historic indigenous elite. Since the upper ranks of the public service in the post-independence period typically have been occupied by representatives of this elite, it is not surprising that the transition to bureaucratization has quite often involved a direct or indirect conflict of interests, and has implied an end to positions of power based upon the status of this elite group.[67] Yet neither the colonial nor later governments have yet destroyed status distinctions, inherent in traditionalistic social systems and remaining in transitional ones, that stress the community over the individual.[68]

The impatient, Messianic political elite, usually from the same class as the bureaucratic elite, has generally found the concept of an impersonal, rule-abiding administrative system inconsistent with its own brand of developmental administration, despite frequent public espousals of the virtues of a rationalized bureaucracy. The political elite has often utilized the technique S. N. Eisenstadt terms "debureaucratization," whereby nongovernmental structures coopt regular administrative structures, either by assuming their functions or forcing them to adapt their operations through goal succession.[69] The natural concern of the political elite with the possibility of an independent power structure (in the form of a bureaucratized administrative system) beyond their direct, personal control is invariably intensified during periods when national viability and their own power are precarious because of external forces or disintegration of the internal order. During such periods of stress, the leader of the political elite historically has tended to "develop strong prescriptive policies toward those strata which he perceived either as opposed to him or as possessing the potential to become independent of him."[70]

This opposition to bureaucratization has naturally resulted in considerable variance between the formal structure of governmental organization and the way it works. This phenomenon, termed "formalism" by Fred W. Riggs, separating effective from formal power within an administrative system, is a characteristic of all transitional governing apparatus fitting Riggs' "prismatic model," wherein the existence of multiple structures and functional specificity tends *somewhat* to replace traditional ("fused"), functionally integrated structures.[71] Under the prismatic model, there is formal stress on bureaucratization, including the transition to an independent, neutral, impersonal, universalistic, and functionally specific administrative system, while in practice each of these particulars of the Weberian model is undermined by both the political and administrative elite. Thus impersonalized authority and universalistic norms compete with, and go along with personalized authority and particularistic norms.

However, in every nation in the world, groups favoring bureaucratization have continued to exist, although frequently they have not been able to articulate and push their demands. This interest persists because of: the scope of contemporary administrative systems—the formal goals of modernization and development require the proliferation both of governmental functions and administrative structures; an intellectual commitment to rationalized, efficient administration; and the necessity for professing impersonal rule both for domestic and international audiences. In some circumstances the military has assumed direct control or exerted considerable influence over operations of the public service. But more common, even in those nations where military influence has existed, is the ubiquitous movement categorized by Francis Carnell as the "romantic revolt" of the masses.[72] This politically docile element in the past is now in many nations for the first time realizing its strength and is coming to be represented by a new nonwesternized local elite, dedicated for the most part to communalism, traditionalism, regionalism, and sacral goals (religion, class, etc.). This movement presents a growing threat from below to the success of the probureaucratization interest in all prismatic political systems. When this threat is combined with an increased tendency toward both administrative concentration and centralization at the top in the form of varying genres of "guided democracy," the chances for Weberian style bureaucratization in most prismatic nations appear extremely slim.[73]

Vietnamese Civil Servants' Perspectives of Their Administrative System

In the Republic of Vietnam the regime relies principally upon its public adminstration system to consolidate, strengthen, and perpetuate its position, and to insure the success of its present economic development and social welfare programs. The administrative system's outlook and morale, traditions and behavior, procedures and actions have, therefore, especially significant implications for future Vietnamese social, economic, and political institutions. They will, for example, be important factors in determining the success or failure of the United States aid program and in deciding the outcome of the communist bid for the peasants' allegiance. The purpose of this article is to see what the high-level—and most knowledgeable—Vietnamese civil servants regard as the outstanding attitudes, behavior, and practices of their public administration system. It is a report of a study of civil servants' perceptions (1) concerning their own roles and those of their peers within a formally bureaucratized structure, and (2) concerning the role of the political elite and other elements of the antibureaucratization interest in developing the administrative system into a highly formalistic operating structure in which there is a wide variance between effective and formal power. It is hoped that such a presentation will contribute to building a theory of comparative administration by helping to fill those gaps termed by Robert V. Presthus the "absence of raw data about the social variables that shape public administration."[74]

The study is based primarily on interviews held during the summer of 1962 with 49 career officials in Class A, the highest level of the Vietnamese civil service, a class roughly comparable to the administrative class in Great Britain. Out of the total of 31,846 career employees, 1,334 are in Class A. The interviewees, selected with the aid of Vietnamese academicians who understood our desire to make the study as objective as possible, constituted probably as good a sample of Class A officials as a foreigner can obtain at present in Vietnam.[75]

Each of those interviewed had a good educational background, having at least a degree equivalent to the second baccalaureate plus some additional university education. Their degrees were overwhelmingly from French-oriented institutions, either in France or (principally) in Vietnam. Two of the interviewees, after receiving the French baccalaureate from Vietnamese lycees, had obtained university degrees in the United States.

Of the 49 civil servants 13 were among the most successful bureaucrats, having reached the top ranks of the civil service; these held such posts as director general, secretary general, director of cabinet, or equivalent. Seventeen were important middle managers. The remaining 19 were young civil servants, junior executives, expected eventually to occupy responsible positions. Only two women, both junior executives, were among those interviewed. A geographical breakdown shows that 20 of the interviewees came originally from North Vietnam (Tonkin), now in communist hands; 13 were from central Vietnam (Annam), now split between the southern, noncommunist Republic of Vietnam and the northern, communist Democratic Republic of Vietnam; and 16 were from South Vietnam (Cochinchina). Forty-three adhered to Buddhism as influenced by Confucianism and Taoism; the remaining six were Catholics, who compose about seven per cent of the total population of South Vietnam. The interviewees represented every major Vietnamese administrative agency except the Department of Justice. In the following discussion and tables, the reader may assume that there are no significant differences among the views of those in the foregoing categories unless otherwise specifically indicated with supporting data.

Every interviewee was asked the same set of questions, in Vietnamese; varying follow-up questions were used to elicit elaboration and clarification. The opening question in each interview was a general one which asked the official to specify what he considered to be the principal features of the bureaucracy. Next followed a number of questions on such topics as public administration during the French colonial period as compared with today's administrative system, centralized versus decentralized administrative structure, leadership of the administrative system, the degree of program orientation of various agencies, the role of the public vis-à-vis the private sector (especially in economic development), the present widespread use of military men in civil administration, relationships between subordinates and their official superiors in the civil service, psychological needs of civil servants, administrative responsibility and accountability, and personnel practices.

The initial, broad question was worded as follows: "What do you consider to be the outstanding characteristics, good and bad, of the Vietnamese bureaucracy?" Although it is difficult to group the multifarious and sometimes overlapping replies into meaningful categories, an attempt to do so is made in Table 1. This table includes only those characteristics mentioned most frequently.

TABLE 1
Perceived Characteristics of Vietnam's Administrative System
$(N = 49)$

Characteristics	Proportion Mentioning (%)
Unwillingness of civil servants to assume responsibility	88
Politicization by the regime	82
Intelligence and trainability of civil servants	82
Diligence of civil servants	67
Separateness of bureaucrats as a class	65
Lack of dedication of civil servants	57
Formalism and legalism of procedures	55
Basic honesty of civil servants	53
Stability and self-control of civil servants	53
Authoritarian behavior of civil servants	51
Centralization of authority	47

A surprisingly high number, 43 out of 49, mentioned "lack of willingness to assume responsibility" as an outstanding characteristic of the administrative system. A fair statement of the consensus of the 43 is: Vietnamese civil servants tend to remain "passive" and "uninvolved," avoiding decisions by referring them to higher levels. Following mandarin and French colonial traditions, the administrative system is autocratic and highly disciplined; unquestioning obedience is expected at every level. Moreover, civil servants are expected to follow rigid, established procedures. Such a system precludes initiative and inventiveness, and encourages the shirking of responsibility. Indeed, civil servants are convinced that their positions and chances for advancement will be jeopardized if they show initiative or make innovations. In the words of the director general of an important department, they have "fallen into an orbit of noncommitment."

The interviewees generally agreed that the civil service does contain some progressive elements, estimated at from 15 to 20 per cent of Class A officials, who would like to break with tradition and apply energy and imagination to pressing social, economic, and security problems. These elements, however, are not organized and consist chiefly of young civil servants who have neither the prestige nor the position to exert a decisive influence.

According to a few officials, young civil servants with western educations sometimes actually retard progress. Fresh from overseas studies and imbued with western ideas, they are impatient for reform. Immediately upon entering an agency, and before they can become acquainted with Vietnamese conditions, they are likely to voice complaints and criticisms. A young official was quoted as saying, after one week in the agency, "Everything is wrong." These young civil servants, it was charged, fail at times to appreciate even meritorious practices that are not in accord with western ways, nor do they understand how to go about changing behavior, and as a result they antagonize the departmental high command with proposals for immediate, radical changes.

At any rate, the attempts of the progressive elements to exercise initiative and to change the existing system have usually been squelched by higher authorities. The young employees soon learn that men get ahead by being "loyal," "quiet," "peaceful," and "orthodox." Either they leave the service or become resigned to the system and adopt, outwardly, an attitude of passivity and acquiescence. Inwardly, however, the young, forward-looking civil servants are "seething with bitterness and frustration."

Closely related to the unwillingness to assume responsibility are several traits which have been grouped under "lack of dedication" in Table 1. These traits were indicated by comments to this effect: civil servants are apathetic and have no sense of purpose; they are not willing to make sacrifices for the betterment of society; they lack patriotism and place personal interests above those of the country; they want rights but not responsibilities; they are obsessed, above all, with private security, so they try to avoid controversies and stay out of trouble. One top official, who had been in the service for 20 years, said, "Most civil servants are ready to surrender to any group—French, Japanese, or the Viet Cong." That civil servants are actually working with less dedication today than they did before independence was indicated by answers to a question asking for a comparison of the present bureaucracy with that of the colonial regime. Out of 39 responses, 25 felt that civil servants are less dedicated now than they were under French rule; only 12 declared there was greater dedication today.

According to 40 interviewees, the regime of President Ngo Dinh Diem has politicized the administrative system and afforded it unsatisfactory leadership. Most of those interviewed believed that the regime had shown initial promise but had lost its "revolutionary spirit." Instead of encouraging innovation, rewarding initiative, and inspiring the civil servants to achieve program goals, the regime, they said, had embraced traditional authoritarian, mandarin attitudes and methods which stifled creativity and originality. Only one Class A official had good words for the regime. The 40 others who were willing to express themselves on the subject found the present regime unsatisfactory, and at least two-thirds of them criticized it scathingly with such adjectives as "unpopular," "unwise," and "arbitrary." Several asked in effect how they could be expected to carry out with enthusiasm the ill-advised policies of an unpopular regime which cannot be changed by the will of the people.[76]

Resentment was also expressed that the president and his family were using the administrative system as a "tool" to further their own interests and perpetuate themselves in power.[77] Numerous illustrations of the regime's manipulation of the bureaucracy for political purposes were given. During the interview this question was asked: "Do you believe the bureaucracy has played an important role in influencing the results of elections?" Forty-three interviewees answered "yes"; one, "no"; and five did not answer conclusively. Those responding affirmatively said the bureaucracy has been obliged to support government-sponsored candidates and to insure their election.[78]

The great majority also mentioned the role of two government-sponsored organizations, one composed largely, and the other entirely, of civil servants. One is the Revolutionary Personalist Labor Party (Can Lao Nhan-Vi Cach-Mang Dang), controlled by the president's brother, Ngo Dinh Nhu, who is also mainly responsible for its creation.[79] The Can Lao is a semi-secret association, composed of the elite of the bureaucracy and the army, plus some businessmen. Twenty-six officials declared that with the exception of the bureaucracy, the Can Lao is the most important organization used by the regime to consolidate its authority.[80] Significantly, this view was shared by only a small minority (three out of 13) of the top-level interviewees and middle managers (seven out of 17); it was mainly the junior executives (16 out of 19) who were impressed with the importance of Can Lao. The avowed purpose of the Can Lao is to support President Diem and combat communism. The interviewees said, however, that another major purpose of the organization is to keep a watchful eye on the behavior of bureaucrats (and others) and to report cases of disloyalty to Nhu.[81] Most Can Lao members joined the organization, according to the interviewees, because membership has financial advantages, constitutes an entrée to the seat of power, and enhances the opportunity for advancement.[82]

The other organization sponsored by the government is the National Revolutionary Civil Servants' League (Lien Doan Cong Chu Cach Mang Quoc Gia), in which membership is theoretically voluntary but actually obligatory.[83] Actual direction and control of the League is exercised by Nhu in the South and the central highlands, and by Ngo Dinh Can, one of Diem's brothers, in the central lowlands. The League's objectives are to promote administrative efficiency, expose communist misdeeds, and to explain and support the policies and programs of the regime. The League conducts a study and political indoctrination program to win supporters for the regime, sponsors parades and ceremonies, and intervenes actively during elections in behalf of government-endorsed candidates. As was the case with the Can Lao, interviewees attached importance to the League inversely according to rank.

A few of those interviewed also mentioned the National Revolutionary Movement (Phong Trao Cach Mang Quoc Gia), a mass organization purported to have 1,500,000 members, whose main purpose is to support the president (its honorary leader) and his policies. The NRM's leaders and most active members are civil servants. Indeed most civil servants appear to regard the NRM and the National Revolutionary Civil Servants' League as virtually one and the same organization. Real authority over the NRM, it was said, is divided on geographical lines between the President's brothers, Nhu and Can.

Another complaint against such political leadership was that it provides "irrational management." The 40 interviewees who declared the leadership to be unsatisfactory agreed unanimously that the President is unwilling to delegate authority, except to members of his family and a handful of cronies. Even such minor matters as issuing a visa to a student for overseas study or a charter for a professional society for public administrators must be decided by the president. Moreover, he insists on deciding many important matters himself, regardless of the resultant bottleneck, which has delayed urgently needed action for months, and sometimes for more than a year. A number of interviewees pointed out that, although the governmental system is centralized, there is no single center of power. And, they agreed, when the president makes a decision, there is seldom anyone to contradict it.[84] However, especially since the president has begun spending an increasing amount of time "philosophizing" and "pontificating" with visitors instead of governing, he has acquiesced, at least tacitly, in the making of numerous decisions by members of his family and a few trusted high officials.[85] Sometimes orders from these power centers contradict each other and cause confusion among the civil servants.[86]

Irrational leadership is exemplified in other ways. Several officials pointed out, for example, that the president allots no fixed time for appointments. Department heads and other high officials are often compelled to drop their work and hasten to Gia Long Palace at the president's behest, only to wait for hours before he receives them, if indeed he sees them at all, for frequently, after a long wait, they may be asked to return later (at which time the same fruitless waiting is likely to be repeated). Some of those interviewed objected to the president's "rule by whimsy." While neglecting important matters, they said, he will suddenly direct prolonged attention to some minor matter such as the contours of a small superstructure on the roof of a public building.

Twenty-seven interviewees felt that legalism characterized the administrative system.[87] Expressions such as these were typical: the bureaucracy is "wrapped up in procedures"; present procedures are "excessive and complicated"; the education of civil servants is "too juridical"; they tend to "think in legal terms"; bureaucrats are prone "to stick to the letter of the law" and to "ignore its spirit"; most of them will adhere to fixed procedures even if it means "sacrificing common sense and humane principles." Also, excessive procedural formalities, it was said, are used as a "protective shield" to inhibit action in controversial matters. One interviewee felt that the rigid, complicated processes were bad enough in the slow-moving society of French colonial days; now, he said, with crucial programs requiring decisive action, such procedures may prove disastrous.

It was the opinion of 32 interviewees that civil servants constitute a class apart from the citizen body. Representative comments were: "the bureaucracy constitutes a united group"; the large majority consider themselves "bound together by common interests" and "separated from the general population"; most bureaucrats "tend to think alike"; they have "about the same attitudes and behavior patterns." Several remarked, in effect, that the bureaucracy was working for its own security and safety and not for the public interest.[88]

One interviewee, however, expressing a view shared by a few others, gave a picture which, at least at first blush, seemed to portray the administrative system as less homogeneous than the others had painted it. The Vietnamese bureaucracy—the system and its personnel—may be viewed, he said, as a "mosaic," resulting from an admixture of traditional Vietnamese, French, and, to a lesser extent, American influences; consequently there are "many different values, philosophies, and abilities." Nevertheless, those officials who perceived the civil service as a mosaic agreed that the greater part of the mosaic had the same tone and color.

Twenty-four civil servants—all who commented on the point—concurred that the unity of the civil service, though still strong, had weakened since French colonial days, principally because of the government's practice of employing a great number of persons under contract. Since the contract employees have no permanent status in the civil service, and since many of them are professional men or specialists who can readily earn a livelihood outside the government, they are less tied to the formal administrative structure and more independent than cadre employees.

Several other unfavorable characteristics were mentioned frequently as features of the Vietnamese administrative system. Twenty-five interviewees declared that Vietnamese civil servants display authoritarian behavior. They described Vietnamese public officials at every level as "mandarins" and "bullies" and charged them with displaying "abject obsequiousness" toward official superiors and "harsh authoritarianism" toward official subordinates. Civil servants were accused of thinking in terms of "prestige and authority," of being "aloof" and impervious to the people's needs and wants. Several interviewees quoted an old Vietnamese saying, "In every Vietnamese there is a mandarin." There was general consensus that civil servants often alienate public opinion through "discourtesy," "unsympathetic attitudes," and "disregard for human dignity." Many persons "fear" or at least "dislike" civil servants and try to avoid them. One middle manager, who had spent most of his career in the provinces, related an incident which he said was far too often typical of officialdom in rural areas. This case involved a malaria team sent by the Health Department to spray the homes and buildings of a small southern village. Because of communist propaganda alleging harmful effects from spraying, malaria teams are likely to encounter hostility even if their behavior is impeccable. In this instance the village mayor, though sympathetic with the activity, pleaded with the team to delay the spraying for a few hours while he explained to his constituents the reason for the intrusion into their homes and offered to advise the team how they might least offend local sensibilities. The supervisor curtly refused the mayor's request, ordering his subordinates to proceed with their work. They entered homes through entrances considered taboo in that region, committed what the villagers considered sacrilege by spraying the family altars, and otherwise acted in such a callous manner that the villagers were in almost open revolt.

Not shown in the table are two other features which ten or more of those interviewed attributed to the bureaucracy as unfavorable characteristics. Fourteen said the Catholics exercised control over the bureaucracy far in excess of their proportionate numerical strength.[89] Twelve mentioned as a leading feature of the service and a barrier to its progress the "outmoded personnel system," under which successful applicants for government employment are given rank, status, and salary in managerial, professional, and important technical positions on the basis of the level and prestige of their diplomas.[90]

Also in answer to the first general interview question, 12 referred to the domination of field administration by military officers as an important new characteristic, which eight asserted was regrettable.[91] However, later in the interview when all were specifically asked whether the increased use of army officers in the administration weakened the bureaucracy, approximately half said "no," and added such remarks as these: "there are very few real army officers; as soon as they change to civilian functions, they really become civilians"; "many army officers are well educated and less bound by stultifying bureaucratic traditions than civil servants"; "military or civilians, they are all Diem's yes men."

Twenty-three civil servants noted that the administrative system was symmetrical and highly integrated, with decision making concentrated in the Presidency. But it would be misleading to say that the majority of the 23 believed centralization of power to be undesirable per se. Though some of the interviewees criticized the failure of high administrative and political officials to delegate authority over even minor affairs, with only a few exceptions they did not advocate a wide, liberal delegation of authority as desirable or practicable. Too great a relaxation of top control, they said, would result in inefficiency because of the incompetence of subordinate officials; also several contended it is "contrary to human nature" for high officials to surrender their power and prerogatives. The principal complaint appeared to be not against centralization itself, but rather against the way in which they thought the country's centralized system was being abused by "the family" for its self-aggrandisement. There were also criticisms of the bottlenecks resulting from poor procedures and faulty communications, which they said nullified many of the advantages of centralization.

Although all 49 interviewees were asked to comment "on the outstanding features, good and bad," of the bureaucracy, only one began with the good features. With only four exceptions the others not only started with the bad features but failed to mention any good features whatsoever until reminded that the question called for them. Nearly everyone had difficulty in thinking of more than two or three commendable characteristics, and no one made more than a few brief favorable comments, all of which concerned good qualities of individuals rather than of the administrative system as an institution.[92] As noted in Table 1, intelligence, diligence, self-control, and honesty of civil servants were mentioned an appreciable number of times as good qualities. Most frequently mentioned was intelligence, ascribed as a characteristic by 40 interviewees. Vietnamese bureaucrats were variously described as "clever," "apt," "able," and as "capable of being trained" into first-class employees. Thirty-three of the interviewees said that Vietnamese civil servants are diligent and industrious, several maintaining that they are the most diligent civil servants in Southeast Asia. Also 26 interviewees declared that Vietnamese civil servants have "self-control." They were depicted, for example, as being "calm" and "prudent." They are not, said one official, "wild and erratic like the Thais and Filipinos." Finally, 26 interviewees named "honesty" as a virtue of Vietnamese bureaucrats (see below, pp. 74–75).

The critical nature of the characteristics described by the interviewees was based chiefly upon their perceptions that the operational administrative system does not possess the qualities of pure bureaucratization. Their description appears quite consistent with that of most qualified observers and students of Vietnamese public administration practices. Excessive dependence upon inflexible traditional procedures and refusal to rationalize such procedures are functions of mandarinic status consciousness and efforts to maintain that status. Aloofness from other societal strata is simply an extension of such status consciousness. Formal sanctions against those who would initiate attempts to rationalize administrative practices, or disregard for their attempts, naturally have resulted in an unwillingness to assume responsibility, and those who feel no sense of responsibility hardly can be expected to develop commitment or dedication to an administrative office.

Respondents' characterization of the particularistic, personalized role of the Ngo family is also consistent with all known facts. The presidential family has worked against the creation of a bureaucratized administrative system and has placed considerable emphasis upon de-bureaucratization through the Can Lao, etc. Further, concentration of decision making in the persons of the small group of top Vietnamese elite, primarily the first family, not only has reduced the independence of the administrative system, but also has led to inefficiency, confused chains of command, and faulty networks of communication. This phase of irrational management has greatly reinforced the unwillingness of bureaucrats to assume responsibility. Finally, perhaps the most interesting characterization is the civil servants' adherence to the centralization (and therefore presumably visibility and impersonalization) of decision-making responsibility, while recognizing the impracticality of concentrating decision making.

In view of the interviewees' predominantly critical appraisal of the administrative system, it is not surprising that they felt morale to be generally low in the service. This perception is evident from their answers, shown in Table 2, to a question asking, "How is morale (*tinh than*) among civil servants at present?"

TABLE 2
ATTITUDES, BY RANK, TO CIVIL SERVANTS' MORALE

	TOP OFFICIALS	MIDDLE MANAGERS	JUNIOR EXECUTIVES	TOTAL	%
High	1	0	1	2	4
Medium	5	8	7	20	42
Low	6	9	11	26	54

A follow-up question, "What factors, if any, contribute to (1) good morale, (2) low morale?" received the replies grouped in Table 3.

In spite of insistent questions on the point, the interviewees did not name many existing factors which they believed were conducive to high morale. A common view was that civil servants were living in discouraging times and had little reason to be optimistic. Only the results of independence from the French were mentioned as contributing to good

TABLE 3
FACTORS INFLUENCING MORALE ($N = 49$)

FACTORS	PROPORTION MENTIONING (%)
Conducive to good morale	
National self-determination since independence	67
Better opportunities than under French	33
Conducive to low morale	
Decreasing living standards	86
Unsatisfied psychological needs	71
Quality of political and administrative leadership	69
Tensions from war and other unsettled conditions	41

morale. The very act of independence had boosted morale, especially initially, and was still a source of gratification, said 33 interviewees. "We now feel we are building something for ourselves and not for a foreign power," was the way a top-level official put it. Second, as 16 interviewees pointed out, ambitious Vietnamese officials have had an important new incentive since independence, because they can aspire to top civil service positions which were formerly in the hands of the French. A higher percentage (nearly 40 per cent) of those who had already reached the top levels referred to the increased opportunities than did the middle managers (29 per cent) or junior executives (26 per cent).

Practically all the interviewees talked at length about the factors which lowered civil servants' morale. The factors most often mentioned are grouped in Table 3 into four broad categories: decreasing living standards, unsatisfied psychological needs, poor quality of leadership, and the unsettled security situation. There is some overlapping among all four factors, and the responses almost inextricably linked psychological needs and poor leadership.

Forty-two interviewees said that the morale of civil servants was being undermined by economic pressures. They complained of low salaries, which had not kept pace with rising living costs, and of the infrequency of pay raises. Government salaries, they agreed, were lower than those paid for comparable work in private business. Many lamented the government's imposition of high taxes and forced donations which reduced their already low standard of living.[93]

Thirty-four interviewees pointed to poor leadership, both political and administrative, as demoralizing. The conservative, self-perpetuating policies of the regime, they asserted, were debilitating the administrative system and in other ways contributing to a loss of the country to the communists. Mentioned especially was the regime's practice of forcing civil servants to participate in various political rallies and activities in which they have no interest or enthusiasm, a practice devised to increase the extent of functional control of the political elite. Moreover, most of the 34 contended that many high-level bureaucrats were incompetent old men who held their positions only because of loyalty to the regime and did not have the respect of their subordinates. The transfer of sovereignty by the French to the Vietnamese, they said, suddenly catapulted a number of Vietnamese civil servants, derisively referred to as "parachutists," into high-level positions for which they were not qualified. A number of interviewees emphasized that morale varied from agency to agency, depending largely on its leadership. It was generally agreed that morale was higher in the provinces than in Saigon because promotions come more quickly there and living costs are lower; also, the provinces are "on the firing line" and "faced with realities."

Placing the responsibility largely upon the political and administrative leadership, 35 interviewees said that the morale of civil servants suffered because certain psychological needs were not being met. Most frequently mentioned was the "lack of opportunity" for a whole-hearted exercise of faculties which would bring personal recognition and contribute to national development. As already noted, regret was voiced that the regime has discouraged creativity and has rewarded principally political faithfulness and conventional comportment.[94] Some objections were voiced by the interviewees to the "paternalism" of the system. "We are treated like children and given no real chance to participate," said a middle manager. He added that in theory civil servants can express themselves in meetings, but in practice they dare not disagree with their supervisors. Also, because authoritative information is not obtainable from agency heads, the Vietnamese bureaucracy is a wonderland of rumors, said a junior executive with a degree from a United States university.

Twenty interviewees mentioned tensions resulting from unsettled conditions in Vietnam as a factor adversely affecting civil service morale. They specified the growing strength of the Viet Cong throughout the country and expressed doubt that the guerrilla war could be won with the present political leadership.[95] Several said they had been disturbed by anonymous threatening letters purporting to come from the Viet Cong. References were also made to the recurring rumors of an impending coup d'état, which some believed to be a distinct possibility.[96] Partly because of the "uncertain future," many civil servants, it was said, are "marking time," and trying to remain as uncommitted as possible.

Also contributing to tensions in the bureaucracy and affecting its morale and efficiency is regional animosity among civil servants from the North, the Center, and the South of Vietnam.[97] Replies to a question asking whether there is antagonism among public employees from the three regions are indicated in Table 4.

TABLE 4
PERCEPTION OF EXISTENCE OF REGIONAL ANIMOSITIES
IN THE PUBLIC SERVICE

ATTITUDE	PROPORTION RESPONDING, BY REGION OF ORIGIN (%)		
	North ($N = 20$)	Center ($N = 13$)	South ($N = 16$)
Agree	55	54	88
Disagree	25	23	6
No opinion	20	23	6

Although a majority of interviewees from all sections agreed that antagonism exists, those from the South expressed it in the greatest number and with the greatest intensity of feeling. All but one of them declared that southern civil servants generally regard the northerners as "too aggressive," and consider them "intruders" without genuine loyalty or devotion to their new homeland in the South. The southerners had only mild censure for civil servants from the Center, and the central interviewees who declared that there was antagonism also reserved most of their criticism for their northern colleagues. A majority of the northern interviewees said that civil servants from the South and Center are resentful because they cannot compete successfully with the more industrious, better educated northerners; after all, they said, during the colonial period the North was the center of learning and culture, and the Tonkinese were the most experienced in high-level administrative responsibilities. In addition, a number of northerners accused the president of giving preferential treatment to southerners. Interviewees from each section accused civil servants from the other two sections of being "clannish," and of favoring employees from their own regions while discriminating against those from other regions.

There was a difference in opinion as to the seriousness of regional animosities. As Table 4 shows, about one-third of the interviewees denied the existence of any significant antagonism. Of the 31 who affirmed its existence, only 12 mainly from the South, believed the hostility to be bitter and intense. The remaining 29, while recognizing that there is a serious problem, believed that regional animosities had reached their zenith during 1955–56, following the sudden influx of approximately 850,000 refugees from the North to the South as a result of the Conference of Geneva in July, 1954, and that friction had steadily subsided after 1956 as the northerners had become increasingly assimilated and accepted in the South.

Also creating dissatisfaction among Class A officials, but to a lesser extent than sectional rivalries, is the conviction that the regime favors Catholics. In answer to a question inquiring whether Catholics received preferential consideration in the bureaucracy, over 40 per cent said "yes." Most of those answering in the affirmative qualified their answer by saying, first, that their comments did not apply to low-ranking officials and, second, that partiality to Catholics, though clearly discernible, was not excessive. Nevertheless, they maintained that the number of Catholics in high positions was disproportionate to their number in the total population.[98] Pointing out that the president himself is a devout Catholic (who once studied for the priesthood), some declared that he feels Catholics are more likely than Buddhists to be anticommunist and personally loyal to him. Ordinarily, they said, whenever the government has a choice between appointing or promoting a Catholic or Buddhist to an important position, it will, all other factors being equal, favor the Catholic. For this reason a considerable number of civil servants were said to have adopted Catholicism in the belief it would give them competitive advantages.

Among the illustrations given as evidence of the weight and influence of the church in governmental affairs were these: all high administrative officials, regardless of their faith, are obliged to attend certain ceremonies at the Catholic church; military vehicles are furnished by the government for Catholic celebrations; Catholic priests frequently determine appointments and cause dismissals of administrative personnel, especially in the field; Vietnam, with a preponderantly Buddhist population, has outdone even the overwhelmingly Catholic Latin countries by prohibiting (at the insistence of Mme. Nhu) divorce altogether except by special dispensation of the president. Those interviewees (34 per cent) who did not feel Catholics were receiving preferential treatment admitted that the charge of favoritism had wide credence but declared it had no substance in fact. They named an imposing list of non-Catholics among the highest placed officials, including, among others, the vice president, the secretary of state for the presidency, and the secretary of state for foreign affairs, who are Buddhists.

There are no accurate figures available to support or refute the common charge that Catholics hold a disproportionately high percentage of important government positions. While the charge received worldwide publicity during the height of the 1963 Buddhist crisis, which led to the arrest of Buddhist leaders and the imposition of martial law followed by strained Vietnamese-American relations, no definitive bill of particulars containing authenticated data of religious discrimination within the administrative system was published by any of the disputants. However, discrimination as described by the interviewees is known to exist, resulting in open violation of the essential secular orientation of bureaucratization. There is considerable question as to the motivation of the top political elite, but even assuming that the rationale stems from the particularistic phenomenon of rewarding the personally loyal (and equating loyalty somehow with Catholicism), the product still involves superimposing ascriptive standards upon an ostensibly rationalized structure. In terms of administrative rationality such a practice can be disastrous, especially as it is exercised in Vietnam, because it epitomizes the administrative evils of formalism. For example, one of the techniques of rewarding the loyal (typically Catholic) bureaucrat is to place him, either openly or clandestinely, in a position of responsibility, vested with more authority than that prescribed for an official (frequently a non-Catholic) occupying an office hierarchically superior to his own.

Fourteen interviewees reported still another area of dissension within the administrative system—between cadre and contract personnel. They said that the cadres' chief source of resentment results from the government's policy of offering attractive civil service positions under contract to Vietnamese educated overseas as a means of luring them home. Several charged that the contracts given to young, inexperienced persons sometimes provide for salaries higher than those received by experienced cadre employees with comparable educations. On their part, contract employees, it was said, often feel they are entitled to many of the benefits, especially tenure and retirement, reserved only to cadres. Only two interviewees, both middle managers, believed that differences between cadres and contractuals "seriously" affected the morale of the service. Several junior executives said that young cadre personnel were demoralized by having daily workers put into certain positions, as high as or even higher than their own.

The administrative system in Vietnam is all-pervasive. It exercises a close control and supervision over social, economic, and political affairs. The following question was asked the interviewees to ascertain what they regarded as the respective spheres of the private and public sector: "Do you believe the bureaucracy exercises too much authority over business, labor, education, and private associations?" Replies are presented in Table 5.

TABLE 5
EXCESSIVE AUTHORITY EXERCISED BY ADMINISTRATIVE SYSTEM ($N = 36$)

SPHERES CONSIDERED	PROPORTION OF RESPONDENTS (%)	
	Who Agree	Who Disagree
Business	44	56
Labor	17	83
Education	17	83
Private associations	33	67

Superficially, the replies indicate an overriding opinion that the public sector does not exert an excessive control in society. Only in the field of business did a strong minority feel that control was too great. On the basis of discussion during the interviews, however, it seems a fair conclusion that most of the "no" answers were an approval of the *degree* but not the *kind* of authority the administrative system exercises. To most interviewees it seemed perfectly natural that the government should have comprehensive regulatory powers, but at the same time they expressed objections and even resentment over the regime's policies and tactics. The policies were frequently denounced as "unsound" and "unnecessarily oppressive." The tactics, it was charged, are often illegal and aimed at insuring the survival of the regime. As an example, it was noted that the government, in addition to exercising its regular legal authority over business and labor, resorted to extra-legal procedures to insure that the leaders of the Chamber of Commerce, press society, labor unions, and other associations would be people favorable to and controllable by the regime. These leaders, they said, serve the regime by explaining and justifying its policies, attempting to engender enthusiasm for the Ngo family and its entourage, and exercising surveillance over the loyalty of association members.[99]

Several interviewees, especially top-level managers, whose replies appear in the "disagree" column of Table 5, said they believed in principle that the public sector was too large and should eventually be reduced. But, they added in substance, it is pointless to consider any appreciable extension of the private sector, because the Vietnamese educational and family systems have not inculcated the strong sense of civic responsibility which is a prerequisite for relying upon private groups instead of the bureaucracy in such matters as economic development.

They suggested that a transfer of responsibility from the public to the private sphere might best be begun in the villages. The villagers, they thought, could be made to comprehend their collective interests in their small communities. After a community consciousness and civic spirit had been created on the village level, they might also be developed gradually on higher government levels, making it possible for new responsibilities to be transferred to the private sector in the districts, provinces, and, eventually, even the nation.[100]

The minority who believed the government was infringing upon the private domain usually expressed their views strongly. They thought that red tape and burdensome, unnecessary restrictions were shackling dynamic entrepreneurs and hindering industrialization, trade, and commerce. One top-level civil servant said that some of the regulations are so illogical and unreasonable they would "stir up resentment even in sheep." A few officials said that greater responsibilities ought to be transferred to private enterprise because the bureaucracy "is full of incompetents."

Asked to name any areas other than those specified in the question where they thought the government was unduly interfering in private affairs, 85 per cent cited the so-called "morality law" as being an unwarranted invasion of private life. Among other provisions of this law (passed at the insistence of Mme. Nhu) is a section that prohibits all dancing whatsoever except between husband and wife in the privacy of their home.

The likelihood of almost complete dependence upon the administrative system for social and economic development during the foreseeable future makes it particularly worthwhile to consider the administrative changes advocated by the interviewees. A consideration of their suggestions will, in turn, bring out several characteristics of the civil service not previously mentioned. The proposals were elicited by the question, "What changes, if any, would you suggest in the civil service system and in the outlook, attitudes, and practices of civil servants that would hasten progress by the government in such important areas as economic development and rural administration?"[101] Changes suggested by one-fifth or more interviewees were as follows: more democratic behavior by civil servants, increased inservice training programs,[102] greater program orientation by agencies, more initiative and greater sense of dedication by civil servants, increased incentives for meritorious service, greater local autonomy, establishment of a system of program control and evaluation, a better public relations program by the government, and improved communications.

Though a discussion and analysis of the suggested changes must await a later study, a few explanatory comments about two of them may be illuminating. The subject matter of one was taken up early in the interview as a separate topic. At that point, 40 officials declared that Vietnamese administrative agencies were not sufficiently program-oriented. Asked to name the most program-conscious agencies, 12 named the Budget Directorate; nine, the Press Liaison Center; nine, autonomous agencies like the national bank and bus authority; and five, Civic Action. All these agencies have been created since the colonial period, most with American technical assistance which stressed bureaucratization of operating structures and procedures. The most traditional and least program-minded agencies, the interviewees felt, were the old-line departments like Finance, Justice, and the civil service agency; these were mentioned by 15, 13 and ten interviewees, respectively. On the suggestion that control and evaluation programs are needed, the interviewees explained that at present there is an almost complete absence of checks, either within or without the departments, to determine whether work is being done effectively.

Of the various questions asked the interviewees regarding personnel practices and administration, perhaps the most fundamental were these: "In general how do civil servants reach the upper levels of the bureaucracy?" and "What is the relative weight of ability, seniority, and political affiliation?"

Table 6 gives a summary of the answers:

TABLE 6
EVALUATION OF FACTORS DEEMED TO AFFECT PROMOTIONS
(IN PRIORITY ORDER)

	POLITICAL AFFILIATION			ABILITY			SENIORITY		
	1st	2d	3d	1st	2d	3d	1st	2d	3d
Top managers	8	4	0	4	8	0	0	0	12
Middle managers	13	2	0	2	13	0	0	0	15
Junior executives	10	1	0	1	10	0	0	0	11
Total	31	7	0	7	31	0	0	0	38

It is evident that a large majority of each category of interviewees regarded the political affiliation, ability, and seniority, in that order of priority, as the means whereby civil servants usually reach the top levels of the service. "Political affiliation" was understood to include loyalty to the regime and influence growing out of political connections. Nearly all the interviewees said that the high levels of the service were available only to those who were designated by or at least acceptable to "the family." They agreed, however, that ability also played a major role in promotions, and that seniority was a relatively minor factor. It will be noted from Table 6 that the interviewees who had reached the highest levels of the service were more inclined than the other categories to believe that the top echelons were achieved by merit. There was a consensus, however, that the government, within its necessary framework of loyalty, was placing an increasing emphasis upon efficiency as a basis for promotions, especially in technical areas.[103]

In view of the inadequate salaries, political favoritism, low morale, and lack of dedication which the interviewees perceived as characteristic of the civil service, their views on the extent of graft and corruption are somewhat surprising. The final question asked during the interview was, "Is graft and corruption in the bureaucracy (a) nonexistent, (b) rare and unusual, (c) moderate in amount as might be expected in most countries, (d) somewhat higher than the average of most countries, (e) common and widespread?" Graft and corruption were defined roughly as money or position acquired in a dishonest or questionable manner by taking advantage of one's official position. A breakdown of responses is shown in Table 7.

TABLE 7

PERSPECTIVES ON EXISTENCE OF GRAFT AND CORRUPTION IN THE PUBLIC SERVICE ($N = 44$)

	TOP-LEVEL MANAGERS	MIDDLE MANAGERS	JUNIOR EXECUTIVES	TOTAL	%
Nonexistent	0	0	0	0	0
Rare and unusual	8	7	5	20	45.5
Moderate amount	4	8	7	19	43.2
Somewhat higher than average of most countries	1	0	3	4	9.1
Common and widespread	0	0	1	1	2.3

Thus the interviewees were of the opinion that Vietnamese civil servants have fairly high standards of incorruptibility. A common remark was that there is less graft and corruption in the Vietnamese government than in any other Southeast Asian country. Also voiced frequently was the belief that relatively few high political and administrative figures, not civil servants in general, are largely guilty of whatever dishonesty there is in public office in Vietnam. One American-educated official said he believed the acceptance of bribes by civil servants for favors was no more prevalent in Vietnam than in the United States.[104]

Although the payment of money to administrative officials for favors was believed by the interviewees to be infrequent, they said the use of political influence in the decision-making process was common. This view was elicited in response to the question, "Are administrative decisions usually made on a universalistic or particularistic basis?" The answers were so hedged with qualifications that no attempt will be made to organize them in a table. However, the prevailing view is that low- and middle-level officials seldom depart from a strict interpretation of the regulations in considering special appeals or conditions; they pass on to higher echelons decisions requiring discretion. High officials also tend to adhere to the letter of the law, but they are inevitably confronted by numerous decisions in which they must exercise discretion. These high officials are flooded with requests for special consideration and favors. Almost invariably, for example, when a Vietnamese applies for a license, permit, visa, dispensation, or government action of almost any kind, he attempts to have an influential person intercede in his behalf. Of course the petitioner hopes the use of influence will induce favorable action, but perhaps a more important reason for seeking intercession is to obviate characteristic formidable procedural snags.[105]

In only a comparatively few cases, estimated by several of the interviewees as five to ten per cent (and even less within the technical services), are the decisions actually determined by outside influence or pressure.[106] Except when there is a question of individual loyalty or national security, decisions are ordinarily objective.[107] A number of interviewees emphasized that even where decisions are subjective and particularistic, they are not necessarily iniquitous. On the contrary, because of the rigidity of the regulations and their lack of provisions for unique or peculiar conditions, intercessions for special consideration may result in equity and inject a needed humanizing element in administrative decisions.

Summary of Findings of Study

The attitude of the top-level Vietnamese civil servants toward the administrative system, as represented by the sample interviewed, is generally dispirited and dissatisfied. They are disappointed in the nation's political leadership, and their deliberate avoidance of commitment reflects their view that the regime is unlikely, or possibly even unwilling, to achieve what they feel are its rightful goals, and that the efficacy of the administrative apparatus is itself impaired by this faulty leadership. Significantly, the only favorable comments the interviewees made were not about the institution, but about certain admirable personal traits they felt were characteristic of most civil servants—intelligence, diligence, self-control, and honesty.

Personal traits the interviewees found less desirable—unwillingness to assume responsibility, emphasis on prerogatives of office, and authoritarian behavior[108]—are partly a concomitant of the stultifying institutional traditions and cultural patterns inherited from the mandarin system and French colonialism. The picture of the bureaucracy that emerges is of an institution with an extremely formal and legalistic structure. Like its French system prototype, the duties stipulated for each office are so narrowly defined that, unless the system also provides for higher-echelon officials to have the right to make overriding decisions, any dealings with the bureaucracy are greatly hampered by the reluctance of civil servants to risk making any kind of decisions at all.

While naturally they did not outline in Weberian terms their perceptions of characteristics of Vietnamese public administration or their attitudes toward the role of existing political elite in operations of the administrative system, their perceptions of the distinctions between effective and formal power confirmed the formalistic nature of public administration. Their views regarding the impotency of the probureaucratization interest revealed clearly the inability of American exogenous influence to eliminate most of the particularistic aspects of the administrative system which they criticized.

Unfortunately, as the respondents see it, the regime has not only failed to grant the requisite responsibility for making decisions, but it has actually nurtured the undesirable characteristics and general insecurity by political interference from above or outside the administrative system. Also contributing to low morale are what civil servants feel are inadequate rates of pay, regional animosities, and tensions resulting from the activities of the Viet Cong.

At this critical period in the short history of the nation, these civil servants find the political leadership limp, uninspiring, arbitrary, even capricious. Their lack of faith in the efficacy of the regime contributes in large measure to their lack of commitment and low morale. They are dejected and resentful over the government's failure to demonstrate responsiveness and responsibility to its people. They regard the National

Assembly, the political parties, the courts, and elections as mere trappings without substance. Although they are sophisticated enough to recognize that the constitutional techniques, traditions, and standards of the west are not necessarily the only path to responsible government in a country like Vietnam, they believe that the apparent direction the present regime has taken can lead only to disaster. Thus civil servants are faced with a dilemma. Obliged to carry out the policies of the regime and to perpetuate it in power, they are expected at the same time to win the allegiance of the people, encourage economic development, and solve the various problems crucial to the survival of a nation threatened by militant communist assault. These two obligations they find incompatible and irreconcilable. Their demoralization is a measure of their perception that the political leadership assumes that the bureaucracy's first priority must be to ensure the survival of the regime.

Conclusion: Formalism of the Vietnamese Administrative System and Comparative Administration Theory

The Republic of Vietnam, despite its uniqueness in certain respects because of individual personalities involved, displays dramatically each of the variables typically involved in the conflict between probureaucratization and antibureaucratization interests in transitional political systems. Its myths and ideologies greatly influence its operational bureaucratic structure, including: the myth of mandarinic inviolability; the person of the great fighter for freedom, Ngo Dinh Diem, the scholar patriot; and personalism, a unique blending of Catholicism, Confucianism, and indigenous, communitarian socialism. The coalition of exogenous and endogenous influences favoring bureaucratization has been impressive. Pressures for developmental administration and the presence of increasing numbers of younger, less legalistically educated civil servants have provided a base upon which a significant probureaucratization interest might have evolved.

French reliance upon contractual commitments, regardless of the static, legalistic, class nature of the bureaucracy which actually reinforced the mandarinic spirit of the public service, did advocate numerous facets of bureaucratization. And American pressure has been tremendous as a force for "reform" through establishment of an operational bureaucratic structure. But American participation as part of the probureaucratization interest in Vietnam has proved the limitations of exogenous influences applied to prismatic political systems. It has given evidence to support the principle noted by John D. Mongomery that

"America cannot easily influence the administrative organization of underdeveloped countries, even when aid funds are involved in a program designed to serve common interests. Only the advice that filtered through the network of local politics could be translated into action."[109] In Vietnam, as the network of local politics is under the personal control and direction of the Ngo family, the filtering process necessary to institute an operational bureaucratization of the administrative structure is a practical impossibility.

The resistance of the antibureaucratization interest, consisting of mandarins and the Ngo family, has proved sufficient to overshadow its potent opposition. Mandarinic goals have emphasized maintenance of as much ritualism as possible in the relationships of the administrative system with other strata of the social system (including the goal of preservation of a distinct mandarinic class).[110] They also stress particularistic norms within the administrative system,[111] for example, evaluation of possibilities for promotion on the basis of degrees rather than performance. The Ngo family resistance to bureaucratization has been manifested in numerous ways. Impersonalized administration is incompatible with their view of the role of the political elite as the guardian of society, whereby the rulers do indeed in an omnipresent fashion direct the implementation of administrative functions. The stresses arising from insurgency have reinforced the reliance of the family upon prescriptive policies and administrative concentration of decision making.[112] Debureaucratization has been utilized heavily to subjugate the administrative system.[113] The survival of the regime has perpetually received top priority from the political elite, forcing the administrative system to relegate all developmental objectives to secondary importance. Even counterinsurgency objectives have received only secondary priorities.

Not surprisingly, formalism has been epitomized in Vietnam. This fact, linked with the considerable American attempts to "westernize" Vietnam's administrative structure, serve to validate at least the first segment of Fred W. Riggs' proposition that "the more exogenetic the process of refraction, the more formalistic and heterogeneous its prismatic phase; the more endogenetic, the less formalistic and heterogeneous."[114] The administrative system's formal organization chart and its formal procedural prescriptions and proscriptions reveal a highly bureaucratized structure. The operational structure, however, underlies the fact that neither the administrative system nor individual occupants of offices in this system are independent or neutral vis-à-vis the political elite. Functional specificity is an operational impossibility because the president and his family have attempted to emulate Riggs' "fused model" as closely as possible. Control by the political elite and by the structures of debureaucratization is highly personal and maintained by particularistic-ascriptive measures.

The probureaucratization interest, while retaining certain force because of exogenous influences, has been completely subordinated. Political control of the civil administrative apparatus is complete. And unlike many other nations, the frequent advocates of rationalized administration, i.e., the military, have been subjected to personal rule equally as much as their civilian counterparts. The Vietnamese military has been coopted by the political elite through debureaucratization measures and by counterinsurgency appointments to offices in local government administrative positions. This latter technique has produced a double chain of command, abetting personal control based upon particularistic-sacral criteria of rewards and punishments relating to personal loyalty rather than performance.

Administrative concentration and centralization in the hands of the Ngo family and its closest allies have been the most striking products of the inability of the probureaucratization interest to influence developments within the administrative system. This has resulted in a completely "guided democracy," controlled by elements of the antibureaucratization interest at the top of the political system. Any potential mass romantic revolt against bureaucratization has remained beyond the pale of lawful political processes because articulation of the interests of those at the lowest levels of the political system by noninsurgency local elites is forcefully precluded.[115] Rather, these feelings have been expressed in the insurgency under the auspices of the National Liberation Front and the military-religious sects.

Formalism in Vietnam, as in any prismatic political system, provides a description of the fate of probureaucratization and antibureaucratization interests at any point in time. Nearly a decade after the Geneva Conference the antibureaucratization interest has balanced the scales in favor of traditionalistic administrative practices. This has occurred because the forces favoring universalism and the like in administration have not amassed a coalition formidable enough to offset the strength of a stratum representing a ritualistic cultural milieu which has acted in conjunction with a particularistic political elite.

As seen by the Vietnamese example, investigation of the activities and relative power of forces competing over the issue of bureaucratization—and of the extremity of formalism resulting from such competition—provides a framework for studying any administrative system.[116] This framework also provides a basis for compiling data on a comparative basis for all administrative systems and for constructing middle-range theories of comparative administration.[117]

South Vietnam's Buddhist Crisis: Organization for Charity, Dissidence and Unity

■ Since the fall of Ngo Dinh Diem the Vietnamese Buddhist movement has played a significant role in southern political processes. As noted in Chapter 5, regimes have been forced from office as a result of actions by so-called "militant" Buddhists, a genuine civil war was narrowly averted because they literally defied the national government in central Vietnam, and the Buddhist leadership has become increasingly active and successful in elections. Still the movement has remained divided by diverse interests, has failed to establish a "third force" as many had anticipated it would, and generally has served as a force against stability. Considering its opponents, however, the instability often has been a product of a more positive approach to social and political questions than that adopted by the Saigon government.

The Buddhist movement has remained a minority one. In fact, as a movement it can claim only a minority of Buddhists as being adherents of its goals. It has also remained more a regional than a national movement with some support in larger urban places even outside central Vietnam. Victories in the 1970 Senate election, the 1971 Lower House election and in local elections in central Vietnam have given the movement a base of power within the formal political system. Attempts to develop organizations for youth, women, farmers, etc., as well as programs for leadership training, have built a stronger infrastructure. The movement has built the framework of a political party which is as strong as any other nationalist party. Through the years, indeed, the place of the movement as a nationalist one has become clear.

It would like political power; its secular leaders at least are not immodest concerning their capability to run South Vietnam. The movement does have something of a political platform though it is less than carefully articulated. It opposes corruption and favors separation of powers with a legislature independent of executive orders. Its position concerning peace has received international attention, but very few know what that position is. From pronouncements and actions the movement has adopted a "progressive" nationalist stance. This means first no surrender to the "communists," a point frequently stressed.

Presumably this means no settlement resulting in a victory for Hanoi or for the NLF. The progressive aspect, advanced more frequently in the early 1970's by other nationalist parties and to some extent even by the Saigon government, is that the NLF should be permitted to participate in future elections following a ceasefire. However, the movement's leaders reiterated its major point immediately after the 1972 Easter offensive began, i.e., independent nationalist opposition must be permitted but all else must be subordinated to preservation of the political system from its attackers.

The Buddhist movement was extremely displeased by the results of the 1971 presidential election. Its leaders were not unified on the best strategy, but they had hoped to make positive gains because of the election. Their support of General Duong Van Minh against President Thieu was never wholehearted. Minh was evasive, demands made upon him by Buddhist leaders were not met to their satisfaction, and few really believed Minh could defeat Thieu. The incumbent had an important power base, presumably had augmented his support in many rural areas, and was unlikely to permit a referendum to throw him out of office. A campaign might have strengthened the movement organizationally, although it also could have been a source of embarrassment if Minh did not fare well. When it became obvious that Thieu did want a two-way race with Minh, one in which he could receive a much wanted majority instead of the plurality he obtained in 1967, some Buddhist leaders were prepared to continue the race if the government made certain concessions. Thieu gave no indication of willingness to appoint movement choices to important government positions. Minh's position on the entire question of the 1971 campaign and even of his relationship with the movement will remain a subject of dispute, but certainly Thieu's obstinacy and known orders to provincial officials to guarantee his reelection were adequate incentives for Minh to withdraw from the race.

Despite the lack of success in obtaining its goals during the 1971 presidential election, the Buddhist movement continued to have advantages no other civil political force possessed. It had a strong local base, trained cadres, better financing than most parties, and actually was the local government in much of central Vietnam. The image as hero of the 1963 coup had not been entirely lost. Its leadership, while severely divided into northern, central and southern factions as well as lay-sacral and youth-elders segments, was more vigorous and articulate than most of its opponents. And it was one national group which conceivably could reach a rapprochement with the NLF. Its leaders preferred not to share power. And few of them were unconcerned about the difficulties of coping with encroachments which a legalized NLF might attempt to make both within the political system and within the Buddhist movement. On the other hand, they recognized

that their future support would be valuable regardless of the type
of political system in South Vietnam. Neither Thieu nor the nationalist
parties failed to recognize their political potential. Although they would
have chosen not to be concerned with the problem, the Buddhist leaders
hoped the NLF also fully recognized this potential. The Buddhist movement by 1973 had become a super-patriotic nationalist force which
could opt to serve as an active loyal opposition, as a militant force
for more representative government, and as the major nationalist peace
party. It continued to qualify its conditions for peace and to adopt
tactics for survival regardless of political developments. Its ultimate
goal of political power, however, still remained elusive.

M ONSIGNOR Ngo Dinh Thuc, dean of the Vietnamese epis-
copacy, archbishop of Hue, founder of the Personalism Training Center,
and chancellor of Da Lat University, ironically initiated the macabre
series of steps leading to the demise of his own clan.[118] His "episcopal
silver jubilee" was the instance for numerous celebrations commemor-
ating his long career as a Vietnamese public figure. A natural and seemingly innocent part of the ceremonies included displaying the white and
gold papal flag.[119] Unfortunately for the Ngo family the occasion for
those celebrations immediately preceded the 2507th anniversary on
May 7, 1963, of the birth of the Lord Buddha. Bird flocks were released
as a sign of charity and mercy, while the combination of horizontal and
vertical red, blue, and saffron-yellow stripes of the Buddhist flag was
prominently displayed. The government promptly ordered the displays
discontinued unless prominence was given to the national flag of the
Republic of Vietnam. Troops then tore down posted Buddhist flags. A
flower dance at the Tu Dam Pagoda, two kilometers from Hue, was
suddenly canceled. Three thousand celebrants then proceeded to the
VTVN radio station in Hue demanding that a commemorative program
be broadcast for the Buddha.

In an almost casual wire from the government delegate for the central Delta, the incident which marked the turning point in President Ngo
Dinh Diem's uncanny fortunes in the game of political survival was described in the following manner: "As such a request [for a commemorative program] could not be met at once a certain number of impatient
demonstrators lost control and assaulted the station. Local security
forces had to use fire hoses to break up the crowd. During the confusion
the grenade was tossed by someone in the crowd."[120] Although the government officially confirmed the delegate's version later, even providing
the added touch that the grenade was thrown by a communist, photo-

graphs by non-Vietnamese showed that troops used tear gas grenades and fired on the demonstrators. The eight casualties that day became the first martyrs who served as a continuing bone of contention throughout the "Buddhist crisis."

Immediate nationwide and international repercussions of the May 8 incident temporarily forced Diem to adopt a compromising tone. He met with an eight-member delegation of leading Buddhists on May 15 and appeared to agree to most of their terms. The legality of displaying religious flags was accepted and payments were agreed upon for families of the May 8 victims. In addition Article 17 of the Constitution was reaffirmed, i.e., "Every citizen has the right to freedom of belief, religious practice and teaching, provided that the exercise of these rights shall not be contrary to morality." From the Buddhists' point of view the agreement was inadequate, as Thich Tam Chau proclaimed in a statement the day after the agreement was announced, because the government did not accept responsibility for the incident. Nonetheless, possibly the announcement would have precluded a continuation of the crisis if a cardinal precept of administration had not been ignored, namely, that promulgation is not identical to implementation. The terms of the agreement were not implemented by the government. This inaction led to the issuance of a pastoral letter on May 28 by Thich Tinh Khiet, monk superior of the General Association of Buddhism in Vietnam, calling for a hunger strike to begin May 30. Tardy action by the regime failed to halt the strike. A May 29 government communique to all cadres requiring religious impartiality and a reaffirmation of Article 17 by the National Assembly on May 31 were given little credence. On May 30, 350 monks and nuns began a 48-hour fast with a four-hour demonstration in front of the National Assembly Building in Saigon, while in Hue the fast continued for an entire week.

The government persisted in handling the situation with less than its usual finesse. It was claimed that communist infiltration had prevented the Buddhist movement from accepting the government's promises in good faith. Further, the regime insulted both the regular Sangha (monastic order) and the sensibilities of the majority of Buddhists by announcing receipt of pro-Diem resolutions from the Buddhist representatives in the provinces of Binh Duong, Phuoc Tuy, Gia Dinh, and Bien Hoa. The insult was only intensified by publication of a letter from the leader of the government-favored Luc Hoa Tang Buddhist sect, stating: "If need be people can tell the President all their aspirations and be sure that with him, who has devoted his whole life for the good of the nation, religious equality is a natural thing."[121] Lack of diplomatic finesse was then compounded when troops using tear gas grenades and blister bombs dispersed 1,200 student demonstrators near the Ben Ngu bridge in Hue, which was within the jurisdiction of Ngo Dinh Can, the president's brother. The hospitalization of some 67 injured students, and the subsesquent maltreatment and death of a number of those incarcerated, added to the fuel, making compromise immeasurably more difficult.

Although events had escaped his control, Diem made a second gesture to negotiate the issue, partly because of considerable American pressure. Once again he called upon the cadres to adhere to the principles of Article 17 and in a VTVN broadcast June 6 appeared more willing to adopt a conciliatory stance than on any previous occasion.

I realize with sadness that some of our compatriots, including the cadres of various branches of the public as well as private services, have not yet reached a substantial degree of understanding and sensitivity regarding their duty towards the people. I therefore have to call upon our compatriots to take full cognizance of their duty as citizens in maintaining public security to strictly observe national discipline, and to seriously study all the problems falling within their competency using only reason, common sense and considering the national cause. Thus, they will effectively help me resolve our problems in conformity with the imperatives of the national policy.[122]

Diem followed this announcement with the appointment of an interministerial committee on June 4. The national government's highest Buddhist, Vice President Nguyen Ngoc Tho, became chairman of the new group. Other government representatives were the influential Presidency Secretary Nguyen Dinh Thuan, and Interior Secretary Bui Van Luong. Buddhist representatives were Superior Monk Thich Thien Minh, the deputy chairman of the Buddhist Association of the central area and commissioner for youth and students of the General Buddhist Association of Vietnam, and Superior Monk Thich Thien Hoa, the chairman of the South Vietnam Sangha. The day after the interministerial committee was formed Buddhist leaders enhanced their bargaining position by agreeing to form an Intersect Committee for the Defense of Buddhism consisting of fourteen Buddhist groups, a step providing more apparent unity than Vietnamese Buddhism had enjoyed in centuries.[123] The Intersect Committee was not only a manifestation of a new Buddhist identity, but also dramatized the unity and identity of the religion and simultaneously singled out the regime as the enemy of Buddhism. A ceremony at Phat Buu Pagoda in Saigon on June 11 focused more international attention on the plight of Vietnamese Buddhists and on the futility of the Ngo personalist regime than any demonstration or reported religious persecution could ever have attained.

From the Phat Buu Pagoda 700 priests went quietly to the front of the Cambodian legation building to observe the execution of a rite older than Vietnam itself. Thich Quang Duc, a 73-year-old monk from Khanh Hoa Province, permitted himself to be saturated with gasoline and then burned himself to death while thousands observed the age-old rite of protest by suicide. Few gestures could have drawn a greater degree of attention to the reality of the Buddhist crisis. The good monk's plea had been simple: "I pray to Buddha to give light to President Ngo Dinh Diem, so that he will accept the five minimum requests of the Vietnamese Buddhists. Before closing my eyes to go to Buddha, I have the honor to present my words to President Diem, asking him to be kind and tolerant towards his people and enforce a policy of religious equality."[124] The deed had a far from simple impact. The afternoon of the immolation Diem presented a scheduled message stating that the discussions of the interministerial committee had restored calm, although unfortunately persons "poisoned by seditious propaganda" had caused "a tragic death." Then almost as though his world could ever be the same, the president of the republic noted:

If, among the Buddhists, some still remain troubled by the propaganda rumors which I have just denounced and are inclined to believe that the public authorities are maneuvering with the design of deferring the settlement of the issue with which they are concerned, and that they are contemplating religious persecution, then I would solemnly remind them that Buddhism in Vietnam finds its fundamental safeguard in the Constitution of which I personally am the guardian.[125]

Six more Buddhists remained "troubled" enough to commit suicide by fire, and each of them made explicit that the president was not an acceptable "guardian" of religious freedom in Vietnam. Diem the man of honor was simply no longer honored.

Indecisiveness marked the handling of the necessary ceremonies for Thich Quang Duc as it had the preceding events in the Buddhist crisis, with conciliation and suppression vying with each other in a confused melee of government uncertainty. Buddhists were permitted to fly their flags at half staff and mourners were allowed to visit the scene of the martyr's state of rest at Saigon's Xa Loi Pagoda. The government attempted to pacify the Buddhists and keep their demonstrations under control by providing transportation for the mourners. But even this gesture was frustrated with failure. The buses were late and thousands of mourners, mostly women wearing white dresses with yellow patches pinned on to denote that they were Buddhists, were prevented from rioting only when the government resorted to the use of barbed wire and other hastily conceived devices of dissuasion.

Then, on June 15, the day before the scheduled funeral for the monk Duc, the government announced that concessions had been made. This announcement was followed the next day by the issuance of a joint communique agreed upon by the interministerial committee and the Buddhist delegation. This communique contained detailed procedures for displaying both the national flag and other flags, including displays on national holidays and Buddhist holidays and displays in pagodas, on ceremonial platforms and vehicles of Buddhist dignitaries, and in processions and private homes. The agreement also provided for the exemption of religious associations from certain statutory controls; the creation of an investigating committee and promise of special clemency for religious dissidents arrested and detained; government guarantees concerning religious activities, properties, publications, and construction; severe punishment for cadres violating the agreement; and payments (rather than compensations because of government guilt) to families of the May 8 incident in Hue. The communication was signed by the three government representatives on the interministerial committee and by Thich Tinh Khiet, Thich Thien Minh, Thich Tam Chau, and Thich Thien Hoa. Monk Superior Khiet extended his full support to the communique, an action which should have considerably alleviated the extreme tensions surrounding the situation following Duc's immolation. In a letter to Diem, Khiet appeared greatly relieved and even confident.

In the name of the General Association of Vietnam, Buddhist associations in the Southern and Central and North Central Areas, the Intersect Committee for the Defense of Buddhism and in my own name, I have the honour to respectfully thank you for having appointed an Interministerial Committee to settle the Buddhists' five wishes and for approving the joint communique sanctioning the settlement.

Like all Buddhist faithful I have the firm conviction that the joint communique will inaugurate a new era and that no misunderstanding, no erroneous action from whatever quarter will occur again, so that the solidarity which binds our people may be further strengthened with each passing day in freedom and justice.[126]

Shortly after the joint communique was issued thousands gathered for the procession and ceremony to accompany the funeral of Thich Quang Duc. Once more the government pattern of concession-suppression dictated events. The June 16 funeral date was postponed at the last minute to June 19, whereupon an inevitable riot occurred. Tear gas, beatings and hundreds of arrests, particularly arrests of teenagers, suppressed the worst riot Saigon had witnessed in years, but these tactics also dispelled any faith that the Buddhists might have had in the joint communique. The government's attempt to save face by claiming that its militant action was necessary to preclude communist maneuvers within the Buddhist ranks satisfied neither the population nor the older Buddhist leaders who had agreed to the joint communique.[127] The regime's tactics, however, were particularly disturbing to the younger Buddhist leaders, who already perceived their representatives' willingness to agree to terms without insisting upon government assumption of legal responsibility for the Hue incidents as a betrayal of the Buddhist revitalization movement. The government's subsequent success in preventing a second riot during the June 19 funeral wrote the final lie to the intent of the joint communique. By building barricades around pagodas, beating and arresting suspect priests, banning a procession, and limiting participation in the ceremony at Binh Chanh cemetery by permitting only 30 busloads of priests and nuns to participate, the regime moved relentlessly to its own destruction. The efficiency of the police tactics rendered compromise impossible and, more significantly, strengthened the hand of the younger and more militant Buddhist leaders against their more concession-prone elders.

From the time of Thich Quang Duc's funeral both sides were hardening their positions. Buddhist willingness to negotiate lessened considerably. On the government side the most significant development was the heightened role of Ngo Dinh Nhu, whose great influence was dedicated to the destruction rather than the appeasement of the regime's opposition. Nhu's hand was clearly visible in the list of complaints Superior Monk Khiet addressed to Diem on June 26 recording in detail the areas where violations of the joint communique had occurred. Khiet specified: that the Information Service had persuaded residents in the provinces to pass resolutions condemning Buddhist activities against the regime; that police made lists of all who visited pagodas; that the Quang Tri pagoda had been blocked off by security police; that flag display difficulties persisted; and that monks and nuns were obstructed when they attempted to visit provinces other than their native ones. In addition, Khiet cited two communique violations which clearly were products of Nhu's handiwork, first, the government's rallying of the Luc Hoa Tang Buddhist sects against the General Buddhist Association, and second, the preparations under the direction of Youth Director General

Cao Xuan Vy for a mass Cong Hoa Youth anti-Buddhist demonstration.[128] Despite Vice President Tho's emphatic denial that the work of the interministerial committee had been betrayed by the president's brother, no one seriously accepted the version of the committee's chairman.

Nhu's most dramatic tactic at this stage was an attempt to embarrass the United States, which he considered a dangerous force favoring concessions to the Buddhists, thus encouraging their dissident activities. On July 5 the government announced that 19 officers and 34 civilians accused of involvement in the abortive 1960 paratroopers' coup would be tried both in person and in absentia. As Nhu had previously accused the United States, and particularly the Central Intelligence Agency, of involvement in the coup and as two former American embassy officials were accused of involvement, the trial was intended as an obvious slap at the presumably soft, compromising Americans. The trial was also intended to convince the Vietnamese military that the Americans could not be counted upon as an effective ally in any attempted coup.

Crude though the tactic was, it might possibly have pressured the United States into accepting Nhu's position in the Buddhist crisis. However, once again careful plans intended to manipulate the development of the Buddhist crisis were made fortuitous by the dramatic action of one man. Nguyen Tuong Tam, the former leader of the VNQDD nationalist party who under the pen name of Nhat Linh ("the mystic one") was Vietnam's best-known poet, committed suicide by poison rather than appear for trial.[129] His eloquent suicide note, written in his home where he had been under surveillance since 1960, pleading for discontinuation of suppression of Buddhists, insured the failure of Nhu's tactic by changing the trial from an exposé to a tragedy. Tam's suicide also intensified the crisis by bringing the always important Vietnamese student groups, among whom he remained a most popular figure, into an active alignment with the Buddhists.

Mid-July was marked by a pattern clearly beyond the control of either the regime or the regular Sangha leadership. Demonstrations, police brutality, arrests and barricades all made the internal situation unbearable and brought worldwide criticism of the Saigon government. On July 16, over 150 Buddhists filed without incident from Xa Loi Pagoda and demonstrated before the residence of the American ambassador to protest nonimplementation of the joint communique. But the next day hundreds were clubbed and arrested at the main Saigon market and at Giac Minh Pagoda and then carted to Binh Chanh cemetery for temporary detention. The suppression-conciliation pattern continued for the next few days. On July 8, security police raided a pagoda and carted off three monks, but the next day barricades were removed from most pagodas, and on July 20 the government released 267 who had been held at the cemetery and permitted those released to go to Xa Loi Pagoda to be welcomed by 600 priests, nuns and laymen. Then on July 23 Saigon witnessed a ludicrously staged anti-Buddhist demonstration by wounded war veterans seated in cyclos (bicycle cabs) carrying progovernment banners demanding more severe actions against religous dissidents.

While these paradoxical events were transpiring, Vice President Tho continued his futile attempts to regain the more conciliatory mood of the joint communique agreement period, proposing a joint commission to investigate instances of previously alleged bad faith in the implementation of the communique and to assume responsibility for future implementation. However, his repeated efforts to persuade Superior Monk Khiet to resume discussions met with no success because the Buddhist leaders now demanded that the government assume responsibility for the Hue affair as a prior condition to negotiations. Buddhist leaders further displayed their lack of faith in government assurances by barricading themselves in the Xa Loi Pagoda on July 25, addressing a crowd of 7,000 at Xa Loi two days later on the nonimplementation of the communique's guarantees and calling for July 30 demonstrations to commemorate the last day of the formal memorial period for Duc in Da Lat, Nha Trang, Quin Nhon, and Hue as well as in Saigon.

The first three weeks of August provided a dismal picture of the vice president of the Republic hampered at every turn in his attempt to instill sanity into a continually deteriorating situation, of the superior monk of Vietnam calling for a limit to sacrificial immolations and being ignored, and of the director of the Political and Social Research Bureau together with many of his well-placed secret police and many important military leaders assiduously plotting a coup which never met with fruition.[130] Ngo Dinh Nhu and Madame Nhu took full advantage of this situation once the initiative had escaped the leadership of all other parties. Nhu's solution was announced in an August 3 interview when he commented that a counter-coup against the religious dissidents was a distinct possibility and that: "The first action of a new Government after carrying out a coup would be to crush Xa Loi."[131] Mme. Nhu's contribution to the debate shocked the world as she castigated "barbecued" monks who used imported gasoline, and noted succinctly that the government should "ignore the bonzes, so if they burn 30 women we shall go ahead and clap our hands. We cannot be responsible for madness."[132] When the "madness" continued with suicides by a student priest on August 13, a nun on August 15, and a 71-year-old priest on August 16, the government showed it assumed no responsibility whatever by cracking down severely on funeral processions and demonstrations in Hue and Nha Trang, although no attempt was made to interfere with a demonstration by some 17,000 in Saigon on August 19. However, the following day an army jeep became entangled in a demonstration in Da Nang, resulting in military casualties and subsequent devastating suppression of the demonstrators.

At this low point when it appeared that the situation could deteriorate no further short of open rebellion, and when the regime appeared to have lost the capacity to cope with what had begun presumably as a relatively minor series of incidents, the Buddhist crisis was "solved" by the superb strategist Ngo Dinh Nhu. In one stroke he moved to still his opposition in the military and to eliminate vocal Buddhist dissidence. On August 21, nationwide raids were carried out against pagodas by troops in full battle gear, and numerous Buddhists were arrested and incarcerated. A state of siege was declared, curfews were established, public meetings were banned, and press censorship was increased. [133] Nhu's counter-coup was brilliant in its simplicity and farreaching in its effect. The military leaders not only were forced to cancel their own coup but at least temporarily shared blame for the militant crackdown about which they knew nothing (except for General Ton That Dinh), as it had been executed by special forces under Nhu's protégé, Col. Le Quang Tung. At this stage the new American ambassador to Vietnam, Henry Cabot Lodge, arrived in Saigon to face a fait accompli under which, according to the Nhu strategy, the United States would only worry about the counterinsurgency campaign rather than about the status of religious dissidents. The Nhu move was so brilliant in fact that it convinced both the Vietnamese military leadership and American diplomats that they could no longer reasonably hope to settle their differences with the Ngo family through negotiations and compromise. The Americans now were forced to rely upon the force of their purse, while the military had no alternative but to rely upon force of arms.

The action which marked the beginning of the end for the Ngo regime served its immediate purpose exceedingly well. The Buddhist movement itself was effectively checked. With the more militant leadership either jailed or in hiding, the elders who had lost the initiative in the evolution of the Buddhist crisis quickly came to terms with the regime. Thich Thien Hoa, chairman of the National Sangha Association, led the way in the capitulation. On August 23 he called upon Buddhists to help implement the joint communique. Hoa noted that it was the government which proposed the "brotherly agreement" but that impediments to the communique had been masterminded by "unidentified provocateurs determined to sow confusion, hatred, division and trouble between the Government and the Buddhists, thus creating the false impression abroad that Buddhists in Vietnam were being brutally oppressed by the Government."[134] A delegation headed by Hoa and including many of the luminaries of Vietnamese Buddhism later paid homage to Diem at Gia Long Palace on August 28. The delegation had the formal blessing of Thich Tinh Khiet, who had recanted publicly three days earlier. In a radio statement on August 25, Khiet recognized his errors, commenting that he had been enlightened about the "true nature of the Intersect Committee's activities" by Hoa. In view of his new enlightened state he said he had decided to give Hoa and his delegation "full powers to repair all the harm caused by the divergences between the Buddhists and the Government to settle by peaceful means all misunderstandings which have caused so many regrettable events in the past three months."[135] The Venerable Thich Thien Hoa performed his new duties well and on September 17 wired the secretary general of the United Nations in his new capacity as head of the Union Committee for Pure Buddhism condemning the fact that "a number of politically minded people" had hidden under "the roofs of the pagodas and monks' robes to engage in extremist activities to satisfy their cupidity, passions and aggressiveness."[136]

The demise of articulate opposition within the Buddhist movement led to what was to a considerable extent a repeat performance of the play which had just ended. Student protests and demonstrations in the cities began almost immediately after the crackdown on the Buddhists. Schools had to be temporarily closed on August 24, student arrests and beatings mounted in numbers, at first in the hundreds and finally in the thousands, and claims of communist infiltration into the student movement became a common government accusation (two female students even were permitted to hold a press conference to announce their communist affiliations). And on October 27 the government proudly announced that it had crushed a student and intellectual plot. Occasional Buddhist activity added fuel to the flame which the students continued to kindle. A sixth and seventh immolation occurred, and potential Buddhist demonstrations, intended to impress Secretary Robert Mc-Namara and General Maxwell Taylor and later the United Nations investigating committee sent to determine facts in the Buddhist situation, were crushed before they began.

The United States, foiled in its attempts to persuade Diem of Nhu's dispensability, halted commercial aid to Vietnam and later stopped assistance to those special forces which had been assigned nonmilitary duties. These sanctions had more of a psychological than a real immediate impact.[137] It is doubtful if they had any effect at all on the Ngos. But the significance of the American moves was not lost on the already thoroughly disillusioned military leadership. The combination of interference in military operations, suppression, bungling in the Buddhist and student affairs, and embarrassment of the military in the August crackdown, made a coup d'etat only a matter of timing. The obvious lack of opposition to such a step from the Americans served as an incentive, although by the end of October little external incentive was necessary. The November 1 coup succeeded because the regime was weakened by its own inadequacies, because it was brilliantly executed through a betrayal more colossal than even Nhu could have envisioned, and as always because luck that day was on the side of the victors.[138] In retrospect it even can be said that the subsequent deaths of Nhu and Diem were the product of Nhu's own brand of "madness" manifested during the early hours of a morning of the previous August. The Buddhists emerged as victors from the Buddhist crisis despite their temporary impotency due to the incarceration of so many of their numbers and to the unwillingness of their top leaders to continue the struggle. Their weakness proved to be their strength just as Nhu's strength made the downfall of the Ngos inevitable.

Emerging from the ruins of the Ngo dynasty as publicly acclaimed heroes and as universally regarded giant killers, it was inevitable that the leadership of the Buddhist movement would henceforth play a more significant role in Vietnamese political processes than had been possible before November 1, 1963. Despite the popularity of the military leadership following the overthrow of the Diem-Nhu-Can combine, the Military Revolutionary Council, as it was initially constituted under Major General Duong Van Minh and as it was reconstituted under General Nguyen Khanh following the "bloodless purge" of January 31, 1964, paid considerable credence to the importance of the Buddhist movement. Early November saw the military releasing imprisoned Buddhists and students, permitting mass street demonstrations, and expressing congratulations to Buddhist leaders. Crowds jammed pagodas to extoll the blessings of the military coup d'etat. Buddhist leaders as an expression of their gratitude to the military utilized their tremendous influence with the students to prevent demonstrations and protests against General Minh's appointment of his old friend and former fellow prisoner,

Vice President Tho, as premier of the new government.[139] Both Minh and Tho then promised that the United Nations declaration of human rights would be assiduously observed and that religious freedom would be assured, including religious freedom for Catholics and the sects.[140]

The Buddhist leaders were far from unanimous in their perception of the most advantageous role for the revitalized religious movement in the immediate post-Diem period. This divergence of opinion was partly a response to the elimination of a common enemy and partly a natural consequence of younger leaders finding themselves in a position of prominence rivaling that of their elder, traditional Sangha leaders. The political milieu in a nation so long encumbered by conditions of insurgency and now challenged by a growing sentiment favoring some form of neutralism for Vietnam also served to divide the more articulate among the Buddhist sacral and lay hierarchies. This division not only took the form of pro- and antineutralism but also involved the debate over what particulars should be included in a policy of neutralism if such a policy appeared inevitable.

But despite variations in opinion concerning both leadership and specific policies, the Buddhists maintained complete agreement on two extremely important points: (1) Buddhism had to be a vital force affecting both public policy formulation and governmental operations, and (2) the Buddhist movement had to display unity and extend its influence on the basis of this unity. On the first point, Tran Quang Thuan, chairman of the Buddhist Student Association and later secretary of state for social welfare in the government of General Nguyen Khanh, was most explicit, stating: "This Government had better have a backing force. What force should this be? The one that brought about the revolution—Buddhism. Buddhism has deep roots among the people."[141] Thuan further noted that Buddhist strength could be most keenly felt as an aid to the new regime among the rural population, precisely the area in which the control of any Saigon government is always at its weakest.

Consensus was clearly visible among the Buddhists, including both the regular Sangha and the various independent groups, concerning the need for unity as a requisite to consolidating and enhancing their political posture. An Independent Buddhist Bonzes' Rally Committee was created on December 25 favoring unification of the sects. This committee was formed as part of the preparations for a most important religious unity meeting, the Vietnamese Buddhist Reunification Congress. The Military Revolutionary Council gave the unity meeting its full support, both because it wanted to be publicly associated with the Buddhist movement and because it recognized the potential for obtaining mass popular support through Buddhist efforts. Eleven sects throughout the nation sent representatives to the Congress at Xa Loi Pagoda, which lasted from December 31, 1963, to January 3, 1964. Thich Tam Chau, chairman of the Intersect Committee, served as chairman of the organizing committee for the Congress.[142]

It was decided by the Congress that Buddhist political and social influence could be best assured by establishing permanent organizations which would administer programs agreed upon by the united Buddhist movement. The most powerful secular force was to be the Institute for the Propagation of the Faith (Institute of Secular Affairs) which was to have representatives in all provinces and in most districts.[143] This organization presumably will expand Buddhist influence among the rural population, as noted by Tran Quang Thuan, by serving as the government of the new Vietnam Association of United Buddhists.[144] Field workers are being trained to implement programs of the Institute for the Propagation of the Faith. Thich Tam Chau is chairman of the Institute, while the Venerable Phap Tri and Thich Thien Hoa are its vice chairmen; Mai Tho Truyen is the lay representative in the organization's chief officer group.[145] Six general commissions, each with a potentially powerful chairman and commissioners, are in charge of various functional categories of Institute activities: religious personnel, faith expansion, rites, financial and restoration affairs, laymen affairs, and youth.[146] A priest is chairman of each commission, while the commissioners include both religious and secular personnel. While considerable importance is given to the younger and more militant leaders, the Institute also provides representation for the leaders of the traditional Sangha as witnessed by the selection of Thich Thien Hoa as an Institute vice chairman.

In addition to the secular orientation of the Institute, an organization to attend to purely sacral matters has been organized. The High Council of the Buddhist Hierarchy includes Thich Tinh Khiet as supreme bonze, thus continuing him as the number one Buddhist religious leader in Vietnam. Other Council officials include a superior bonze, two elder bonzes, a secretary general (Thich Tri Quang), and three deputy secretaries general.[147]

Lines of authority between the more secularly oriented unit and the sacral hierarchy have not been keenly articulated, and remain potential vehicles for magnifying the considerable political differences among the Buddhist leaders as do the several divisions of the Institute. Despite these possible handicaps, the existence of unity in the Vietnam Asso-

ciation of United Buddhists and the establishment of a permanent organization provide the Buddhist movement a greater opportunity for
effectively exerting its overall influence than it has enjoyed in several
hundred years. The 2507th birthday of the Buddha marked the beginning of the end of a powerful regime, but in terms of long-range impact
on Vietnam its greatest heritage may yet prove to be the revitalization
of Vietnam's principal religion.

3

Electoral Behavior in South Vietnam: A Case Study of the 1967 Elections

Introduction

This case study of the 1967 election is an attempt to provide a comprehensive statement of the one event where nearly all nationalist political forces in South Vietnam competed in the open. This election to a great extent is a microcosm of Vietnamese nationalist politics since the end of World War II and even of many types of struggles since the beginning of the century. The goals of the case study include taking a photo of the vast variety of centrifugal forces in the only occasion where their activities have centered on a single process. Another goal is to provide a careful observation of that process itself. Although the event was unique in many ways it is representative of the electoral experiences in nearly all underdeveloped nations.

The host of actors competing in a non-clandestine struggle which they really did not fully comprehend, the inability of communal and other interest group forces to join together even once for a common objective, the process of electoral behavior in a quasi open but still quasi dictatorial milieu—these are representative of electoral experiences in most of Asia, Africa and South America.

Since 1966 especially, South Vietnam has had an unprecedented series of experiences with popular elections. Few underdeveloped nations have undertaken such a broad experiment in electoral processes, and there is certainly no historic example of such wide-ranging use of the franchise in time of war. Historians may prove this was an experiment in folly. Certainly, for a number of sociopsychological reasons, many have observed electoral behavior is antithetical to traditional Vietnamese norms and that it has proved an exercise in insignificance, occurring as it has during the most bloody war of our era. Yet it has been unique, something that could not lack interest for anyone absorbed by Vietnamese politics.

The area in which the extremely diverse interest groups in South Vietnam competed was nationwide, though proving once again that perhaps nothing is truly "national" about Vietnamese politics. Nonetheless, in 1967 elections provided a forum for those groups. The forum was not open, and it was conducted under traumatic circumstance. But it was an opportunity previously excluded from Vietnamese politics. It did not necessarily set a pattern for future electoral enterprises. Yet it did provide a broad spectrum of nearly all interested political personalities, and a canvas for comparison with attempts by other underdeveloped nations that have utilized elections as a phase of what their leaders perceived as political development.

VIOLENCE has rarely been absent in Indochina since 1940, though varied plebiscites have been held to provide legitimacy *a posteriori* for a mandate obtained by nonelectoral means. Almost without exception the various attempts to prove the representative nature of legislative or executive leaders or of decisions have been show pieces—manifestations either of the assumed political maturity of a governing group in an underdeveloped nation state or of the assertion that the Mandate of Heaven had truly passed to the more deserving. Paul Mus, for example, has noted that the image created by the Viet Minh in eliminating village councils and other elders, replacing them by supposedly elected administrative committees, was not strengthened so much by their temporary presence as a local power as by their perceived mandate as the successors to the Nguyen dynasty and to the French colonial rulers. But Mus has suggested a more basic hypothesis concerning Vietnamese perception of electoral, i.e., majoritarian, processes in general, one that questions the universality of western assumptions of representative government.

We have problems and we have solutions and we feel that we have done our duty toward the Vietnamese by giving them our solution to the problem. But there is no communication. We want the Vietnamese to exercise the right to vote and we preached the doctrine that a man is a man only insofar as he has the ballot, otherwise he is a subject, not a citizen. This is a principle which we must convince Asians to accept if the world is to become a worthwhile place in which to live. That, you see, is the terrible problem. We have our problems and our solutions, but the problem often does not exist for the Asians. I am speaking here of the average Asian, the average Vietnamese. This is how he reacted: "Why should we get involved? Why should we add our voice, our vote? If the program is bound to succeed, the Americans or the French, our counselors, would involve themselves and take credit for its success. If they 'pass the baby' to us, if they want us to vote on those issues about which we know so little, it's because it will fail and once it has failed, they will tell us, 'Well, you asked for it.' "

To summarize, I am giving you a serious warning about your good will even though you are basically right. You are right, but there is no communication. Do not be hasty and do not believe that such a thing as the right to vote is the solution. It is the problem. It is a solution only in the long run. For the time being, you have the problem of convincing the Vietnamese that it is the solution. And although they should understand that it is a solution, they are not prepared for it.[1]

During the pre-World-War-II domination of Indochina by France a series of limited electoral devices was utilized, particularly in the colony of Cochinchina, to provide a pretense of indigenous involvement and to legitimate the power of the extremely influential colons. The most important example was the Colonial Council of Cochinchina formed in 1880; representatives were selected by an extremely limited electorate, including initially three-fourths Frenchmen who were government personnel who voted their own budgets. "In 1880 the French set up a Colonial Council, composed of six Frenchmen elected by universal suffrage by their compatriots, communes, two delegates of the *Chambre de Commerce* (Trade Council), and two members appointed by the governor."[2] Later the Vietnamese representation, being somewhat expanded, provided the only even limited popular referenda experience during the prewar period.

In the 1920's, the Constitutional Party, favoring close relationship with France but also supporting programmatic reforms and a greater Vietnamese role, won seats on the Council. Due to colon opposition this party's electoral success was short-lived, and the Constitutionalist Party, together with other parties favoring gradualism, was discredited (see Chapter 2: "Patterns of Political Party Behavior"). I. Milton Sacks notes that "attempts to reform the French administration by a small group of nationalists—without links to the mass of the population and inhibited by a heavy-handed colonial authority—opened the way for the attempt to seek through revolutionary means the desired road to freedom."[3] A possible resurgence of Vietnamese representation oc-

curred again in 1939 when 80 per cent voted for and elected to the
Council three Trotskyite candidates—a party permitted to operate
openly during the Popular Front period but struggling against assimilation and soundly defeating both Constitutionalist and Stalinist opposition
in the election.[4] This followed a combined Trotskyite-Stalinist victory
for the Saigon Municipal Council two years earlier. Saigon, Hanoi, and
Haiphong had elected mayors in addition to elected councils. Other
councils such as the Grand Council of Economic and Financial Interests
and the Tonkin and Annam Chambers of People's Representatives provided a "semblance of consultation with the people" but were only advisory with operational power remaining in French hands.[5]

Elections from the end of World War II to the termination of hostilities formally ending the First Indochina War in 1954 were mostly
stages of larger political strategies. Nonetheless, the role of political
parties was for the first time formalized. In 1945 the Viet Minh held
elections for people's committees in villages under its control, allocating
considerably greater powers to the new bodies. On January 6, 1946,
the first truly general election in Vietnam's history was held (in Tonkin
and Annam) for a National Assembly. The results were predetermined,
owing to a compromise by the Viet Minh and the Nationalist Chinese
army of occupation whereby 70 seats (50 VNQDD, i.e., Kuomintang,
and 20 Dong Minh Hoi) out of 350 would be held by opposition nationalist parties. Ellen Hammer, noting widespread irregularities, characterized the election as one where the forces favoring independence
inevitably would have won in landslide proportions even if a completely
open vote had been possible.[6] This legislative body, or more specifically
a special committee of the elected National Assembly, continued as the
manifestation of a representative regime for the Democratic Republic
of Vietnam (DRVN) throughout the First Indochina War.

An agreement between the DRVN and France on March 6, 1946,
presumably also laid the foundation for an election in Cochinchina to
determine whether it would join the two former protectorates of Tonkin
and Annam. After Admiral Thierry d'Argenlieu initiated a Republic of
Cochinchina by proclamation and France finally adopted a postwar constitution including it as a colony, fulfillment of the promise to the Viet
Minh became part of the price of the ill-fated attempt to broaden the
base of popular support through the Bao Dai government. The vote
in Cochinchina on April 10, 1949, was hardly the popular mandate envisioned in 1946. A territorial assembly selected by indirect means, involving no more than 700 Vietnamese voters, included "the professional, syndical, and corporate organizations of the French, such as the

Chamber of Commerce and Agriculture."[7] It also included local and provincial councilors. It was this group that "legally" brought Cochinchina back again as part of Vietnam.

The only vestige of a true electoral process under Bao Dai occurred in 1953, but this election did not result in the formation of a National Assembly. Municipal and village councilors were to be popularly elected, and they were to select provincial councilors who in turn would select members of the national body. Despite the lateness of this attempt to involve broader numbers in the process of legitimation of the government, observers did find that the quite limited procedure stimulated more nationalist sentiment and simultaneously disturbed the Viet Minh more than the previous cynical attempts by the French and Bao Dai at popular cooptation. The municipal elections of January in some ten per cent of the nation's villages witnessed in most jurisdictions a 60–70 per cent turnout of the approximately one million voters.

Political activity was greatest in Tonkin, where the Dai Viet Party attempted to expand its base. Ngo Dinh Diem's brother, Bishop Ngo Dinh Thuc, joined with the Tonkinese bishoprics in urging a high vote among Catholics, and "declared in a pastoral letter that any Vietnamese Catholic who did not exercise his right to vote would be guilty before God, before the Church, and before the country."[8] Saigon, as in succeeding elections, hardly displayed universal voter interest, but in Hanoi the election produced a most unusual result, i.e., the more-or-less official candidates were soundly defeated.

In Hanoi, an antigovernment (but also anti-Viet-Minh) faction, headed by an ebullient French-trained dentist with American sympathies, Hoang Co Binh, and also by a former companion of Ho Chi Minh, Nguyen The Truyen, ran on a more "political" platform demanding: (a) universal suffrage for national elections; (b) replacement of appointed mayors by elected ones; (c) elimination of French council members and creation of strictly French chambers of commerce in Haiphong and Hanoi; and finally (d) an end of the war. Binh won a smashing victory over the government's candidate, Ngo Thuc Dich, and received twenty-three out of twenty-four elective seats on the city council. French political experts rationalized Binh's victory by the fact that his probity was known and because of "his political virginity and good organization." Indeed, Binh's supporters were at most polling stations, watching the ballot boxes and immediately reporting any attempts to meddle with them.[9]

The 1953 victors, Hoang Co Binh and Nguyen The Truyen, were to figure again in the scenario of electoral processes in South Vietnam. Ellen Hammer observed that the Hanoi experience was the product of a potentially important coalition. "The Nguyen The Truyen list was elected with Catholic support and was made up of so-called nationalists of the Left—doctors, lawyers, journalists, and intellectuals generally. They were critics of the Tam government and stood for a genuine unification of the country, for free national elections, and for an end to the war."[10] Thus the electoral proceeding, an isolated footnote in Vietnam's history, actually created a limited amount of life in the *attentiste* force. But it was not only too little by far and too late by several years, it also was quickly sabotaged by Bao Dai's substitution of his own appointed national council for the assembly that was to be elected by the elected councilors.

The most important proclaimed election was never held—the 1956 election on reunification noted in the Geneva Agreement. It is difficult to assess the exact intention of this proposed referendum. In one sense it was little more than a repetition of the DRVN-French agreement of 1946, an unsatisfactory conclusion to perhaps the most tragic colonial war in history. Interpretations of the intent of the provision, unfortunately, are mostly contingent upon the interpreter's orientation to the events leading to the Second Indochina War. The Final Declaration (July 21, 1954) of the Geneva Conference was not signed by anyone but was "taken note of" by conference participants, and the State of Vietnam under Ngo Dinh Diem protested against the declaration, openly refusing to be an active party to its implementation. Article 6, dealing with elections, is vague, although presumably the participating powers intended that an election concerning the unification of the two "zones" would be held in June 1956. It mentions that a "settlement of political problems, effected on the basis of respect for the principles of independence, unity and territorial integrity, shall permit the Vietnamese people to enjoy the fundamental freedoms, guaranteed by democratic institutions established as a result of free general elections by secret ballot."

Speaking in favor of Diem's decision to ignore this particular article, Frank N. Trager states: "The State of Viet Nam had indicated that it would accept elections only if the country were not partitioned and if the United Nations would supervise such elections so as to ensure their freedom and genuineness. Obviously such conditions never were met. And by 1956, the Viet Minh organs of repression within the Democratic Republic of Viet Nam had made it well-nigh impossible to hold free elections within that Communist country."[11] On the other hand B. S. N. Murti has argued: "The entire negotiations at Geneva were based on the assumption of one Vietnam and the cease-fire line was purely a military arrangement in order to bring about cessation of hostilities and to provide for actual unification which was to be accomplished through the medium of general elections."[12]

Of the post-Geneva elections held in the two Vietnams prior to the fall of Ngo Dinh Diem certainly none were prototypes for obtaining representative government. Political parties became more secondary factors in electoral proceedings than previously, except for officially sanctioned parties in both "zones" or "nations." Yet the elections of March 4, 1956, in South Vietnam, for a National Assembly to draft a constitution for the newly promulgated Republic could formally, as Murti has noted, be perceived as providing a de facto regime according to the so-called "doctrine of legitimacy," regardless of Article 6 of the Geneva Final Declaration.[13] Diem's 98.2 per cent as opposed to Bao Dai's 1.1 per cent compared with Ho Chi Minh's 1946 electoral victory. The one-sided nature of this mandate continued for the three other elections during the Diem era, i.e., the National Assembly elections of August 30, 1959, and September 27, 1963, and the April 9, 1961, presidential election.

Nguyen Thai, observing that many Vietnamese were prepared to accept the government's vigorous intervention in the first two elections because of the severity of the national crisis and the need to create a viable political system immediately, is extremely critical of the continuation of a practice explicitly designed to control electoral activity. "For those who tried to find out for themselves in 1959 whether the second legislative elections were intended to raise the representative standard of the National Assembly, it soon became clear that the leaders of the regime did not see representation as an important feature for the legislative body of South Vietnam."[14]

Of the several elections between 1954 and 1963, the 1961 presidential election was the most telling example of an approach that viewed the electoral process as a technique for legitimating the position of the national leadership. The National Revolutionary Movement and Can Lao Party as well as the National Revolutionary Civil Servants' League were actively supporting Diem, as were other specific interest-group organizations established by the government. Political parties *qua* parties were not overtly represented by the candidates, a practice followed also in Assembly elections. The government's military and bureaucratic personnel were active in the campaign and in maximizing voter turnout. Opposition candidates were restricted and even harassed in their campaigns. The two competing slates were not genuine threats. The vote for Diem (89 per cent) represented a large plurality received primarily in the provinces, with his vote highest in insecure areas where government manipulation was easiest, and lowest in the fairly open election in Saigon. The two opposition slates were (1) Nguyen Dinh Quat and Nguyen Thanh Phuong, the former a businessman and rubber planter and the latter a former important Cao Dai political and military leader, who received only 4 per cent, and (2) Ho Nhut Tan (a once prominent nationalist and oriental medicine practitioner) and Nguyen The Truyen (who fared so well in the 1953 Hanoi election) with 7 per cent.[15]

Electoral processes under Diem may have been his greatest single failure. They undermined the view of him as the completely honest, disinterested mandarin who claimed the Mandate of Heaven through constant perseverance and good works. This was not irrelevant to the Vietnamese in general, who to a great extent smiled at his 1955 and 1956 electoral victories and his refusal to hold a 1956 reunification plebiscite, as the actions of a clever and strong man who was defeating his enemies and solidifying the country by the means at hand. But once the fortunes of the Ngo family turned, the elections were increasingly resented as fraudulent, hypocritical displays of democracy, used to perpetuate the assumed Mandate of Heaven and ignore reforms. Analyzing the abuse of electoral proceedings, Joseph Buttinger has observed:

The Diem regime failed because it not only opposed the political aspirations of the Communists, but also because it trampled underfoot the justified aspirations of the entire people. It could have succeeded in suppressing Communism only if it had abstained from suppressing everybody else. Not less but more democracy, a basic condition also of social justice, would have made the Diem regime politically effective against Communism.[16]

Elections for the National Assembly in North Vietnam on May 8, 1960, and April 26, 1964, were even more controlled by the state than those in South Vietnam, where the machinery for population control was considerably less sophisticated and ubiquitous.[17] In both instances the option was not one of openly and rationally selecting among alternative leaders or parties. Rather the Vietnamese experience with elections served to reinforce the facade of representation and to augment the claims to legitimate power of incumbent holders of political power. As Robert Scigliano has observed, both Ho Chi Minh and Ngo Dinh Diem "permitted elections only to the extent they could control the results; both have used elections to mobilize mass approval of the regime; and in each, minor parties exist only as fronts for the ruling group."[18]

In a sense the preliminaries for national elections for a new president, National Assembly, and constitution began almost immediately after the deaths of Ngo Dinh Diem and Ngo Dinh Nhu on November 2, 1963. The preliminaries required approximately four years. For those four years, South Vietnam had neither an elected chief executive nor an elected National Assembly. Instead, power once centered in the Ngo family was assumed by a series of military tribunals beginning with the Military Revolutionary Council, first headed by General Duong Van Minh, the initially popular hero of the anti-Diem coup. The Assembly elected in 1963 was replaced by numerous appointed councils. For a brief period after the first coup until the second coup led by General Nguyen Khanh, i.e., from December 1963, to February 1964, representation was vested in an advisory Council of Notables. This was a collection of 60 civilians who had previous prominence as leaders of parties, religious groups, etc. Despite the advanced average age of this group it included people who were later to play prominent roles in South Vietnamese governments, including about one-third who became ministers, two (Tran Van Huong and Phan Huy Quat) who became prime ministers, and one (Phan Khac Suu) who became chief of state. The succeeding group, the High National Council (September–December 1964), had only 17 members, of whom eight had been members of the Council of Notables. This second body, including Le Khac Quyen, the advisor to militant Buddhist leader Thich Tri Quang, wrote a provisional constitution, elected its chairman, Phan Khac Suu, as chief of state of the provisional government, and appointed Tran Van Huong as prime minister.

The provisional constitution, like the one proclaimed by Khanh in August 1964, soon became a dead letter. The High National Council became involved in the political struggle within the military hierarchy surrounding Khanh and in a Catholic-Buddhist struggle. A number of its members were temporarily detained, and it was purged by the military in favor of an Armed Forces Council. This was followed by an abortive attempt by the American Embassy in Saigon to restore what it apparently perceived as "civilian" rule under the High National Council and its appointed chief of state. Following a period of particularly stressful militant action against Huong by the Buddhists, the Armed Forces Council pacified the Buddhists temporarily by replacing Huong with Dr. Phan Huy Quat and appointing a National Legislative Council (that lasted from February to June 1965) representing each of the major regions and religions in Vietman as well as the military itself. Although the Armed Forces Council indicated willingness to disband, providing power formally for the Quat government, the prime minister, while temporarily retaining Buddhist support, was opposed soon by a

Suu-Catholic-Cao Dai-Hoa Hao coalition. Quat resigned in favor of the group that "mediated" the dispute, i.e., the military.

Perhaps the most significant act during the Quat period went almost unnoticed, primarily because candidates who discussed mostly "local" issues were less likely to be considered newsworthy by the world's press. On May 30, 1965, South Vietnam held elections for provincial and municipal councilors. For the first time since the limited village and municipal elections of 1953, Vietnamese were provided an opportunity to vote for local leaders. Diem had agreed to have appointed provincial councils late in his period of rule, but these were only advisory. The new councils were also advisory, but they represented the first step in representative government and were sought by many leading civilian politicians. Seventy-two per cent of registered voters, i.e., 3,466,523 voters, elected 471 councilors. Dr. Phan Quang Dan was elected in Gia Dinh Province, Dr. Hoang Co Binh in Saigon, and Buddhists, Catholics, Hoa Hao, Cao Dai, and Chinese won in regions where their respective strength was predominant. Commenting upon what was generally considered a successful example of popular consultation, Denis Warner noted: "To be sure, the Councils elected in the May, 1965, vote have not had a wide or important influence on political affairs. Even so, the more energetic and influential ones have succeeded in creating at the lower levels of the society a consciousness of the value of representative government that could begin to challenge the Vietcong at the grass roots."[19] Before the end of their first term, however, a high percentage of the provincial councils had become inactive.

Generals Nguyen Van Thieu and Nguyen Huu Co and Air Marshal Nguyen Cao Ky formed a National Leadership Committee following the fall of Quat. It then expanded to ten members, and an Executive Committee was appointed to serve as the government. Because of their positions in the newly appointed bodies, Thieu became chief of state and Ky became premier in June 1965.[20] Formal resumption of military power over the operations of South Vietnam's government, while displeasing to most political interests and to the American policy of development of a state legitimated by manifestations of broad-based support, was followed by a brief period in which violent political upheaval was absent. However, demands for election of a popularly selected group of leaders increased measurably by the beginning of 1966. The National Leadership Committee vowed support for electoral processes as a means of legitimating a government for South Vietnam. Developments were swift and brutal during much of 1966, forcing the military leadership to proceed with steps leading to implementation of this promise.

In January the Leadership Committee stated that a Democratic Building Consultative Council would be appointed to draft a constitution and that a referendum would be held in November 1966 to approve the new document, followed in 1967 by election of a new government. Neither the timetable nor the continuation of a military government was acceptable to significant interest groups, especially the militant Buddhists. Following dismissal of General Nguyen Chanh Thi as commander of I Corps in central Vietnam, where the militant Buddhists were strongest, this volatile group began a series of violent demonstrations of their power. Saigon was forced to rely upon military forces to prevent civil war. A National Political Congress was appointed and called for an election. An Electoral Commission was then appointed to set steps in motion for a Constituent Assembly election. This Commission temporarily included militant Buddhist representatives, who left once it was decided that the election would not result in creation of a new government but that this task would be determined by a second election. This meant the military leadership automatically would remain in power for an extended period, a contingency unacceptable to the Tri Quang forces.

The first national election since 1963 was held on September 11, 1966, for the 117-member Constituent Assembly. Despite the refusal of both militant Buddhists and militant Catholics (led by Reverend Hoang Quynh, formerly military leader for Bishop Le Huu Tu of Phat Diem), the voting was heavy. The Constituent Assembly, which elected Suu as its chairman,[21] was to write a new constitution (promulgated on April 1, 1967) and to approve the guidelines for the 1967 national election. In many ways, the Assembly proved to be an independent group, although the military leadership greatly influenced its important decisions. Under Suu's direction the Assembly disregarded the regime's wishes and remained in session after completion of the Constitution, becoming a Provisional National Assembly until the newly elected National Assembly took office.

Precampaign Politics

Although it is not possible to state precisely when the 1967 presidential campaign began informally, the political activities of the leaders of the government, numerous leaders of the Constituent Assembly, and other South Vietnamese politicians intensified toward the end of 1966.

By spring there was indication that most of the military leadership was prepared to support Ky. He retained considerable support among younger officers. He was known to be the candidate of General Cao Van Vien, the minister of defense, one of the most important members of the directorate. In addition, General Nguyen Duc Thang, the minister for revolutionary development, was an enthusiastic supporter. Tactically, one of the problems Ky faced during this period was his frequent promise not to run for the presidency if Thieu was a candidate. In the spring a number of the generals attempted to persuade Ky to announce his candidacy prior to Thieu. The chief of state was holding his own counsel, refusing to make a public declaration of his candidacy.

It became increasingly clear that Ky, although he had previously stated he would not be a candidate, giving as an excuse the demands of his wife and the demands of the Air Force as well as his lack of taste for civilian governmental matters, indeed wanted to be the first elected president of the Second Republic. He had been mending fences in various areas of the country and had made obvious political gestures toward a number of the more important groups in the nation. It was revealed in April that Dr. Nguyen Huu Chi, a Ph.D. from Michigan State University, formerly Quang Nam Province chief and a public affairs officer under Ky, had been conducting polls. One poll was taken in Hue and Saigon. The question asked was "Whom do you prefer, General Ky or General Thieu?" A second question was, "Why?" Of the 68 per cent answering, 75 per cent responded in favor of Ky. In another poll over 3,000 persons were queried about support for the Ky regime vis-à-vis the NLF. One of the questions was "Do you agree with the work of the government of Vietnam or do you want change?" Another question was "Is your life better under Viet Cong or government control?" The poll showed "90 per cent said it was better under government, no one said under the Viet Cong, 7 per cent said they didn't know, and 23 per cent said they didn't care."[22] Thus the premier's poll showed that not only was he more popular than Thieu, but the communists provided no competition in a popularity contest with him.

Although rivalry between Ky and Thieu intensified, early in May both generals supported a single election for the presidency rather than a run-off in the event no candidate received a majority. In the Assembly the Democratic Alliance bloc (a progovernment faction), headed by Le Phouc Sang, led the debate for a single election. Dr. Phan Quang Dan proposed that any winning candidate should receive at least 33 per cent of the vote in the first election. Others favored even a smaller percentage. After considerable debate, the Assembly agreed not to require a minimum percentage for election.

The government also was involved in Assembly debates concerning subsidization of presidential candidates. Forfeiture of the equivalent of a US$1,700 deposit, and return of the $80,000 (1.7 cents per voter) provided by the government for his campaign, was required for anyone receiving less than 10 percent of the vote. This was the sum provided during the Constituent Assembly election. The military attempted to keep the sum available to each candidate at an absolute minimum, but government forces did compromise and agree that military candidates would resign or take extended leave during the election. The progovernment votes proved adequate, although their control was far from complete over the proceedings. The single vote proposal, for example, received only 44 votes out of 80 persons present.

The Ky forces were particularly active during May in seeking support from civilian politicians and from members of the government, both civilian and military. Tran Van Huong was approached concerning his availability as a vice-presidential candidate on a Ky ticket. He refused. Brigadier General Nguyen Ngoc Loan, director of security and the national police, held conversations in Washington with exiled General Nguyen Chanh Thi concerning his support for the Ky candidacy. Rivalry between the two chief generals became so severe that General Cao Van Vien, fearing the debate would split the military hierarchy, decided against formal armed forces support for any given candidate. When Thieu mentioned his possible support for General Duong Van Minh (a move that proved to be a stalking horse), General Vien apparently became convinced the armed forces should remain neutral.

Ky and Thieu continually attempted to reinforce their positions through arrangements with province chiefs and other military officials. The practical result was that provincial officials were frozen in their positions, as all were identified as being proponents of one or the other. The most dramatic example was in IV Corps, where the new corps commander, Lieutenant General Nguyen Van Manh, failed in an attempt to remove ten existing province chiefs for inefficiency and/or graft largely because of the political situation. Still, at different stages during the year both Ky and Thieu restated their promises to eliminate corruption in the military and provide efficient and honest local government. Toward the end of the campaign, in fact, a number of persons were removed from official positions being charged formally or informally with corruption. These late attempts at reform often touched persons opposed to the candidacy of the military ticket.

On May 12 in Da Lat, Ky announced his candidacy. He stated that he would never oppose Thieu, but noted that there was no possibility

Thieu would become a candidate. That same day, Thieu's office formally stated: "The General is still considering running and is still a possible candidate"[23]—a possibility confirmed by Thieu himself the next day in Saigon. At this point there was speculation that the chief of state had been outmaneuvered and was simply making last minute face-saving comments. On May 13 too, Ky compromised his position with a typically controversial statement, that if a communist or a neutralist were to be the head of the next government "I am going to fight him militarily. . . . In any democratic country you have the right to disagree with the views of others."[24]

A week later (May 19) Thieu formally announced his candidacy. The government then notified information personnel that unkind comments exchanged between the two generals were to be censored. Even then Thieu's stand remained ambivalent and he appeared to back down, while the Ky camp spread rumors that Thieu would not be a candidate. Apparently this angered Thieu. On June 14 he again publicly affirmed that he would run, and a member of his official entourage asserted also that "General Thieu's decision to run is irrevocable."[25] In addition to these separate announcements, an obvious sign of the split occurred on June 19 when leaders of the military regime met to provide a public review of their two years in office. Thieu was absent, reportedly "sick." Ky presided and in the atmosphere of military camaraderie announced: "If I fail, I would return to the front to combat the enemy side by side with my comrades-in-arms."[26]

The premier at this point appeared to be well ahead of his chief rival. His campaign slogan, "The government of Nguyen Cao Ky is a government of the poor," was plastered on billboards in the major cities. In addition, he began to act like a politician. He systematically made appeals to the tribesmen, the Chinese, and other important elements in the population. On June 24, he announced he would double the budget for education during the next fiscal year—an extremely important gesture in a nation with over 26,000 university students and over 2,000,000 public and private school students. (Under the Vietnamese system of education most of the students are weeded out French-style after the fifth year, through national examinations.) Doubling the US$38 million educational account would be a significant step forward in a nation where only 5 per cent of the national budget was earmarked for educational purposes. "Two-thirds of the nation's population are illiterate, one-third of the school age children have never seen a classroom, 85% of all school-age children will never get beyond the fifth grade under the present system."[27]

The new education commitment followed another significant decision by Ky. The Diem regime had confiscated properties of non-Vietnamese following a decree that only nationals could undertake business in eleven defined functional areas.[28] On June 16, Ky announced, appropriately enough in a Cholon restaurant, that properties of Vietnamese citizens of Chinese descent would be returned to them. He also added a new element to his running commentary on the possibility for peace discussions. He noted he would be willing to have a debate before the United Nations: "Israel fought for only four days, but that conflict was brought before the United Nations for discussion. Why has the Vietnam war dragged on so long without it coming before the United Nations? If the United States does discuss the war, I would be going there myself to present the South Vietnamese point of view."[29]

Ky's campaign activities were not restricted to positive gestures toward important interest groups. During the spring and early summer the Ky government was active in arresting certain dissenting voices. These joined many thousands of others, including militant Buddhists arrested during 1966, most of whom were not brought to trial and were not formally charged. Ngu Tang, an important businessman, and Nguyen Si Hong, a writer, were arrested. The most controversial arrest, however, was that of Vu Hanh, who had been accused by the newspaper *Song,* of procommunism. He was exonerated by the Propaganda Ministry and attempted to bring suit against the newspaper. He was arrested by General Loan and accused with being involved in "helping the Communists in their attempts to conquer South Vietnam."[30] The newspaper *Song* was a pro-Ky instrument and many of the essays were written by members of the Ky government; the typical Saigonese suspicions claimed that Vu Hanh was arrested to protect the newspaper from a slander suit.

Government control of the press in South Vietnam has a long history, and the censorship applied early in the campaign was not unusual. During the French era, and under Diem, it was an important factor in manipulating news. There was some relaxation following the fall of Diem. However, succeeding juntas retained varying forms of censorship over the press. A number of newspapers were allowed to exist because of their progovernment leanings. In the campaign for the presidency, however, this control became a matter of some embarrassment. All newspapers and magazines were published only with governmental consent, writers were accredited by the government, and specific articles were censored. This precedent became less than relevant when censors under the Ky administration tended to be overenthusiastic. On June 26,

Thieu said, "I myself have been a victim of General Tri's [Nguyen Bao Tri, minister for information] censorship." He noted in the same interview, "I would never use the police or the pacification workers or put pressure on the province chiefs to solicit votes," for an unfair election would result: "The people will lose confidence in the government. And they will not cooperate with the government. And the Communists will win the war politically in two or three years."[31] The object of Thieu's insinuations had not escaped the attention of the American embassy, the military leaders, or the increasing number of foreign correspondents in Vietnam. The Ky administration's resourcefulness in utilizing the instruments of government for political objectives played into the chief of state's hands. The other military members of the Leadership Committee considered this an affront, as they did Ky's illegal open campaigning before the agreed dates.

Ironically the question of campaign irregularities outlined by Thieu was to become perhaps the major issue in the forthcoming campaign. But a second issue he discussed on June 26 became the topic underlying most substantive discussion. Thieu observed that it would not be possible to have negotiations concerning peace at least until three years following the presidential election. He was later to adjust this position dramatically. On the same day Ky also said, "It is always time to stop a war. But first we must have a strong stable regime; not a strong man, but a strong regime."[32]

On June 27 occurred an event that may well have been significant in finally resolving the struggle between the two principal generals. General Duong Van Minh (Big Minh) announced from exile in Bangkok that he would be a candidate for the presidency. The next day the directorate decided to refuse his request for a visa, and Major Generals Linh Quang Vien, minister for defense, and Nguyen Van La went to Bangkok to discuss the matter with him.

On the day of Minh's statement both Thieu and Ky announced their running mates, thus appearing to solidify the division within the military ranks. Nguyen Van Loc, chairman of the Army-People Council, a 43-year-old lawyer, would be running with Ky; Thieu's running mate would be Nguyen Huu Le, an important member of the Hoa Hao, who added a new dimension to the Thieu campaign. Foreign Minister Tran Van Do, who had been considered a likely running mate for Thieu, announced his candidacy for the Senate. As an appendix to his announcement, Thieu went out of his way to note that Ky's candidacy did not have the blessing of the United States, but his comments were censored in the newspapers.

The National Leadership Committee, fearful of the consequences of the growing dispute and other pressure from the American embassy, began marathon meetings. Rumors of troop movements and of conversations among the Leadership Committee were rampant. There seemed some possibility that other members of the directorate, perhaps Lieutenant General Thuan Xuan Chieu, secretary general of the Leadership Committee, would assume the position of premier during the election. It also seemed possible General Vien might assume chairmanship of the Committee in place of Thieu. An alternate rumor was that the I Corps commander, Lieutenant General Hoang Xuan Lam, just promoted by Thieu, might serve as premier. During this period Colonel Tran Canh Thang, Loan's deputy, became director of the Military Security Service in place of Loan. This obviously was a compromise permitting the man who had been instrumental in the censorship of Thieu's previous remarks and in the handling of Ky's campaign to back down without actually losing power.

On June 29, Assembly speaker Suu confirmed receipt of two telegrams from Big Minh, and it was also rumored that Nguyen Xuan Oanh would serve as Minh's running mate. The ruling directorate "for security reasons" refused Minh's visa, but on June 30 he was formally filed as a candidate by his announced running mate, Tran Ngoc Lieng, a 44-year-old attorney.

At 11 A.M. on June 30, just before the deadline for filing, Ky announced he would not run for the presidency. Instead he agreed to serve on a Thieu ticket as the vice-presidential candidate. Reportedly, he had not consulted with his aides. "If necessary," he stated, "we must make sacrifices in order to realize unity. I feel I have lived up to those standards and feel qualified to ask you to live up to the same spirit. We must also prove the prestige of the armed forces. The armed forces can only carry out its mission if it is united. If we can sacrifice our very lives, we can do anything else, including the renunciation of titles. I would like you to have this attitude in the elections."[33] Apparently the development was unplanned:

On Wednesday [June 29] a routine Corps commander meeting was scheduled with General Cao Van Vien, the chief of the Joint General Staff, in Saigon. These four generals controlled the four military areas under which South Vietnam is divided for war purposes.

After their military meeting they adjourned to a small room near Vien's office at the Tan Sonhut air base just outside of Saigon and a political meeting was soon in session. They asked both Thieu and Ky to join them in the talks.

Finally, this morning [June 30], Ky made his dramatic offer to stop his own race for President and run as Thieu's vice-president.[34]

Despite formal US denials of involvement, Ambassador Ellsworth Bunker had applied considerable pressure to Ky. It was reported that "he did tell the Premier in blunt language that his abuses of power were threatening to make a mockery of the elections."[35] The ambassador's attitude and pressure combined with Thieu's spade work among the other generals, who were becoming increasingly perturbed at Ky's actions, removed the most significant source of actual and potential support for the premier. Apparently the military leaders had intended to have both generals give up their posts temporarily during the campaign assuming that no compromise could be worked out. They were encouraged in their actions by private briefings from members of the American embassy, assuring them that the United States was not supporting either of the leading contenders.

With the split within the military leadership settled at least publicly, the stage was set for the existing governmental power structure to compete with any opposition. On July 1 the Constituent Assembly gave its approval to the tickets of 17 contenders for the presidency. By a vote of 72 of 85 members present, General Minh's slate was also approved, although the government had written to the Assembly noting that Minh was considered a security risk. The assembly also approved 66 slates (660 candidates) for the Senate race. The approved lists were to be posted a second time on July 19, at which point additional objections to specific candidacies were to be considered. Thus little had been resolved, particularly as it was noted in the Assembly discussions that Minh's running mate Tran Ngoc Lieng lacked the required certificate of military service.

On July 4 a report that Big Minh was missing from his normal domicile in Bangkok led to speculation that he very well might attempt to slip into South Vietnam surreptitiously. His acceptance by the Constituent Assembly still had to be ratified by the Central Election Committee. It was known that the American embassy was attempting to persuade the government to permit Minh to return and to permit the Central Election Committee to approve his candidacy. Minh's support among southern Buddhists, his probable ability to reach an understanding with the forces supporting Tri Quang and his continued support among elements of the armed forces continued to make him a most potent opponent.

The government allowed fairly good coverage to Minh's candidacy, but its willingness to permit candidacies from potent opponents was taxed not only by Big Minh's announcement but also by the candidacy of former Minister of Economics Au Truong Thanh—unquestionably the most highly praised Vietnamese higher public official in 1966—at least by Americans. His efforts at improving economic conditions in South Vietnam, including measures against inflation and to provide fair distribution of rice, had met with considerable success. However, the former cabinet member was categorized as a so-called peace candidate—an orientation he did not deny, while government innuendos suggested a communist orientation. Thanh's opinions were by now well known:

Vietnam has two choices. We can achieve peace or our country can be destroyed. The people should be permitted to make that decision. The junta represented by Thieu and Ky offer the platform of more war. We offer a platform of peace. Whoever heard of the Vietcong asking for a cease-fire? They will never do that because the war creates the conditions under which their terrorism and their brainwashing can be effective. It is our duty to express the desire of the people for peace. That is the way we can appeal to what is in their hearts and in their minds. That is the way to defeat the Vietcong.[36]

Thus, Thanh opposed not only the position of the government but that of the NLF. In addition, he expressed fear of American over-involvement in the sovereignty of South Vietnam. He believed it would be difficult to arrive at a stage for negotiations but that the elections, under the proper auspices, conducted fairly, and with a proper winner might indeed provide what he called "a climate" for negotiations. He was under constant and increasingly close surveillance by Loan's police. "The only security I have is the American press."[37] On July 7 the security police accused Thanh of being procommunist. Thanh's reaction was: "If I am a Communist or a pro-Communist the three prime ministers who included me in their cabinet—including Premier Ky—were also blind men." Although Loan was later to admit publicly that he did not consider Thanh, a close friend of his, to be a communist, the former minister had been arrested in 1959 and had signed some form of confession. Furthermore, one Le Van Lam Paul claimed that in 1959, Thanh had refused his request to join the communist party. Paul also noted to the police that he had met Thanh again in 1965 and that their views regarding peace at this later date were far from dissimilar.

It was difficult to assess the exact nature of the government's attack upon its former minister. An economist, a southerner, educated in France, Thanh was a wealthy man and a professor at the University of Saigon. While once a prominent member of the Ky government, he did resign in protest, during 1966, to protest southern underrepresentation in the Ky cabinet. As the question of southern sympathies was of extreme importance, and as there was a far-from-insignificant southern movement favoring a peaceful settlement, it is possible the regime did indeed consider Thanh to be a threat. Thanh himself also claimed that he had refused Loan certain favors in 1965, including a distributorship for gold sales and permission for police to serve as exclusive tax-collecting agents.

Despite the government's announced intention of limiting the electoral process by opposition to the Minh and Thanh candidacies, other steps were taken during the precertification period to liberalize the conduct of the election and the regime's control over opinions expressed in the campaign. Premier Ky announced new censorship policies. In the past, newspapers submitted page proofs to censors by 9 A.M. Blank pages or more likely blank sections appeared with considerable frequency. The new program was as follows: By 1 P.M. editors send a copy of their paper to the censors; the censors could request seizure of the day's edition. Before the campaign ended and after the September 3 election it was proved that censorship, while definitely relaxed, did not permit the nation's editors a free hand. Practically, however, seizure of an edition was not likely, as official publication time for the 27 Vietnamese and seven Chinese newspapers in Saigon was 3 P.M.

Censorship was relaxed on the day the campaign officially opened, August 3. On the surface this was a senseless action—the new Constitution prohibited censorship—but in practice the government's formal agreement was extremely important, and represented a reversal of a decision publicly announced by Ky on June 4, that censorship would continue throughout the election period. This relaxation was partly the result of pressure group demands, including petitions by members of the new Dai Viet party, the VNQDD, the Catholic journalists and writers, the National Youth Association, and the Joint Schools Association, which noted: "The minimum condition (for free elections) is freedom of speech, of press and of publications. A lack of freedom of speech, press, and publication has made the people extremely confused and has caused them to lose completely the confidence in the assurances to carry out democracy made following the Honolulu and Manila conferences [between Ky and President Johnson]."[38] As the Constituent Assembly had previously requested Ky to comply with censorship relaxation, presumably it was Thieu's insistence that prompted the Ky reversal.

The importance of the new attitude toward press restrictions became apparent by July 11, at which time it was obvious candidates other than Thanh would be considered peace candidates. The leading civilian candidate, former Premier Tran Van Huong, previously considered a potential leader of a "southern" solution, mentioned the possibility of nationwide elections within five to ten years. "The war has lasted for a long time. Everyone is tired of it. Everyone wants peace. Americans also want peace in 1968. People on both sides have suffered. I think the leaders of the two sides have a duty to find a means to put an end to it. If peace is reached, there is no winner and no loser." His proposal involved a ceasefire, a program for refugee resettlement, and several years of negotiations. At the end of this period he stated: "The people will have the right and freedom to choose the government they want. It means that if the people will find the nationalistic (South Vietnamese) government is good, they can support it. If they like Communism, they can follow it."[39] Newspapers, while not reporting Thanh's position, were permitted to quote Huong.

On July 18 the Constituent Assembly refused to accept the candidacies of seven tickets, including those of Big Minh and Thanh. In a show of independence the Dai-Viet–influenced committee appointed to review applications and report to the full Assembly decided at first to refuse acceptance of the governmental ticket, but reconsidered and decided to recommend neither for nor against Assembly acceptance of the Thieu-Ky slate. The initial decision of the committee caused the military leaders some concern. The generals met and a special police alert and a reserve battalion alert were made known. The minister of information said: "If the Assembly does not accept the candidacy of Thieu and Ky, the government will dissolve the Assembly."[40]

A procedural problem did begin with the committee. Unlike the other candidates, who appeared in person, the government ticket sent Nguyen Van Loc to testify. The committee refused to accept the credentials of the governmental candidates' representative, requesting that he return again bringing proper documents. He did not bother to do this. The question of both governmental candidates refusing to resign their positions was also raised in the Assembly debate. Dai Viet and southern bloc representatives spoke against the candidacy of the generals, but they received 56 votes from among the 70 Assembly members present.

Minh lost officially on a formality. Tran Ngoc Lieng, his vice-presidential running mate, a French citizen between 1950 and 1955, was disqualified under the Constitution, which required Vietnamese citizenship from birth. The Minh ticket was defeated by 54 negative votes. The Constitution also bars neutralists and communist sympathizers and Thanh was accordingly disqualified.

Five other tickets were deemed inconsistent with the Constitution by the Assembly and were disallowed: (1) the Moving Hands ticket of Ly Dai Nguyen, a young writer from Bac Ninh, and Vu Dinh Manh, who had been chairman of the Southern Veterans Association; (2) a ticket with two newspaper reporters in central Vietnam, Luu Quang Hong and Nguyen Manh Hai, whose symbol was "The Will of the People is the Will of God"; (3) the Rising Sun ticket of Dr. Nguyen Dinh Luyen and assistant prosecutor of the Supreme Court of Appeals Tran Van Thoan; (4) an "Emancipation" slate of central Vietnamese teacher Tran Thuong Nhon and Nguyen Van Hung; and (5) a Cao Dai ticket, the "White Star of Liberation above the Earth," of Hoang Chu Ngoc, the 37-year-old secretary general of the Cao Dai Central Committee, and Tran Van Xuyen, a Central Committee member.[41] It is unlikely any of these five would have received a high number of votes.

As he had done on previous sensitive occasions, General Loan visited the Assembly during the debate. He was present during discussion of the Minh candidacy. He also gave indication of considerable interest in the discussions relative to the qualification or disqualification of the governmental candidates. Loan, who had hoped Premier Ky would be elected president, was not especially pleased by the Assembly acceptance of the military ticket.

In an attempt to placate his followers, Ky met at Da Lat with Loan and 50 other police officials. He explained his reasons for accepting second place on the ticket, and also discussions were carried out relative to the probability of this group retaining its power. Due to the limited range of jurisdiction permitted the vice president in the new Constitution, Ky noted expressively that his own position would range far beyond that envisioned by the Constitution. Ky had demanded the right to name the new premier, who, both candidates had earlier publicly agreed, would be a civilian. While this and similar meetings did not satisfy his followers, his forces agreed to make the best of the fait accompli. Their attention was focused now on the role of Ky and the range of discretion remaining to his supporters after the new government took office.

Although the premier was playing the role of second man, he found it difficult to avoid embarrassing his ticket by making statements bringing into question his willingness to release the reins of authority. He indicated the possibility of drastic steps if his plans were not fulfilled:

"If the crooked and the corrupt use other tricks to win in the Presidential election, I will stage a coup d'état."[42] This was a step beyond statements previously made by both candidates that a civilian government would have to "live up to the aspirations of the Vietnamese people." Both had also mentioned they would not stand for a neutralist or procommunist government. As a "kitchen cabinet" was being formed, composed of generals that would, in effect, form the military committee provided for under the new Constitution, there was question that either general or the military leadership would accept defeat at the polls with grace.

The military ticket was obviously hesitant to abdicate formal responsibilities even for a provisional period. Two days prior to the formal opening of the presidential campaign Tran Van Huong did call upon them to resign. He said he would appeal to their conscience "to act according to the wishes of their people." Huong agreed the new Constitution permitted the two military men to retain their governmental positions because they had taken military leaves of absence. However, he felt that the "legitimacy" of the election would be brought into question if they retained power: "Ky and Thieu had said they would have honest, free and fair elections, but as long as Ky and Thieu are still running the government, and organizing and controlling the elections, I leave it up to you to decide how free and fair the elections will be. Do you expect a judge to be as fair in a verdict involving members of his family as with others?"[43] Yet as neither was willing to heed Huong's suggestion, the campaign guidelines had been set before the campaign even began. It was to be a race of the military–government candidates against ten opponents. It was surprising that the military ticket displayed on the whole a solid front. But the existence of ten other slates was evidence of the unwillingness of nationalist, perennial oppositionists to unite behind an agreed-upon ticket or program.

The Presidential Campaign: An Abortive Beginning

In many ways the 11 slates contending for president and vice president were quite imposing. Most were known nationalists who could boast proud records. A number were acknowledged heroes for their opposition to Diem. Combined, their record of public service was impressive, although for most this service had been of rather limited duration, due to the traditional short tenure of Vietnamese governments. A few had questionable personal backgrounds, and a number had found reason to work with the Viet Minh, the French, Bao Dai and Diem at some point in their careers. A few also were considered superannuated, and more than one was suspected of entering the race for reasons other than anticipation of victory. Yet, unquestionably at a different time and under slightly different circumstances several of the slates could have provided formidable opposition to any possible ticket that could have been devised in South Vietnam.

The eleven tickets were:

Ticket No. 1: Phan Khac Suu and Dr. Phan Quang Dan

Both members were among the best-known and most popular nationalists in South Vietnam. Each achieved a certain martyrdom under Diem due to his imprisonment and physical maltreatment following the 1960 abortive coup. Suu, an agricultural engineer and a former civil servant, was imprisoned for five years by the French for revolutionary activity in 1940. He was a member of Diem's first cabinet and of Bao Dai's as well, but he broke with Diem during a crisis involving the sects; he was an advocate of revitalized organization for the Cao Dai. He served on the Council of Notables, as chairman of the High National Council, as chief of state, as an elected member of the Constitutional Assembly from Saigon, and as chairman of the Constituent Assembly. Dan had worked with the Dai Viet in North Vietnam early in the First Indochina War, had formed a Republican Party and then a Democratic Party, and served as a vocal critic of the Diem government. He had been elected to the National Assembly in 1959 despite Diem and Nhu's harassment, only to have his victory disallowed. (Suu was the only oppositionist candidate actually to be seated in the National Assembly.) A nationalist with an independent bent, Dan had refused to join with Suu and the other Caravellists. Instead his criticism of the regime was based to a great extent upon editorials in his newspaper. The Harvard-trained M.D., who operated a Gia Dinh medical clinic, was elected to the Gia Dinh Provincial Council by a landslide in 1965, becoming its chairman, and to the Constituent Assembly in 1966 by an equally imposing plurality. He also served on government-appointed councils, and held the chairmanship of the National Political Congress that decided upon elections for the Constituent Assembly and the presidency.

Ticket No. 2: Ha Thuc Ky and Nguyen Van Dinh

Both Ky and Dinh were former civil servants who had fought against the French. Ky, a former Viet Minh, was secretary general of the Revolutionary Dai Viet Party, having served on the Council of Notables and for a few months as minister of interior when Dai Viet leader Nguyen Ton Hoan was deputy prime minister under Nguyen Khanh. He resigned when the Dai Viet attempt to infiltrate all levels of government failed. Ky served a five-year jail term under Diem; he claimed to have attempted to assassinate the former president. His running mate had served as deputy prefect of Saigon and as a province chief.

Ticket No. 3: Hoang Co Binh and Lieu Quang Kinh

Binh, a northern dentist, was a Caravellist, a member of the Council of Notables, and was elected in the 1965 municipal council election to the Saigon Council. He led the Social Democratic Bloc. His principal distinction had been his 1953 electoral victory in Hanoi.

Ticket No. 4: Truong Dinh Dzu and Tran Van Chieu

Both had been active in the Tan Dai Viet Party, in fact claiming to have worked since 1963 in building a nationwide organization in anticipation of the election. Dzu professed to have plotted a coup against Diem, who did have him arrested briefly, allegedly for irregularities in his financial dealings. A former director of the Rotary Club of Southeast Asia and president of the Saigon Rotary Club, as well as an exponent of the Moral Rearmament Association, Dzu's financial fortunes had been enhanced by marriage and allegedly by a once close relationship with Ngo Dinh Nhu. He was even presumed to have played an important role in the so-called family code of Madame Nhu, whose brother was once Dzu's law partner. He was a well-known lawyer, who was blacklisted by the American embassy, and had defended Nguyen Huu Tho (NLF Chairman). Chieu was a well-to-do merchant, a former civil servant, and former president of the Chamber of Commerce of Saigon.

Ticket No. 5: Tran Van Huong and Mai Tho Truyen

This was the only combination that could claim to compete with Suu-Dan in terms of national respect for services in the nationalist cause. Huong, a former teacher and civil servant, was the imperturbable grand old man, whose respect in Cochinchina was considerable. He had been mayor of the Saigon Prefecture under Diem and under Khanh. Resigning from the former's service, he performed clerical tasks for a livelihood in a pharmacy. He also was the Vietnamese Red Cross' secretary general. A former fighter with the Viet Minh, he was also a Caravellist, a member of the Council of Notables, and a prime minister. Truyen was in many ways the most respected candidate of all 22. A former civil servant and inspector general, he had been the prime mover, as lay leader, of the Buddhist revitalization movement. Over the years he had remained basically apolitical, although he had been imprisoned during the 1963 Buddhist crisis. His organization had been active in public services, education, and every aspect of Buddhist training throughout much of Cochinchina. His international reputation was considerable, and when his Southern Buddhist Association broke with the Tri Quang group due to their emphasis upon political action after Diem's downfall, a significant number of southern Buddhists had followed him. Truyen had also served on the Council of Notables, the High National Council, and the National Political Congress.

Ticket No. 6: Pham Huy Co and Ly Quoc Sinh

Co, an M.D., was a leader of the Free Democratic Party during a long exile in Paris and was prominent among the Vietnamese anti-Diem expatriots in France. His party once was connected with Dan's during the Diem era and had been involved in anti-regime terrorism in South Vietnam.

Ticket No. 7: Tran Van Ly and Huynh Cong Duong

Ly had once been a prominent lay Catholic leader in central Vietnam and an early ally of Diem, working for a nationalist oriented "Bao Dai solution." He served as chairman of the Annam Administrative Committee after World War II, and later as governor of central Vietnam. A Caravellist, he refused portfolios offered by Diem, and was temporarily arrested on two occasions.

Ticket No. 8: Nguyen Van Hiep and Nguyen The Truyen

Both were old-time revolutionaries. Hiep, Quat's minister of interior, was one of the founders of the VNQDD, and a leader of the anti-French Mekong Delta uprising. Truyen had once been an associate of Ho Chi Minh in Paris, was a member with Suu and sect leaders in the Popular Union for Independence in 1949, was elected against the official slate in the 1953 Hanoi election, and was a candidate on a ticket opposing Diem in 1961.

Ticket No. 9: Nguyen Van Thieu and Nguyen Cao Ky

Both entered the military during the First Indochina War. Each rose rapidly in the ranks. Thieu, a Catholic from central Vietnam, joined the French Army in 1948, receiving training in both Vietnam and France (and later in the United States). He served as a division and Corps commander, on the original post-Diem Military Revolutionary Council, and as chief of the Joint General Staff. During the first half of 1965 he was second deputy prime minister and a vice prime minister for the armed forces. He was also chairman of the Armed Forces Council. Due to his position as chairman of the National Leadership Committee he succeeded Suu as chief of state in June 1965. Ky, from northern Vietnam and a nominal Buddhist, had the reputation of being the nation's most flamboyant soldier-politician, but also came to be generally regarded as a competent administrator. His position as air marshal and commander of the Air Force placed him in a powerful position during each coup attempt after the death of Diem. He was temporarily minister for youth and sports, and a leading figure in the military leadership's final firing of General Nguyen Khanh. He became prime minister when Thieu became chief of state because of his position as chairman of the Central Executive Committee of the National Leadership Committee.

Ticket No. 10: Vu Hong Khanh and Duong Trung Dong

Khanh was a founder of the VNQDD in 1927. He fled to China in 1930 after the Yen Bay revolt against the French, perhaps the most legendary action of the colonial period. In China he led a VNQDD splinter group. His group was supported by the Chinese, together with the Viet Minh and the Dong Minh Hoi, as members of a provisional government in exile. Moving into Tonkin with Chinese occupation forces in 1945, the VNQDD created a series of local governments, fought the Viet Minh, but then joined with them in the new Vietnamese government. Khanh became foreign minister temporarily. After the VNQDD leaders fled the combined wrath of the French and Viet Minh, Khanh from his exile in China worked with various nationalist groups opting for the Bao Dai solution. With the collapse of the nationalist regime in China, Khanh (then a general) led some 10,000 troops into Tonkin, slipping past French defenses, but he finally surrendered. He was a member of the Committee for the Study of Unification of the National Armed Forces that met in Da Lat in 1950 in an attempt to create an indigenous military force for the Associated State of Vietnam. From 1952 to 1954 Khanh was secretary of state for youth and sports under Prime Minister Nguyen Van Tam. Arrested in 1960 after the abortive coup and imprisoned until 1963, he had been in opposition to Diem even in 1954. Khanh's running mate, once a member of the Hoa Hao military, was secretary general of the Social Democratic Party and had been elected to the National Assembly from Vinh Long Province in 1960.

Ticket No. 11: Nguyen Dinh Quat and Tran Cuu Chan

Quat, the rubber plantation owner with a sense of humor, was known for his 1961 race aginst Diem. He was elected to the Constituent Assembly and was a member of the progovernment Democratic Alliance Bloc. His running mate had served as minister of education and youth in the autonomous Cochinchinese state formed by the French after World War II.

This was obviously an experienced group. Two of the candidates had been born before the turn of the century, ten between 1901 and 1909, nine between 1917 and 1923, and one (Ky) in 1930. The median age for both presidential and vice-presidential candidates was 58. Ten had been born in the Mekong Delta, eight in North Vietnam, and four in central Vietnam. One was a Cao Dai (Suu), nine were Buddhists, five were Catholics, one a Hoa Hao, one a professed Confucianist, and five claimed no religious persuasion. Ten were professionals (doctors, lawyers, engineers, teachers), nearly all had previous administrative experience, most had been both anti-French and anti-Diem, and while only two claimed the military as their occupation, a significant number had been involved at one time in their careers in military or quasi-military activities.

The campaign began formally on August 3, with a television show on which 21 candidates appeared (notably, Ky was absent), and several briefly articulated positions they were later to develop. Thieu announced a three-point platform of (1) democracy building from the hamlet and village levels and promoting political parties, (2) social justice including the elimination of corruption and development of an efficient civil service, and (3) postwar economic planning. He indicated peace would come when the communists recognized the futility of their intention to conquer South Vietnam. Co proclaimed a policy of peace through military victory, while Dzu opted for termination of bombing of North Vietnam to be followed by immediate talks with Hanoi. Several speakers, unaccustomed to the electronic media, found themselves almost literally speechless. And the *Saigon Post* observed without further explanation that "a light touch was added to the serious event when Mr. Nguyen Dinh Quat told the audience of 'my poverty because of my opposition to the dictatorial regime of Ngo Dinh Diem.' "[44] The wealthy Quat had the buffalo as a symbol, despite Suu's previous adoption of this typical Vietnamese work animal, because his buffalo was female. "I was waiting to see if there were any candidates worthy of the country. Since there aren't any, I will have to run for President myself."[45]

As each ticket was allowed only five minutes for its presentation, the television program was more of an introduction of the candidates than a discussion of issues. Both Suu and Huong held separate press conferences on the first day. Both of what were then considered the leading civilian contenders touched upon the peace issue. Dr. Phan Quang Dan observed that a de-escalation and negotiation at all levels would "include the National Liberation Front—not as a government but as part of the vast Communist organization."[46] He also outlined a program to provide parcels of land to the peasants, to eliminate taxes until termination of the war, and to sponsor creation of political parties. He felt only such parties could make pacification work. However, Suu appeared to compromise his running mate's position, noting that the NLF was "a tool of Hanoi, so we are not going to negotiate with them. If negotiations ever take place, we will only deal with Hanoi." Suu also stated "there must be a de-escalation of the bombing in North Vietnam and a similar move by Hanoi, to send less men and material into South Vietnam."[47] Huong said he would not negotiate "until we have freedom on our side." Both Huong and Mai Tho Truyen emphasized that any negotiations would have to be an entirely Vietnamese affair. Huong stated: "America should avoid treading on the footsteps of the French who concluded the Geneva Agreements in 1954 without the concurrence of the Vietnamese."[48]

On August 5 Trong Dinh Dzu and Tran Van Chieu formally inaugurated their campaign. Immediately they were labeled the peace ticket. Dzu said: "We should stop bombing for 24 hours to give Hanoi a chance to show her willingness to negotiate. If Hanoi shows no willingness, then we resume the attacks. Six more months of bombing and the North Vietnamese people will start to revolt against the Hanoi government." The "white dove" candidate claimed he would not have direct negotiations with the NLF: the Constitution forbade such discussions and the NLF represented only a "segment" of the total population. Dzu also said "we will propose to Hanoi that we will stop military activities if they stop infiltration into the South." And again, "if Hanoi agrees, we will ask the Russians and the British to convene another Geneva-type conference." Concerning the NLF: "But to be realistic the National Liberation Front does represent some people in this country and they control some villages. We will invite them to a private conference and I will ask them to present to us their reasonable propositions. But they must be reasonable."[49]

According to the procedures agreed upon, the 22 candidates were jointly to take a 22-province tour and appear before audiences that the candidates' organizations could gather and that the government would encourage. The first scheduled appearance was to be August 6. The military candidates supposedly were to travel with the other candidates. The representatives of the other ten tickets waited for an hour and a half at the Saigon airport for a government representative. None appeared. At Quang Tri, a crowd of perhaps 1,000 awaited the candidates, who were transported from Saigon in an Air Force C-47, which landed at Dong Ha, an airport some seven miles from Quang Tri. There was no transportation waiting. US marines volunteered to drive the candidates to the meeting, but they refused, and after a 45-minute wait flew to Da Nang. (The province chief sent transportation which arrived 15 minutes after their departure.) In Da Nang, Ha Thuc Ky, leader of the Dai Viet Party, phoned General Huong Xuan Lam (I Corps Commander) requesting transportation. Quang Tri Province is historically a Dai Viet stronghold. Lam said he was unable to provide such transportation. Nguyen Dinh Quat said "This proves that the government does not want to participate in this election." Once in Da Nang the candidates voted 6–3 (with one abstaining) to return to Saigon rather than continue their trip. Dan wanted to remain in Da Nang. "It would be disastrous for the candidates to give up now. The prestige of Vietnam depends on this election and so does the American support of the war." The Dai Viet leader said "Ky and Thieu agreed in advance to play this trick on us." VNQDD candidate Vu Huong Khanh said the incident was a "sabotage of the election."[50] During news conferences held upon the candidates' return, Dzu said, "I had the impression they (Ky and Thieu) must be trying to eliminate as many civilian candidates as possible by such tactics," and Huong claimed that "The government purposely arranged the trip to humiliate us and make clowns out of us."[51]

Nguyen Van Loc represented the military ticket at a meeting of candidates. The government claimed there had been a misunderstanding. And General Lam pleaded bad weather as the cause of the incident. Ky, while not appearing at the candidates' meeting, let his views be known: "What did they expect, a Mercedes? They are not Presidents yet, but already they are acting like big bosses." And again, "I can't imagine what it would be like if one of them became President. What would happen to the poor people and to the military? They would have ceremonies all the time, all day, and then no more fights." Ky was unmoved by the joint communique signed by all civilian candidates, except Co, holding the government "absolutely reponsible for the Dong Ha incident."[52]

On August 10 the civilian candidates voted not to continue the tour until they received a letter of apology from the government. They never did receive such a formal statement. Instead, the Central Election Committee, accepting responsibility for the Dong Ha mishap, drew up an abbreviated schedule which the candidates considered for several days. Southern candidates displayed temporary unity, issuing a joint communique claiming the government "has not answered our letter and therefore is not willing to assume responsibility for the security of the candidates." The communique alleged "government authorities have taken measures to prevent voters from contacting candidates, have given instructions to civil servants and plainclothesmen to occupy all the seats in the theater where the public talks by candidates will be held and has placed barbed wire on the roads leading to the auditorium where rallies will be held."[53] Huong in a press conference made an important accusation that in the Mekong Delta "there are organized bands of hooligans charged not only with insulting our campaign workers, but also with mistreating and beating them up."[54] Apparently unperturbed by the refusal of the candidates to campaign or by the various accusations, the military candidates resumed so-called nonpolitical tours. And Huong Co Binh, the former Hanoi councilor, began to campaign separately from the other candidates.

Despite disclaimers, the military ticket was perturbed by the impasse in the electoral proceedings. Ironically the most potent weapon available to the civilian group was withdrawal of their candidacies en masse. This would have placed the government in a most delicate situation vis-à-vis Vietnamese interest groups, the American embassy, the US Congress, and world opinion in general. Even at this juncture such a contingency appeared unlikely, as it would have required unprecedented cooperation among the ten opposition tickets. However, Thieu and Ky gave assurances that campaign procedures would be improved in order to persuade their competitors to begin competing. According to Thieu "we explained that we have no responsibility according to the electoral law, but we will continue to supply any needs of the candidates." And again, "we have no intention at all to sabotage the election." The prime minister stated "a couple of months ago I had a meeting with all the chiefs of police from all the provinces. And I told them not to intimidate or use their authority to crush the people. Until now, I had heard nothing about this."[55] Ky also attempted to clarify his previous comments concerning a possible coup against an elected government with which he might disagree. "If we were elected this time and failed to carry out our plans for a social revolution, I am sure that the people—including the armed forces—would ask us to go home."[56]

Although not providing a formal letter of apology, the government agreed to provide added security, transportation via Air Vietnam rather than via military transport, and open air programs (a procedure the candidates demanded to prevent the government from packing auditoriums). With the exception of Co and Binh, the other eight candidates agreed on August 12 rather grudgingly to accept these conditions and the 11-stop abbreviated campaign schedule proposed by the Central Election Committee.

The candidates did not, however, alter their previous criticisms. On the day he agreed to begin campaigning, Huong in particular elaborated on his accusations. "There is a wide-spread campaign of intimidation against my people. Ordinary peasants have told us about this but they will not dare admit this to you, because they are terrified. Some people are afraid to say my name." He stated that in Chuong Thien, Phong Dinh, Vinh Long and Go Cong provinces his supporters had noted increased pressures during the past few days. "In Go Cong the province chief called on two of my supporters, who are lower government officials. You have families he told them and you are being paid by the government. You'd better be careful. Think of Kennedy. He was a President and he had all those people protecting him. Think what could happen to you. You're alone." The prime minister replied, "We'll punish anyone who is found guilty. What more can I do?"[57]

The civilian candidates were quite candid in publicly informing both Ky and Thieu what they could do to improve the electoral process. On August 13 Ha Thuc Ky, Dai Viet leader, called upon the United States to persuade the military leaders to resign. He said "otherwise, there is no chance of an honest election. If the generals stay in power during the campaign, they will go on cheating and using the government positions to unfair advantage and there will be no way to stop them."[58] He stressed the need for a transitional government directed by a civilian. He also recommended that the elections be postponed for one or two months, a recommendation similar to one by Senator Jacob Javits and several other American congressmen.

These charges and demands received a great deal of visibility during a live radio press conference with all candidates except the military on August 14. Dzu stated that the July 16 meeting between Ky and police officials in Da Lat was a sign of the government's intention to behave illegally during the elections. Dzu charged that Ky told police to rig the election "by whatever means at your disposal."[59] He also charged that Ky gave An Giang Province peasants envelopes including US$25 as well as a picture of Premier Ky. (Later it was found that a certain percentage of Ky's contributions did not filter down to the population through the provincial administrative hierarchy.) Dang Duc Khoi, press officer for Ky, denied these charges, and repeated the premier's earlier statement that the Da Lat meeting was held for the purpose of ensuring a free and open election. Dzu also stated at the August 14 news conference that "Ky told them to use all means in their power to bring pressure on the voters. He told them that if they were successful they would be given a reward and advanced one rank—from Captain to Major, for example." According to Dzu, Ky also told the police officials they could provide income for one agent in every village at a salary of US$35 a month and two agents at the district level and four at the provincial level with salaries of US$65 a month. "I charge General Ky to deny this. With whose money is he going to pay everybody—the taxpayer's or American aid dollars?"[60]

Other important accusations were made at the August 14 news conference. Binh, for example, stated that he had lost workers outside Saigon due to government pressures. The Saigon Council member also claimed Thieu and Ky retained their positions illegally. Phan Quang Dan commented in a fairly moderate tone of criticism, one he maintained during the entire campaign:

To allay the suspicions of the people I wish that the military ticket would take part cheerfully in the campaign with the other candidates, instead of using government resources to campaign alone to the detriment of all the civilians. The electoral law and the decisions of the electoral committee provide for joint campaigning. The generals should not use the pretext of official business to campaign alone while little rallies are set up for the rest of us.[61]

The various accusations of irregularities did not go unnoticed in Saigon or in Washington, which had in effect launched its own campaign to disprove the contentions of the civilian leaders. Ambassador Ellsworth Bunker added his prestige to the Washington public relations program, cabling the White House that "a strong crosswind (at Quang Tri) had convinced the pilot that the landing would be dangerous, and that he then went to the nearest field (Dong Ha)."[62] The telegram, among other things, was specifically to allay fears of Senators Symington and Pastore, both friends of the administration and both "hawks" who had previously indicated their support would be contingent upon a fair election. The ambassador's cable testified to the fairness of the election and to the exaggerated nature of charges of rigging and corruption. In addition General Maxwell Taylor and Clark Clifford visited Vietnam and reported their evaluation of the electoral proceedings directly to the White House. Clifford told newsmen: "We took a personal message from President Johnson to Ky and Thieu on the subject and said as bluntly as it can be said that if there was any one act on their part which could be calculated to alienate the American people, it would be a rigged election in South Vietnam."[63] And finally President Johnson himself on August 16 strongly expressed satisfaction with the election proceedings, at a ceremony honoring American civilians who had distinguished themselves in Vietnam.[64]

In Saigon, the military ticket decided to have its campaign manager, Nguyen Van Loc, answer the mounting criticism. He noted that Ky had instructed provincial officials to provide full cooperation to the other candidates. He denied each of Huong's criticisms, including: that members of the military had been issued two voting cards, that official facilities were being used by the military candidates and their organizations, that American helicopters had been used to transport the military candidates' campaign workers (in one case), that his workers had been under surveillance and that his poll watchers as well as his hamlet agents had received threats, and that lower level governmental officials were under instructions to deliver votes.

Huong had cited six provinces as scenes of flagrant violations: Dinh Tuong, Go Cong, Kien Giang, Bac Lieu, Binh Tuy and Vinh Binh. At this point it appeared possible that Huong might pull out of the campaign. He stated that "voting frauds in faraway places where the foreign press does not go" would be where the government would exert greatest pressure. "We think that when people in power continue to apply intimidatory methods, and to put pressure throughout the country on the electors and the campaigners for civilian tickets, our Constitution for the establishment of democracy becomes ineffective." During a news conference he also said that he would not accept the position of premier under Thieu. He noted the campaign had destroyed "the bridge of mutual understanding." Huong further criticized Major General Thang, the pacification director, who had stated that leading the nation was a responsibility of the armed forces. "By saying this he implied that the constitution is useless, the national assembly a luxury and the elections a waste of time. If the generals would make themselves more explicit, then we will all withdraw and leave them to do whatever they please."[65] (General Thang's comment was "the future of this country totally depends on the armed forces. If the country should fall into Communist hands, history will hold the armed forces responsible.")[66]

The Presidential Campaign: Rallies and Interviews

The interval between the formal beginning of the campaign and the second attempt to conduct a series of joint public presentations was not a period of lost time for any of the candidates. The civilians had articulated a set of legitimate grievances, and they had received wide attention—to a great extent because of the Dong Ha incident. Their accusations had been widely circulated by radio, television (in the cities and provincial capitals), and in the press. Particularly in Saigon where the press circulation was some 867,000 (27 Vietnamese papers, 2 English and 2 French papers) the candidates' comments were generally known. At the same time the military ticket took advantage of this period to continue their "nonpolitical" visitations in various sections of the country, particularly in the Mekong Delta. While the civilian candidates had limited their discussion primarily to a critique of the conduct of the election, Thieu and Ky had spelled out in increasing detail their "reform" program. Each of the civilian slates had established a platform of sorts but had not yet stressed their positions on the question of peace and other topics. The exception was Dzu, who was rapidly receiving more attention than his competitors because he had been vehement in his criticism of the regime and also because he had stressed more than others the possibility of peace gestures. In fact, he had devised a four-point peace plan including a three-day bombing pause over North Vietnam, a cessation of hostilities, a roundtable talk between Hanoi, Saigon, and Washington (and separate discussions with the NLF), and finally a Geneva-type conference.[67]

Two days before the campaign began again in earnest the Suu-Dan platform was distributed to the press. This "manifesto" was issued by Dr. Nguyen Xuan Oanh, chairman of the Phan Khac Suu for President National Committee. The manifesto called for a civilian government under Suu, whose experience, impeccable record and moral character qualified him for such a role, and noted that "only with this ticket will peace and prosperity be attained without delay and failure." Oanh's statement further called for a Government of National Reconciliation and Union with the presidential election as the first step. Implicit in this government would be a willingness to bring all interests into the councils of policy-making, because "to love and serve one's country cannot be the monopoly of any one person or group."[68] In short, the Suu-Dan ticket would not exclude the NLF from participation in the movement for National Reconciliation and Union.

However, it was the military ticket that provided the foremost set of election promises, partly in response to their competitors' allegations and to American pressure but primarily because Thieu was beginning to play fully the role of the politician. Thieu's position on the peace question remained ambiguous but it evolved quickly during the first half of August. On the one hand, he continued to state: (1) "Personally I am convinced that Hanoi will not negotiate until it is convinced it cannot win militarily and politically"[69] and (2) "We shall only negotiate on the realistic basis that there now exist two Vietnams with two sovereign governments."[70] But he also announced that one of the first things he might do would be "to ask Hanoi if they want to hold peace talks with us—a legal, elected government." He mentioned he might even request that the United States temporarily stop bombing the DRVN if "I learn privately this would bring a good response." He also noted, "If we deal with the NLF it would mean this is an internal war and not an invasion"; and the NLF "exploits the people of South Vietnam to support the war initiated by the North."[71] Thieu and Ky also pledged reform and streamlining of government and administration. For example, Thieu announced on August 11 that a reorganization of the military vis-à-vis the pacification program would be undertaken. Of the army's ten divisions, four would be broken down and placed directly under the province chiefs and given responsibilities for protecting pacification workers. At this time some 50 per cent of the regular army, i.e., 53 battalions, were protecting the pacification teams. Thieu stated "The province chiefs will be given more power and more responsibility in the pacification program, with a better chain of command and better use of regular forces and regional forces within the provinces."[72]

Ky also expanded upon pledges to purge the military of corruption. According to Ky, Major General Nguyen Duc Thang had received a new assignment to "cleanse our ranks." "He will not only get a free hand, but also the support of the army's commanding generals."[73] The minister of pacification was appointed chief of staff of the Joint General Staff of the armed forces. This presumably permitted him to direct both political indoctrination and internal military security matters, although he was supposedly to retain operational control over training of the pacification teams. In addition, the popular forces (145,000) and the regional forces (145,000) were to be under his direction. The new appointment, when added to Thieu's claim that as many as half of the province chiefs would be removed for either corruption or incompetence, was indication the government was seriously considering administrative reform. This task quickly proved vastly more complicated than implied in the election pledges, and General Thang (who was generally acknowledged to be incorruptible) soon became disillusioned with his assignment.

In effect the outline of the debate between Ticket No. 9 and its rivals was determined by August 15. The civilians, except for Co, wanted peace, but Thieu had also advocated a version of a peace plan. Both Thieu and Ky and the other ten slates promised to eliminate corruption and provide for what is unquestionably the most discussed and least articulated concept among Vietnamese, i.e., "social justice." But by August 16 the preliminaries were over. The civilian candidates had agreed to finish the campaign. Now the stage was set for the pledges to increase, the criticism to become even more caustic, and the personal rivalry to intensify.

On August 16 the formal campaign rallies began again at Bien Hoa. Approximately 1,200 attended a meeting in the courtyard of a girl's elementary school. About three-fourths of the crowd consisted of civil servants and soldiers, as each unit and branch of the military and civil service sent representatives. Campaign workers also were present in number. This was hardly a startling turnout for a city of 60,000 people in a province with 174,000 registered voters, but it proved not to be atypical. Fifteen minutes were allowed for each candidate, at the termination of which time an elder rang a red-handled brass dinner bell. He continued this procedure until the candidates ceased to speak and sat down. Huong appeared to draw the greatest response from this particular crowd. The military ticket was represented by a local politician, Dr. Vo Van Cuu. A *New York Times* reporter present at the rally interviewed a civil servant and a soldier, among others. Each denied pressure to attend the meeting. A council member from a nearby village told him "we had a seminar at the province chief's office weeks ago. I did not see any attempt to intimidate us, but the officials intimated that we could vote for those who have distinguished themselves in serving the nation. We knew they were hinting at the military slate."[74]

Sharp questioning of candidates did occur, as at later rallies. Suu was queried as to whether he might hand over the government to the NLF, as he had to the military in 1965. And Dan was questioned about the old accusation that he had wept during a court trial under Ngo Dinh Diem. Dan was asked if he would be likely to weep if he were to be in trouble again. He of course denied the truth of the original accusation.[75] Huong cited further irregularities, particularly in Vinh Binh where he claimed Nguyen Thien Nhon had ordered officials to support Premier Ky. This accusation met an immediate rebuttal. Nhon, serving in Loc's absence as the Thieu-Ky campaign manager, observed he did not mind "the remarks of an inconsistent doddering old man." The accused even offered "my head to anyone who can prove that Premier Ky is corrupt to any degree or has indulged in traffic of influence."[76]

On August 17 the presidential candidates appeared at a public meeting in Qui Nhon, capital of Binh Dinh Province (a city of approximately 50,000). Air Vietnam passenger planes brought the group to the northern city, a caravan met them and a band played. Despite this, accusations by Ha Thuc Ky stated that posters and leaflets printed by the government had not arrived. In addition, he said certain of his campaign workers had not been permitted to campaign in town. Suu made an apropos appeal to central chauvinism: "The people of Central Vietnam are much more politically conscious than people in Saigon and the Delta. Most of the country's political movements have originated here." Dan condemned governmental corruption and unwillingness to prosecute corrupt officials. He also commented that the military candidates had not resigned from public office as they had previously claimed they would: "If they are true to their word, why are they running for office?"[77] Dan also criticized the government for spending $300,000 for rebuilding Independence Palace, which had been bombed in 1962. One original concept was offered by Nguyen The Truyen: a National Guerrilla Academy would be created if his ticket won. He also announced that his running mate, Nguyen Hoa Hiep, would personally lead the graduating classes in guerrilla activities.

During the second rally, Ha Thuc Ky, a native of Hue, and Dzu, who was born in Qui Nhon, were favorites. This is Dai Viet country. Both touched on one of the most delicate issues in central Vietnam. At the end of July Thieu had signed a decree approving the charter for a United Buddhist Church and in so doing had sided with the Northern Buddhist leader, the "moderate" Thich Tam Chau, in an intense dispute over control of the Buddhist community with his rival, the central Vietnam "militant" leader Thich Tri Quang. As a result of unrest against Thieu and Ky in 1966, Tam Chau had gained control of the Vien Hoa Dao (the main center of "revitalized" Buddhism), while Tri Quang was forced to maintain headquarters in Saigon's An Quang Pagoda. The new charter provided that electors of the United Buddhist Church were to come from the various branches of the Buddhist church. Previously representatives for conventions came from specific provinces. Although Chau was a northerner, the scheme of representation by branch gave additional power to the southern segments of the church, and this was where the northern Buddhist refugees resided. A new charter also stated that the formal United Buddhist Church headquarters remained the Vien Hoa Dao, although Thich Tinh Khiet, the elderly patriarch, resided at An Quang. Tam Chau responded by having the Vien Hoa Dao appoint a new supreme patriarch, Thich Lam Em.

Following the debacle of 1966, however, the militant Buddhists were considerably weakened in terms of esteem (see Chaper 2: "Patterns of Political Party Behavior"). They at first repeated only their previous insinuations concerning the discriminatory practices of the Catholic chief of state. But on August 14 the militant Buddhists again began overt attacks upon the government. Some 1,000 followers gathered to protest acceptance of the new charter by Thieu. This "illegal charter," it was stated, was the work of "a minority of religious traitors and a plot to topple the supreme patriarch." Thich Thien Minh, noting that the Buddhists did not want any trouble, stated "If General Thieu pushes Buddhism to the wall we will be forced to fight him."[78] Thich Thien Hoa said "How can we prevent Thieu and Ky from getting elected? Only the United States Armed Forces are in a position to do that." He also stated "if the government pushes us against the wall, we will have to adopt self-defense measures. But we want to emphasize we Buddhists prefer non-violence and we will never harm the national prestige."[79] Public attacks continued but, unlike previous struggles against the government, met with no enthusiastic popular response. By introducing this issue so vividly into the presidential campaign, Ha Thuc Ky and Dzu were making a direct appeal to the Buddhists of central Vietnam, although Tri Quang did not proffer support for either of them.

On August 18 for their third joint appearance the candidates appeared in Gia Dinh before 1,500 people. The rally was attended by numerous government workers and plainclothes police agents. The small size of the crowd drew criticism from Huong. "The Government shows a lack of goodwill in organizing such a shabby rally. I know personally that the government has told agents here in the crowd to ask me unfriendly questions. But I don't mind." The former premier was upset by a comment by Ambassador Bunker to the effect that the election was fair. "Why should Bunker give the answer when the charge was directed at Thieu and Ky?" Commenting on the possibility of peace Huong observed "many of our brothers in the National Liberation Front are true nationalists." Such NLF members are "eagerly awaiting the establishment of a clean and effective government in Saigon to make the life and death decision to break away." After observing that he had once fought with the Viet Minh he stated, "One of my sons joined the resistance. I haven't heard from him in years." Discussing negotiations Huong commented: "There must be negotiations, but to tackle them we must have enough strength. We must get our own house in order first."[80] He said the NLF was "nothing but a North Vietnamese tool." In short, he ruled out a coalition government and negotiations with the NLF.

While the civilian candidates were in Gia Dinh, Ky was in Da Nang attending the annual convention of the local branch of the Vietnamese Confederation of Labor. The teamsters, fishermen, and pedicab drivers (approximately 2,000 union members) were enthusiastic. Local union leaders were even more enthusiastic although the national president of the union, Tran Quoc Buu, ostensibly had not opted for any of the presidential candidates. Ky condemned the civilian politicians, observing that many of them lived in luxury in the capital and on the Riviera. He made a dramatic appeal: "I am not asking you to vote for me. I came neither for honors nor for money. I am rather tired and wish I could go back to the army. I wish there could be a good government. Especially, I want no rigging of the election in my favor." He then stated "a weak, dictatorial, partisan or corrupt government will lead the country to perdition."[81] All in all, considering the troubles of 1966 in Da Nang it was a very good day for Ky and his "policy for the poor."

This trip, billed as nonpolitical, was his ninth barnstorming trip since the campaign began. Typically such trips involved aid to flood victims, free rice to the needy, hospital dedications, and distribution of land titles in the Mekong Delta. Upon his return from the Da Nang trip Ky told newsmen: "You know, I've been number two man in the government for two years. Now I am number two man on the campaign ticket. But I still get all the criticism." He also noted: "I took the number two spot in the interest of the army and the nation. I am not going to try to upset that unity." He observed that charges of irregularities were "plain ridiculous" and stated "we don't need to rig the election to win." He also said he would join the candidates for a joint appearance, but "I don't know when."[82]

Ky was showing signs of strain in the compromise with Thieu, as his remark on his second place role indicated. But Thieu also commented indirectly upon his running mate the day after the Da Nang labor meeting. He attempted to counteract Ky's much criticized comment that the military might attempt a coup d'état if the election resulted in a non-military regime. Thieu said: "The army has no right to plan a coup to disturb a freely and fairly elected civilian President. I don't want the army to interfere in political affairs. It is against the interest of the nation." Elaborating upon his position, he managed not to overlook the Armed Forces Council: "the most important thing now is frank understanding between the army and a civilian President to give the army any responsibilities which the civilians cannot carry out, such as national defense."[83] He also said Huong and Suu were the two men most likely among the civilian candidates to win. Both men he categorized as nationalists.

In a news conference in Saigon on the same day Dan attempted to broaden discussion to a significant policy question, observing that land reform was the most important issue, rather than communism. "Over 80% of the people in the city do not own their own houses, landlords follow the troops in the countryside and collect the back rents.

Land reform is the most crucial problem. We have plenty of land in this country which can be distributed to the people. Some people think this is Communist, to hell with them."[84] He was of the opinion that an effective land reform program would bring about a favorable change in the course of the war.

On August 20 the civilian candidates made an appearance in Nha Trang in the soccer stadium before a crowd of some 3,000. Huong commented quite favorably on the role of local authorities in publicity and other activities relative to the rally but attacked the government for questionable increased voter registration (some 390,000 increase in one month). He believed it was due to fraudulent distribution of two voting cards to military personnel. He claimed to have Big Minh's support. Dan, while noting that two cards had been distributed, blamed it upon mismanagement of the electoral proceedings. Dzu again attacked Thieu for recognition of the Tam Chau group, but his true contribution was his statement that "Democracy means the people's ability to kick out such worthless and ineffective people as Nguyen Van Thieu and Nguyen Cao Ky."[85]

While the other candidates were in Nha Trang, Thieu in Saigon told the press he would either return to the armed forces or serve in a new administration led by one of his rivals. Ha Thuc Ky also held a press conference criticizing Thieu's prior reference to the need for military direction of the armed forces and promising an amnesty for all political prisoners (except hardcore communists) and authorization for the return of all exiled general officers.

In a radio address the following day, Ky promised the elections "would be completely honest and impartial." In a cable to Speaker of the House John W. McCormack and Vice President Hubert H. Humphrey he defended the fairness of the elections: "We hope that the people of Vietnam will entrust us with further responsibilities on the basis of our past performance. But should the people decide otherwise, we shall readily accept their verdict."[86]

On August 21 most of the civilian candidates were in Banmethuot, but Huong campaigned in Cholon, appealing to the Chinese business community. However, he did state that Chinese should serve in the military as well as the Vietnamese. In addition, he appeared to retract his accusation that Ambassador Bunker was interfering in internal affairs. Yet Mai Tho Truyen added to his ticket's criticism of US activities; he was "sorry that with an intelligence network as large as the US maintains in Vietnam, Washington is so badly informed about what is going on here."[87] A very serious criticism of the electoral proceedings was made in Saigon on this date by Ha Thuc Ky concerning police activities in Thua Thien province. He claimed 19 Dai Viet members were arrested and his party flag was torn up during a meeting. Government officials denied Ky's charge and spelled out a policy to fine anyone voting twice up to US$170 plus 1–12 months in prison—fines would be doubled for civil servants.

On August 22 the candidates ventured to Tay Ninh, citadel of Cao Dai strength. Huong stated that peace would be possible only as a "civilian solution." He said "we cannot say that if we have large amounts of ammunition, whether we kill 300 of the enemy today or 500 tomorrow, that we will have peace." The only incident at Tay Ninh was Ha Thuc Ky's displeasure when Skyraiders flew over during his speech; he termed the disruption "sabotage." Dzu pleased his audience with his plea to "resist the pressure of hooligans and reject the military ticket."[88] On the same day General Loan warned that "an act of sabotage" in the electoral proceedings would result in the perpetrator being shot on the spot.

For their seventh appearance, on August 23, the candidates appeared at Can Tho. Huong commented, "Who installed the present government? Only chance and false alarms." His running mate stated, "If you do not organize fair campaigning, the future government will not represent anyone. It will not be in a position to negotiate peace and the war will go on."[89] Only 1,000 of the city's 118,000 residents appeared at the rally. Dzu expanded upon previous charges. He stated that the Corps commanders in three areas were influencing provincial and district chiefs to get out the vote for the military ticket. He accused the government of "buying support" from five Saigon newspapers, and displayed a slip he said was being distributed by the government, recommending six Senate slates. Dzu noted sympathy for the militant Buddhists who were holding a convention protesting the charter obtained by Tam Chau. The An Quang Buddhists had agreed at their meeting to join nine candidates in calling for resignations by Thieu and Ky. Dzu's most bitter comment at Can Tho was that Thieu "played a decisive role in the death of the late Ngo Dinh Diem and betrayed the Dai Viet party which put him in power June 1965."[90]

The rally on August 24 was held in Rach Gia, a city of 45,000 in Kien Giang Province, before an audience of 2,000 people. Despite advance publicity Thieu did not appear. A high proportion of the population of the province is Catholic and approximately 30 per cent are of Khmer extraction. Nguyen Van Loc represented the military ticket and drew only favorable questions from the audience. Despite the fact that some five men asked nearly all of the questions, Nguyen Dinh Quat received the greatest ovation. He was asked, "If you are elected president will you ask the Americans to leave Vietnam?" The 1961 presidential candidate observed, "It is up to you, the people. If you want them to go then I will ask them to go."[91] Huong received little sympathy from this audience. Thieu was criticized by Dzu as a "traitor both contemptible and miserable."[92] Dzu commented that Thieu's treachery to Diem had led to his death, although the former chief executive was a friend and sponsor. Dan criticized Ky for his statement that he would follow policies of the junta regardless of who was elected. "That is queer indeed. It's because we disagreed with those policies that we decided to run against him." Suu received cheers when he observed that he had served in this town while a member of the Viet Minh. Huong stated to his critical audience, "There have been pressures to make you vote for certain tickets. Please don't give in to any pressure, because this is perhaps the last opportunity for you to help to build our nation."[93]

Dzu's comments at Rach Gia led to an immediate rebuttal by Ky. Referring to the peace candidate as a dog and a horse, a reference to a self-effacing letter Dzu allegedly sent to Diem in 1963, Ky noted he "would have a cage made at Independence Palace to lock the scoundrel in."[94] Also in a Long Xuyen speech, Ky urged the Hoa Hao to stress religion and refrain from political activism and attacked the Venerable Tri Quang as "an extremist who should be blamed for the disintegration of Buddhism as a political force."[95]

On August 25 in Saigon Ky observed that he would be willing to participate in the decapitation of "bad election officials." However, on the same date both Ha Thuc Ky and Vu Hong Khanh raised new accusations. The former stated that 19 members of the Dai Viet party had been beaten and jailed near Hue, Khanh that seven members of the VNQDD had been arrested by police. The Dai Viet leader gave a strong warning. "If repression and fraud continue then we will stage demonstrations to protest against them. We are not afraid of violence. We are used to meeting violence with violence and there will be bloodshed."[96] Khanh made a similar threat regarding potential VNQDD retaliation. Considering the militancy of these two nationalist parties and their traditional use of armed party militia, such statements could not be considered idle gestures (see Chapter 2: "Patterns of Political Party Behavior").

On the day these accusations were made, Thieu indicated that approximately 50 officers would be brought before a disciplinary committee of the military. This was part of the previous steps in military reorganization, when General Thang became chief of staff under General Cao Van Vien, the chief of the Joint General Staff. Officers reported and later confirmed to have been dismissed included: Brigadier General Pham Dan Lan, once director of the Saigon port; Major General Bui Huu Nhon, previously superintendent of the military academy at Thu Duc; Lieutenant General Truyen Ngoc Tam, liaison officer to the Free World Military Assistance; Brigadier General Ton Phat Xung, who once commanded the Rangers; and Colonel Truong Quang Xuong, who was commander of the Regional Forces.

The next day, August 26, after 15 nonpolitical trips, Thieu met at a rally with the civilian candidates. The site was My Tho, a city of 67,000. During the rally Dzu stated: "I consider Nguyen Van Thieu's signing of the decree recognizing the new Buddhist charter as an utterly unconstitutional and illegal act." Huong, who had been a teacher in this city, received the biggest applause. Ha Thuc Ky said of the premier, "He made fun of the Constitution when he was not elected. He is likely to ignore the Constitution after he gets elected."[97] Approximately one-half of the audience of 2,500–3,500 were soldiers who had received leave to attend. When Thieu spoke he made no reference to his running mate. He commented:

Please do not consider me only as a candidate but as the Chief of State for the last two years and as a soldier who has been fighting the last 20 years. As a soldier and a Chief of State, I know what I am talking about. We must end the war by a victory over the Communists and through a buildup of the pacification program. If you ask me what I have done so far I could say I have accomplished some things but because I am not God, don't expect me to achieve everything overnight. To build up the country one must have at least 10, maybe 20 years.

Thieu also mentioned his position relative to negotiations: "If necessary I will agree to stop bombing North Vietnam for one week to show good will for peace. If Hanoi does not show good will for peace we will continue the war."[98]

Following his speech one questioner asked, "What about the statement that if any hooligan is elected the military will overthrow him?" Thieu's reply was "that statement was made by Premier Ky. If I am not elected I will go back to the army and fight with my comrades."[99] In Saigon a number of questions were presented to Ky during a press conference the day Thieu appeared in My Tho. The animosity between the two candidates was obvious. Ky observed: "I do not think there will be much political trouble after the election. As to the second part of your question—please ask General Thieu, who is the Number One Man if our ticket should be successful."[100]

The next day approximately 3,000 of the 116,000 registered voters of Da Nang's 253,000 persons attended the candidates' rally. Only five presidential candidates appeared. Ha Thuc Ky criticized the government for lack of support for villages and observed that such protection would have precluded attacks such as the one at Hoi An, capital of Quang Nam Province, on August 15 when 1,200 prisoners were released. The Dai Viet leader stated, "South Vietnamese troops have been used as a sacrifice for the Ky military junta."[101] He also criticized the government's recognition of the Tam Chau group. This was a very popular statement in Da Nang, a Tri Quang stronghold. Mai Tho Truyen observed: "a number of voters know that these questions are deliberate attempts to heckle me and do not agree with the hecklers." Dan also commented upon the "needling questions." The military candidates' representative received no applause, although the audience did applaud when hostile questions were asked of him, e.g., "Will the government pardon those arrested when the struggle movement was crushed?" "Why is the government antiBuddhist?"[102]

While the Da Nang rally was being held, in Saigon Thieu expanded on his peace proposals. "We are ready to meet any who are representatives of the front. If they want to see us, we are ready to welcome them. But we will not invite them. If they want to see the Saigon government, to discuss some problem, we are ready to welcome them and say, 'come here'."[103] Thieu spent part of the day in Cholon addressing an audience of about 5,000 in the Chinese section of Saigon with an electorate of approximately 200,000.

Appearing on a broadcast for the American television program, "Face the Nation," Ky also spoke on possible peace and the role of the NLF: "In the past we had many pauses in bombing. We saw no result. Why do we have to pause again? I think we must accept a pause in bombing in the North only if we see some good will from the other side to respond, because what happens after the pause—going to continue to fight or meet together? What happens?"[104] Ky also noted he would not under any circumstances accept the NLF as a government even if it were freely elected.

The next day Ky decided finally to appear at a joint rally. He picked perhaps the most hostile territory for his only appearance with the civilian candidates. A crowd of 6,000, many of whom were university students, appeared in Hue. Ky denied he called all Buddhists communists. He repeated his campaign slogan of being the government of the poor. According to Ky, "We have never thought of ourselves as saviors, as being resolvers of the dangers and problems of the country. There is a great deal left to do in helping the underpriviledged and consolidating our ranks against communism. We wish to continue." Dzu challenged the premier: "I can assure you Ky will never win the election if he is not going to cheat." The premier replied, "If you had been following the activities of the country you must know that a cheating policy is not our aim."[105]

Within 24 hours of the Hue rally, candidate Huong echoed the opinion held by increasing numbers of Vietnamese about American intervention in internal sovereignty. He characterized an American observer team sent by President Johnson as causing the people of Vietnam "grief and humiliation." However, Huong said that his previous criticisms and those of other candidates had reduced the "pressures and intimidation." He continued that "this does not mean that the coming election will be entirely honest, because intimidating campaign voters is one thing and cheating at the polls is another." He repeated again that two voter registration cards had been given to members of the military. Criticizing the discrepancy in facilities provided the candidates, Mai Tho Truyen said that Ky had cheated. The premier had flown to Hue in his private plane, the civilians by Air Vietnam. Huong considered the chief of state's pledge to end corruption as a trick. He stated that Thieu's pledges were really intended as "a threat to military officers to get them to tell the men to vote for the military ticket or else."[106]

Suu also held a press conference on August 29. He observed that "after 20 years of war, we are afraid of the military and military dictatorship. We need a civilian." Expressing fears of possible rigging he stated: "I do not have enough people for the polling stations, and I am joining with the other civilian candidates to have enough people watching the polls." He did claim: "I have many students, many young people who are volunteers. I have more than 1,000 in Saigon and thousands—I don't know how many—outside of Saigon." The claim undoubtedly was accurate, as Suu was the leader of one of three youth groups of the Cao Dai, a group stationed in Saigon. Suu stated he anticipated support from the Cao Dai, the Hoa Hao, and the Buddhists in the Center. Commenting upon possible peace moves, Suu said: "It's useless to start negotiations unless you have a good army and a good political policy. The most important thing now is to have a government with popular support that can move ahead on reform and create a sound army. I like to call it the 'new people' policy. Just like the New Deal under Roosevelt." Answering another question Suu said: "The NLF is only a tool of Hanoi. If negotiations can ever take place, it can only be with Hanoi."[107]

While the civilian candidates were being interviewed, Thieu spent August 29 in Banmethuot where he promulgated a declaration of minority rights. Over 3,000 highlanders were present for the ceremony, including FULRO representatives. Ky and Paul Nur, commissioner for montagnard affairs, were also present for the "nonpolitical" venture. For the highlanders, this particular trip was quite important. For them the election was of value to the extent it persuaded political leaders to implement programs for reform and increased autonomy (see Chapter 4: "Administration and Political Warfare in the Highlands").

Upon his return from the highlands, Thieu appeared once again with the civilian candidates. This time, on August 30, the rally was at Quang Trung before some 8,000 draftees. Thieu was received with little enthusiasm. Most questions were asked by regular army officers. Thieu said: "I did not want to remain in power but injustice still exists in the armed forces and corruption continues to be a problem so I decided to sacrifice myself and run for President." Criticizing the ineffectiveness of Vietnamese political parties he stated, "So the armed forces have had to play a political as well as military role." Dan criticized the Vietnamese draft system and noted "in Cholon there are Chinese youths who pay 6,000 piasters [about US$51] for deferments while you are drafted."[108] Dan also criticized the military system of promotions and the extreme emphasis upon education for promotional purposes.

The next day (August 31) there was a rally in Cholon before only 600 rather unenthusiastic persons, half of them children, and later a press conference. Dan emphasized the enormity of the problems facing Saigon. He said the city is not a city: "It grows more foul-smelling with each passing day as the mounds of garbage get higher and higher." Dzu condemned inflation and promised to lower egg prices. Huong said that the city was threatened with "thousands of hoodlums and robbers who imposed their will on our capital city." The press conference was attended by Thieu, although he arrived an hour and a half late. The proceedings were broadcast live on the radio. Thieu claimed that "Anyone who uses two voting cards must be punished. I've told local officials that if they commit fraud in the elections, they will be punished. If I were elected and the elections were fraudulent, I would not accept the presidency."[109] He also observed: "We could have stayed in power without any appeal to the public. But we have decided to organize these elections to see whether the people really were with us. If I really wanted to cheat it would be difficult for the people to find out about it. But

I have ordered officials at province, district, village and hamlet levels not to do anything illegal."[110] Dan listed several electoral abuses, including: "Voters with more than one poll card, which enabled them to cast more than one ballot; villages whose population has vanished, but that are still carried on the electoral rolls with several hundred residents, and inadequate procedures to safeguard sealed ballot boxes."[111] Dan condemned both the United States for bombing populated areas in Hanoi and the Viet Cong for recent raids in the Delta. Huong again criticized the American observers: "The foreigners will never understand the subtleties of governmental manipulation. It was shrewd of the government, because it is to the government's advantage." Concerning the war Huong said: "From North to South bombs and shells are devastating our land. All these sufferings that we have endured for so many years—are not even they enough to pull us out of the bad dream in which we see only disunity? Peace must be secured. The two governments of Vietnam must sit down to find a way out for the people."[112]

Thieu admitted during the press conference that mismanagement had resulted in certain members of the military receiving two voting cards, but that he had ordered such persons to return one card. He responded to a query concerning his absence from previous rallies. "There is a question of security for a Chief of State or a Premier. If I die on the battlefield, that is not significant, but if I die in a city, the Vietcong would boast that they had assassinated a Chief of State. Because of our national prestige and need for continuity of leadership, I reluctantly did not join them more often."[113] He also denied supporting any specific set of Senate slates.

The final rally of the campaign was held September 1 in Lam Son Square, Saigon. The rally began at 5:30 P.M., an auspicious time to receive the greatest attention. A crowd of approximately 2,000 was present. Nguyen Van Nam, who represented the military ticket, was booed when it was known that the major candidates were not present. He was asked, "Are pacifists guilty? Why aren't President Johnson, the Pope, and foreign pacifists who favor peace in Vietnam guilty? Why aren't Vietnamese pacifists who call for an end of the Vietnam war expelled from South Vietnam to North Vietnam or put into jail?" Nam was booed when he refused to answer and stated that he would refer the questions to the candidates themselves. Ly Quoc Sinh, running mate for Pham Phuy Co, was also booed. The hawk slate had a slogan of victory at any price. Dzu, following Sinh, said "I am encouraged by the response you have just given my rival."[114] The crowd booed down Huyen Linh Tu when he queried Huong concerning an injury he had ostensibly received during the Buddhist crisis when the candidate was prime minister. Nguyen Dinh Quat added to the general anti-American flavor and received a favorable response. His principal vignette was: "The United States provides everything from cigarettes to toilet articles to its troops here. They provide everything to its troops except sex, and that's what the Vietnamese people are here to provide." Huong revealed his thoughts at the beginning of the campaign. "At the beginning of the election I thought of the possibility of serving as Premier if Mr. Thieu or Mr. Ky asked me. But now—seeing what they have done—I will not serve under them as Premier." Dzu condemned the Thieu-Ky slate: "We have got to get rid of these dictatorial militarists." Dan proved himself to be a peace candidate, stating "Military escalation is not the way to stop this war. We need a political solution, a solution that will give our people better and more prosperous lives."[115] His statement was favorably received.

Military Ticket Campaign Strategy

The presidential campaign ended in the midst of the traffic and noise of Saigon during its busiest hour. At times it had seemed a farce. Certain actions of the candidates simply reinforced a Vietnamese tendency to ridicule, ingrained as part of a cynicism learned through experience bordering on tragedy in the lives of most of the electorate. General Duong Van Minh at one point referred to the election as a "contest between a giant and ten dwarfs." This was both unkind and untrue. But his observation that "If the dwarfs are to have a chance, they must unite"[116] was obvious from the moment of the Thieu-Ky compromise. It was this division that made the contest unequal. Minh might have proved to be a formidable foe, although this is uncertain due to the expedient rapprochement of the military candidates. A contest pitting Thieu vs. Ky vs. Minh vs. the entire civilian contingent would have been impossible to predict. However, a test of strength between a united government-military slate and a highly divided civilian contingent was quite predictable. Resources were unequal, ability to bargain with constituencies was unequal, and the influence of one ticket upon the electoral machinery was great.

Of course, the candidates Thieu and Ky were good politicians. Ky's combination of flamboyance, personal charm, administrative ability, and ability to work with specific groups and to command loyalty from devotees was formidable. Thieu's subtlety, finesse within the councils of power, perception, and balance also did not escape the attention of many citizens. Since 1965, the Thieu-Ky team had provided a certain amount of order, hardly enough of an incentive to rally enthusiastic support among the peasantry or among South Vietnam's approximately 45 per cent urban dwellers. But after the perpetual holocaust and the Minh, Khanh, Buddhist, Catholic, Huong, Quat, coup and demi-coup era of 1963–65, order is not the lowest of Vietnamese priorities. Still they did not really provide true order. The NLF-DRVN complex, the Buddhist upsurge, the shuffling among the military leadership, the trauma of a shifting group of ministers (southerners vs. northerners, etc.) would have been considered signs of considerable disorder in most political systems.

The strategy of the military ticket was to remain fairly aloof from involvement in debates with other candidates, to mend fences nationally on "nonpolitical" excursions, to respond to specific allegations by the opposition, while at the same time articulating a political platform with the broadest possible appeal. This platform took the form of pledges stated modestly at first and then expanded. Promises to eliminate corruption, to work for efficiency in administration, and to support economic development plans naturally were received suspiciously but were consistent with the desires of the electorate. Thieu's declaration on the possible peace initiatives was partly a measured response to his civilian critics. But his pledges on this point were never extreme enough to alienate his important support within the Armed Forces Council, the militant Catholic community, or the sects. Finally, and perhaps most important, Thieu was determined, as part of his election tactics and of his general strategy, to govern under the best conditions possible and to follow proper procedural steps to provide the election with an aura of openness and honesty. Despite numerous irregularities, he succeeded to a great extent in developing such an aura. This was vital for the Second Republic to be considered legitimate by interest groups within South Vietnam. It was also vital as a response to his foreign critics and allies, especially the Americans.

Administration of the national elections was assigned to the Special Commissariat for Administration (SCA) and its respected Commissioner Nguyen Van Tuong. Under any circumstances his task would have been extremely difficult. During a period of war, the SCA's problems proved enormous. The NLF harassed voting officials, threatened voters and even candidates, escalated terrorist activities, and especially plagued district and provincial capitals with shows of force to discourage voter enthusiasm. But the SCA's prime problem was the enormous logistical requirements of balloting and counting. Paper ballots totaled

460,000,000. Each voter was provided 59 ballots. Once the voter made his decisions he placed one ballot in the presidential box and six senate ballots also in this urn. Each of the ballots for the senate carried the names and photographs of each member of the slate, along with the campaign symbol of the ten candidates. In order to produce the 1,000 tons of ballots the minister stated, "I had to muster 60% of Saigon's printing capacity to do the job, starting July 22. Every printer had to print issues of all 59 ballots. If I gave the order for all one ticket's ballots to the best printer, there would be charges of discrimination from the others."[117]

Printing, ballot distribution, incidental expenses, and campaign subsidization for candidates (about one-half of funds appropriated) cost some $3,400,000, monies budgeted for and administered by the SCA. Ballots delivered to the 8,824 polling places were carried by truck, airplanes, and naval vessels. Thirty air cargo planes were involved, as well as 100 trucks that carried ballots to the Delta and to the Saigon suburbs. Each of the 5.8 million voters registered by the SCA was provided a registration and identity card and a voting card. The latter card had four marked corners, one of which was torn off once a ballot was cast. Voting was not permitted if the presidential corner had been torn off.

A nationwide system to control. conduct of the election was created.[118] The Central Election Council—consisting of the presiding judge of the Court of Appeals, the dean of the Saigon Bar Association, the State Council chairman, an Assembly delegate, and an SCA representative—validated candidacies, reviewed complaints, and checked out allegations of questionable balloting. The Council determined Senate victors and submitted recommendations to the National Assembly relative to the race for president. Campaign committees, providing candidate representation, local election councils, and special election day committees were appointed to aid in conducting the election and reviewing irregularities. In addition, watchers were assigned to each polling place. The procedure was complex, both for election officials and the electorate. Observing the problems of his task, Tuong stoically stated:

Many candidates' local representatives blame me for anything that goes wrong, but under the law I am like the handyman in the theater. I announce the title of the play. I raise the curtains. I try to keep order in the audience. After the play I lower the curtain. If the play is a hit, I shall get no credit. I did not write it, and the candidates are the actors.[119]

In general, Thieu's objective of proper procedural steps as implemented by the SCA was accomplished. Even the candidates who later claimed wide-scale irregularities rarely attacked the SCA's role but rather made allegations concerning actions of the regime beyond SCA control. Thieu succeeded less in his second objective, i.e., persuading his American critics and allies of the honesty of the electoral proceedings. South Vietnam's national elections had become a significant American political issue despite President Johnson's pronouncements that the plebiscite was both important and honest.[120] In order to allay fears of excessive irregularities the Saigon government invited United Nations observers (a request refused by Secretary General U Thant), and issued a blanket invitation to the world press, promising to "put all facilities at the disposition of members of the international press."[121] Owing to the impact upon American politics, manifested for example in testimony before the Senate Foreign Relations Committee reviewing the 1964 Tonkin Resolution, and in a special report by a subcommittee of the House Committee on Government Operations highly critical of the Vietnamese elections, President Johnson decided to send American observers. The group of observers finally selected represented the Congress, State Houses, urban areas and numerous interest groups ranging from the VFW and the AFL–CIO to Catholic bishoprics and the Junior Chamber of Commerce. It was these observers who drew heavy criticism from Huong as being instruments for interference in the internal sovereignty of South Vietnam.

The presence of this group appeared to aid Washington's case that the election was relatively honest. None appeared to witness irregularities in their nationwide tours, and most claimed September 3 was a day of considerable moment in building democracy in South Vietnam. A number of the observers candidly stated that their temporary vantage point was appreciably less than adequate for a thorough analysis of the proceedings. However, nearly all experienced news correspondents also agreed that procedurally election day went more smoothly and with far fewer gross irregularities than they had anticipated, although newsmen received information about specific problems that witnesses felt less than willing to quote to the official observers.

That failure of even the most sophisticated foreign observer to recognize the subtleties of electoral manipulation was pointed out by Nguyen Xuan Oanh. Acting as chairman of the Suu National Committee, Oanh spelled out potential irregularities in a speech the entire text of which was carried by the *Saigon Post* the day before the election. He noted that election day rigging had taken numerous forms and could be duplicated on September 3, including secret orders and intimidations, threats, especially among the illiterate, illegal displays of military ticket emblems in voting places, violations of secrecy of the ballot, ghost ballots, changing ballot boxes, multiple voting by military personnel, misreading and falsifying names on ballots, ballot mutilation, ballot box stuffing, voting booths within military compounds, and false reporting of results. Oanh warned that a military victory in less secure areas, opposed to a closer race in secure sections, should be viewed with considerable suspicion.[122]

The Referendum and Its Challengers

On September 3, 1967, the polls in South Vietnam's 50 provinces and municipalities were open from 7:00 A.M. to 4:00 P.M. During these nine hours 4,868,266 persons voted. This was an 83.8 per cent turnout of the 5,853,251 registered voters. Only 3 per cent of the ballots were invalid, presumably an indication that no high percentage of voters was prepared to disavow the entire proceedings. Percentages of those voting ran as high as 93.9 per cent (Ninh Thuan Province). Lower percentages were recorded as in the past in the cities, particularly Saigon (63 per cent).[123] Total votes and percentages for each of the candidates are shown in Table 8.

TABLE 8
RESULTS OF THE 1967 PRESIDENTIAL ELECTION

SLATES	TOTAL VOTES (%)
Thieu-Ky	1,649,561 (34.8)
Dzu-Chieu	817,120 (17.2)
Suu-Dan	513,374 (10.8)
Huong-Truyen	474,100 (10.0)
Ky-Dinh	349,473 (7.3)
Quat-Chan	291,718 (6.2)
Hiep-Truyen	160,790 (3.5)
Khanh-Dong	149,276 (3.2)
Binh-Khinh	131,071 (2.9)
Co-Sinh	106,317 (2.2)
Ly-Duong	92,604 (1.9)

Dzu was the true surprise, as few initially considered him a serious contender to Huong or Suu. Presumably the major reason for his support was his strong advocacy of a peace platform. The Thieu-Ky ticket received a plurality in each of the four zones, with slightly less than an absolute majority in General Vinh Loc's rather tightly controlled II

Corps. Suu carried the cities of Da Nang and Hue and Thua Thien Province. Tri Quang, who apparently wanted to support Huong but found it practically impossible due to the former prime minister's earlier crackdown on Buddhist demonstrations, opted for Suu-Dan in central Vietnam. Huong received a plurality over Thieu in Saigon; his vote there might have been better except for Dzu's unexpected third-place race and the respectable showing of Suu, Ha Thuc Ky, and Quat. Huong also ran a good race in Da Lat, but did not do as well as expected in the Delta. The surprising Dzu carried five provinces: Quang Nam in I Corps; Binh Duong, Hau Nghia, and Tay Ninh in II Corps; and Kien Phong in IV Corps. In addition, Dzu ran no lower than second in all provinces of IV Corps and III Corps except Gia Dinh, where Huong was in second place behind Thieu. While losing, Dzu ran a good race against the military slate in the provinces of Long An, Phu Tuy, An Giang, Chau Doc, Vinh Long, Ba Xuyen, and Kien Giang. Other perhaps unexpected developments included the relatively good races at least vis-à-vis other civilian candidates: Ha Thuc Ky in IV Corps outpolled Suu and ran close to Huong, and in III Corps he ran fifth but was only slightly behind Suu in several provinces; Quat ran a surprising race in I Corps (where his "female" buffalo was on occasion confused with Suu's "male" buffalo), and he placed fourth in II Corps.

The loss by Thieu of six provinces and three cities, having 1,640,053 registered voters and casting 1,333,582 votes was significant. Thieu's 26 per cent in the six autonomous cities, as opposed to 34.8 per cent nationally, was also important. His margin was only 5 per cent over Huong's 21 per cent in these six constituencies; Suu received 16 per cent and Dzu 13 per cent in the six. However, when Thieu's vote in the quite urbanized province of Gia Dinh is added, his plurality increases greatly. The differential between Thieu's national and city vote was much less than the discrepancy during the Diem period. But the cities provide the most dramatic example of the limitations placed upon opposition to the Thieu-Ky combination due to the number of civilian candidates who proceeded to cut deeply into others' total votes. That Thieu received an absolute majority in only seven provinces and less than 30 per cent of the votes in 13 provinces makes this even more obvious.

Thieu received good support among the military and government personnel, the highlanders, elements of the Hoa Hao and Cao Dai, portions of the Chinese, Catholics, moderate Buddhists, and labor. Militant Buddhists, while supporting Suu in central Vietnam, appear to have opted for Huong further south. Dzu apparently was popular with ele-

Republic of Vietnam: Provinces and Tactical Zones

TABLE 9
Presidential Election Returns by Tactical Zones, Cities (C) and Provinces

Cities and Provinces	1 Suu/Dan	2 Ky/Dinh	3 Binh/Khinh	4 Dzu/Chieu	5 Huong/Truyen	6 Co/Sinh	7 Ly/Duong	8 Hiep/Truyen	9 Thieu/Ky	10 Khanh/Dong	11 Quat/Chan	Total	Registered Voters
Tactical Zone I													
Hue (C)	20,394	5,054	368	1,503	1,937	301	389	499	8,162	501	4,227	43,335	54,827
Da Nang (C)	34,061	5,045	1,258	5,160	4,770	1,284	1,039	2,072	22,496	3,215	9,494	89,894	116,053
Quang Nam	20,716	15,764	3,776	12,779	5,289	3,018	2,381	4,790	28,378	17,187	16,584	130,662	153,393
Quang Ngai	31,468	8,806	4,582	44,323	7,073	2,830	2,491	4,288	41,609	2,911	17,244	167,625	202,664
Quang Tin	10,538	6,538	3,098	7,147	7,827	2,257	1,950	4,503	34,045	3,234	5,971	87,102	94,483
Quang Tri	14,287	16,008	2,197	8,991	2,580	2,020	1,482	2,630	20,911	8,016	9,335	88,457	107,281
Thua Thien	41,203	35,382	2,408	5,168	4,347	1,610	1,311	2,961	33,804	3,710	19,972	151,876	183,160
Total	172,667	92,591	17,687	85,071	33,823	13,320	11,043	21,743	189,405	38,774	82,827	758,951	911,861
Tactical Zone II													
Cam Ranh (C)	4,717	1,287	450	921	978	538	559	1,203	7,324	524	2,642	21,143	24,353
Da Lat (C)	2,314	1,672	508	2,846	5,561	497	539	773	9,723	768	1,310	26,511	34,765
Binh Dinh	27,151	17,601	5,522	46,076	10,293	5,809	4,940	13,021	118,232	5,922	15,790	270,357	302,260
Binh Thuan	6,169	4,867	2,006	19,588	7,766	1,992	1,995	3,531	37,924	2,811	5,226	93,835	106,375
Darlac	3,209	2,691	1,550	3,552	6,014	1,344	1,410	2,788	38,554	1,770	2,911	65,793	78,099
Kontum	1,431	1,443	583	5,700	1,427	368	359	1,169	25,707	607	976	39,770	47,998
Khanh Hoa	30,043	7,199	2,732	9,270	7,619	2,929	2,919	4,897	56,192	2,946	14,313	141,059	166,240
Lam Dong	2,312	1,505	540	1,039	979	475	410	880	12,043	825	1,332	22,340	26,839
Ninh Thuan	5,749	3,348	1,309	4,696	5,020	1,569	1,525	2,410	30,502	1,730	4,123	61,981	67,409
Phu Bon	1,197	992	716	1,116	1,248	416	309	2,377	11,717	548	2,376	22,956	27,052
Phu Yen	23,261	5,931	2,827	9,176	3,279	2,320	1,855	3,960	30,067	2,327	13,311	98,314	116,107
Pleiku	3,885	3,528	1,934	7,164	3,507	1,505	1,577	3,592	29,466	1,569	3,030	60,757	77,572
Quang Duc	948	706	333	697	505	424	444	540	8,519	440	733	14,289	15,503
Tuyen Duc	2,124	1,502	718	2,728	2,107	684	590	1,192	21,463	1,049	1,428	35,585	41,696
Total	114,510	54,272	21,728	114,569	56,303	20,870	19,391	42,283	437,433	23,836	69,495	974,690	1,132,268
Tactical Zone III													
Saigon (C)	59,371	34,007	13,995	87,670	137,962	13,159	10,010	14,910	135,527	15,300	23,700	545,611	765,340
Vung Tau (C)	2,227	1,767	646	3,657	4,015	553	469	977	13,456	889	1,083	29,739	35,787
Bien Hoa	7,878	7,102	3,140	31,494	13,546	2,965	2,531	4,343	55,488	3,570	5,991	138,048	179,450
Binh Duong	7,106	6,196	3,062	23,499	8,576	2,529	2,290	3,698	19,275	2,904	5,719	84,854	113,065
Binh Long	1,945	1,396	880	3,936	1,616	1,007	982	1,272	7,732	980	1,454	23,200	28,218
Binh Tuy	761	1,496	499	5,143	639	427	488	1,101	11,237	566	845	23,202	27,068
Con Son	49	21	30		85	4	16	25	658	17	19	940	1,019
Gia Dinh	36,472	21,580	9,078	63,934	69,949	7,968	6,774	11,694	171,123	10,422	15,904	424,898	562,190
Hau Nghia	3,044	3,082	1,555	19,430	3,837	1,256	1,175	1,608	10,425	1,483	2,761	49,656	63,439

Long An	4,544	4,235	2,071	15,535	9,220	1,812	1,831	1,879	15,608	2,407	3,485	62,427	75,303
Long Khanh	2,580	3,975	1,159	5,746	3,270	898	823	1,961	25,624	1,403	1,977	49,416	61,155
Phuoc Long	832	802	599	1,008	961	617	556	895	11,004	514	654	18,442	20,981
Phuoc Tuy	2,176	2,170	1,120	12,002	4,268	933	820	1,291	15,705	1,229	1,826	43,534	50,768
Tay Ninh	6,696	5,013	3,607	39,947	6,543	2,284	2,157	3,133	30,830	2,825	4,344	107,379	130,395
Total	135,681	92,482	41,427	312,831	264,487	36,412	30,922	48,787	523,692	44,509	69,756	1,601,346	2,114,178
Tactical Zone IV													
An Giang	11,502	22,456	6,567	43,483	12,215	3,546	3,291	4,737	62,035	4,968	7,752	182,552	224,274
An Xuyen	1,523	1,476	832	6,444	2,491	760	652	3,593	14,326	789	1,131	34,017	42,245
Ba Xuyen	4,601	6,378	2,896	20,574	8,823	3,553	2,662	3,665	21,738	3,878	5,428	84,196	103,280
Bac Lieu	4,241	5,290	1,923	9,729	6,191	1,902	1,555	2,582	15,717	1,954	3,539	54,623	69,780
Chau Doc	9,372	11,023	5,341	40,019	8,043	3,692	3,084	4,336	65,374	4,117	7,136	161,537	184,301
Chuong Thien	2,472	2,423	1,405	7,909	2,018	724	724	824	22,488	997	1,846	43,830	53,298
Dinh Tuong	6,352	6,844	2,977	14,240	15,492	2,479	2,288	3,955	29,732	3,265	4,285	91,909	112,934
Go Cong	1,657	1,726	892	2,879	4,581	798	583	1,543	17,594	1,238	1,294	34,785	38,588
Kien Giang	6,602	6,729	2,975	28,364	8,258	2,567	2,002	3,072	39,130	2,647	5,771	108,117	132,967
Kien Hoa	6,920	6,942	3,509	14,069	9,056	2,815	2,775	4,035	40,845	3,621	6,758	101,345	118,793
Kien Phong	4,850	6,351	3,332	34,160	3,812	1,891	1,750	2,524	28,448	2,301	3,933	93,352	111,110
Kien Tuong	648	557	396	4,283	732	321	283	434	6,126	414	595	14,788	17,200
Phong Dinh	10,772	9,007	5,393	24,103	11,846	2,825	2,697	3,403	28,072	3,336	6,209	107,663	145,332
Sa Dec	5,200	6,703	3,254	13,246	5,068	1,702	1,765	1,861	43,760	1,934	3,224	87,667	97,662
Vinh Binh	3,572	7,340	2,839	13,745	5,550	2,488	2,066	3,224	32,246	2,726	3,388	79,184	95,791
Vinh Long	10,232	8,523	5,698	27,402	15,311	3,652	3,121	4,189	31,401	3,972	7,351	120,852	148,389
Total	90,516	109,768	50,229	304,649	119,487	35,715	31,248	47,977	499,031	42,157	69,640	1,400,417	1,694,944

SOURCE: "The Presidential Election," *Vietnam Report*, 7 (Washington: Embassy of Republic of Vietnam, 1967).

ments of the militant Buddhists, the Cao Dai and Hoa Hao. And Huong received a high proportion of the Chinese votes, but Suu appeared to have received minimal support from the Cao Dai.

Owing to Dzu's unexpected showing in outlying jurisdictions, a number of government officials hinted he might have benefited from NLF votes. He did run second in heavily NLF provinces—including Kien Hoa, Long An, Phuoc Tuy, Phuoc Long, Binh Long, and Kontum. Three unsuccessful Senate slates affiliated with Dzu's Tan Dai Viet Party also did well in NLF-influenced areas. However, Thieu carried these provinces. But Dzu also ran well in relatively pacified provinces such as An Giang and his home province of Binh Dinh. The National Police conducted an inquiry into alleged NLF threats to voters to vote for Dzu in Kien Giang and Kien Hoa provinces without reaching a definitive conclusion. The Tan Dai Viet Party was particularly perturbed by the claim of NLF support for Dzu. A communique of the party stated "being an anti-Communist organization, we do not have in our ranks pro-Communists or Communist sympathizers."[124] The Tan Dai Viet had provided better organization than had other civilian candidates. Khanh relied upon sections of the divided VNQDD, Ha Thuc Ky on the Revolutionary Dai Viet Party, Suu upon his Cao Dai youth group, and Huong upon a Mekong Delta group. Yet these were quite secondary structures compared with the government-military complex.

The mandate for Thieu and Ky was challenged immediately—in fact before final votes were announced. Suu termed the election "fraudulent and pre-arranged," adding he intended to "join with other tickets in a collective protest to be sent to the Provisional Legislative Assembly due to rigging of the elections." On September 4 seven of the ten civilian candidates lodged complaints with the Assembly. Dzu bitterly observed: "The election was a nationwide fraud. I consider this government illegal and incompetent and I do not accept the results of this election. I will never serve in the Thieu-Ky government."[125] A Huong aide said "the Generals apparently do not want a normal political life in South Vietnam," and Ambassador Bunker said the elections "went remarkably well."[126]

Both Suu and Dzu said that in Gia Dinh and My Tho the ballots ran out because troops had been taken to overcrowd the booths. Dzu also charged certain soldiers had multiple voting cards. Suu claimed that in many areas his campaign workers believed only 10 per cent of the voters turned out for the elections. "How then can anyone believe that the turnout was more than 80 per cent almost everywhere, as the government reported this morning?" Dan claimed the vote was absurd, observing he had treated more patients than he received votes in Gia Dinh Province. And a Huong spokesman commented: "It wasn't enough for them to rig the elections. They wanted to humiliate Mr. Suu and Mr. Huong in their homeland, the Delta."[127] Despite these allegations, the new vice president said: "If Dzu has proof that there was fraud, let him go ahead. If there was a fraud we would have had a much larger margin. During the campaign, Mr. Dzu made many charges, but none of them was proved."[128]

On the day after the election the NLF also broadcast its responses. It termed the winning ticket as "dirty lackeys of the Americans." It also referred to them as "running dogs, traitors, and country sellers." The broadcast stated:

> For our people, the existence of the puppet Saigon administration only means that the American's tyrannic yoke of domination will continue to weigh heavily on our compatriot's life and that the Americans will continue to carry out the war intensification policy in an increasingly fierce manner. The highest office of the Americans is still in the hands of the two dirty traitors whom the compatriots have insulted and wanted to be overthrown. Such is the truth about the Presidential and Vice-Presidential election farce of the United States–Thieu-Ky clique. Therefore, no matter what fine words the United States–Thieu-Ky clique uses and what percentages—80%, 90%, or even higher—they announce, these will be a 100% deception.[129]

Any vestige of unity among the defeated presidential candidates disappeared quickly after the initial comments on September 4 and 5. Eight of them formally filed charges on the election, but they were not joined by Ha Thuc Ky or Huong. Dan also refused to make a claim against a rigged election. In addition to signals of disunity, the Nguyen Dinh Quat–Tran Cuu Chan slate made formal allegations against Dzu; it was claimed Dzu "has campaigned on the Communist line and denounced our ticket to be favorable to the government, which was very detrimental to our ticket in terms of ballots cast for us."[130] By September 10, the Provisional National asembly had received 15 formal complaints of presidential election irregularities. (Representatives of 25 defeated Senate slates also filed claims.)

The winning ticket was encountering as much difficulty maintaining a facade of unity as its opponents. On September 8, Thieu refused to appear on the television program "Meet the Press" with Ky. Thieu also commented that the responsibilities of the vice president were clearly defined in the Constitution. And certain pro-Ky newspapers began to question whether Thieu would keep commitments made when Ky withdrew his candidacy for the presidency. A newspaper controlled by General Loan, *The Masses,* advocated the Constitution be amended so that Ky could become premier. The paper said "Ky's supporters voted for the military ticket because they thought the vote would bring General Ky a higher position. They did not think their special affection for him would bring him a major defeat."[131] The *Saigon Post,* generally sympathetic to Ky, stated in an editorial on September 11 that Thieu was a "minority President" who needed all the help he could get. This editorial noted the "gentleman's agreement" with Ky, observing Thieu could not "go his own way." Commenting on the television program incident, the editorial even commented that Thieu's "drug of success [electoral victory] may have gone up his head."[132] In a second editorial the following day, the *Saigon Post* was no less complimentary. "The danger is also real that flatterers could make him think he is what the Vietnamese would call the center of the universe."[133] Emancipation from the ill effects of such flatterers, according to the editorial, could best be found in development of a true opposition including the less-than-successful AVB (All Vietnam Bloc), a primarily pro-Ky structure, and perhaps the defeated presidential candidates and the politically oriented religious leaders. The American embassy attempted to persuade Thieu to find a method for retaining Ky's support. One of Thieu's advisers responding to this attempt asked an American newsman: "Ky's men already demand that the Constitution be amended. Do the Americans want amendment too?"[134] Considering the US insistence upon such a Constitution, the postelection position of the embassy obviously was cause for confusion to Vietnamese politicians.

After formal protests were initiated but before the Provisional National Assembly acted upon these claims, Suu and Dzu were joined by militant Buddhists and student organizations in demanding invalidation of the elections. Suu centered his attention upon creation of a new political party and continued to serve as chairman of the Assembly. Dzu, on September 15, appeared before a group of about 500 university students. Several days earlier, during an entrance examination at the University of Saigon Medical School, several hundred students had launched a protest against the election, denouncing Thieu and Ky and destroying examination papers. In his Saigon address to the student group Dzu stated that the military ticket had "sold out Vietnam's national sovereignty. The purchaser was the United States. Who let the Americans come into our country and install big bases? Wasn't it Thieu and Ky? Now what did the election prove? It proved that the Vietnamese people demand peace and the overthrow of these corrupt elements." Later, denying any anti-Americanism, he told an interviewer that "my speech was to answer propaganda from Thieu and Ky. That I am the American's man, that I have American money, that I am a pawn of American agents."[135] Dzu's comment was not entirely specious, as Saigon rumors had connected him with the American Central Intelligence Agency.

Dzu also attended rallies of the militant Buddhists at the An Quang Pagoda, condemning the trampling under of South Vietnam's internal sovereignty. The Tri Quang group was demanding rescision of Tam Chau's charter, invalidation of the national elections by the Provisional National Assembly, and postponement of Lower House elections. One An Quang Pagoda pronouncement was: "General Thieu himself did not give a damn about the religious aspirations and beliefs of Buddhists who have adopted a moderate line of action. Consequently, if such a line would be discarded in the future, we shall hold General Thieu entirely responsible for it."[136] The militant Buddhists also sponsored antigovernment demonstrations in Saigon, Da Nang, and Hue. As these demonstrations were considered illegal, it was assumed General Loan, Ky's friend, permitted them to occur.

On September 28, Buddhists marched in both Hue and Saigon. In the capital 700 monks and nuns were led by Tri Quang to Independence Palace. Thieu and Ky met the group outside the front gate. Thieu said "I hope we can find a solution to get the Buddhists unified. We will do anything in our power to see that the Buddhists get together."[137] Tri Quang remained on the grounds in front of Independence Palace although most of his supporters left. It was clear the argument was more one of recognition of Tam Chau than of the election.

Tri Quang met with a three-man delegation headed by General Pham Xuan Chieu. Government officials unsuccessfully attempted to arrange a meeting between Tri Quang and Tam Chau. Thieu refused to concede recognition that the charter was illegal. Again, as in 1966, Tri Quang lost an encounter. He continued his vigil until after the Assembly acted upon the formal list of allegations, and then left following an ambivalent pledge by Thieu to the supreme patriarch of An Quang to look into a satisfactory method for resolving the difficulty.

Dzu was also finding his plans thwarted. Immediately after the election, judicial proceedings against him that had been suspended for the campaign were reinitiated. In the first of several steps required for conviction, he was fined US$29,500 and sentenced to three months' imprisonment on a 1962 charge and to six months on a 1966 charge, concerning respectively an alleged fraudulent check for US$12,488, and US$11,480 allegedly transferred to a bank in San Francisco. He was acquitted on a charge of collecting a US$1,270 fee from a person whom he had not defended. Dzu denied all three charges, asserting he was being persecuted because he was an opposition leader. He claimed that Ngo Dinh Diem had him arrested for plotting a coup. Regarding the 1966 charge, he claimed friends of his in the United States had deposited the money on behalf of his two children in universities there. On September 28 he refused to visit police headquarters as requested. He noted on this date, "I thought I had the necessary majority in the Assembly to invalidate the elections, but I don't know now because Ambassador Bunker spent the afternoon with Premier Ky on Tuesday and the same evening Ky invited 58 deputies to have lunch with him on the following day."[138]

Dzu was arrested on September 30. Also arrested was Vu Hong Khanh, who was traveling with Dzu in an automobile, but who was immediately released with Loan's apologies. The charge against Dzu was defamation of the judicial system. His wife attempted to schedule a news conference but was prevented from doing so, whereupon Mrs. Dzu and Phan Khac Suu marched with linked arms in front of Dzu's campaign headquarters. Dzu was later released under house arrest pending additional trials.

The police had followed a much more impolitic course than in the Dzu case, one that proved a major source of embarrassment. At 8:10 P.M., September 21, Vietnamese police broke into the home of Au Troung Thanh. The former minister of finance had previously invited newsmen to his home after noting police cars in front of the house. Before the affair was over reporters scuffled with the police and General Loan himself entered the home. The police carried a slip of paper requesting Thanh to go to headquarters the next morning for a talk with General Loan. The disallowed presidential candidate had applied for an exit visa. Loan said "when a man who is political applies to leave, asking to take his whole family with him, I must ask him to explain himself." Loan continued "Thanh is not a Communist. I am his friend. But it is my job to investigate."[139]

On his way to the police station on September 22 Thanh stopped at his office. Apparently police following him misunderstood and handcuffed him in addition to pushing him around. Loan gave his apologies to a man "of his rank and position." A press conference was held during the one-day interrogation, and in response to questions Thanh stated: "I strongly protest against what has happened last night and this morning and I am very sorry for my country. If this can happen to me, what can happen in the countryside where the peasants are helpless. Americans and Vietnamese are fighting here for freedom and democracy, but alas, where are freedom and democracy?" Loan emphasized that the former minister was not under arrest. Thanh observed "I would like to go to America and I would like to tell the American people what is really happening in my country." Loan said he did not have to provide reasons for detaining and questioning anyone. "The people I ask to come to see me never know the reason why. I don't put the reason on my invitation. It is not for a lunch or a dinner."[140]

Nguyen Van Bong, National Institute of Administration rector and a contender for the premiership, explained the Thanh case as one where Ky, through Loan, had Thanh detained in order that Thieu would not offer the former minister a post in the new cabinet. Such an offer was later denied by Thanh who, after an 18-hour detention, was placed under house arrest like Dzu.

As a prelude to the Provisional Legislative Assembly debate on validation of the election, the Assembly's Election Committee (a heavily Dai Viet group) voted 16 to 2 against validation. Four major complaints were presented to the Assembly by the Committee: mishandling of election organization, campaign procedures, casting of ballots, and ballot counting. The Assembly rejected these complaints, and debated for some 15 hours until nearly midnight October 2, its constitutional deadline, on the question of validation itself, finally voting 58:43 for, with 2 abstentions. Police guarded the National Assembly Building; and once again General Loan's presence was a cause of some discussion. A few blocks away a militant Buddhist demonstration against validation was broken up. Suu resigned as Chairman of the Provisional Legislative Assembly in protest against the actions of the body, devoting his attention to building the Democratic Front as an opposition bloc. Nguyen Van Loc was appointed prime minister, and Thieu and Ky were inaugurated on November 1. The new president promised administrative reforms, drastic steps against corruption, and a proposal to Hanoi to talk peace and recognize the now fully legitimate Republic of Vietnam. The 1967 presidential electoral process had ended.

Expanding the Electoral Experience

Owing to the international attention paid to the presidential election, four other important 1967 electoral processes in South Vietnam received relatively little coverage. Yet as examples of electoral experiences in an underdeveloped nation at war these other elections carried at least the germ of development of a representative form of government. They included referenda in all "safe" areas and resulted in the election of representatives of all levels of government, except municipal and provincial councillors who were elected in 1965. Combined with the presidential elections, the hamlet, village, Upper House (Senate), and Lower House elections provided a set of opportunities for popular selection previously unknown in Vietnam. As in the presidential election, and perhaps more so in the hamlet and village elections, these four votes were not without procedural and other irregularities. Further, they were complicated and limited only to areas not under direct NLF influence. This was a considerable proviso. But the millions of ballots that were cast, particularly in hotly contended Senate and House races, resulted in representation of a cross section of all of South Vietnam's complex matrix of religions, ethnic groups, political parties, and interest groups. This was no small achievement.

Village and Hamlet Elections. The village elections in "safe" areas (Phase I) were held on five consecutive Sundays between April 2 and 30, involving 40 per cent of South Vietnam's villages—984 villages with 3,233,000 registered voters (see also Chapter 5: "Political, Military and Constitutional Areas"). There were 12,719 candidates for the 9,964 seats, a ratio of only 1.4:1; all candidates were required to be village residents for one year. Percentages voting varied from 98 per cent in Sa Dec Province to 49 per cent in Gia Dinh Province, where most persons worked in the capital. In Phan Nhan village on Saigon's outskirts, only 23 per cent voted. The national total of 2,511,000 votes was 77.6 per cent of registered voters.

Village councils varied in number from 6 to 12 members, with the member receiving the highest votes becoming village chief. Each village council appointed an administrative committee chairman who appointed commissioners for economy and finance, security, propaganda and civic action, social welfare and agricultural affairs. This last commissioner ostensibly assisted in land reform. The constitution also required government assignment of two civil servants to each regional entity.

Despite provincial control of budgetary matters, the formal delegation of local legislation and policy making to Village People's Councils was a significant decentralization procedure. Training courses for elected officials offered under the auspices of the Special Commissariat for Administration was another attempt to implement decentralization.

Local campaigns were generally mild with little campaigning and little political party activity except in such areas as Quang Tri Province; officials at the province, district and pacification-team levels solicited for the candidates. Personal reputation and family interests weighed heavily in voter appeal. In certain villages a family representative was permitted to vote for family members. A majority (57 per cent) of those elected to village councils were farmers. Village and hamlet officials (13.1 per cent) were next, and merchants (11 per cent) were third. The average age was 40.

Hamlet elections were also held during 1967 by steps (five from May 14 to June 11) in Phase I for "secure" hamlets. Only hamlet chiefs, and deputy chiefs in hamlets with a population of 3,000 or more, were elected. A total of 4,608 (33.3 per cent) of South Vietnam's 13,085 hamlets held elections. Phase II elections began in July but occurred only after revolutionary development teams deemed a local situation secure. A total of 2,310,000 voted in Phase I, 78.7 per cent of the registered voters. Candidate-to-position ratio was 2.3:1. Elected were: 2,261 farmers, 1,676 former village or hamlet officials, 300 southern highlanders, 142 Cambodians, 30 Chams, 17 northern highlander refugees and 4,493 Vietnamese. Though restricted, the new hamlet organization permitted the chief to represent the village chief and to supervise activity of the hamlet administrative committee handling security, propaganda and civic action.

Upper House (Senate) Election. Sixty members of the Senate were elected on September 3.[141] Although both the presidential and Senate elections were administered by the SCA, different rules for the campaigning applied for the 48 slates (480 candidates) whose applications were approved. The Central Election Committee made determinations as to which slates won. Radio and television time was provided, as were facilities for public appearances. Voting was nationwide, requiring each voter to select six of 48 ballots, and the six slates receiving the highest votes won. Unquestionably, many voters agreed with Ky's description of the Upper House election as a big lottery. But many of the candidates were well known nationally, and a high percentage had the organizational support of particular parties and groups in specific districts.

The campaign began on an embarrassing note. The day before, La Thanh Nghe, former minister of crafts and industry under Premier Ky, was accused of accepting pay-offs. Nghe headed a ticket composed of several members of the Constituent Assembly, presumably a pro-Ky slate. An official from the controller's office of the Agency for International Development (AID) stated that the former minister had received "illegal kick-backs and importer commissions" amounting to nearly $900,000 between 1956 and 1966, and had deposited the money in American and Swiss banks.[142] The director of AID in Vietnam also stated that drugs Nghe had imported were often found in the hands of the NLF. The former minister was under investigation by the minister for economic affairs. The government was attempting to determine if he had illegally deposited moneys in foreign banks rather than repatriated funds as required by law. It was also reported that Ky had persuaded the election commission to reverse its decision to invalidate the application for candidacy of Nghe and his slate. Despite this beginning and other incidents, such as a later accusation against one candidate of misusing funds, the physical beating of Pham Huu Thiet by soldiers in Quang Nam while campaigning, and the American embassy's embarrassment when a mimeographed list sponsoring the military ticket and six senatorial slates appeared in Gia Dinh and Binh Hoa on obsolete USIS stationary, the campaign ran relatively smoothly. Considering the number of candidates, in fact, it proceeded with a minimum of confusion.

The 48 slates ranged over all of Vietnam's political persuasions. In many ways the total list read somewhat like a Vietnamese political *Who's Who,* although several slates were drawn up so quickly many candidates were unacquainted with other ticket members. Many were ministers in Vietnam's numerous post-World-War-II cabinets. Post-1965 cabinets were especially well represented, as were members of the Constituent Assembly and provincial councillors and former administrative or legislative members of the Diem government. Militant Buddhists had been disallowed but a Tam Chau-supported slate did run. Professors and former military leaders were well represented among the candidates.

Included among the more important slates were, of course, the six winning tickets:

1. the Farmer-Worker-Soldier slate, which won 23 of 50 provinces and cities, was headed by former General Tran Van Don, planner of the 1963 coup, and included former General Ton That Dinh (instrumental in the anti-Diem coup), Dang Van Sung (farmer-labor alliance advocate), Pham Van Tan (1961 vice chairman of the Ngo Dinh Nhu-initiated National Unity Committee), and FULRO member Ksor Rot.

2. National Leadership Committee member Nguyen Van Huyen's Lily slate—Catholic (southern) Citizens Bloc—included former Diemists, e.g., Tran Huu Huong (once minister of finance and National Bank chairman), and Le Van Thong (formerly president of the Veterans Association).

3. Nguyen Gia Hien's Bright Star slate represented northern Catholics

in the Greater Unity Force (a group active in the fall of Quat's 1965 regime).

4. the Sun slate of former General 'Huynh Van Cao, who favored Diem in 1963 but temporarily commanded I Corps during the 1966 Buddhist crisis, represented a group close to Nhu and included Nguyen Manh Ba (Confucianist Studies Association) and General Nguyen Van Chuan (former I Corps commander and friend of formerly militant Buddhist-supported General Nguyen Chanh Thi).
5. a Revolutionary Dai Viet slate, affiliated with Ha Thuc Ky and led by Nguyen Ngoc Ky.
6. Tran Van Lam's ticket—he was National Assembly president under Diem but broke with him—which included seven former Diemist officials, but also Tran Trung Dung (an early leading Diemist minister who broke with his Ngo relatives but was in charge of the Diem-Nhu funeral).

There were numerous other important tickets. Among these were: Phan Ba Cum's Hoa Hao ticket, including Ta Chuong Phung, a signer of the 1960 anti-Diem *Caravelle* statement and once governor of Binh Dinh, and Ba Cut's former chief of staff, Truong Van Cu, an early anti-Diem Hoa Hao maquis leader; La Thanh Nghe, whose ticket embraced pro-Ky personalities, including the government forces' Constituent Assembly leader Le Phuoc Sang; eminent economist Vu Quoc Thuc's "Professors Slate"; a pro-Ha Thuc Ky slate headed by Nghiem Xuan Thien; the three "Coconut" slates headed by Huynh Van Nhiem, Tran Van An (whose record since the Japanese occupation has read like an adventure novel due to his anti-French, anti-Diem actions and his position in post-Diem governments); and Nguyen Thanh Danh's ticket favorable to Dr. Dan. These tickets each ran respectable races. Many other slates had prominent personalities: Tran Van Do (South Vietnam's foreign minister, whose ticket included several Caravellists), Truong Luong Thien (a Cao Dai sect leader), Truong Cong Cuu (whose slate was heavily Can Lao), Nguyen Van Truong (leader of a group of the Movement for the Renaissance of the South), Phan Khoang (leading a pro-General Vinh Loc slate), Nguyen Tuong Ba (son of Nguyen Tuong Nam, a once-important VNQDD leader who committed suicide as an anti-Diem protest in 1963), and Pham Thai (principal candidate of a pro-Vu Hong Khanh VNQDD slate). The voters definitely had a choice but perhaps an overwhelming one.

In fact it was this range of choices that made the senatorial race, if anything, too representative of the multitude of disparate interests in South Vietnam. The host of highly personalized, basically nonideo-logical groups, parties, and quasi-parties with no tradition of com-promise and with a historic tradition of shifting alignments provided choices for practically everyone. But the extent to which this was a meaningful choice is a different question. This has been the reason each post-Diem government, the 1967 Constitution and Thieu claimed that a two-party system must be a goal of nation-building.

Certain attempts at viable party formation resulted from the Upper House campaign. General Don's party represented a variety of interests. However, the main attempt to create a nationwide political party was the development of the All Vietnam Party (the Toan Viet). Its program professed: "With the genuine determination to unite and create a strong position on the national political scene, with the pooling of abundant means and talent, the Toan Viet Bloc will seek to realize long-range and short-term programs in every field of activity, at the regional as well as at the national level."[143] A pledge was also made to provide technical aid to workers and peasants. The party held a national convention August 7–8, which began on a note of division. Hoa Hao leaders, re-ferred to by the *Saigon Post* as "local bosses," wanted to support the three coconut tickets and plan for the campaign, but VNQDD repre-sentatives from central Vietnam wanted a statement of principle first. It was finally determined to support the coconut group, but the Hoa Hao professed they could join only as individuals. It was claimed that over 200 groups belonged to the party, including, in addition to ele-ments of the Hoa Hao, certain segments of the VNQDD, a portion of eastern province Cao Dai (Thua Thien, Quang Nam, Quang Ngai, Binh Dinh Provinces), 30 Young Democrats, and many civil servants. A claim was made that the party had 1.5 million adherents. It also was known Ky was not unsympathetic. Yet the coconut tickets finished eleventh, seventeenth, and twenty-third in a field of 48. The closeness of many of the tickets in the final tally and the dispersal of votes meant the party slates could have won with only slightly additional support. But the All Vietnam Party lost for the same reason many other slates lost, i.e., inadequate organization as compared to the Catholic groups.

The true lack of organization or propensity for unity or for com-promise, however, was epitomized in probably the most dramatic event of the senatorial campaign. It was a debacle characteristic of numerous other national "congresses," councils, etc., in Vietnamese history called to adopt a common position acceptable to most of the active political groups. Representatives of each of the 48 slates for the Senate met on August 29 at Dien Hong Palace. The meeting almost turned into a small riot. Instead of criticizing jointly the government for sponsoring certain slates the candidates argued among themselves. The list of slates supposedly supported by the government differed according to the speaker. Dinh Thanh Chau, a member of a slate accused of being sponsored by the government, began to plead his innocence. He had little opportunity.

The debate never really started for in the ensuing tumult, nobody could hear anything. At one point, the official secretariat of the Central Election Campaign Committee was nearly ousted. And a cut of electricity at 5 P.M. immediately resulted in charges of "sabotage."

Mr. Nguyen Gia Hien, a Catholic leader, accused of collusion with the administration, then withdrew to the waiting hall, challenging "whoever wants to struggle to get out to the street." His challenge was not accepted.

When Dinh Thanh Chau started distributing a different list of senate tickets which, he said, "are really those endorsed by the government," Tree, and the Gun and the Plow—one representative of one of these tickets came and spat on him.

The assailant, Captain Nguyen Huu Khang, immediately withdrew after the surprise attack but he was pursued by Chau who counterattacked by what Vietnamese reporters called "saliva fire."

Chau missed his target and his "saliva round" hit one of the reporters nearby.

The session recessed.[144]

When the election was held a week later one of its most interesting features was that, regardless of whose set of "government slates" one used, the tickets considered progovernment did not fare nearly as well as anticipated.

Total votes for the winning slates ranged from 980,474 for Tran Van Don's ticket to 553,632 for the Revolutionary Dai Viet ticket led by Nguyen Ngoc Ky. On the whole, with the exception of Don's victory, the spread of votes for a majority of slates was not great. Pham Dinh Ngi's slate was last of the 48, receiving only 279,122 votes. But clusters appeared and only a few thousand votes separated most tickets, except for the top seven, from the ticket receiving the next highest number.

The tallies were a slow process for the over 5,000 personnel of the Central Election Council. For several days preliminary announcements added and subtracted from the six winning tickets. On September 8, Tran Van Lam noted it was extraordinary that he lost 54,000 votes in two separate announcements by the SCA. He presented a severe indictment: "Reasons given to explain the drop cannot hide the illegality, the dishonesty and lack of seriousness (of those in charge) and are good grounds for the people to think that the Senatorial contest has been pre-arranged to mar the real meaning of the elections" (see also Chapter 5: "Political, Military and Constitutional Arenas"). Lam outmaneuvered the government by arriving with a contingent at the closing and opening times of the main office handling the count, bringing supporters and reporters and demanding to see and count returns immediately. Twenty-five formal complaints were made, but these did not change the final vote.

The Upper House—with its majority of Catholics whose election was primarily a function of the bloc voting by organized Catholic interests in the nationwide election, its former Diemist officials (many of whom had broken with Diem before the 1963 coup) including former Can Lao members, and its northern and militant representation—was not truly representative of national interest groups. One Chinese and 2 highlanders were members; 10 were Dai Viet adherents. And while 11 (of 59 who ran) were former Constituent Assembly members, one-fourth had no previous government experience. It was a relatively young group, with an average age of 48, and a majority were professionals (11 teachers, 11 lawyers, 5 doctors, 1 architect, 2 pharmacists, and 6 engineers); 11 were former military leaders.

Lower House Elections. The October 22 Lower House election did provide broad representation. This election was on a district rather than a nationwide basis. The ratio was 9 candidates per office in a field of 1206 (originally 1650 filed) for the 137-member body, including 16 ethnic minority seats. Saigon's 15 seats had 236 candidates, though only 57.8 per cent of registered voters cast ballots in the capital. Nationally the turnout was 72.9 per cent. A high percentage of former officials won—30 military, 29 civil servants (7 former province chiefs), 19 Constituent Assembly members (of 50 candidates) and 9 elected councillors.

Many were professionals—26 teachers and 10 other professionals (mostly doctors), with an average age of 39, as compared to 49 for all Lower House candidates. Some 42 per cent had no previous experience as officials of government in any administrative or legislative capacity, but 46 of the 137 members had been elected previously to the National Assembly during the Diem era.[145] Known regional origins were 32 from North Vietnam, 44 from central Vietnam, and 59 southerners. Those elected included 6 southern and 2 northern tribesmen, 6 Cambodians and 2 Chams. Known religious affiliations were: 46 Buddhists,

35 Catholics, 13 Hoa Hao, 6 Theravada Buddhists (Khmer), 5 Cao Dai, 2 Protestants and 4 Confucianists.

The various South Vietnamese parties, groups and sects were represented. Included were 10 members of General Don's party, 12 MRS adherents, 8 militant pro-Tri-Quang Buddhists (including representatives from Hue, Da Nang, and Saigon), and 15 militant Catholics (including Nguyen Khac Tan, attorney for Major Dang Sy who was in charge during the beginning of the 1963 crisis in Hue). Labor won only four seats but ran close races in many districts. However, the Don group's record was not impressive. At least six of the pro-Tri-Quang members probably would have been disallowed as candidates if the government had not seen fit to pacify the Buddhist leader after his Independence Palace siege.

Thus, the Lower House had voices for each of the religious, regional, ethnic and political interest groups.

Products of the Electoral Process

The five electoral experiences of 1967 did not provide South Vietnam with a dose of instant democracy. Perhaps they served as a beginning: at the very least, electoral processes were beginning to have some meaning to the Vietnamese. Many perceived the elections as an attempt to force the population to provide legitimacy to a group of leaders whom they considered illegitimate power holders. Many voted because they feared nonparticipation would result in unfavorable sanctions being applied against them. Numerous officials did nothing to disillusion this fear.

Voting as a rational act of selection among alternatives and of choosing in one's own interests was difficult. In fact the Senate race was indeed something of a lottery, a development permitting one highly structured interest group to make gains far beyond what its numbers seemed to demand. At the village and hamlet levels personal factors were significant in the voting, but overt or covert pressures by officials for favorable candidates were often even more important. The Lower House elections were the best examples of political party and interest group competition in limited geographical areas.

The major group excluded was the NLF, its front associate parties, and its communist arm, the People's Revolution Party (PRP). Tactical terrorism reaching large proportions of the voting population rendered the NLF's presence known during the campaign periods and on election days. The NLF did not attempt, however, to stop the elections or to win electoral victories. It had the capacity to disrupt the balloting, although not the ability to dictate voting nationally. The other group with a potential for changing the results of the several elections also remained outside of the electoral process except for the Lower House, i.e., the militant Buddhists. Owing to internal strife the Tri Quang group could claim at best a limited ability to elect candidates even in a completely open referendum. In the center, it could influence electoral decisions greatly, although even here it had to contend in particular districts with the VNQDD, Dai Viet Party, and the Catholics.

Charges of voting irregularities were numerous. In II Corps the Thieu-Ky ticket's large plurality was questionable, but none of the other candidates offered real inducements to the highlanders. The government had been delinquent in fulfilling commitments to residents of the central Vietnamese Highlands. But FULRO and local constituencies had pledges from Thieu and Ky. In addition, tribal representatives elected to the Lower House and Senate meant that the highlanders would at least have some voice in Vietnamese public policy formulation. In other areas irregularities also occurred. Many of these were the result of the complicated balloting system and were more inadvertent errors of electoral administration than voting manipulation by design. Blatant rigging was alleged by the losing candidates: there was ample evidence of this. Whether these examples were related more to an excess of enthusiasm on the part of local officials or to direction from superiors varied with jurisdictions. It is possible that the number of such instances was minimized by the fact no one assumed the military ticket could lose. The Thieu-Ky combination did not have a show-piece landslide victory, and their urban percentage was not so much less than their national one as to be over-suspect. In the final analysis it seems most unlikely Ticket No. 9 would have failed to receive a plurality even if no irregularities had occurred at all. The large number of competing slates almost mandated that the incumbent leaders would win.

Despite the limitations upon the press, the degree of freedom enjoyed during the election was not insignificant. For the first time important public personalities openly advocated negotiations for an end to hostilities, including even discussions of sorts with the NLF. And criticism of the government was not only open but often vehement. Charges of corruption, inefficiency, incompetence and favoritism were made. Direct appeals to the electorate and promises to specific interest groups made for a lively campaign. Most important the programs, allegations, and promises of the candidates were read in the newspapers, seen on television, and heard on the radio. News conferences carried live on the radio had large audiences. The programs of candidates also were presented to the electorate through campaign workers who were active throughout much of the country. Campaign organization for most of the candidates was hardly elaborate, but factions of political parties did support several of the tickets.

Interest group activity was at least as important as that of the political parties. Catholic bloc vote victories in the Senate were the most dramatic and the most successful. Labor support of General Don's Senate slate and its showing in the Lower House election was indication of effective organization. Hoa Hao, Cao Dai and militant Buddhist-sponsored slates did well in specific races. Ethnic Chinese candidates did well in predominantly Chinese districts. In a sense the expected occurred with each of Vietnam's minorities providing support for members of its own group. Attempts to create coalitions of these minorities met with difficulties. As these groups are not cohesive but are controlled by factions, they are not as serious electoral threats as they potentially might be. Even the Catholics are not part of a monolithic bloc. Instead village priests, individual bishops, and lay leaders can often deliver specific blocs of votes. Because of the numerous factions of the many interest groups, the Lower House election might have resulted in an overrepresentation of Catholics, due to their relatively greater cohesiveness. Catholic leaders deliberately attempted to prevent such an occurrence after their Senate victories.

Composition of the Lower House and of the Senate showed the importance of another, primarily Catholic, group. Former officials of the Diem regime did extremely well. Many, of course, did lose, and several of the winners were known for having broken with Diem. Others were only on the fringes of the ex-president's ruling party. Many belonged to the legitimate and traditional elites in their districts. On the other hand a post mortem of the Diem political image became more prevalent as the American presence increased. For example, editorials expressed a hardly universal but increasing viewpoint that though Diem was an autocrat he was also a Vietnamese nationalist. As the claims of US interference in internal Vietnamese affairs became louder, a surface respect for the man who held fast to his own counsel despite American urging simultaneously became greater.

Much had been learned. Both candidates and the electorate gained experience. Techniques for administration of electoral processes had been improved. These were not small achievements. However, South Vietnam was not simply an underdeveloped nation experimenting with the trappings of democratic government. It was a nation torn by a prolonged struggle. Even the question of its continued existence as a separate nation had not been resolved. Election of a government does not provide stability, and South Vietnam's history hardly was one to make its electorate optimistic about the possibility of stability.

The 1967 electoral experience was followed by numerous other local and national elections, as described in Chapter 5. There were Senate elections in 1970 and Lower House elections in 1971. As in 1967, the numbers of Senate slates and of House candidates were large. Many incumbents lost, including numerous progovernment representatives. The Buddhists and the Progressive Nationalist Movement made significant gains. Voting turnout was quite high and as usual was less suspect in urban areas. Inevitably plurality victories were the rule in contests where rival parties splintered both the opposition and the progovernment vote. At the village and provincial level, there were many highly contested races and nearly all groups gained some representation among the thousands of council members elected. In general the process of elections did appear to have gained increased respect as a method for selecting holders of public power. And, in general, the numerous groups and parties appeared prepared to accept the method as at least one avenue for seeking power locally and nationally.

However, the NLF, which continued to be excluded from the process, gave no indication of agreeing to such a method as a means for bestowing legitimacy upon policy makers. There was even question as to whether the national government was willing to adopt electoral processes as definitive solutions to questions of succession. Frequent government pressures upon specific electorates and candidates as well as continued military bureaucracy influence in civil affairs certainly did not add to the stature of referenda generally. Nor did Thieu's near-unanimous 1971 re-election in an uncontested presidential race.

Thieu actually wanted an opponent. He wanted to win a genuine majority rather than a plurality as in 1967. If this had occurred he would have had a more legitimate claim to power. He knew this and so did most Vietnamese. When neither Big Minh nor Nguyen Cao Ky would agree to participate in what they rightly considered to be an electoral trap, Thieu followed the route of obtaining a plebiscite favoring his administration. Except for some begrudging respect he received for being able to manipulate his total number of votes, Thieu was a loser in 1971. The process of elections was also a loser as was the political party system.

The electoral process was also seriously hampered by Thieu's actions in 1972 and 1973. By eliminating village elections even temporarily, using the Easter offensive's effects as an excuse, legitimacy of local elected officials was lessened. By placing severe restrictions on procedures for political party formation, genuine electoral competition became increasingly difficult to achieve. And by advancing the Democratic Party with support by the entire machinery of government, Thieu assured his favored slates would win the 1973 Senate election in a race with almost no competition and very little campaigning.

Despite such serious handicaps, the seed sown in the 1967 elections did prepare the way for an important harvest in terms of political development in South Vietnam. Elected hamlet and village councils and the elected National Assembly have been important. Considering the horror associated with the war, there had been advances made in electoral procedures and in somewhat more representative government which were unpredicted before 1967. Like all things in Vietnamese politics such advances were extremely qualified and perhaps temporary ones. Elections were recognized by many to be a substitute for violence as a route of decision making and of leadership succession. Exclusion of the NLF did not have to be a permanent deficiency. With local power bases all parties and groups did have a claim to have their demands recognized by the national government. Such claims were advanced further in the National Assembly. Though not totally respected, these claims definitely received more attention than they would have if the numerous elections had not been held. This may prove to be a small gain. But it may prove to be one twig to which the body politic can cling in the storm of war and of domestic political dissension.

4

Revolutionary Warfare Politics

Introduction

The two Indochina wars have defied many textbook explanations of what is an appropriate way to conduct warfare. By all standard odds the Viet Minh should not have defeated a European power. While there are many explanations—and excuses—as to why a powerful French expeditionary force could not defeat the army of Ho Chi Minh and Vo Nguyen Giap, none is satisfactory except as an apology for France's defeat. France had itself just been rescued from colonization. In 1945 a Chinese-British-American power play was at work in Indochina, and France was forced to reenter its former colony with caution, losing valuable ground and time in the process. Only after 1950 did the United States come to the aid of its wartime and cold-war ally, and then more because of Korea than because of Indochina. By that point the new rulers of China were providing the Viet Minh with vast quantities of material aid. According to this rationale, China and not the Viet Minh defeated France. As in most arguments, there are threads of truth in such a rationale. But such threads disintegrate readily upon analysis.

It was the Viet Minh who defeated France just as years afterwards the latter day Viet Minh defeated the United States. These victories undoubtedly would not have been possible, at least in the form which they took, without considerable external assistance. Nor would they have been possible if their opponents had possessed the ability to compete in a truly political war. But this, of course, was the entire point in 1945, 1950, 1960, 1970 and when the Paris accord was signed in 1973. Certainly the Viet Minh was never the romanticized maquis its publicists claimed and most of the world assumed. It always had a regular force contingent, one which expanded rapidly as the First Indochina War progressed. However, it also always had, first, a political orientation to warfare and, second, a constantly developing irregular force that could have cut the ground out from under any conventional European-model military force.

The Viet Minh was greatly aided by the insistence of French admirals and generals that they were dealing with an inferior opposition that could never perform what a modern army would consider as miracles. The later American force, bound as it was to the most burdensome logistical system in history, also aided its Vietnamese opponents by adopting the same presumption. Faced with a contending military force that could call upon irregulars almost at will but which further could amass conventional forces for grand scale set-piece battles which were entirely to its advantage, both the French and the American expeditionary armadas proved incapable of defeating their enemy. The genius of this Viet Minh strategy was that it could build upon a foundation carefully constructed by revolutionary warfare strategy, and it was to be used as the coup de grâce against the French Union Forces.

Throughout the Second Indochina War, North Vietnam and the NLF opted for a near repetition of the successful developmental strategy of the first encounter. As noted in the essays in this chapter, the strategy once again proved to be a provocative approach to warfare, often brilliant in execution and invariably impressive in tactical application. This did not necessarily guarantee success nor did it testify that the NLF-Hanoi methodology was without flaws. Despite its obvious appeal to a significant proportion of the population residing in South Vietnam, the indigenous opposition was considerably stronger than it had been in the 1945–54 period. Despite the weaknesses of the Saigon government, it had a greater linkage with the population as a whole than did either the French or the numerous Bao Dai cabinets. The army of the Republic of Vietnam, the ARVN, experienced the types of debilitating problems discussed in Chapter 5, but it also possessed assets the French military did not have. Highland groups, religious and regional forces struggled against the claims to suzerainty of both North Vietnam and the NLF. Finally, despite the inherent weaknesses of the American expeditionary force, it did have access to seemingly unlimited financing, supplies and firepower.

Revolutionary warfare during the Second Indochina War also ran head on into programs of "counterinsurgency" and "revolutionary development." Such programs had a very checkered history. For the most part they were failures, or at least they were unsuccessful until the very end of the 1960's. Alone they could not cope with the NLF's revolutionary warfare strategy and they could be decisively harmed by conventional warfare. In combination with military defeats of the NLF and North Vietnamese regular military forces, "revolutionary development" could and did provide significant competition. By 1972, as described in the introduction to the first essay in this chapter, the Saigon government's efforts to encourage local political and administrative development, as well as a local presence by the national administrative system, had made greater strides than I had assumed it would in any of the next three articles. Nothing could be more important in revolutionary warfare than a political counterattack. This was the substance of what happened in South Vietnam from 1966 to 1972. South Vietnamese political processes provided the overlay necessary to counteract the revolutionary warfare tactics of an NLF that had been weakened by military measures.

The depth of penetration of the political process changes undertaken by the government and the diverse interest groups prior to 1972 definitely still remains an important question mark. In fact it is the most significant question for the future of South Vietnam. The Easter offensive of 1972 had a major impact upon those political process changes. If the South Vietnamese government were to further weaken the local and national institutions which did experience at least limited success in terms of political development, there is no doubt that a revitalized NLF (operating under North Vietnamese guidance) could tear down the fragile infrastructure so important to southern interest groups and political parties. However, if the processes of political party development, elected institution development, and public administration development should produce an infrastructure at least somewhat less fragile, many equations present in revolutionary warfare politics would be changed. In terms of a political system including the NLF these changes would be particularly important for political behavior in South Vietnam.

The problem with such a possibility is that it has always been the whole point of the Second Indochina War. Revolutionary warfare is political warfare. Only politics can cope with political warfare. Bullets, artillery and tanks cannot in themselves defeat an idea nor can they completely eliminate overlapping, parallel hierarchies. If South Vietnam had a viable political system, which it does not have, revolutionary politicians (as opposed to conventional warfare forces) would have no option if they hoped to gain political power except to participate in political processes which are legitimate within that political system. In the absence of such a viable system, revolutionary politicians can be anticipated to continue political warfare at various levels of intensity they consider expedient and appropriate until they can gain political power.

The Organization Theory of Revolutionary Warfare

■ Revolutionary warfare in South Vietnam reached new heights in sophistication during the 1960's. The National Liberation Front achieved goals in a near textbook fashion. It is doubtful if there has ever been a better example of a successful operation of the genre: parallel hierarchies, shadow and de facto local governments, clandestine cell networks, skillful training programs, paramilitary programs capable of keeping the Saigon government constantly off balance, a developed and highly competent regular army quite able to stand up to the army of the Republic of Vietnam, infiltration of governmental and nongovernmental and military and nonmilitary intermediate structures and groups of all kinds, selective and measured application of terrorism, a highly trained set of urban commando cadres. Each classic requisite for revolutionary warfare had been carefully honed and had been patiently set in operation or assiduously developed as a reserve for the right moment. The cadres had been well trained, were highly motivated, had enjoyed tremendous victories, their morale was excellent, and the future of their cause appeared to be extremely bright. Indeed, in 1965 an NLF victory seemed to be inevitable. The forces of the revolution had earned justifiable respect for their prowess and stood head and shoulders above their competitors in the Saigon Government.

Many factors altered NLF potential as a political force in South Vietnam after 1965. Luck and sheer perspicacity combined with an unlimited supply of material support from the United States permitted the Saigon government to become increasingly secure. Although it hardly appeared to be the case during the later 1960's, the GVN also became more stable. Despite numerous reversals and a shift from Nguyen Cao Ky to Nguyen Van Thieu as occupant of the highest place in government, basically the same central governing apparatus continued from 1965 until the 1973 ceasefire, a period nearly as long as that of the Ngo Dinh Diem regime. The American buildup and the buildup of the ARVN, and massive influxes of goods and technicians gradually hurt the NLF. And then the direct intervention of North Vietnam in all NLF affairs, as the PAVN (People's Army of Vietnam) replaced the NLF as the main force in the revolution, undercut the NLF drastically. The war ceased to be a revolution and became instead a conflict between the northern and southern zones of the Vietnamese fatherland. By the time of the Tet offensive in 1968 most military action was being undertaken by the PAVN and not by the NLF. The PAVN-NLF combination had not won a major military victory in two years despite the presence of large numbers of PAVN regulars. The NLF had been hit piecemeal and was badly hurt during the 1965–67 era. It had been greatly "northernized" and quite simply was not nearly as viable as it had been.

The Tet offensive came near to delivering the coup de grâce for the NLF. It carried the burden of the conflict during the major drives, although the PAVN assumed the role of attacking force later in the campaign. The NLF won significant victories and provided an exemplary performance in terms of purely military actions. However, perhaps unlike what might have occurred in 1964–65, the NLF did not receive the one type of support which was absolutely essential for a strategic victory as opposed to a string of single tactical victories. Much of the NLF dogma had assumed the inevitability of a popular general uprising to carry it to ultimate power once a general offensive had begun. Carefully constructed cells had been covertly established for this happening. In 1968 the NLF failed to carry the population with it despite its excellent organizational system. With cover dropped, with much of its cadre leadership lost, with reserves sapped and with regular NLF forces suffering vast losses, the NLF was put back a decade. The theory of revolutionary warfare had been applied brilliantly. But it was not enough. The NLF in effect was caught by American firepower, by a weakened but tenacious Saigon army when the crunch came in 1968, and by surbordination to Hanoi's policies. The latter was unquestionably the most serious problem for the NLF. It was not in top form in 1968. Considerable rebuilding would have been necessary for the NLF to succeed in achieving its goals. The PAVN had been secondary during the main push and had in effect let the NLF suffer grievous losses as part of a grander strategy which was unsuccessful.

Unlike the PAVN in the early 1950's, when its regular forces also had severe losses in a series of serious defeats against the French, the NLF did not have an impenetrable sanctuary equivalent to that of the Viet Minh in the northeastern highlands of Tonkin. As a result, from 1969 to 1972 the GVN was able to destroy much of the NLF infrastructure. Weakened by the Tet offensive, the NLF was further weakened daily by GVN incursions into terrain previously ruled by it. Owing to its serious weakness, northern influence increased even more and reliance upon the North became essential for survival and not merely as a means to improve its logistics. Main NLF forces went to Cambodia, while recruiting within South Vietnam became more difficult as recruits were taken from younger and younger groups.

The basic apparatus of the NLF continued, and selected base areas remained at its disposal. It continued to constitute still a guerrilla and terrorist threat. Rebuilding occurred, slowly and with difficulty, but it became more of a chore to compete with recognized political parties locally. When Hanoi in 1972 called upon the NLF to follow another grand strategy and prepare the ground for uprisings the NLF could not or at least did not comply.

The 1972 winter-spring offensive was a PAVN affair. In the Mekong Delta, NLF forces, mostly from Cambodia, could harass the GVN; but this was a far cry from the role of the NLF in 1968. The NLF made immediate gains where historically it had been strongest and it supplemented PAVN activities in selected areas. Reinfiltration was possible in some villages where the South Vietnamese army had left the self-defense forces the task of village protection while it moved to encounter the PAVN elsewhere. But these were distinctly supportive rather than totally independent actions. For the NLF perhaps the greatest change brought about by the 1972 offensive was that its localized apparatus became even further northernized. Thus, the most successful and ambitious attempt ever to apply systematically the tenets of revolutionary warfare was a failure. Even complete defeat of the GVN would not have acquitted the NLF. Such a defeat would have been due to the sheer firepower of 130-mm. artillery and tanks of the PAVN and to the sheer strength of the northern force. In effect the NLF to a great extent was sacrificed upon the altar of big power industrial might, a product of modernity available and used without reservation in the later stages of the Vietnamese conflict.

Despite this ironic turn of events, the NLF at its height represented a model of revolutionary warfare. It is unlikely to be emulated simply because no other national situation is likely to be identical to that of South Vietnam during the 1950's and 1960's. Still the principles perfected by the NLF show undeniably that organizational genius can effectively challenge forces much more superior materially. The combination of organizational sophistication, intensive ideological indoctrination, selective terrorism and gradual paramilitary and regular force buildup is a combination which can shake the foundations of most of the world's nations. External assistance was important to the NLF as it would be to any revolutionary movement, but this aid was of secondary importance (except for well trained regroupees infiltrated from the North) until the stage of large-scale American intervention. What set the NLF off from other so-called liberation movements was first the sheer talent of its organizers and of its proselytizing units. And of equal importance, a factor which could rarely be emulated, the NLF local leaders and the rank and file as well consistently displayed tremendous courage under conditions where all objective odds were not in their favor. It was no doubt this latter factor which permitted the NLF to survive as a potential force even during the darkest of its hours following 1968 when the strategic policies of Saigon, Washington and Hanoi placed it in a vise which pressed from all sides with a magnitude no conceivable organizational weapon could withstand. By 1973 the NLF was still adequate to continue political warfare and the 1972 offensive improved its potential in this regard. Unquestionably it would remain a factor of importance in the political processes of South Vietnam, but the scope of its future role had become even more highly contingent upon political decisions made in Hanoi.

DESPITE the power of the drama, it was a long time before observers began to study the nature, structure, and modus operandi of the Viet Minh during the First Indochina War.[1] These aspects of the anti-French guerrillas have never been fully explained, although there is significant documentation to provide a vivid picture of the stages and competing forces involved in the prolonged post-World-War-II conflict.[2] There is also adequate evidence on the philosophy of the revolution, the organizational and administrative structure of the Viet Minh political-military apparatus,[3] and the military tactics which whittled away and finally defeated the French defenses.[4] But those who have analyzed the Viet Minh phenomenon have rarely delved into the intricacies of leadership, the roles played by organizational structures especially created by the leadership for the purpose of obtaining commitment from a varied population, or the rationale for explaining the failures (and they were many) suffered in the prosecution of revolutionary guerrilla warfare among numerous groups of potential adherents.

This lack of solid information and, more significantly, the lack of positive theory to explain the strengths and weaknesses of Viet Minh revolutionary warfare strategy and tactics, particularly the efficacy of the concept of total population involvement, have meant that an important historical era has remained a blank page to many observers. Above all, it is the theory gap which has precluded the articulation of an effective response to revolutionary warfare in Indochina. The Viet Minh simply refused to behave according to the theories of conventional warfare. They refused to be subdued by a technically superior opponent or to meet him on grounds where he might make the best use of his assets. They refused also to draw any limits whatever—either sociological, economic, political, or military—to the scope of the struggle. Their strength lay in their ability to capture and control the energies of entire populations.

The Viet Minh theory was simplicity itself. It was to direct such vitality along channeled, disciplined lines in every conceivable arena against the opposition, whose total effort of necessity had to be more limited in scope. If the control system were maintained, primarily through organization building and the techniques of group dynamics, the movement would be invincible. In time, the opposition would crumble; perhaps not tomorrow, but inevitably it would crumble. A myth of ultimate success served as a stimulus for those who might otherwise have faltered.[5] This myth, when combined with perpetually maintained group pressures and with the pervasive indoctrination of the population, provided constant reinforcement to insure commitment to the organization and to guarantee the best possible use of efforts spent in organizational activities.

The failure to grasp the organization theory of revolutionary warfare as exemplified by the Viet Minh during the First Indochina War has resulted in a serious lack of understanding of the nature of revolutionary warfare in South Vietnam since the Geneva settlement of 1954. The nontheoretical interpretation of events since that date has adversely affected major policy decisions, and has led to what is often popularly conceived of as an inexplicable situation.[6] Surely there have been few conflicts with respect to which so much controversy has raged over such questions as, Who is the enemy? How does the enemy maintain his forces in increasing numbers in face of the superior technology used against him? Why does the enemy retain such an impressive constituency despite his many failures to fulfill promises and despite his generally alien philosophy?

For the first time a comprehensive answer to such questions has been provided; and, more importantly, a catalogue of revolutionary warfare organization theory has been presented by Douglas Pike in his highly provocative *Viet Cong: The Organization and Techniques of the National Liberation Front of South Vietnam.*[7] This work is unquestionably the most thorough examination ever made of the National Liberation Front (NLF), its origins, evolution, structure and functions, techniques of organization building, relationships with its constituency, with external organizations, and with foreign capitals, and its political philosophy and changing strategies.

Relying upon vast personal experience, extensive documentation and the collation of original source materials on the NLF, and on a keen perception of Vietnamese life-style, of the principles of self-actualization through the interactions of microcosmic social organizations, and of deepseated societal divisions, Pike has captured the essence of a milieu so very propitious for the success of a clandestine organization. He has also grasped the core of NLF organization theory for capitalizing upon the characteristics of this milieu, for harnessing the natural propensities present in such a milieu, and for controlling and guiding societal behavior along lines dictated by democratic centralization and operational decentralization. His book is thus a sophisticated analysis both of a Vietnamese case study in implementing the theory of revolutionary warfare, and of the possible universal applicability of this organizational-administrative theory of how to obtain societal controls.

Pike presents many themes. But the two most significant concepts developed and documented throughout his seminal contribution are, first, the importance of the organizational weapon in NLF revolutionary warfare; and second, the perennial role of the Democratic Republic of (North) Vietnam (DRVN) and of the Lao Dong Party in the South, which role increased over the years from being participants in, to controllers of, revolutionary warfare in South Vietnam. He could hardly be more explicit in his position on the latter topic:

It is the thesis of this book that the DRV was indeed the godfather of the NLF, that its support over the years was developmental, from lesser to greater, that until mid-1964 this was largely confined to two areas—doctrinal known-how and leadership personnel—and after mid-1964 it supplied antiaircraft weapons and certain other types of military hardware not available through capture, but at all times from 1960 on *it stood ready to help the NLF in any way that was absolutely necessary.* (p. 321)

Nor is he any less explicit in his description of the primacy of the organizational weapon to the NLF:

The most important task, one that took precedence over all other activity, was organization building. Once created, the organization became the instrument for managing the social movement propaganda work and the agit-prop activity to nullify the GVN administration (the political struggle) and to destroy the ARVN by a combined assault of persuasion (military proselyting program) and coercion (the armed struggle). (pp. 215–16)

The NLF Organizational Weapon

The creators of the NLF began with an appreciation of the historic role played by organization in Vietnamese society.[8] This role was manifested by associational activities in the village, by clandestine multifunctional organizations concerned with protection and religious practices, and by the omnipresent sense of Confucian filial piety, all of which resulted in the Vietnamese generally becoming, as Pike notes, "organizational animals in the same way that many Americans are political animals—instinctively so." (p. 6) This appreciation was supplemented generously by the accumulated experience of the Viet Minh in organization building.

Although the theory of organization adopted by the NLF involved a variety of constituent elements, its central focus was always the enmeshment of individuals in a framework of action prescribed by the organizational leadership. The central technique involved agitation-propaganda activities "conceived as a servo-mechanism by means of which the rural Vietnamese were indoctrinated with a certain set of values and beliefs as the necessary first step, the formation of the masses into an organizational weapon." (p. 121) A first objective was individual involvement, in effect *membership,* including contributions toward the attainment of organizational goals.[9] The broader objective was the development of membership commitment to the organization itself. Once this was achieved, contributions could be channeled along desired paths, norms affecting the vocational and avocational activities of members could be influenced, dogmas and concepts including objects of admiration and hate could be taught, and eventually a member's expectations concerning his own behavior and that of others (both members and nonmembers) could be manipulated and controlled. In short, the NLF theory of organization called for engulfing the waking hours of its membership with prescribed and proscribed patterns of behavior.[10] "The individual became submerged, the group became the unit, and great social pressure was brought to bear against the deviant, thus achieving the ultimate NLF objective—a self-regulating, self-perpetuating revolutionary force." (p. 125)

An involved methodology was devised for implementing the NLF organization theory. Specific methods were applied for developing a sense of organizational solidarity and community; for mobilizing members for struggle movements by generating discontent with a stereotyped "other" (the opposition) that fell outside the organizational orbit; for controlling the input of information through specific structures and through a highly articulate indoctrination program; and for isolating members from contact with groups and ideas not identified with the revolutionary movement. (p. 125)

Unquestionably the foremost method was the creation of "liberation associations," whose purpose was not only to embrace as large a number of Vietnamese as feasible, but also to provide an organized group framework for as many activities as possible of the individual Vietnamese.[11] Such associations included the ubiquitous functional liberation associations, that is, separate associations for farmers, women, workers, youth, students, and intellectuals. (ch. 10) The functional liberation associations maintained their own hierarchy, on occasion involving a complex of interlocking directorates from the national NLF to the village, and were tied locally to the administrative liberation committees. Utilizing such groups as a vehicle, the NLF could intensify its general appeal by capitalizing upon local and specifically meaningful grievances, while increasing the identification of particular clientele groups with its programs, and increasing its control through an intermeshing system of cells and through a structure facilitating agit-prop activities.

Other associations served basically the same role of developing and reinforcing membership identification and commitment. These included several political parties,[12] organizations for Vietnam's numerous religious and ethnic groups, and diverse but important groups such as the Former Resistants Association. (ch. 11) Many organizations were indeed "front" groups that might or might not have a bona fide constituency. These structures served to provide legitimacy for the NLF in its quest for support from varied audiences. But to the extent that these groups, such as elements of the Cao Dai, Hoa Hao, and Binh Xuyen sects, contributed their energies and resources to the struggle movements, they were very important to the cause, particularly during the early period of revolutionary warfare.

Two principal structures were created to direct and coordinate the activities of the complicated system of interlocking associations, namely, the NLF command structure and the People's Revolutionary Party (PRP).[13] Basically the NLF command structure was organized as though it were a de facto government, following the typical pattern of communist administrative organization (congress, central committee, presidium, secretariat) at the central, interzonal, zonal, provincial, district, and village levels. (ch. 12) A military structure was associated with each level of the NLF, and this structure was responsible to the political leadership at the appropriate NLF headquarters.[14]

While many of the subordinate organizations existed only on paper, and while there were variations in the importance of different subdivisions in different parts of the country, frequently the standard administrative services were provided, such as health, education, and so forth.[15] In the "liberated areas," such functions did become significant. (ch. 16) But all such functions were adjuncts of the overriding organization-propaganda-violence functions, that is, to the political and armed struggles, combined with training and indoctrination, which were understood to be the primary raison d'être for the leadership at each rung of the hierarchical ladder. In fulfilling these latter functions, the NLF organization theory laid special stress at each level, for reasons of discipline and control, on the dual concepts of democratic centralization of policy formulation at a higher structural level, and decentralization of policy implementation at lower structural levels.

The second nationwide control and coordination structure, the PRP, grew in significance as the political struggle became subordinated to the military struggle, although the southern Lao Dong Party had never been absent from the scene and was instrumental in initiating the struggle movements and, indeed, the NLF itself. This party, the "vanguard" unit, maintained a structure similar to that of the NLF, including a military structure where political officers provided coordination and control analogous to their counterparts in the de facto government command structure. It also instituted its own cell system and urban structure, and sponsored the so-called Youth League and the Vanguard Youth League. This avowedly communist party organization provided leadership through the democratic centralization concept,[16] served to provide ideological reinforcement and support for communists in the South, limited the possibilities for doctrinal deviation within the NLF, and apparently attempted to hold southern chauvinism in check. (ch. 8)

Thus the organizational theory and structure of the NLF called for the existence of parallel hierarchies.[17] The product was a complex matrix of overlapping organizations, formal and informal, including the administrative structure of the NLF, the PRP, the military structure, the numerous functional and other associations (including the front groups), and, to an increasingly significant extent, the administrative and military structures of the DRVN as well. Each hierarchy attempted to observe and check the activities of others. The several hierarchies together provided a set of overlapping structures covering diffuse functions in an attempt to provide simultaneously a diffracted but totalitarian society. Masses of people were organized as group members, but the groups themselves were so structured as to preclude independence of action. An intensive program of training and indoctrination in each hierarchy served to develop a sense of group identification, cohesiveness, and commitment. The control of available information attempted to preclude the input of any information not provided through channels of an NLF association. "The chief effort was communication; the chief medium was the especially created organization; the chief daily activity of the cadres was agitation and propaganda work." (p. 32)

The PRP was as essential to the parallel hierarchy system as the NLF program, insofar as it provided inspectors to report on individual and group activities. Such inspectors could maintain presumably tight controls over elements of the NLF in order to insure administrative and fiscal accountability, which was more and more important as taxation and other demands upon all the structures became increasingly heavy after 1963. The PRP proved essential because it could demand ideological purity and the acceptance of changing strategy and tactics from each of the hierarchies. In performing this role, its influence increased markedly vis-à-vis the other hierarchies. It reported on the loyalty of officials to the directives of the national leadership, and perhaps also to the directives of Hanoi as well, and it expanded the overlapping nature of the parallel hierarchy system by systematically substituting its own members for officials in leadership positions in other hierarchies.

Organizational Control of Revolutionary Warfare: Tonkinese or Cochinchinese?

The evidence presented by Pike concerning the DRVN's role in the creation, leadership selection, evolution of strategy and tactics, access to resources, and development of parallel hierarchies of the NLF appears undeniable. This role is even more visible in connection with the growth of the PRP as a parallel hierarchy control agent. Yet even Pike's thorough documentation of the growth and adaptation of revolutionary warfare structures in South Vietnam admittedly omits a clearcut explanation of the initial alignment of forces, the posture of the DRVN relative to the earliest phases of insurgency and to the struggle forces' leadership prior to 1959–60, and the ability of the NLF to evolve so quickly after 1960 as a nationwide organization.

The explanation of the rapid evolution of the NLF is complicated by the relative weakness of the Viet Minh in the South in 1954. At the time of partition, the Viet Minh were estimated to have exercised some form of organizational control over approximately two million people south of the partition line, including important Annamite and Cochinchinese base areas. But Viet Minh strength in the southern highlands prior to 1953 was not great, and even then was more of a military position than a true example of population control. In the South, nationalist forces—primarily the sects—precluded the Viet Minh from duplicating their organizational successes in the Red River Delta, although a wide area was constantly "contested." Discipline and organization in the South remained much less effective than in the North. Adventurism, vacillation, and an apparent unwillingness completely to follow Tonkinese doctrinal dictates resulted in far fewer sucesses for the Viet Minh in the South than in the North throughout the 1945–54 period. In fact, while the prominence of the Viet Minh in Tonkin was unquestioned by the time of partition, they were markedly further from victory in the South in 1954, a factor which undoubtedly had a bearing on their decision to accept partition.

But when the Viet Minh formally withdrew from the South, they did retain much of their previously existing organizational structure.[18] As has been spelled out in detail in numerous sources, they left trained cadres "submerged" among the population, hid caches of arms, took large numbers of southerners to the North for training, and even retained significant base areas. The Lao Dong Party also maintained a clandestine organization, with liaison among southern party members. In short, at the time of partition the DRVN certainly did not forsake completely their concept of a nationwide Vietnamese revolution as opposed to a Tonkinese revolution, nor was the DRVN at any point an uninterested neutral observer of events in South Vietnam.[19]

The Fatherland Front and other instrumentalities in Hanoi kept up liaison with the South and made plans for unification.[20] Nonetheless, despite these DRVN actions, and in spite of the early infiltration of Southerners, the exact position of Hanoi in the organization of the struggle movement prior to creation of the NLF in 1960, and even prior to the formal announcement of creation of the PRP in 1962, is far from clear. The concept of a thoroughly DRVN-programmed development of southern insurgency attributes too much omnipotence to the DRVN leaders, and also underestimates the Cochinchinese (a weakness in approach demonstrated through the years by the Viet Minh and then by Ngo Dinh Diem as well). The explanation of DRVN strength rested more in its ability to continue organization building, to take advantage of propitious conditions, and to respond rapidly to demands for action.

Commenting upon the 1955–60 period, Pike notes: "Lao Dong Party cadres living in North Vietnam, mainly Southerners who had served in the ranks of the Viet Minh, went South, and, with dissident elements in South Vietnam, the most numerous of whom were the Cao Dai, began a political-paramilitary organizational effort that culminated on December 20, 1960, in the creation of the National Liberation Front." (p. 74). The sects certainly were not subject to Lao Dong discipline, but did contribute substantially to the initial alignment of forces and were dominant in some zones of operation. In fact, much of the early recruitment was carried on in regions formerly controlled by the Hoa Hao and Cao Dai.[21] The Former Resistants Association originally was headed by a Cao Dai, and such groups as the Allied Forces of Religious

Sects Against the Americans and Diem, a primarily Hoa Hao organization in Long An Province, were of considerable importance in the violence struggle program against the Diem regime.[22]

It was the presence of these noncommunist elements that gave the earlier period something of the appearance of a "conventional" civil war. But such a conclusion omits the tremendous significance of the organization theory of revolutionary warfare. From no later than 1959, DRVN emphasis upon organization became the dominant ingredient of the struggle movement. "The struggle became an imported thing. But it was not military hardware that was imported at this time. It was something more necessary and valuable: expertise, doctrinal guidance, insurgence know-how, and, above all, organizational skill." (p. 78) In 1960, when the NLF was formed, such skill was definitely in evidence: "It was an organizational steamroller, nationally conceived and nationally organized, endowed with ample cadres and funds, crashing out of the jungle to flatten the GVN." (p. 76)

Following formation of the NLF, the course of revolutionary warfare passed through several stages carefully outlined by Pike. These were the social movement propaganda stage lasting until 1962, the political struggle movement phase of 1962 and 1963, and the legitimization-militarization stage beginning in the summer of 1963 and continuing to the present. Organizationally, after the initial organizing stage the NLF underwent a time of expansion until 1962, followed by a season of internal strengthening until the downfall of Diem, and finally a "refinement period" in which Marxism was stressed and many noncommunist elements of the Front were eliminated. (ch. 6) Pike's primary thesis concerning post-Diem developments is that the NLF apparatus has undergone a "Tonkinization" process, characterized by a shift from the concept of a general uprising to the concept of a special war, by a shift from emphasis upon political struggle to emphasis upon military struggle, and by a shift from a relatively permissive control orientation and alignment with "fronts" to a coercive control orientation exemplified by doctrinaire requirements for uniformity and regularization enforced by the PRP. Most significantly, as Pike has documented, personnel in leadership positions increasingly were northerners. By 1965, at least half of all cadres infiltrated to date were from the North; and nearly all newly infiltrated cadres were northerners. (p. 324) Such "Tonkinization," of course, greatly expanded DRVN operational control over the NLF, even down to the village level, and perhaps far from incidentally helped to prevent separatism and compromise by the southern cadres. (p. 116)

There can be no doubt that, by the end of 1965, many important developments had altered appreciably the total picture of revolutionary warfare in South Vietnam. The American military presence was by then an accomplished fact, and Hanoi could no longer hope to eliminate the Americans by historic military tactics. The western force could not be defeated by the NLF or by the limited use of regular PAVN units. Ancient maquis were no longer immune places of refuge. Yet occupation of these zones by the GVN had not been accomplished, and NLF units could still develop new maquis and avoid annihilation. But militarily the NLF movement was now both on the defensive and operating more and more as a negative force. These were significant alterations attributable almost completely to the increased American presence. The Viet Minh timetable was clearly disrupted. The morale, physical well being, and general security of the insurgents were adversely affected. Infiltration and thereby the reinforcement of leadership cadres, military forces, and materials had become increasingly difficult. The total Indochina pattern had been changed. Laos continued to serve as a Viet Minh base; but civic action successes and military thrusts against the Pathet Lao, combined with increased pressure on the DRVN itself, prevented the Pathet Lao from exploiting the position they had held a year previously.

The post-Diem developments proved that the organizational weapon as constructed by the NLF was far from invincible. Its doctrinal underpinnings were based upon indoctrination programs and structural devices which provided a significant sense of identity but not an impregnable commitment in face of the growing number of vicissitudes heaped upon the civil population by both sides. The loss of many important sect connections after 1963 meant a break in the cohesiveness of the rebel alignment. Diem's fall and the subsequent dissolution of the Can Lao and the National Revolutionary Movement eliminated devil figures formerly so visible and readily available as objects of the omnipresent NLF hate themes (see Chapter 2: "Organizing Bureaucrats"). Fear of southern, primarily Cochinchinese, chauvinism and separatism led the DRVN increasingly to strain the legitimacy of revolutionary leadership in the South by infiltration of an overlay of Tonkinese civil-military "colonizers." On occasion this took the form of actual physical annihilation of previous allies by assassination and military pogroms. More typically the northern presence simply asserted control over organizational activities in the South.

When, in addition to the presence of the alien Tonkinese, the overt propagation of alien communist ideology was pushed during 1966, the bonds linking the old organizational system were radically altered. Leadership changes, a greater emphasis upon discipline, and the substitution of "unification" goals for "reform" action inevitably modified existing patterns of interaction, varied the established networks of membership dependency upon the organization, revised channels of control and communication, and most dramatic of all, altered perceptions and commitments relative to the formal unit. American and South Vietnamese military pressure resulted in demands for protection which the NLF could not provide. In a situation where the organization proved incapable of meeting popular demands, while at the same time increasing measurably its own demands upon the population, the previously institutionalized arrangements gave way to a new set of relationships. Taxation rates, for example, became usurious. The recruitment of southerners ceased to be on the basis of indoctrinated commitment and often became a variant of corvée. Relative permissiveness vanished, and was replaced by pervasive coercion. Immediately identifiable goals such as land reform, education, and the like were succeeded by much less immediate goals. Promises of ultimate victory following protracted struggle supplanted promises of less expensive, more rapid success. And more difficult for even the indoctrinated sympathizer to comprehend was the subordination of geographically perceivable objectives in the Mekong Delta for the vaguer goals of a broader strategy further north, which meant the imposition of hardships in Cochinchina in order to provide material and financial support for the more "conventional" struggle in the highlands and coastal regions.[23] Nevertheless, to the credit of the earlier organization builders, the organizational weapon survived such drastic policy changes without collapse of the system.

Despite the considerable evidence Pike presents, by 1967 the controversy still remained unsettled as to the exact power positions of northern vs. southern leadership within the NLF. Jean Lacouture has provided interesting evidence to the effect that the southern element maintains considerable autonomy, although his thesis was published prior to the big PAVN influx and the historic PRP *coup de force* in the administrative hierarchy of the NLF.[24] The testimony of captured and *chieu hoi* ("open arms" or repatriation plan) prisoners has made clear that there is increasing bitterness over the dogma of protracted struggle and over the growing influx of Tonkinese into the South. There indeed appears to be a difference of opinion among many southern and northern cadres concerning long-range goals, although this policy dispute differs in various sections of South Vietnam.

DRVN influence has clearly become paramount in the highlands. It is also clear that the ties between the Center and the North have been strengthened markedly since 1964. The disputed evidence relative to

the Mekong Delta region rests upon several factors not carefully documented, including the continued presence, or lack of presence, of sect
elements within the NLF struggle apparatus, and the degree of Cochinchinese operational control, or lack of control, over specific programs
and associations of the NLF. Pike dismisses the post-Diem participation
of the sects. But it is unlikely that the sects rallied as universally as he
appears to imply. On the other hand, whether those who have not
rallied continue to have a policy voice in the NLF is an entirely different question.

The failure to prevent Tonkinese and Lao Dong interests from gaining domination over an organization of the typically chauvinistic
Cochinchinese has thus far not been satisfactorily explained. If the
southerners completely abdicated power, and if "nationalist" Cochinchinese interests which the Viet Minh proved unable to control even
during the First Indochina War were conceded with such a minimum
of resistance, then the years 1964–66 must have included events no ana-
lyst has yet dealt with. It would appear that the truth lies somewhere
between a complete southern abdication and the thesis that the southern
struggle movement has remained autonomous.

By 1966 the evidence of a northern steamroller sweeping over all
but the Cochinchina element of the NLF—the principal element from
the beginning—was overwhelming. In Cochinchina, the old Viet Minh
base areas also undoubtedly became PRP satrapies. This leaves only
the populous delta region itself and the cities to be accounted for. The
prevailing confusion is over who controls what in these, the most important areas of South Vietnam. Such confusion can lead honest men to
tell different stories after observing the revolutionary movement
throughout the nation. It was here that noncommunist—in fact, even
reactionary—elements worked jointly with the communists in a front to
unseat Diem. It was here that the Viet Minh had to rely initially after
1956 upon interests it suffered but no doubt despised. On the other
hand, the officially announced leadership of the NLF, a leadership almost exclusively from this region, while not formally promoted as communists, were representatives of groups long sympathetic to the Viet
Minh. (Exceptions to this were those Central Committee members who
appeared to have little following among the groups they claimed to
represent, or who represented nonexistent groups. It is difficult, for example, to imagine more paradoxical, opportunistic pronouncements
than the NLF's laudatory comments about the repressed, liberty-
loving, "religious" Binh Xuyen and its NLF Central Committee
representative.)[25]

The NLF leadership was never widely popular, or even especially well known. Central Committee members were rarely leaders of large followings. It is true, of course, as Bernard Fall has pointed out, that the presence of extremely well known charismatic elites has never been a prerequisite for success in revolutionary warfare.[26] It is also true that a primary function of the organizational weapon is to inspire a commitment to the system, its goals, and its activities, rather than to individual leaders. According to communist dogma, commitments to individual organizational spokesmen rather than to the organization *qua* organization may even be considered dysfunctional, at least during the militant struggle phase.

Nonetheless, leadership (noncharismatic, perhaps) is vital in forging the organizational weapon. And the leadership of the NLF was from the outset supplemented, reinforced, and finally largely substituted for by southerners well trained in the North, and then by northerners infiltrated from the DRVN. These cadres possessed skills of the association creator, of the propagandist who reaches out into the body politic in order to obtain closer and closer ties to the organization itself. These professional organizers spun the web of interassociational functions and purposes until the net caught whole village populations in a maze of commitments. Presumably there were few escapes from this net. Yet despite its tenacity, the web ultimately suffered breaks and then open gaps. It required constant reinforcement because it was ultimately a myth—a myth woven with considerable talent, but also without what the communists are so fond of categorizing as an "objective" foundation.

Forging a Counter-Organizational Weapon

There is a particular irony in the fact that the reliance which the Viet Minh and NLF placed upon organization building has been so difficult for most western observers to appreciate.[27] For Americans so attuned to the "organizational society," this irony is especially paradoxical. And because of this lack of appreciation of revolutionary emphasis upon the organizational weapon, the responses since 1945 have been almost entirely geared to secondary activities of the insurgent leadership. Military operations against forces of the opposition have continually been frustrating. Despite the frequency of success in immediate tactical terms, the impact of the military method has too often proved irrelevant. The sheer magnitude of human and material resources introduced by the United States most certainly has damaged the NLF measurably, forcing a major alteration in the DRVN-NLF strategy.[28] Further, when dealing with purely military operations involving PAVN regular forces, no response except a military one is feasible. Indeed, in coping with a violence struggle movement such as that of the PAVN in 1966–67, which operates without an organizational base but relies solely upon force of arms, a military response can even be adequate. But even complete victory over, or complete retreat by, regulars from the North would at most provide a solution to the "second war," and would be no guarantee of success against the organizational structures guiding revolutionary warfare.

There is no question that the NLF has been seriously damaged indirectly because the pressures of opposition have affected the morale and communications system of the organizational apparatus. It has also been badly hurt directly by personnel losses among leadership cadres (notably among agit-prop cadres). And considerable damage can be caused by successful military actions against base areas. But even assuming that, by the sheer size and number of military offenses, the NLF is destroyed as a struggle force (of the violence variety), such a strategy has two definite disadvantages. First, it is expensive to an extent that was unimaginable even after the fall of Diem. Second, although the overt infrastructure conceivably can be destroyed eventually by frontal attack, such a procedure can never eliminate all vestiges of this infrastructure. Nor can such a procedure by itself eliminate the struggle movement in its political phase or even in its terroristic violence phase.

There appears to be only one method for rooting out the deepseated NLF infrastructure, and that is through counter-organization sponsored by an effective administrative system. Moreover, the present Rural Development (RD) program is only one basis for such an approach. And the RD operation can become meaningful in this context only by becoming political. Becoming political means forging an adequate organizational weapon. The revelation that Dai Viet Duy Dan party elements were serving as instructors at the Vung Tau training camp, and providing indoctrination in the ideology of this old nationalist group, apparently was a shock to many. Yet, while the Duy Dan is perhaps not the ideology of Vietnam's future, some group or groups which stand for a positive program and for some definite ideology must become the mainstay for any counter-organization attempt.[29] In the vernacular, it is not possible to fight something with nothing.

The localized successes of the VNQDD (Vietnamese Nationalist Party) since the fall of Diem, and similar successes of the Dai Viet Party against the NLF, both since 1964 and even before during the

First Indochina War, testify that an ideologically oriented, nationalist struggle movement, when organized and capable of indoctrinating its members, can cope effectively with the communists. In those instances where organizational techniques have been relied upon to mobilize Vietnamese opinion and support among noncommunist forces, the results have frequently been phenomenal. The 1963 Buddhist movement against Diem was an organizational coup. The movement had no military forces and no methods of general population coercion. But it had organization, and it displayed amazing propaganda talents (see Chapter 2: "South Vietnam's Buddhist Crisis"). Against a regime that could counter only with military strength, the match proved uneven. The successes of the sects against the French, the Viet Minh, the GVN (during the broader front era of the NLF), and against the NLF after 1963, were functions of commitment to organizations. Similar examples of Catholic groups and tribal organizations and even of the Vietnamese Confederation of Labor further prove that the NLF organization theory is not the only theory of organization capable of obtaining identification and commitment from important segments of the population of South Vietnam (see the next section).

By creating structures that are visible and that have appeal to the predilections of local residents, alternatives become available. Once it is clear that such a structure can possibly provide security and administrative services, the NLF position can be measurably weakened. Agit-prop success is contingent upon the structure it supports being the only visible alternative. Such diverse groups as tribesmen and Cao Dai would never have opted for the NLF if any tangible alternative appeared plausible to them. The NLF gained its position relatively cheaply. A certain amount of terror, mixed with an optimum amount of propaganda against the Diem regime, which had no appreciation of how to use organizations effectively, plus a maximum amount of promises, were small expenditures. Matched against almost any viable organization, such methods would be inadequate for achieving NLF goals.

Naturally no organization is created in a vacuum. A base is essential. This can be a functional base (for example, the unions), a religious base (such as the Hoa Hao), a primarily ideological base (the Dai Viet), and so forth. The possibilities for taking such a base and developing it into a viable organization are to a great extent a function of leadership.[30] For example, such leadership can be provided through the administrative system, or through functional organizations for various occupations. Or such leadership can be provided by the natural leaders of community interests. The potentialities of the latter are contingent upon many factors. But provincial, district, and village elections can provide a vehicle whereby these personalities can gain access to, and commitment from, individuals belonging to organizations supporting their candidacy and their cause.[31] Decentralization of administrative responsibility to elected village and other local officials also expedites their ability to assist in the creation and development of local organizations, particularly of the functional variety.[32]

Much depends ultimately upon the effectiveness of the administrative system.[33] The creation of a system of organizations to include as wide a range of the population of South Vietnam as possible can serve eventually as the foundation for grass roots administration. But in order for such a system to be coordinated, and in order for the Saigon regime to become an effective governing mechanism, dramatic advances must be made in the Vietnamese system of public administration.[34] Approval of a federal, or at least a less unitary and centralized, system of government in the new constitution would simplify the administrative system and provide a much larger number of interests with sizable local constituencies with increased access to local policy-making authority.[35] Heavy emphasis on the training of additional administrators, particularly for provincial and local government, would help make government visible and would go a long way toward closing what Ellen Hammer has called South Vietnam's leadership gap.[36] Few developments could be more important, a factor recognized by the NLF, which fears competing leadership more than any other single phenomenon.

When budgetary priorities are given to civic action programs and the institution of administrative services, especially local police administration to assure minimal protective services, and when commensurate priorities are provided for training administrative talent for such programs and services, a new emphasis will be possible.[37] A GVN-sponsored social and political struggle can become the first order of business. This development, relying upon organization building as the primary instrument of implementation, is one methodology that can eat away at the foundations of the floundering NLF organizational apparatus.

Forging this organizational weapon must be first and foremost a Vietnamese activity stressing Asian, not western, ideology; relying upon religious and ethnic predilections where necessary; coopting indigenous leaders and interests where present, and creating them when they are not.[38] Potentially, of course, American organization specialists can play valuable advisory roles. It would be difficult for those charged with the task of implementing a theory of counter-organization to find a better set of guidelines than those provided by Douglas Pike's *Viet Cong*.

Administration and Political Warfare in the Highlands

■ Tribal elements in the highlands of South Vietnam have made mar-
ginal gains since this essay was written. Montagnard representatives in
the National Assembly and a special Ministry for Ethnic Affairs, which
has had a tribal group member as its minister since its beginning,
have provided some protection for highlander interests. Voting rights
have been extended, a greater number of public services have been
provided, and increased numbers of highlanders have become involved
in government and politics. All these changes have been a thin layer
of advancement. Little has really changed.

Vietnamese have not accepted inhabitants of the vast inland terrain
as equals. Even the steps toward increased autonomy initially granted
to tribal groups in North Vietnam have been partially and gradually
rescinded by Hanoi. In the South, withdrawal of American forces
represented a loss of what at most was a minimum protection from
excessive lowlander encroachments. II Corps, where most tribesmen
have lived for years, has been more of a fief of the commander than
other corps areas. Rich Vietnamese have managed to manipulate land
claims and have obtained additional wealth through obtaining title
to large tracts of property formerly owned by highlanders. Vast numbers
have been moved to new locations, ostensibly for security reasons,
where amenities have been absent, vocational activities have been more
controlled, and personal liberties as well as tribal customs have been
threatened. Because of the location of their territory, PAVN infiltration
was not stopped and true security was never achieved in the highlands.
While opting to serve with the ARVN, a majority of the tribal irregulars
have still never been an equal participant in material benefits received
by the ARVN.

Tribesmen have been permitted to serve as defense forces of the
GVN at their discretion and have maintained the right to leave government military services at any point of their choosing. During the 1972
PAVN invasion of the highlands, many did exercise this right, although
typically only after the ARVN shield was removed. What has happened
to the highlanders is the cruelest fate of all. They have been caught
between two contending Vietnamese armies. They have suffered from
both PAVN and ARVN artillery as well as from American aerial
bombing. Their presence is simply an annoyance to the two local
superpowers. Being in the middle, considered as aliens and inferiors
in their own homeland, the highlanders are trapped.

Peace would be welcomed by them, but their future does not appear
to them as being a bright one regardless of the probable form such
a peace might take. Their hope continues to be to obtain as much

autonomy as possible regardless of who rules in Saigon. Conceivably a genuine application of provisions already in the constitution of the Republic of Vietnam would provide them needed protection. A strong Ministry of Ethnic Affairs, elected village and provincial chiefs and councils, decentralization to the point where finances and home security could be determined locally, increased quotas at the National Institute of Administration, and extensive subsidies for health, education and other public services are essential if the tribal groups are to survive even in the absence of warfare.

Considering the history of Vietnamese-highlander relationships there is still no cause for optimism that such developments will occur. Specific reforms might be anticipated as a result of future political processes, especially if highlander votes should become more sought-after prizes by Vietnamese politicians. Highlander leaders might again attempt to win concessions by force of arms, but probably such a course would be suicidal. Local political power might become a reality permitting local leaders to formulate public policies in line with highlander customs and ambitions. These things are possible. But, unfortunately, it is much more probable that any Vietnamese government will not follow through on formally promulgated reforms. It is quite likely that the highlanders will continue to find most reforms to be much more form than substance.

VIETNAMESE nationalism is especially weak in the highland area of South Vietnam, which covers some 50 per cent of its territory.[39] This area, referred to variously as the *Pays Montagnard du Sud* (PMS), the central Vietnamese highlands, the high plateau, or simply the highlands, is very little known even to the Vietnamese, although it is in many ways the most vital region of the country in the struggle against the Viet Cong. Situated along the important infiltration routes from eastern Laos and Cambodia, the heavily forested highlands have provided sanctuary for insurgent forces and for clandestine Viet Minh and Viet Cong cadres for two decades. The indigenous highlanders have been forced to see their domain serve as a battleground between forces whose objectives appear to have little relationship to their own ambitions for the future of the highlands.

While anthropologists and other students of the area have obtained only a slender file of data on the indigenous population, it is known that there are at least 50 tribes in the highlands, with a large but undetermined number of subgroups; that these tribes use over a hundred languages and dialects; that the tribesmen are mostly of mixed Malayo-Polynesian stock (Papuans, Negritos, Melanesians, Indonesians); and that their total may exceed 700,000. A considerable number of the highlanders in South Vietnam live in plateau sections of the central Vietnamese lowlands and to the south of the central highlands. But the large majority live in the seven provinces of the central Vietnamese highlands: Kontum, Pleiku, Darlac, Quang Duc, Tuyen Duc, Lam Dong, and Phu Bon. The major highland tribes are limited to a single or at most two or three provinces. The Jarai in Pleiku Province (numbering perhaps 100,000), the equally numerous Rhade in Darlac Province (particularly around the Banmethuot area), the Koho in Tuyen Duc and Lam Dong provinces (more than 100,000), the Bahnar in Kontum and Pleiku provinces (75,000), and the Sedang in Kontum Province (over 40,000) are the largest tribal groups in the highland region. The highlander population, especially around Banmethuot, was also supplemented following the Geneva partition by several thousands of White and Black Thai, Tho, and Man tribesmen who escaped to the South.[40]

Viewed traditionally by the Vietnamese as *moi* or savages who were wastefully misusing valuable lands which might better be employed to improve the economy of the more civilized lowlands, the highlanders have for many centuries faced the possibility of eventual extermination. They have been prey to Khmer, Cham, and Vietnamese military encroachment, to regional wars among their more powerful neighbors, and even to slave raids. Cut off from the technological advances and cultural development of the lowlands, these various tribal groups have maintained their primitive animist religion, and continued their traditional agricultural pursuits.[41] A few tribes remain nomadic, but most, even those practicing what Gerald C. Hickey refers to as "shifting ray" agriculture, have devised landholding systems whether along communal lines such as the clan-based system of the Rhade or along individualistic and family lines.[42] They have also developed rules, both among tribe members and between members of various tribes, for every form of social relationship, including the settlement of disputes, treatment of criminals, and inheritance of personal property. None of the highland legal systems are sophisticated codes of law, but they are sufficient to provide the basis for a social order considerably in advance of that usually accredited them.

Despite the historic march to the south of the Vietnamese after the end of the 1,000-year era of Chinese suzerainty, and the victories of the Vietnamese over both the Chams and various tribal groups during and following the course of this southward migration, the imperial regime at Hue never succeeded in permanently penetrating the highlands, where the tribesmen went to seek refuge and to maintain their communal identity. As Joseph Buttinger has noted, the last emperor of Vietnam, Tu Duc, did make a futile attempt to extend Vietnamese governmental authority into the highlands after 1863, but this effort failed entirely of enduring success.[43]

The Pays Montagnard du Sud

It was left to the French to open up these virgin territories, to establish cities in the highlands and commercial links with many of the tribesmen, and to create a government for the region. Relying heavily upon local leaders, the French were able to establish the rudiments of an administrative system in the highlands, although the region never formed an integral part of Indochina. Kontum, Pleiku, and Darlac were governed by French residents, while the districts and cantons of these three provinces were governed by highlanders. Some schools were established, as was a medical service, and a court system was created to administer tribal justice. No attempt was made to "Vietnamize" the tribes or their leaders. Nor were tribal rulers involved in colonial political institutions. Communications with the rest of the nation remained almost nonexistent. A few arteries were developed for commerce, tourism, and administration, but these routes ran only to a few cities and left untouched the vast regions ruled by nature and the numerous tribes.

Typically, the French adopted a patronizing attitude toward the highlanders. The region was subject to some economic exploitation, and it also provided an immense recreation area. But the highlands were never systematically tapped as an economic resource. Frenchmen did receive monopolistic concessions of one sort or another, and rubber and coffee plantations were established. But the plantations, and commerce in forestry and agricultural products, were actually secondary efforts. To this day, the tremendous economic potential of the highlands remains largely unexplored. The poverty of the region is a function of the backwardness of the tribal inhabitants, their wastefulness as primitive agriculturalists and nomadic farmers, and the lack of either investment from or exports to the outside world. During the French period rice production, which was left to the tribesmen, remained insufficient to feed the population.

One result of French rule was that the tribesmen remained apart from the Vietnamese nation. They were, if anything, even more anti-Vietnamese than before the French arrived. Relatively greater contact with the Vietnamese, whom they encountered as exploiters and money lenders, exacerbated traditional antipathies. Anti-French movements were also recorded in the highlands, but the tribesmen never played a part in Vietnamese nationalist activities. French plantations, which encroached on tribal land holdings and exacted corvée labor after World War I, stimulated new highland revolts during the 1930's.[44]

The goal of the tribesmen was independence from Vietnamese imperialism. Articulate exponents of tribal autonomy initially appeared to favor some continued connection with the French, in order to protect the highlands from Vietnamese land settlement and the alternatives of *moi* slavery or annihilation, which more than a few Vietnamese accepted as the ultimate solution to the "*moi* problem." At the Da Lat Conference in 1946, the French proposed that the PMS become an autonomous region in the Indochinese Federation, an act implemented later by the creation of the position of commissioner of the Republic for the mountain populations of South Indochina. This autonomous region was matched later by the creation of a Thai Federation for northern Tonkin.[45] Both acts were obvious attempts to weaken the Vietnamese independence movement. Later both the northern and southern autonomous regions were made crown domains under Emperor Bao Dai.

The relative success of the French in the highlands during much of the First Indochina War is vivid testimony to the vehemence of tribal hatred of the Vietnamese, whether under the Viet Minh flag or not. In Tonkin, Thai forces operating between the Red and Black rivers defeated the Viet Minh at their own game for half a decade.[46] In the south, Viet Minh success was never complete in any section of the highlands or among any major tribal grouping, although substantial advances were registered during the later phases of the war. The Viet Minh campaign of late 1953 and 1954 against the highlands, which formed part of the offensive leading to Dien Bien Phu, was devastating in its impact on the highlands.[47] General Vo Nguyen Giap has termed the campaign a victory over the French "subjective estimation" of the total military situation.[48] In a sequence which reads somewhat like the headlines of 1965, the Viet Minh took Dak Doa, then northern Kontum Province, advanced to Road No. 19, and then took An Khe. They also captured the city of Kontum itself and attacked Pleiku. Nothing of this magnitude had been seen in the highlands before. The French, weakened by their efforts to implement the Navarre Plan, simply were overpowered as Giap used the great bulk of his forces in the Viet Minh Fifth Zone in a concerted attack on the highlands.

The relative success of the French during the entire period prior to 1954 was also a function of their ability to appeal to local tradition and the local power structure. Giving arms to tribal armies, respecting their laws, working through their leaders, and paying tribute to tribal groups *qua* groups had two results. First, it provided a source of support for the French against the common enemy. Second, it reinforced anti-Vietnamese sentiment throughout the plateau country. In a number of instances, French efforts were supplemented by Catholic priests and their proselytes among various tribes, a presence later found valuable by many American Special Forces teams.

The Viet Minh played much the same game as the French. Systematic implementation of their slogans of eating with, living with, and working with the indigenous populations produced many Viet Minh adherents. The Viet Minh typically went further than the French in promising tribal autonomy and in supporting notions of manifest destiny of one tribe against its historic tribal enemies. The Viet Minh also promised continued respect for the tribal traditions of each tribe, and its survival as a separate group. But, despite these tactics, Viet Minh success in the southern highlands was limited. Their failure was acknowledged by their action in taking a large number of southern tribesmen (probably at least 25,000) north with them after the 1954 Geneva Conference. After intense indoctrination, most of these were infiltrated back to the highlands either as individuals or as organized military units during later years.

The Failure of Assimilation

The record of Vietnamese relations with the highlands during the Ngo Dinh Diem period was hardly such as to modify historic tribal opposition to Vietnamese nationalism. Once Vietnamese ruled Vietnam again, their distaste for their backward, uncultured, "inferior" stepbrothers did not diminish. Teams of the Michigan State University Advisory Group who studied the tribesmen pointed out the opportunities for coopting tribal leadership into the overall structure of the Vietnamese nation and for building a strong military force among the tribesmen, but few positive steps were taken by the Saigon government. Gerald C. Hickey, in his 1957 report on the high plateau, warned especially of the continuing Viet Cong threat to the highlands. "One important element in the High Plateau situation is the presence of Viet Cong agents abetting the unrest and utilizing it in their propaganda to the detriment of the Government's prestige and programs. This propaganda stresses the Government's lack of good faith in failing to keep promises. In addition, Viet Cong agents reportedly are making the tempting offer of autonomy if the Mountaineers support their cause."[49]

The prophetic warning, like Hickey's detailing in the same report that 5,000 to 6,000 Rhades had gone north from Darlac Province after partition, that Hanoi broadcasts in the Jarai language were having an adverse effect in Pleiku Province, and that Viet Cong agents were operating in Darlac, Pleiku, and Kontum provinces, went unheeded by the Saigon government. A similar warning published in 1956 by Roy Jumper, with the information that Laos and the Mekong River were open infiltration routes for returning Viet Cong as early as 1955, and that Viet Cong battalions 307, 310, and 313 were operating once more in the delta (on the side of the sects), received no more attention than Hickey's.[50]

In the Democratic Republic of Vietnam (DRVN) after 1954 an attempt was made, with more than a little success, to win the loyalty of previously hostile tribesmen and to guarantee the continued adherence of those mountain tribes which had worked closely with the Viet Minh during the First Indochina War. Two autonomous zones were created by the DRVN: the Thai-Meo Autonomous Area adjacent to the Yunnan Thai Autonomous Region, and the Viet-Bac Autonomous Area bordering Laos.[51] But implementation of regional autonomy has not proved simple in practice, as elimination of the Lao-Ha-Yen Autonomous Zone has shown, because of administrative difficulties in maintaining autonomy and control simultaneously.[52] The DRVN has also on a number of occasions found it necessary to use military force in dealing with the highlanders.

Nonetheless, the policy of autonomy appears to have given the DRVN a greater opportunity to work with the tribesmen than any attempt to communize or assimilate them. Obviously, the political independence of the tribesmen is nowhere as great as DRVN propaganda asserts, and the tribesmen have not yet reached the stage where they are willing to accept DRVN programs passively unless they are adapted to local conditions. The fact remains, however, that tribesmen have been placed in positions of considerable administrative responsibility, tribal laws have been accepted for the most part as separate rules for the particular region, tribal languages are employed in schools, and tribal members have been given important military positions.[53] Administrative training and the full military use of tribesmen, including service in Laos, have been stressed. On the other hand, attempts to communize the mountain regions have been deemphasized, and even the oppressive "land reform" programs have not been implemented among the patriarchal tribesmen.[54]

In the South, Saigon also considered the highlands as a separate case for administrative purposes. However, emphasis was more upon "handling" the tribesmen than upon drawing them into the nation. Tribal fears of being considered as *mois* forever were hardly without foundation. Vietnamese were named as provincial and district administrators, and exacted tribute from the highlanders with little in the way of service programs as compensation. Education and other public services, particularly the much needed medical program, have remained woefully inadequate.[55]

Saigon's highland resettlement program also backfired. Designed primarily to relieve economic pressure along the central coast and to settle refugees from the North, the program did not resettle enough persons to have the desired impact upon the coastal economy. Nor was it effective in establishing a nucleus of lowlanders in the Kontum-Pleiku area and providing a stable population against the threat of insurgency and a foundation for eventual assimilation of the tribesmen. The outcome was quite different in the South, i.e., in the lowlands, where many aspects of the land reform program under Wolf Ladejinsky were considerably more successful.[56]

In the final analysis, the most important aspect of the highland resettlement program was that it confirmed the worst suspicions of the tribesmen concerning the Vietnamese. If the Vietnamese were to settle large areas of the highlands and close off areas vital to the shifting ray agriculture of the nomadic tribesmen, eventual tribal extermination was the probable result. As Frederic Wickert has noted in an analysis of Diem's highlands assimilation policy:

If there is no Communist invasion of Free Viet-Nam, it would look as if the tribespeople will gradually lose more and more land, and more tribal villages will deteriorate and die out. The stronger tribes to the north may be able to hold off the Vietnamese invasion for a while, but in the long run all the tribes people will have to integrate themselves economically and politically into the larger, more aggressive Vietnamese culture. The total assimilation of the tribespeople is not going to be easy for anyone.[57]

The Diem regime also alienated many tribesmen with its policy of sharp reprisals for a variety of alleged misdeeds. Numerous tribal groups previously allied with the Viet Minh were driven to take arms again against the Saigon government, and not infrequently to abandon village sites in face of government pressure. Wilfred G. Burchett claims, with his typically jaundiced perspective, that this was an initial phase of Viet Cong insurgency of South Vietnam after 1954.[58] Saigon's military forces naturally enough sometimes failed to discriminate between communists and noncommunists in specific villages, and their actions not infrequently alienated entire villages. All this was a major cause of eventual insecurity in much of the highlands.

The NLF Highlands Program

The National Liberation Front (NLF) and the DRVN were acutely aware of tribal discontent with the Diem government, and fully prepared to take advantage of it. Tribesmen who had previously been sent North for training and indoctrination systematically infiltrated into the South. Tribes which had taken to the maquis to defend themselves against the Vietnamese, particularly those formerly aligned with the Viet Minh, welcomed such professional assistance.

The old military-administrative interzonal hierarchy of the Viet Minh was reactivated, including an elaborate provincial and district committee system supplemented by a village and hamlet cell scheme. The provincial and district committees were connected administratively with the Provincial Central Committee of the NLF insurgency operations in both the central coastal regions and the highlands were placed under the direction of the Interzone of South-Central Vietnam (Interzone V) commanded by General Nguyen Don. Both Interzone V and the Nambo Interzone were tied directly to the Committee for Supervision of the South of the DRVN Central Committee.[59] The Interzone V command, which has survived attack thus far, is situated conveniently in the Quang Ngai-Kontum border area. Moving rapidly from this region, the Viet Cong can carry out attacks both along the coast and in the highlands, and attempt to recruit in Quang Nam and Quang Ngai provinces, particularly, but also in Binh Dinh and Phu Yen.

The tried and true carrot-and-stick tactics of the past were put to use again: terrorism, kidnapping, selected assassinations, sabotage of Saigon government facilities, and attacks upon isolated military installations were combined with promises and actual assistance to tribal leaders.

An autonomous high plateau region was promised, presumably to be independent of both Hanoi and Saigon. In order to lend a measure of reality to the "coalition" nature of the NLF, tribesmen were included among the NLF leadership group, and appointed to important positions in de facto provincial, district, village, and field office administrative units. Ybih Aleo, a Rhade from the Banmethuot area, now serves as chairman of the committee dealing with minorities, as a member of the

NLF Central Committee, and as an NLF vice-president. He also is the leader of the so-called "Movement for Tay Nguyen Autonomy."[60] Numerous areas in the highlands under NLF administrative control have been given special treatment, including acquiescence in many tribal customs. In villages where the NLF serves as the operational government, all of the usual services are provided, including education, public health, and the like. "Reactionary" practices are often not tolerated, however, and young people have been taught to look with disfavor upon many traditional tribal ways.

Yet the Viet Cong score card remains far from perfect. The vast majority of the tribesmen are still unconvinced that the Viet Cong are much more than pirates and roving bandits or that the NLF movement is not only another manifestation of the historic Vietnamese drive to extend control over the highlands. By almost any analysis, the limited success of the NLF has been more the product of the Saigon administration's failures than of its own popular appeal to highland groups. One of the clearest proofs of this is the fact that over 150,000 highlanders have sought refuge in South Vietnamese-controlled areas since the beginning of the intensified Viet Cong highland campaigns of 1962 and 1963.[61] While official claims in 1963 that at least 50 per cent of the refugees were able-bodied males can be viewed skeptically, and while all tribal refugees to the "secure areas" certainly did not join the exodus voluntarily, the exodus did occur. This proves, if nothing else, that a high proportion of the highlanders regard the operational program of the NLF (as opposed to its promised one) as being the worse of two perceived evils.

Special Warfare, Strategic Hamlets and the Tribesmen

To a certain extent Saigon's administrative failures in the highlands have been countered by two important factors. The work of the Republic of Vietnam Army (ARVN) II Corps command (aided greatly by MAAG) and of the American Special Forces teams, has provided a foundation for gaining the loyalty of the tribesmen and, at the same time, has been a bulwark preventing the Viet Cong from walking away with the highlands.

It was long a priority recommendation of the American aid mission that the highlands be treated as a special case. Most of the tribesmen were noncommunist in the sense of having no commitment to communist ideology, and many had served well in fighting the Viet Minh. They were known as rugged fighters whose natural habitat admirably fitted them for guerrilla warfare. Strongly anti-Vietnamese in sentiment, they could hardly be attracted to Ho Chi Minh or to appeals from the North for unification. These proud people cooperated well before 1962 with American investigative teams and with American aid agents. The Central Intelligence Agency and other American agencies interested in developing effective tactics for counterinsurgency also recognized the potential importance of the highlands both as a battleground against the Viet Cong and as a field for training and experimentation in special warfare tactics. While inevitably this interest led to experimentation with all kinds of gimmicks in the highlands, some useful and others futile, the enterprise provided much helpful information applied later at special and staff training courses.

After the Taylor mission in November 1961, it became possible to expand the American role in the highlands beyond the experimental, semi-secret activities which hitherto had been pursured on a severely limited scale. Taylor's recommendations called for an accelerated political as well as military war. Insofar as his recommendations concerned the highlands, they called for the AID mission to carry out a crash program of economic and social welfare services, and for Special Forces teams to live with, eat with, and work with the tribesmen. The CIA also operated in the region.

Such a broad program had little chance of success if American forces operated alone in the highlands; Vietnamese government support was also essential. But as the policy of President Diem and his brother, Ngo Dinh Nhu, toward the highlands ruled out effective participation by the tribesmen in the government of the region, the American program encountered innumerable obstacles and was not completely successful.

Once Diem and Nhu, under American pressures, permitted an expanded program for the highlands, the Americans not only had to win the cooperation of the tribesmen through special warfare techniques, but also to gain the support of Vietnamese military units operating in the area. Fortunately, General Nguyen Khanh and his II Corps subordinates accepted the American program and facilitated its implementation to the extent possible considering the hostility of Saigon. General Khanh, who had played an important part in saving President Diem during an abortive military coup in 1960, was a capable and aggressive officer, and this made him popular with the Americans. On the whole, his command in 1962 and 1963 did not face the rugged opposition from Viet Cong battalions which periled the Seventh Division and III and IV Corps. This meant that defeats in the II Corps area did not result in the high casualty rates recorded (or not recorded to pacify Diem) by government forces farther south.

Special Forces training programs began to show results rather quickly, beginning early in 1962 with the development of the Sedang and Rhade rangers.[62] Tribesmen responded well to the Americans, as have the Meo tribesmen in Laos.[63] The day-to-day conduct of Special Forces troops, especially their ability to work closely with tribesmen and their heroism in battle gave new hope to many who otherwise might have abandoned the fight against the Viet Cong. The tribesmen appeared to appreciate working with the Americans, although their attitude toward Vietnamese regulars did not change perceptibly. Banmethuot, Pleiku, and Kontum were strengthened as strongholds against the insurgents, not withstanding increasing Viet Cong pressures. Many villages regained their former ability to ward off Viet Cong political penetration and military onslaughts. For the first time the insurgents had to anticipate severe harassment when moving into or from point to point in the highlands. Viet Cong sanctuaries no longer were impenetrable.

Unfortunately, a great deal of the good will engendered by the American military-civilian project was destroyed by the techniques of Ngo Dinh Nhu for implementing the strategic hamlet program in the highlands. Once again, a potentially effective program led to extremely adverse consequences, despite the work of the USOM Office of Rural Affairs in planning and assisting in the construction of the strategic hamlets and in bringing civic action programs to hamlet inhabitants.[64] The administration of the program in the highlands was as bad as, if not worse than, in the lowlands.[65] Villages were uprooted, forced labor was commonplace, severe punishment was meted out to those who withheld cooperation, crops went unharvested, material assistance was slow in coming from Saigon and frequently did not arrive at all, and protection against the Viet Cong was often not available, due to overexpansion of available resources. In short, the job directed by Political Counsellor Nhu was botched.

Many tribesmen naturally turned violently against the Saigon government. Entire villages disappeared from newly established hamlet concentrations. One group of tribesmen trained by American Special Forces even attacked Plei-Mrong in December 1962. The Viet Cong information system improved while the government's communications with the population dropped measurably. For many tribesmen, the neutralist concept of a third force became increasingly attractive.

Deterioration in the highlands during 1963 was in no way comparable to the decline of government strength in the Delta, although the tactical position of the Viet Cong in the *Pays Montagnard du Sud* had improved measurably by the end of the year. Thereafter, even larger units of regular DRVN forces infiltrated the area with relative ease.[66] Elements of the DRVN's 325th Division were reported as having crossed over from Laos, and as taking part in the 1965 summer siege of Duc Co and in the Dak To attack. Like other reports of this character, such as the official Vietnamese government claim (later proved inaccurate) that the 325th Division was involved in the October 1960 attack on the Kontum border, it was extremely difficult to judge with any accuracy the movements of DRVN regulars in the highlands, although evidence appeared to substantiate the fact of their presence.[67]

The Highlands During the Post-Diem Period

Their hands freed somewhat by the November 1963 revolution, Special Forces teams in the highlands were given a new lease on life. Khanh was able to provide more overt help and the CIA and other American agencies to provide more material assistance. The American counterinsurgency program gained considerable momentum during 1964, with over 10,000 highlanders receiving Special Forces training. One ironic consequence was an event the Vietnamese had long feared. In September 1964 a major uprising occurred among tribesmen trained by the Special Forces. This unfortunate development left its mark on the Saigon government. During the revolt, which lasted for over a week, Rhade irregulars captured the Banmethuot radio station and demanded the creation of an autonomous highlands nation. Over 3,000 American-trained highlanders were involved. In addition to political autonomy, Rhade demands ranged from insistence on the replacement of Vietnamese officials in the local government to appeals for representation in the Saigon regime, and called for American officers and economic aid officials to replace Vietnamese officers among highlander forces. Other requests ranged from improved medical services and instruction in tribal languages in highland schools, to land reforms to permit tribes to regain lost properties, and to freedom for international travel by highlanders. Before the revolt ended a black-red-green horizontal striped flag with three white stars representing major tribes was flown at five camps.[68]

General Khanh, partly acceding to the urging of Ambassador Taylor and others, halted his military response to the Rhade uprising. Although a number of Rhade tribesmen and ARVN troops were killed, the revolt ended before the Saigon government launched a major offensive against the tribesmen. American Special Forces advisers at Bonsarpa, Buonmoprong, and other camps were largely responsible for negotiating a settlement with the Rhade. The revolt, which undoubtedly was stimulated at least in part by NLF agents, was primarily a product of historic tribal discontent aggravated by Vietnamese behavior toward the irregular forces. Unhappily the settlement was not satisfactory to any of the parties concerned. The underlying problems remained untouched, and highlander grievances have since been permitted to continue with only minimal effort by the government to deal effectively with them. Another limited revolt in 1965 testifies to this continued failure.

Although the Rhade revolts increased Vietnamese-highlander strains, tribesmen have continued to deal with the Viet Cong on much better terms than during the days of the Diem-Nhu period. The fact that a number of Special Forces training camps were overrun and many more attacked by the Viet Cong, both in 1964 and in 1965, in itself indicates that the highland rangers and other specially trained tribal forces are having a decided impact upon the NLF plan of operations.[69] Tribal forces have gained in mobility, and the regular Vietnamese military forces almost despite themselves are finding them a significant ally. The regular 22nd Division operating out of Kontum and the 23rd Division operating from Banmethuot would have had a considerably more difficult time coping with increased infiltration from Laos and across the seventeenth parallel if the current equivalents of the *Bataillons Montagnards* had not been organized. This is particularly true in view of the expected scope of operations throughout the I and II Corps areas since November 1963, and the rapid turnover of Vietnamese officials in both military and combined military-civil positions during this period.[70]

Even with intensified DRVN assistance to the NLF, the post-Diem period has witnessed at most a stalemate in the highlands. This outcome could not have been achieved without the special warfare program. To be sure, strong Viet Cong centers feeding infiltration routes to the South remained and grew in strength; the Interzone V command continued in the Quang Ngai-Kontum section despite ARVN attacks, and the bases in Binh Dinh near Kontum, on the Cambodian-Pleiku Province border, on the border of Phu Bon and Pleiku provinces, and in southern Darlac Province were strongly reinforced before the 1965 monsoon season.[71] The attack on the airfield and American billets at Pleiku on February 6, 1965, in which there were over a hundred American casualties, and which served as the prelude to American bombing of DRVN territory, proved the continued vulnerability of highland strongholds to historic Viet Minh-Viet Cong tactics. Yet despite these ominous signs, such indicators as the ability of the Bahnars and their American Special Forces advisers to hold out against a grueling 70 days' siege at Duc Co on Route 19 during August 1965, until a large relief force managed to work its way through a Viet Cong encirclement, have provided continued evidence that the Viet Cong cannot yet count on the highlanders to provide a "sea of people" in which to swim constantly upstream. The presence of the United States First Cavalry Division in the highlands in late 1965 immeasurably increased the difficulties of the Viet Cong in this respect.

Political Action and Administrative Adaptations for the Central Vietnamese Highlands

The main task ahead remains what it always has been. Neither the Saigon government nor the Americans can develop close cooperation with the highlanders until effective counterinsurgency tactics are supplemented generously with a political strategy aimed directly at the needs and aspirations of the highlanders themselves.

Counterinsurgency in the central Vietnamese highlands can be greatly advanced militarily by the American Special Forces teams. Tribal military forces with a commitment to protect their own group and their own cultural and religious beliefs and institutions can serve usefully as anticommunist bulwarks. Despite all their weaknesses, Hoa Hao and the Cao Dai successes against the Viet Minh testify to this fact. The ability of certain Catholic communities—such as the area under Colonel Le Roy against the Viet Minh, the territory of Father Hoa against the Viet Cong, Major Trinquier's special program in the northern highlands, and the activities of pro-French tribal groups in the southern highlands—all give striking evidence of the vulnerabilities of Giap-type warfare when it it not possible for agitation-propaganda units first to win over a population by political means.[72]

The competence and potential of American Special Forces working with irregular units in the highlands have been proved. But the scope of their ultimate success is a function of political actions beyond their control. To a great extent USOM, both through its agencies in Saigon and its local advisers, can provide many of the tools for effective political action in the highlands.[73] By providing much needed services in medical care, education, agriculture, administrative training for highlanders both at the National Institute of Administration and in (or near) the highlands, and other social and economic fields, real political progress is possible.[74] Social and economic problems in the highlands are so immense and in many ways so unusual that it might even be appropriate to entertain the possibility of creating a separate USOM for this region. This would be a striking departure from the usual procedure, but the potential advantages are so great that radical administrative innovation is surely justifiable. Ambassador Henry Cabot Lodge's own sophisticated approach to political warfare, together with the appointment of Major General Edward Lansdale as Lodge's special assistant for pacification, have been promising signs in recent months that administrative adaptations for political action are entirely possible.

Ultimately, of course, political success in the highlands is contingent not upon what American military and civilian personnel do, but upon what the government of South Vietnam does. Conquest and assimilation have failed as techniques for solving the continuing highlands minorities problems. Regardless of the potential merit which might have been ciaimed for it at one time, assimilation as a national policy is no longer conceivable. The hostility of the highlands and the attractiveness of proclaimed NLF policy, as well as the expanding presence of the Viet Cong, signify that any policy aimed solely at the convenience of the Vietnamese is no longer tenable. Only a policy aimed at the highlanders themselves is now feasible.

The central Vietnamese highlands must soon be granted administrative autonomy. This is not an argument for secession of the large plateau region from the Vietnamese state. Rather it favors a reasonable political solution for an extremely dangerous situation. Administrative autonomy within the Republic of Vietnam would permit the highlands to remain politically an integral part of the nation. It would provide for needed administrative flexibility, permitting highlanders a much wider participation in their government, and allowing wider possibilities for solving unique highlands problems through implementation of programs geared specifically to tribal conditions. It would be the most effective technique for winning the cooperation of tribal leaders, by accepting local forms to the extent possible, and by giving tribal and village chiefs and headmen as well as village councils, elders, and even sorcerers a good deal of formal responsibility to serve as the operational government within their own territories. This delegation of authority to de facto tribal leaders would bring them within the framework of the administrative apparatus now operating throughout the highlands. They would be directly responsible to other highlanders who would assume higher administrative positions on both geographic and functional bases.

Such administrative autonomy would involve numerous obvious

difficulties, particularly those associated with disagreements among various tribes. To some extent this could be alleviated by creation of a number of administrative regions in the highlands based primarily upon the traditional geographic areas of supremacy of the larger tribal groups. It also could be resolved partially by creating divisions within each administrative region to deal with the needs and problems of each important tribe in the region. A highland council also could be created in time to coordinate the activities of government throughout the central Vietnamese highlands. If a national legislature is eventually created, appropriate representation on both a tribal and a regional basis should be guaranteed for the highlanders.

But such a system can work ultimately only if the central government assumes more responsibility for the welfare of the highlanders, and if the highlanders themselves are persuaded to assume the responsibility of fulfilling their own political obligations to the national government. One of the most expeditious methods for developing this sense of joint responsibility would be the establishment of a Ministry for the Highlands, which could coordinate Saigon's relationships with the highlanders. Such a ministry, combined with special highlands divisions in each of the present ministries, could fairly quickly provide the bona fide administering government which the highlands have so long lacked.

While no doubt this proliferation of administrative structures at the national and local levels is susceptible to criticism on the basis of numerous presumably sound administrative principles, the times demand striking administrative adaptations in order to cope with the political realities of contemporary South Vietnam.[75] These adaptations are essential in order to give the highlanders something to defend, something to which they can become committed, something comprehensible to them which respects their cultures but which gives them an opportunity to improve their lot, something which will inspire confidence in their individual and tribal future and which provides them with the opportunity and the challenge to assume the burdens of administrative responsibility, something which will permit them to defend themselves night and day throughout the year. Certainly leadership is not wanting in the highlands. The abortive revolts of 1962, 1964 and 1965 demonstrated once again that the ordinary tribesmen will follow their leaders in attempts to preserve tribal identity and to gain self-government for the tribes. Nor is the desire for self-improvement or community advancement lacking. Given the guarantee of a political context in which their economic and social potential can be improved, and given the material and advisory assistance for expediting such improvements, there is every reason to assume that

the indigenous population of the highlands will take advantage of such
opportunities.

The Ubiquity of the Administrative Role
in Counterinsurgency

■ Perhaps the major premise of this essay is that governments which
could cope with viable insurgency situations do not have them. In
South Vietnam the opposite of this theme has always been of paramount
importance. Evidence seems increasingly clear on this one point: a
potent political system could have precluded the rise of the NLF in
the 1950's. The combination of Diem's autocracy and personalized
rule plus American naiveté in political-economic terms and the American Korean syndrome in military terms laid a path the NLF genius
for revolutionary warfare could exploit readily. As the GVN weakened
in the mid-1960's, the NLF came near to supplanting the South Vietnamese regime outside the main urban centers. Only when the governmental administration and the political party system expanded in
strength after 1968 did the NLF strategy falter. It then faltered badly.

The administrative role became truly significant simply because the
Republic of Vietnam locally was providing government rather than simply rule from Saigon. Cause for optimism by the Saigon government at
the end of 1971 had real merit for the first time. The countryside
was not the bed of roses many in Saigon and Washington increasingly
assumed. But improvements in terms of local participation, of delivery
of public services and of overall security were human as well as statistical facts.

However, there is another thesis not presented in this essay in adequate detail which is of great significance. Actual administering can indeed fare well in a revolutionary warfare conflict. But public servants,
regardless of their merit, can never challenge sheer firepower. Tanks,
artillery and mortars can destroy overnight what a decade of administrative development has brought to a village. Walls crumble, wells are
destroyed, schools and hospitals and markets are demolished. Local con-
stabulary can be slaughtered as can even the most dedicated self-defense
forces. In short, "traditional" or conventional warfare is no respecter
of village political, social and economic development. In a brief period,
this type of warfare can create large numbers of homeless, can destroy
economies and can make a shambles of an administrative system. The

winter-spring offensive of North Vietnam during 1972 turned back the clock of administration in much of South Vietnam.

It is a dramatic case study of how irrelevant both revolutionary warfare and counterinsurgency can become when the rules of the game change completely. This did not mean that everything built up through processes of political development had been destroyed. Indeed, the nationalist forces undoubtedly were much more able to assume self-preservation under strained conditions because of that development. It did mean that any village which became the direct target of conventional warfare stood to lose everything.

Certainly neither the Saigon government nor the NLF could continue unabated without qualification their prior claims to power once the invasion by northerners began in earnest in 1972. The cycle continued. The march to the South by the Viets was at another stage of its historic evolution. No southern force, whether representing the GVN or the NLF administrative systems, could escape the immediate consequences of this northern movement. These consequences would require rebuilding once again, they would require redevelopment of much of the infrastructure which had been destroyed, and they would require enlarged administrative programs to resolve the vast number of immediate human and physical problems resulting from the invasion. These were consequences no government could escape.

There is, of course, one additional factor. Nearly all observers, including myself as can be seen in the three essays in this chapter, have continually underestimated the ability of the residents of South Vietnam to survive, to build, and simply to cope with the incredible pressures they have experienced. Despite the odds they continue to face, it is not at all impossible they can somehow commence again and again the procedures necessary for survival and perhaps for political development as well. This process may defy counterinsurgency manual procedures. From a western perspective it may appear rather as a bungling-through of a series of steps that do not seem to constitute a total developmental system. For all I know it may even defy the law of gravity. But the political interest groups in South Vietnam may find a path which adapts current administrative practices to the necessities of Vietnamese political behavior. The rule book on political warfare may indeed need to be rewritten.

ONE of the most disquieting commentaries on South Vietnam—and on American involvement in South Vietnam—is William A. Nighswonger's *Rural Pacification in Vietnam*.[76] This analysis by an articulate and sympathetic participant-observer of legitimate government revolutionary counterinsurgency warfare lists a series of programs which failed.

Yet it is not the failures that are overly disturbing. Nor is it the specific inadequacies that lead to a generally pessimistic evaluation of the fortunes for revolutionary development in South Vietnam. Specific inadequacies can be found to a degree in any project analogous to those pursued in the Vietnamese setting; comparisons with Malaya and the Philippines, while admittedly overexaggerated, are analogous enough to prove the point.[77] But such inadequacies are problems of detail, whether of great detail or small. Problems of this sort should be susceptible to solution if they are accompanied by an expanded commitment of resources, both human and material, and by minimal administrative adaptations permitting increased flexibility and coordination of effort, and by some requisite minimal amount of luck. And luck in counterinsurgency, typically, is opportunity seized upon in an expeditious and opportunistic manner.

What is disquieting about Nighswonger's list of social, economic, political, military and administrative project failures is that there was nothing intrinsic in the concepts underlying their initiation which automatically precluded their success. Certainly most of them had and continue to have enormous potential for attaining counterinsurgency objectives. It is even possible that almost any one of the failures could be taken off the shelf, given a small amount of procedural dusting, and tried again successfully under more auspicious circumstances.

This latter thesis rests upon the assumption that the concepts and types of projects applied thus far in revolutionary development in South Vietnam actually have been relatively adequate to the task. (This point is made most advisedly.) It assumes further that circumstances have remained inauspicious for success *because the government and administration of South Vietnam have been inadequate structurally and functionally to cope with the problems of development, of insurgency, and even of governing.* And most certainly nearly all of the problems continue to hinge upon the many failures of governing itself. Due to this failure, South Vietnam provides the most dramatic and expensive case study supporting Davis B. Bobrow's general hypothesis concerning so-called "civic action" or "revolutionary development."

Indeed, the general implication of our hypothesis is that the local armies and governments best suited to the official American image of civic action are those already best qualified to meet popular aspirations and frustrate Communist maneuvers. Those indigenous armies and governments whose unsatisfactory behavior gave rise to the American adoption of the civic action doctrine are the least willing and able to use this strategy effectively. The irony of this situation points to the unremoved need for American efforts in many cases to modify either the local military or government or to reconcile ourselves to a curtailed set of objectives for the future of the developing nations.[78]

Bobrow's theme is a corollary of Edward W. Weidner's general hypothesis for development administration, a hypothesis that could have been written following analysis of the United States counterinsurgency role in South Vietnam: "The programs of technical assistance in public administration have been successful in direct proportion to the clarity and preciseness of the development goals of the host government and the firmness and determination with which it has worked to attain them."[79]

Considering that development goals provide the foundation for auspicious conditions associated with revolutionary counterinsurgency, Weidner's thesis is of special value. All hope for the Revolutionary Development program rested upon clear, precise development goals implemented with firmness and determination by the Saigon government, by its various ministries, and by its military and local governmental administrative apparatus. As Professor Nghiem Dang has noted, "the effective role of public administration seems to be the supreme hope of Viet-Nam, and its endeavor to promote the social and economic well-being of the nation."[80]

The year following the Honolulu conference (February 1966 between President Johnson, Thieu and Ky) did provide reason for quite cautious optimism in this regard. Premier Ky's government at least survived the period and all of the programs of revolutionary development indeed were initiated and advanced with varying degrees of success (see Chapter 5: "Struggle Politics and the Bigger War"). The GVN was formally committed to the doctrine and modest progress toward overall development goals was manifested in solid electoral and civic action steps. Caution, however, requires mention that the projects were really not more than extensions or adaptations of the projects Nighswonger evaluated with fairness and objectivity. Further caution requires mention also that the official evaluation of post-Honolulu programs remains rosier than the facts and that the government is only relatively, rather than absolutely, more stable than its predecessors.

The Lack of Ubiquity of Public Administration in South Vietnam

A hypothesis central to counterinsurgency policies (i.e., "revolutionary development," "revolutionary warfare," "modern warfare," etc.) is that only effective administration can cope with insurgency conditions.

Revolutionary warfare operations have the greatest potential for success in areas that historically have not been subject to the operational administration of a particular nation state. In South Vietnam, the regions of greatest NLF strength generally have been locales that have not been effectively governed by the central regime since World War II. Further, large areas within both Vietnam and Laos cannot be considered as having ever been under de facto governmental control. The mountain areas, particularly, have proved to be beyond the scope of Chinese, Thai, Vietnamese, or French administration. In such sections insurgents find their natural abodes.

Operating within a rural milieu, an insurgency organization finds either alienated residents or, more frequently, residents whose entire socialization has omitted little but the most occasional reference to an outside government. Living in comparative isolation, knowing central rule only casually in the form of an infrequent but corrupt mandarin, or having encountered government only in the guise of some past military maneuver near their village, many peasants naturally have no commitment to the regime operating out of a national or provincial capital. This does not signify anarchy or lack of commitment to established order. Actually, within the bounds of locally accepted mores, village government not infrequently provides more relative economic security and social stability than does the national government in the regions it in fact does govern. But the very existence of established governing local elites whose judgments are acceptable to village residents provides opposition to the legitimacy of a nonadministering regime's claim to govern even in the abstract.

The elite whose legitimacy is accepted locally often plays a vital role in the plans of insurgents. Local elites, if they can be persuaded by some means, are likely to adopt the course they deem essential for personal and community survival. The insurgents may or may not lay claim to the right to govern in a village, but even if they do not make such a claim they will demand acquiescence in matters of importance, such as disobedience to national directives and provision of stocks from the community-controlled supply chests.

As the only viable administration, village elites are likely to take such steps as they consider necessary to pacify those who threaten the community. Being practical local politicians, they also may permit themselves to be coopted by the threatening forces. Such a tactic would be categorized as quisling in developed societies, but is rather simple logic when neither local leadership nor its constituency has any commitment to the lawful national government. Once coopted, the village elite have reason to work more closely with insurgents if the cooptation experience proves profitable to the community. It provides the basis for development of a commitment to an external force. Finally, the experience of cooptation and subsequent commitment subjects the community to potential reprisal from the central government. While the entire process is one of being damned if you do and damned if you don't, the choice of potential retribution from an occasional visitor as opposed to imminent destruction by physically present insurgents is rarely a difficult one to make.

Successful counterinsurgency in Vietnam, as one instance of the general hypothesis, has always been contingent upon whether the Saigon government could become an "administering" regime. As Sir Robert Thompson has observed: "Unless an effective administration is maintained and steadily improved by the recruitment and training of the best young men in the country, national policies become meaningless because, without the functioning of an effective administration, no policies can be carried out."[81] As principles of government go, this is as simple as any rule can be. But in an underdeveloped nation, the principle is far from simple in application. In the final analysis, lack of administration has always been the core of National Liberation Front success. Insurgency is relegated to mere terrorism when it operates against a "governing" regime. And terrorism, although an important ingredient, is insufficient in itself to produce an insurgency-motivated state of emergency. The people are a "sea" for revolutionaries only when the "people" live in a vacuum.

China fell to the forces which thrived in such a sea because the Chiang regime became nothing more than an urban faction. The Republic simply failed to administer territory. Gaining first where government was least, the communists provided an administrative system of their own. Edgar Snow's description of the socialist regime even during its dark days in the mid-1930's depicts an administered territory with a population identifying itself with and committed to an administrative system.[82] The "sea" was a group accepting the norms and goals of a government which provided services, protection and a legal order.

The situation in certain rural areas of South Vietnam is somewhat similar to that of China before 1949. Certain sections in Cau Mau peninsula and Zone D have been under Viet Minh administration almost continuously since World War II. These sections are in many ways identical to those in the highlands of Tonkin under Viet Minh control during the anti-French war. Bernard Fall's description and analysis of Viet Minh administration during that struggle could serve as a textbook on government and administration in areas of the South today.[83] In most of the South, however, the NLF is not the day-to-day government, but it is a force in policy making by local elites. Through terror, threats, bribery, cajoling, persuasion and, most important, organizational successes, the NLF has become an external power to which village leaders must be accountable. NLF members may become part of the local officialdom and NLF guerrillas may bring to task publicly those decision makers who choose courses deemed detrimental to NLF interests. These tactics are effective only to the extent that the legal government lacks administrative controls operationally in a given village and area.

Many of the difficulties of operational control are directly traceable to the evolution of Vietnamese public administration. To a great extent, the fortunes of the NLF are equally traceable to this evolution. The overlay of Chinese, French, and American concepts of administrative theory upon the Vietnamese administrative system has resulted in a complicated governing process. Unfortunately, the French overlay reinforced the nonactivist aspects of Vietnam's administrative practices while destroying the foundations of the popular acquiescence to a Confucianist literati philosophy of emulation and harmony. The pre-French period witnessed gradual development of a sophisticated, fairly rationalized system cf mandarinate rule.[84] But this system, emphasizing as it did proper protocol roles for rulers and ruled, remained limited in scope. Regional autonomy (particularly southern provincialism) and village autonomy, as well as problems of communication, continually delimited the local presence of the Vietnamese government. The long French era *subordinated* the position of the Vietnamese within the governing scheme, *extended* greatly the structures and functions of government beyond the caretaker activities of the imperial regime, and *created* an aura of contractualism and bureaucratism.[85] Yet the French developed no universal presence of government and administration.[86] This failure as much as any other single factor doomed colonialism after World War II.

Since 1954, South Vietnam has not recovered administratively from the vacuum left from the French era. It would have been a herculean chore to provide a universal presence of government and administration immediately following the destruction of the First Indochina War and the withdrawal of the French governing apparatus.[87] Evaluation of the initial successes of the Diem government varies widely, but regardless of appraisal of the rather phenomenal occurrence of GVN survival, the fact of long-range importance is that the Diem era did not witness establishment of an administrative system capable of governing the entire territory of Vietnam. However, Diem did attempt to govern below the district level. His much condemned abolition of village elections even carried the seed of a truly revolutionary extension of national government. But the Republic was not geared to implement such an ambitious possibility, and Diem was unable to pursue the goal effectively. Whatever potential for creation of a nationwide network of administration existed was dissipated after his first years in office. As Malcolm W. Browne has remarked: "the biggest factor in the disenchantment of the Vietnamese people with the Diem regime was his failure to do anything to change the French colonial system of administration. And this fatal flaw appears to be no less true of Diem's successors."[88]

The problems of administration faced by Diem and his successors were to a great extent, although not universally, the product of the so-called "*fonctionnaire* spirit." This phenomenon, hardly unique in an underdeveloped excolonial nation, has been described in the following uncomplimentary manner by Nguyen Thai: the *fonctionnaires* "manifested a certain reluctance to lead and act; they tended to avoid decisions and to advance procedure to cover their unwillingness to assume responsibility; they were more concerned with their civil service status and its petty privileges than any national program of administrative activity."[89] The characteristics frequently attributed include the following:[90]

Corruption: a legacy of French destruction of the philosopher king, traditional ethics concept of the mandarinate and of the breakdown of controls during the Indochina War; family protection; *ung ho* (bribery).

Legalistic orientation: a product of French training and continental administrative law emphasis; highly procedural.

Personal aloofness: Vietnamese administrators in white suits looked down upon their constituencies but had lost their Confucianist-inculcated sense of responsibility; authoritarian behavior; status consciousness.

Cadre system: basically an employee classification system guaranteeing position, promotion, and salary on the basis of degrees.

Attentiste: hesitated to commit themselves, to assume responsibility or to make decisions; survival primary goal.

Parachutists: rapid advancement of lower level cadres during last days of French and after 1954; mostly *fonctionnaires* and not mandarins.

Urban elitists: represented small proportion of population.

Static, nonactivist: little initiative; buckpassing.

The structural-functional problems that have also plagued the GVN would have rendered administration difficult even in the absence of insurgency conditions. The imperial civil service in effect had been dismantled by the French. The French personnel system, geared to its complicated governing scheme of a unitary government, tutelary control, integrated administrative structure and centralization, assumed close administrative controls and a high degree of professionalism. Recruitment, advancement, and position were contingent upon a cadre scheme based ultimately upon pre-entry education. Financial as well as structural controls were highly proceduralized and legalistic.[91] The ministerial system, combined with subordinate local governments, required overlapping jurisdictions, numerous lines of administrative responsibility, and a complicated set of checks and balances prior to and following many decisions. Local and national government structure changed drastically after 1954, further complicating the personnel assignments and the matter cf jurisdictions. Offices to implement technical programs continued to proliferate after 1954. Personnel shortages, in both generalist and technical cadres, were critical. Training procedures were incompatible with functional requirements. Most important, the entire system inherited from the French was one that allowed the state simply to rule the population. Service functions were always subordinate. In short, the role of government and the structural-functional apparatus created to carry out this role had little relationship to universal administration to and for the total constituency. It was the Diem regime's principal weakness that this role was not changed.

Administrative inadequacies were compounded measurably during the later period of Diem's rule, when increased centralization of decision making rendered a bulky structure almost inoperable under the insurgency crisis condition (see Chapter 2: "Perceptions of the Vietnamese Public Administration System"). To an extent, the problem of centralization in decision making was ameliorated following the coup of November 1963. The rapid turnover of leading personnel and the reinstatement of the regional delegate system under the corps commanders in fact provided an overcompensation for that important fault of the Diem period.

Few of the inadequacies of administration were altered by post-coup events, though the entire Revolutionary Development (RD) program can be viewed as a procedure for working toward building a viable administrative system.[92] Perhaps this is impossible under insurgency circumstances. While limited, the progress in Vietnam toward improvements in government and administration since Honolulu seems to testify that the task is not necessarily impossible. But the potential for success remains contingent upon GVN commitment to developmental goals.

Civil and Military Administrative Structures and Political Functions

To a great extent, implementation of the commitment to RD goals—assuming it is a sincere commitment on the part of the GVN—will be a function of the type of government established under the 1967 Constitution. A representative regime elected by popular mandate, permitting greater administrative decentralization and elective councils at local levels, potentially can overcome many obstacles of local leadership and popular opposition that have historically hindered Vietnamese administrative processes. However, pragmatically, within the framework of a representative government, implementation of RD goals also will be a function of the specific administrative organizations assigned responsibilities for each subgoal.

In South Vietnam the all-important operational phase, i.e., the actual administration of programs, will continue to be a weak link in counterinsurgency. Stable and unstable governments, civilian and military regimes, and regimes that have appeared to support materially as well as formally the various RD goals, have encountered this problem.

In addition, under the new system of government as under each of the previous ones, certain fundamental axioms of organization theory will be applicable which will create problems in RD implementation. Inevitably and properly, administrative organizations (1) will vie to have internal goals elevated to the highest policy priorities, (2) will advance logic to stress the necessity of receiving allocation of as many resources as possible, (3) will request optimum jurisdiction and substantial autonomy for operations, and (4) will insist that the goals and operations of alternate administrative organizations be subordinate in the arenas of their interests.[93]

To the dedicated, such priorities are perceived as just. Objectives to which organizational professionals devote their vocational endeavors and reputations are naturally not only right, in and of themselves, but are also more important and effective problem-solving ends than those of others. The rights, powers, facilities and resources of subordinates within the organization must be protected and enhanced regardless of the impact this has upon the operations of the other organizations. This does not necessitate overt conflict with other organizations operating within the same geographical or functional area. Cooperation may in fact be deemed desirable, as it may be useful or even a prerequisite for goal achievement.[94]

Activities of many administrative structures may be ultimately directed toward identical general public policy objectives, e.g., eliminating poverty, eradicating conurbation problems such as those of the Saigon metropolitan area, or winning a war. The question to the principal decision makers of one organization rarely will be whether other structures should exist or function. Instead, the relevant questions are: (1) Do the other organizations function as supplemental or as primary units in general and in particular fields? (2) Do the other organizations have a primary, joint, or secondary position in strategy formulation, in specific tactical decisions, and in access to superior policy formulating structures? (3) Do the other organizations have more, equal, or less of a posture for making demands upon the allocation of various resources? (4) Finally, and in many ways often less concrete, is the "orientation" of other organizations perceived by superior policy makers, by clientele groups, and by any other relevant organizations as the principal "orientation" in the policy area?[95] In agricultural policy, for example, this "orientation" difference between administrative structures may be the distinction between an "owner" and "renter" orientation. In revolutionary counterinsurgency warfare, the perennial competing orientations are "political" and "military."

Owing to these two orientations, administering against revolutionary warfare typically is considered to be either of the civil or military variety. As Marion J. Levy, Jr., has observed: "The focus on armed force organizations as things apart from general civilian concerns—as a necessary evil at best—has obscured attention to what may be the most efficient vehicles for the maximization of modernization with a minimization of the uncontrolled spread of side effects."[96] The underlying supposition is that the military apparatus must remain in a position subordinate to the civilian one.

One problem in revolutionary warfare, however, cannot be resolved by a simplistic civilian-military structural division. The raison d'etre of revolutionary warfare is primarily, if not exclusively, related to political functions. The division functionally is not between civil-military but between political-military. In all warfare, political factors ultimately must be given priority. In revolutionary warfare, political factors are not only primary priorities, they are the hub around which the wheel of all activities turns. Military activities supplement according to a political timetable.[97]

Military administration, where necessary and feasible, also can provide for regular civil functions to be performed.[98] When an area has been cleared, a period of military administration is almost inevitable. The skill with which such administration is carried out is of tremendous importance in terms of obtaining a political commitment from inhabitants. It is entirely possible that anti-insurgency organizations can be initiated by special divisions of the military itself after an area is cleared. Special agit-prop teams should arrive almost immediately following the retreat of insurgency contingents. These teams may be military or civic action, but their tactics are standard:[99] population census; extensive interviewing followed by intensive interviewing; creation of provisional government to provide basic services with minimum disturbance of previous civic functions; provision of relief to the needy, grain to farmers, etc.; initiation of a *lien gia* (inter–family group) system with both secret membership and an open membership for purposes of creating a local government; and indoctrination. Services should first emphasize those functions (road building, well digging, etc.) that the former de facto regime was unable to provide but had promised. Most important for this stage, however, is the creation of an organization for activating energies, resources and commitments. The elite to be coopted through assignment of organizational leadership roles may be known prior to the clearing operation or may be determined as a result of the intensive interviewing procedure, or may be former leaders brought back by the government.

Given the primacy of political functions, civil objectives must always be of highest priority. But this can easily assume a much too limited scope for specific structures. In most instances where functional differentiation indeed is an identifiable political and cultural characteristic, the civil structures can be relied upon to implement development as well as "regular" public functions. Yet to deny such functions to appropriate military structures would be to defy significant historical example as well as the nondifferentiation characteristic of an underdeveloped society's politics. For example, Eisenstadt's and Witfogel's lists of military structures performing diffuse societal functions including large-scale developmental administration activities present a vital element in maintaining stable, viable civilizations.[100] Certainly contemporary cases are equally numerous.

First, the goals of development, harsh as they frequently are, can buttress a society from overwhelming immediate deprivation. Second, despite the inconsistency of military supremacy with the typical western democratic model, it would be a mistake to assume that such supremacy is inevitably less representative or less capable of sharing operational power than predecessors or plausible alternate elites. Despite its "guided" nature, Pakistan's system is more inclusive of diverse political interests than was the regime it displaced.[101] An argument can be made for many other military-led governments, including Egypt, Ghana, Indonesia and South Korea.

The extent to which military-guided political systems have been successful has been a function of several features: (1) capable, relatively efficient, and relatively incorrupt administration, (2) cooptation of significant interests, e.g., local and religious concerns, students, etc., and (3) articulation of an ideology acceptable to nationalist orientation but pragmatic enough to retain ability for needed operational (and foreign policy) adaptations.

Thus, the formal public administration structures assigned developmental functions realistically can be civilian or military or a combination of the two. But in a developing nation, and particularly in one experiencing revolutionary warfare, it is essential that personnel at all levels directing both civil structures and military structures involved in RD be subject to public and development administration training.[102] When possible, this should be formal training, but it should be continually reinforced by inservice administrative training programs. The significant element is that the orientation of the structure(s) must be a political orientation. As a general rule, military administration will display less of a propensity for a political developmental role. Because this is the primary role for government in revolutionary warfare, it follows that civilian administration rather than military administration typically is a more propitious instrument for construction of a viable political system. However, when the civil apparatus proves inadequate, rational administration may require a shift in structures responsible for development. Unfortunately, such a shift is no guarantee of rationality.

In fact, situations where the civil leadership is corrupt, incompetent, and inattentive to requirements of legitimate political interests are the very instances where leadership substitution is likely to result only in a change of faces.[103] Generally it is this presence of legitimate complaints against weaknesses of administration that serves as the foundation for rallying already alienated populations to the banner of insurgency. Governmental structures without a political orientation toward adopting and implementing policies directed at ameliorating conditions of poor administration will actually add fuel to the torch lit by insurgent leadership.

When the actions of government are predominantly nonpolitically oriented, a regime is increasingly at a disadvantage as insurgency moves to the phase of bona fide revolutionary warfare.[104] Unfortunately, this was the case with Diem. During this advanced stage, an astute opposition leadership will have created an organizational base involving diverse interests and functionally responsible for obtaining mass commitments. Once this occurs, the legitimate regime will encounter constant political opposition. A polarization will exist wherein each act will be countered with a political retort rendering that action unenforceable. Since the early 1960's, this polarization has rendered objective conditions in South Vietnam difficult and frequently impossible for the administrative system.

Organization Theory for Revolutionary Development

Presumably South Vietnam will soon have a civilian government. Politically this should have many advantages even if current military leaders assume major roles in the new regime. Greater popular acceptance of government should be possible and the existence of a bona fide political arena should serve as a pressure toward greater administrative efficiency.[105] Responsibility should also be shared by greater numbers, with the potential for developing commensurate greater commitments.

There is a potential danger in the shift in that the turnover at the ministerial and perhaps local levels as well may lead to temporary confusion in terms of civil and military administrative organization activities. A further danger is that the role of military administrative organizations in RD programs may suffer initially. And the greatest danger is that the new government and its administrative system may prove inadequate enough to tempt a further military assumption of power.

The objective must be not only to survive despite these dangers but also to mesh in a coordinated fashion the activities of civil and military administrative organizations in such a way as to implement RD goals effectively. Public administration in a counterinsurgency situation therefore must not be conceived of as either civil or military. Rather, public administration must be the implementation of political functions, a task in fact always assumed in Vietnamese history. Due to the multifaceted nature of revolutionary warfare, appropriate diverse structures indeed are necessary. The real object is to create a *system* of interstructural coordination rather than a series of disjointed projects. But such a system is unlikely to be developed in Vietnam if implementation is left solely to national civil or military public administrators.

The NLF has created a sophisticated network of parallel horizontal and vertical intermediate structures to enmesh populations and to retain commitments. Throughout, the organizational weapon has remained the key to Viet Minh and later NLF success (see the second section of this chapter). Utilization of a perfected instrument has permitted insurgents to saturate the rural body politic with a matrix of political controls. These controls have then been used to prevent civil authority from governing and to manipulate populations in "struggle" activities.[106] The success of the NLF as organization-builder is an experience that cannot be ignored. Kenneth E. Boulding's commentary is appropriate: "Frequently, indeed, the character of an organization is determined by the nature of its enemies, for its enemies are the most important part of its environment."[107] Experience displays vividly that the Vietnamese can cope with the Viet Minh challenge when they have what to them is a cause worth a commitment. Frequently in the past, the totality of this commitment, e.g., among the tribesmen groups, has been limited due to lack of an organizational foundation.[108]

The absence of significant intermediate structures to articulate the interests of substantial publics in the community is a problem faced by most underdeveloped nations. This leaves a vacuum between national leadership and its citizenry. The latter remains an amorphous mass which can be reached only by direct governmental actions.[109] At the same time, national leadership cannot receive support from aggregated interests but must rely upon single exponents of specific interests. This means, in short, that only the most influential can be given full consideration and that the vast majority remains without a continuing source to provide access for their views (see Chapter 2: "Patterns of Political Party Behavior"). It means further that constant efforts must be made to educate the masses concerning programs about which they could not possibly have been consulted at the initiation stage.

The problems present under such circumstances are tremendous. A government faced with crises stemming from these conditions can ameliorate them only by itself serving as the charter member of new intermediate structures. Such government-originated groups may become genuine focal points for determining views of particular publics or they may simply become vehicles for enforcing uniformity in governmental programs. In South Vietnam under Diem, the latter alternative was selected, generally following but expanding upon an old French technique of program implementation (see Chapter 2: "Organizing Bureaucrats"). Such facade structures cannot cope with the NLF infrastructure. The organizations created must be bona fide ones, for, as Pye properly observed, it is actually necessary to "conceive of the problem of political development and modernization as essentially the creation of adaptive and purposeful organizations."[110]

Public administration in Vietnam must be involved as an integral element of RD in the creation of an infrastructure of linking and overlapping organizations. A *system* of interstructural coordination could incorporate public (civil and military), semipublic and private structures in social, economic and political administrative roles. As George K. Tanham has stated: "It is critical that the people be organized so as to contribute to the counterinsurgency effort and to their own social, economic, and political development."[111]

Without such organizations the counterinsurgent's strategic problem, as outlined by David Galula, cannot be resolved, i.e., "To find the favorable minority, to organize it in order to mobilize the population against the insurgent minority."[112] The election of council structures at each level of government provides a significant beginning. This vertical hierarchy supplemented by horizontal economic and social structures will, it is to be hoped, form a link between national policies, local implementation, and population acceptance of the legitimacy of government and administration. If such a link is not created and if the Saigon government cannot become an "administering" regime utilizing both civil and military structures for this end, neither the RD program nor any similar program has any chance of success.

5
Vietnamese Political Processes Plus a War

Introduction

Both the First and the Second Indochina Wars were political struggles. Undoubtedly all wars are enmeshed ultimately in a web of political variables, but the encounters in Indochina are especially noteworthy for their political component. Other factors, economic and ideological ones, have not been irrelevant. But politics has been so all-pervasive in the two Vietnams and in Cambodia and Laos as to make the seemingly unending warfare almost unique. There exist many precedents of wars that have been relevant primarily to localized situations. However, the Indochina wars have made Clausewitz appear to be an amateur. Neither France nor the United States—nor China nor the Soviet Union—ever fully appreciated the political nature of Vietnamese warfare. Although a Viet nation has never incorporated all of the contested territory which has been fought over since even before Pearl Harbor, nationalism has always been a dimension (indeed a vital moving force). Disparate as the factions were and remain, a positive orientation toward a fatherland, even toward a race, has pervaded the troubled annals of all Vietnamese history since they initially resided as a race apart in southern China long before the birth of Christ. Compared to other developing nations where nationalism has been a Johnny-Come-Lately, Vietnamese have always been "nationalists" in the most chauvinistic definition of this concept.

Historically the question has never been whether the Vietnamese are the chosen people—even more than the Chinese the Vietnamese begin all discussion with this assumption. The question has always been, who will rule the nation? More specifically, which elite of which region will rule? Centuries have made regional divisions significant to all Viet-

namese. Communism, socialism, capitalism, et al. are primarily rationalizations for reinforcing one nationalist group vis-à-vis its competitors.
Religion and parties have supplemented regional orientations. In South
Vietnam as in North Vietnam the only universal query has always been:
Will we control the other zone or will it control us? Civil war was inevitable under such circumstances, and given the background of Vietnamese history, the next question was, inevitably: Do we invade them
or do they invade us? There is no identical situation. Germany and
Korea could be divided and the leaders of each divided zone could covet
the territory of the other zone. But in Vietnam division simply perpetuated what had existed since before the French arrival.

Vietnam remains, at the very least, a divided nation, as it has been
for centuries. The North would like to fulfill its manifest destiny and
conquer the South. The South would like to rule northern terrain but
does not possess the skill even to attempt to bring about a united fatherland, especially one subjected to southern rule. After the folly of the
Americanization of the war in 1965, the North turned the war into a
truly traditional conflict. The standard ingredients of the traditional
struggle were (1) throw out the foreigners and (2) North vs. South.
Washington fell into the trap easily because of the organizational opportunism of the US military. Following the failure of the American position, epitomized by the 1968 Tet and post-Tet campaigns, when the
USA irrevocably lost "its" war, the Indochina war returned to its North
vs. South dimensions. It became a test of wills between Hanoi and
Saigon. The American presence—though steadily diminishing—lost all
pertinence. It was no longer germane to the fight being fought. The USA
could be the supplier, it could use its massive air and sea power to punish the North and protect military forces of the South, it could pressure
for changes in the political system seemingly popular with sundry American constituencies, but the war had reverted. It had, of course, never
changed; there had been a temporary intrusion of a historically insignificant third party. The two perennial enemies were finally face to face,
aided by their "client suppliers." Even the once tremendous potential
of the National Liberation Front of South Vietnam became secondary
as the northerners placed it on the shelf for the truly important battle,
the attempt to consummate the ambitions of the march to the South
which had begun in earnest during the eleventh century.

The political struggle had turned toward Saigon's favor by the beginning of the 1970's. Politically the GVN, despite its perpetually fragile
nature, established more of a presence than it had experienced in a
decade. NLF withdrawals and infrastructure losses were factors. But
political system changes in South Vietnam were even more significant.

Refugees were increasingly resettled. More important were the quasi-autonomy of local elected councils, their power over budgetary affairs, augmented provincial council authority, a wider constituency role by National Assembly members, and land reform. Greater local roles by political parties (both civil and religious ones) began to expand political involvement. Many other things had not changed—corruption, military leadership in many spheres, centrifugal pressures by the host of interest groups, retention of centralized mandarinic administration even though forms of decentralization to village and provincial levels had an impact, tea house politics, patronage in appointments to ARVN leadership positions and to province chief posts.

None of the things which did not change aided the GVN's cause, although indirectly each was a factor in increasing Nguyen Van Thieu's power. Manipulating both GVN strengths and weaknesses, Thieu outdistanced all his rivals. His uncontested reelection in 1971, a product of design and of his misjudging his opponents, both added to and detracted from his preeminence. He lost some face, but his opposition looked foolish in the eyes of many Vietnamese. Ironically, nearly all observers assumed he definitely would have won in either a two- or three-candidate race. However, a majority in a three-sided contest was definitely not a certainty. Regardless, the high-handed methods used to insure him a large vote did not result in increased instability. Six months after his reelection South Vietnam was relatively stable, "secure"— relative to a decade or even a few years previously—and was surviving the phasing out of the American military presence. Still, gut weaknesses and potential for chaos remained inherent in the Thieu-led political system. The loyal and the not-so-loyal, but legal, opposition was biding its time, waiting and watching for Thieu to stumble, for some unanticipated peace agreement, for the impact of American withdrawal to have some effect which might give them an opportunity for experiencing a day of glory and of power. Party building continued under less than advantageous conditions but under conditions where this was at least plausible.

In short, when the People's Army of Vietnam (PAVN) invaded from the North during the 1972 winter-spring campaign, it attacked a more complacent and self-satisfied political system than it had known previously. The truth was that the South Vietnamese were actually getting cocky about their relative success. Even when the fact that all regular PAVN divisions were involved outside North Vietnam became apparent, relative complacency continued among most of the southern nationalists. Only when Quang Tri city fell and the southwestern provinces were genuinely threatened did the real import appear to be recognized. One should never be complacent about the heirs of the Tran Hung Dao squadron formed by Vo Nguyen Giap in the northeastern highlands of Tonkin in 1941.

After initial losses due to the sheer firepower of the opposition and then to inept military leadership the GVN pulled its forces together for the biggest military struggle of its history. And by then many of the gains of the 1969–71 period had been imperiled. Refugee totals again swelled astronomically. Local governments in many locales were eliminated. Highly vaunted reconstruction projects were destroyed. In many areas self-defense forces were routed by vastly superior forces. All parties, including "militant" Buddhists, did rally to the nationalist banner. But Thieu, after placing the nation's leading nonpolitical general in charge of I Corps and thereby reforming the northern front for a counterattack, then placed a most political general in command of the Mekong Delta. The latter immediately appointed close friends as province chiefs while the PAVN steadily moved from Cambodia to disrupt the advances which had occurred in the far south after 1969 and to assist the NLF in regaining some of the ground it had lost in the previous few years. All sides had once again moved around the rims of the seemingly endless circle of Vietnamese politics.

In Chapter 5 the web of political processes and warfare in South Vietnam is traced from approximately 1965 to 1973. It has been a highly complex political history. If there had been monolithic forces opposing each other, the story could have been described much more simply. But simplicity is one characteristic notably absent in the Vietnamese experience. Each essay covers slightly more than one year. Because changes are treated in sequence there are no introductions for the annual political-military analyses. The final essay in Chapter 5 provides some generalizations covering events leading to and including the Easter invasion or winter-spring offensive of 1972 and the 1973 ceasefire. This may enlarge upon a broader perspective of the sequence of events in the seven-year period.

Struggle Politics and the Bigger War

Struggle was the keynote for 1966 in South Vietnam.[1] It was ubiquitous within the structures representing the military, the administration, re-

This essay was co-authored with Dr. John C. Donnell.

ligion, political parties and even those structures directing the insurgency. An avenue for increased political participation by legitimized political interests was opened. As this avenue widened, historic regional differences were voiced once again. Even within the National Liberation Front (NLF) the perennial regional animosities were heightened. If South Vietnam had advanced little toward either tranquility or stability during the year, at least political apathy had lessened. And even if the administrative system remained incapable of implementing the goals of reconstruction and political action, many administrative and organizational activities of the NLF were for the first time hardly more successful than those of the Saigon government.

Politics of Religion

Two interrelated issues dominated South Vietnam's political process during 1966. First was the question of developing some form of representative base for the legitimate political system. Second was the actual struggle and the broader preparation for potential struggle over the issue of interest group access to and control over the administrative and policy formulation structures of the present and future governing apparatus. During the year the alignments relative to these issues shifted dramatically though religious and regional interests, represented within the military as well as in the administration and in the general political forces of the community, dominated the sometimes violent debates. Throughout the year the leadership of the Armed Forces Council managed to maintain its position but only by adopting the expedients (1) of acquiescence to demands for creation of a procedure for expanding representation and (2) of increasingly providing varied interests with formal access to the administrative system.

Recognizing the requirements for coopting nonmilitary elements and for responding to external pressures to provide some vestige of "self determination" as President Johnson mentioned in his State of the Union message, the National Directorate (at the time consisting of ten military leaders including the four semi-autonomous corps commanders) announced in January that a procedure would be created for an eventual new constitution. On January 18 Deputy Prime Minister Lieutenant General Nguyen Huu Co outlined steps for such a development, including appointment of a Democratic Building Consultative Council to draft a constitution, a November referendum on the constitution, and general elections in 1967. A further commitment to these steps was made in the February Declaration of Honolulu in that a "democratic constitution" was to be formulated followed by "ratification by secret ballot."

Through uncertainty over the speed with which the military actually would relinquish power and over the extent to which specific interests would be included or excluded under a constitution written and promulgated through military auspices most of Vietnam's political forces adopted either an *attentiste* stand or covertly opposed the Directorate's program. Opportunity for the more militant interests to resolve this uncertainty was presented by the Directorate itself on March 10 when, following a bitter clash between Prime Minister Nguyen Cao Ky and I Corps Commander Lieutenant General Nguyen Chanh Thi and Ky's threat of resignation, General Thi was removed for reasons of "health." Although this ostensibly increased the authority of the national regime over an area operated often independently of Saigon, the removal of the popular hero of the abortive 1960 anti-Diem coup immediately raised several issues to the surface. Particularly, questions of the roles of central Vietnam and of the United Buddhist Church (UBC) under any future constitution appeared to be at stake.

The Venerable Tri Quang, symbol of the overthrow of Diem and contender for power within the UBC as well as for power to influence the national government, provided the catalyst for both centrist and Buddhist militancy. Following the rapid rise of Buddhism as a political force during the 1963 crisis, after centuries of decline and a three-decade "revitalization movement," with Tri Quang as the most visible leader among his competitors, a new Buddhist power structure operating through the UBC had served as a government-toppling *enfant terrible* during 1964 and 1965. The Buddhist movement, despite internal dissension within the UBC and opposition of powerful southern Buddhist interests, appeared to be second in overt influence only to the shifting military leadership group. Within days following General Thi's removal, the UBC initiated a series of actions to obtain control from the military over both the timetable and the format of the proposed constitution and referendum. Demonstrations and strikes led by "struggle committees," including NLF-infiltrated student units in Hue and Da Nang, against the government of Chief of State Nguyen Van Thieu and Prime Minister Ky began in mid-March. Many civil servants and I Corps troops joined with the dissidents, a factor which, combined with the vacillation of division commanders in the center, led to temporary de facto secession of Hue and Da Nang. Civil war appeared imminent and even continued United States support for the Ky regime became questionable as the demonstrations increasingly emphasized anti-American sentiments.

Ky and the Directorate alternately made concessions and ordered displays of force. A succession of I Corps commanders, five in 11 weeks, proved unable or unwilling to obtain unity in the center. On April 3, the Directorate called for a National Political Congress composed of leading figures of all interests, but on the same day Ky stated he would "liberate" Da Nang from "communists" and shoot Thi's appointee as mayor. Two days later Vietnamese marines were landed in Da Nang by US planes, but Ky and Major General Nguyen Van Chuan (Thi's replacement as I Corps commander) agreed to avoid force. Ky agreed to retract his statement concerning communist control of Da Nang. In spite of this detente, demonstrations increased in intensity until the National Political Congress, under the chairmanship of Dr. Phan Quang Dan, called for an election. On April 14 Ky agreed to a Constitutional Assembly election within three to five months and Thieu issued a decree creating an Electoral Commission. This appeared to appease Tri Quang who, claiming Ky's move meant the government would be replaced after one quick election, was more or less successful in quieting the struggle committees, though dissident groups continued many of their activities.

The Tri Quang-Ky truce was of very limited duration. Electoral Commission approval of two elections on May 11, four days after Ky stated he planned to be in office for at least one year, was followed by the occupation of the headquarters of Lieutenant General Ton That Dinh (who had replaced Chuan) and of Da Nang itself on May 15. Despite suicides, the placing of altars in the streets of Hue and in other cities, violent demonstrations in Saigon and in Hue (including destruction of the USIS Library and the American consulate), and even a fast by Tri Quang, government forces moved methodically against Hue, against diehard remnants in Da Nang's Tinh Hoi Pagoda, and finally against the UBC's Secular Affairs Institute in Saigon. Tri Quang's removal from the Hue municipal hospital on June 20 cleared the Vietnamese political stage, at least temporarily, of Buddhist militancy.

Although experiencing phenomenal success since 1963, the Buddhist attack upon the Thieu-Ky government had proved to be a bitter failure. By 1966 the militant tactics of the UBC, its political orientation, and its inability to present constructive alternatives had exhausted much of the reservoir of good will among the general population. It had alienated important elements of the Buddhist community, particularly Mai Tho Truyen, chairman of the South Vietnam Buddhist Studies Association, who opposed the 1966 political activities of Tri Quang and who insisted upon "pure religious activities." Tri Quang's attempt to define the nature of the new constitution had alienated southern interests, important elements of the sects, and Catholic interests, despite his attempts to create a workable coalition with segments of these important forces.

Owing to his opposition to Ky, Rev. Hoang Quynh, the militant Tonkinese refugee leader, did join with Tri Quang as well as sect factions to oppose an election once the UBC in the summer decided to boycott the two-election system which retained Ky in power for at least another year. But the Archdiocese of Saigon remained opposed to the upheaval of Buddhist militants and refused to accept Hoang Quynh's Front of Citizens of All Faiths as a representative institution. In central Vietnam the struggle committees were actively opposed by village Catholics and were violently opposed by the Vietnamese Nationalist Party (VNQDD) and by the Dai Viet (Greater Vietnam) Party. Assassinations of VNQDD leaders and sacking of party offices were met by reprisals by party irregular forces (including American-trained Political Action teams) and by anti-Buddhist demonstrations.

Also devastating to the cause of the Tri Quang forces was the struggle for power within the UBC itself. Thich Tam Chau, leader of the Tonkinese refugee community and director for secular affairs, had in effect outmaneuvered Tri Quang for control of the national Buddhist movement. Like Tri Quang, but also like the Archdiocese of Saigon, Tam Chau openly regretted the absence of civilian rule. He opted for noncooperation with the government and issued orders for demonstrations in Saigon under pressure from Tri Quang's Saigon representative, Thich Thien Minh (the UBC commissioner for youth, who survived an attempted assassination on June 1). Yet Tam Chau hardly appeared displeased that the Saigon Students Union refused to join the militants as it had in the past. His attitude appeared clear when he told a group of 283 released on July 5 not to be "incited by anyone." He also decided to retire to Vung Tau during the election campaign, leaving Thich Thien Hoa (the leading southern Buddhist in the UBC) as acting chairman.

The split within the Buddhist movement was widened even further when Tam Chau returned from Vung Tau. Tri Quang, having terminated his fast, had joined with Thien Hoa in an appeal to Superior Tinh Khiet, and on October 30 the 86-year-old superior bonze appointed Thien Hoa to replace Tam Chau. This was splendid irony, for it was Hoa who supported Diem and condemned Tri Quang following the 1963 government pagoda raids. Thus a movement that in a brief three-year period had created the conditions leading to the fall of Ngo Dinh Diem, had influenced measurably the policies of successive governments, had established a university and expanded educational and social-medical-welfare facilities, and that had a greater potential for establishing cohesiveness than perhaps any other national institution, was reduced to becoming another of Vietnam's numerous factionalized parties.

Politics of Co-optation

If the competing forces in the South Vietnamese political arena were the principal obstruction to the militant Buddhists' drive to unseat the Thieu-Ky regime, it was due to a combination of political acumen and occasional good fortune that the American-supported Ky proved capable of balancing the diverse interest groups and thereby maintaining his own position. This was no inconsiderable task. The important interests which had no intention of permitting Tri Quang to dominate the national scene also overtly or covertly opposed or were lukewarm to Ky, and manifested little faith in vague assurances of a "democratic" Constitutional Assembly. Ky's trump card throughout the crisis was the fear of Tri Quang shared by southern and various party and religious interests.

The April National Political Congress was a convenient instrument for numerous political groups to influence the possible future structure of government and to call for elections and freeing of prisoners, while also condemning illegal demonstrations. Dr. Dan's leadership undoubtedly helped to legitimize the Congress as an intermediate step toward an elected government despite the absence of important Buddhist, Catholic, and Cao Dai elements. The Electoral Commission, chaired by Le Van An, who led the Japanese-sponsored Phuc Quoc-Cao Dai coalition against the French during the 1940's, gave many groups an opportunity to expand the legitimization process. Even the Buddhists sent representatives to the Electoral Commission and their delegation, headed by Tran Quang Thuan, walked out only after the Saigon government occupied Da Nang rather than after the Commission approved the two-election scheme.

The appointed organizations provided a procedure for coopting varied interest groups as supporters for the succession-to-power program advocated by the military leadership. In order to obtain shorter-range support the National Directorate was increased on June 1 from ten to 20, the increased number being civilians—two Buddhists, two Catholics, a Cao Dai, a Hoa Hao, a Dai Viet, a VNQDD, and two notables. Two weeks later a People-Military Council of 80 members (one-fourth from the military) was decreed to serve in an advisory capacity to the cabinet. Tran Van Van, a 70-year-old, noted southern separatist, was appointed chairman of the advisory body.[2]

The Ky government also attempted to gain support among southerners and Catholics through ministerial appointments and other means. Although Chief of State Thieu is a Catholic and Deputy Prime Minister Co is a southerner, Ky and other Tonkinese appeared overrepresented in ministerial, provincial, and military-administrative positions. This was hardly a favorable situation for a regime facing potential centrist secession. Among other important steps to meet southern criticism, Major General Nguyen Bao Tri was transferred from III Corps to head a major ministry (Justice, Information, Interior) and to supervise the conduct of the September 11 Constitutional Assembly election, and Dr. Nguyen Luu Vien (an important Mekong Delta Buddhist) was appointed a Deputy Prime Minister. Other Catholics were appointed to important positions in addition to General Tri, but as he was one of four Catholics on the National Directorate and presumably a former member of the Can Lao, his appointment was of especial importance. After the election Ky also promised the Catholic clergy a review of instances of political imprisonment after the revolt against Diem, and on October 26, nine political prisoners, including the once powerful Dr. Tran Kim Tuyen, director of social and political studies under Diem, were released.

These various efforts of Prime Minister Ky met with measurable success particularly during the Buddhist crisis and the election campaign. However, with the election over and the Constitutional Assembly debating, southern interests greatly increased the pressure upon Ky. The prime minister compromised several issues with the Cochinchinese but acquiesced to demands for increased southern representation through the government. The issue of a southern presence was intensified prior to the Manila Conference, when Brigadier General Nguyen Loan, head of the National Police, arrested the Deputy minister of health, Dr. Nguyen Tan Loc, who had criticized his superior for preference for Tonkinese. The resignation of Loan, a close friend of Ky who had an active role in the election and who led the government occupation of Hue in June after replacing Thi's appointee as police head, was demanded in a petition signed by 11 of 12 southerners in the cabinet.

Ky was able to delay threatened resignations until the termination of the conference. Four ministers did resign, including Minister of Finance Au Truong Thanh, who had directed the successful economic reforms earlier in the year and who was a potential candidate for national office in any election held in 1967. The prime minister, having persuaded several southern ministers to remain, then took the bold step in November of transferring powerful southerner Lieutenant General Dang Van Quang from his IV Corps fief to the cabinet. As a quid pro quo, six new southern cabinet ministers were appointed to replace the four who resigned, including Dr. Nguyen Van Tho, who was deputy minister of health under Diem, as minister of education. Also a number of southerners were placed in positions of responsibility throughout the governing military apparatus.

The Election and the Constitutional Assembly

Despite the struggles in the streets, the perennial coup plot rumors, and the dramatics of intraministerial and intra-Directorate antagonisms based primarily upon personal and regional issues, the election of September 11 for members of the Constitutional Assembly was unquestionably the most significant symbolic and perhaps actual political event of the year. It was opposed by the UBC and by Rev. Hoang Quynh's organization, subjected to harassment by the NLF—all ingredients less than auspicious for a free popular plebiscite. Nonetheless, the Vietnamese turned out at the polls in numbers certainly not far short of the official figure of 80.8 per cent (4,274,812) of registered voters (5,288,512). Percentages varied but all were consistently high, e.g., 83 per cent voted in the entire Delta, 87 per cent in I Corps (91 per cent in Hue and 81 per cent in Da Nang), 73 per cent in Gia Dinh, and 66 per cent in Saigon. As under Diem, varying but relatively low numbers cast blank ballots as a safe form of protest. However, as in 1953 when voting for legislative representatives and as in 1965 when voting for provincial and municipal councillors, residents of all regions found the opportunity to participate in a referendum proved a potent incentive.

The procedure where slates and proportional representation were used was complicated, and special representation procedures were provided for the tribesmen, Chams, and Cambodians. The special treatment for the tribesmen, who have been involved in several abortive revolts, was begun early in the year following the Honolulu Conference, with the appointment of Paul Nur as special commissioner for montagnards affairs, and was given added emphasis during October when a significant number of FULRO (Front for the Liberation of Oppressed Peoples) irregulars rallied, somewhat unenthusiastically, to the Vietnamese regime, which once again promised improvements in public services and citizenship conditions.

Police and civil servants registered voters and delivered registration cards when they were not claimed. Government seminars were held in nearly all communities, and civil servants worked actively on "information" programs. A house-to-house canvass was made wherever possible by government officials as well as by NLF agents. In certain areas military bloc votes were reported and there was covert pressure to vote, especially in Major General Vinh Loc's II Corps area, the assumption being that nonvoters might be denied certain privileges. Nonetheless, objective observers appear unanimous that the election of September 11 was freer than any other in Vietnam's history.

Statistics on those elected to the 117-member Constitutional Assembly reveal that nearly all of South Vietnam's major interest groups were represented. The UBC was the primary exception, although 34 Buddhists were elected. Thirty Catholics, ten Hoa Hao, and five Cao Dai, as well as nine tribesmen and Cham, and four Khmer were also elected. The average age was under 40, with the 25–34 age group larger than any other group. A high percentage were professionals of various types, 23 were provincial or municipal councillors, and only 20 of 64 military candidates won. Party affiliation was not a quotable statistic, given the personalized, shifting alignments of politics characteristic of South Vietnam, but ten admitted to being VNQDD members, eight were Dai Viet—both party groups being primarily from the Center—and two were adherents of FULRO.

Following a slow start wrangling over procedural matters, the Constitutional Assembly began to provide the appearance of fulfilling much of its promise. Phan Khac Suu, a 65-year-old southerner, former chief of state, who defied Diem and suffered imprisonment, and who had led an unsuccessful attempt earlier to combine the diverse sects of the Cao Dai, was selected as chairman. Dr. Phan Quang Dan, who was attempting to build a bloc among the councilors, refused to be a candidate for chairman, as did Dr. Dang Van Sung, who was working with Dr. Dan and Tran Quoc Buu of the powerful 300,000-member Confederation of Vietnamese Workers to form a farmer-labor alliance before the next election. Suu's principal opponent was Tran Dien, a Dai Viet from Thua Thien Province, who cooperated to some extent with Dr. Sung's attempt to build a political organization.

The capacity of the Constitutional Assembly to present views greatly at variance with the Directorate remained unclear. The Directorate formally could veto effectively any part of the proposed Constitution unless two-thirds of the membership voted to override it. Despite Thieu's apparent assurance to Dr. Sung that such vetoes were improbable, the military leadership refused to relinquish this prerogative. Once the Constitutional Assembly began its work in earnest, attempting to complete its work by March 1967, several features probably acceptable to the majority of members as well as to the Directorate appeared to have general acceptance, e.g., the American pattern of an elected president and a bicameral legislature. Regardless of the specifics of the proposed new government or of the nature of rapidly emerging new political alignments, the principal impediment to a viable political system naturally remained the continued presence of the "competing government," the National Liberation Front.

The Military Struggle

The war escalated rapidly during 1966. US ground forces outnumbered the 317,000 ARVN regulars by September and were scheduled to total 385,000 by the end of the year. The GVN had another 260,000 men in its Popular and Regional Forces plus National Police units, which also were being assigned to paramilitary functions. Attempts to enlarge the ARVN by another 100,000 men were largely frustrated by leaks at both ends of the system: draft dodging remained a serious problem and the total of desertions from all GVN forces by early December was estimated at over 120,000, though it was hoped that they would decline after harsher penalties were introduced in October. (Some authorities claimed most deserters eventually returned to the ranks, but other observers contended that the returnee rate was as low as 10–15 per cent.)

The NLF estimated total strength was 250,000 men, including some 110,000 regular troops, obtained by locally recruiting some 1,500 men per month and by receiving streams of northern infiltrators. The infiltration increased from an earlier rate of about 4,500 to 7,000 per month, totaling 48,000 by late November.

North Vietnamese statements began to emphasize a "single Vietnamese nation" view of the war and claim the demilitarized zone between North and South had lost its significance as a result of US/GVN air attacks on the North; and northern infiltrators tended increasingly to move across the DMZ though many still traveled down the circuitous, punishing "Ho Chi Minh" trails through Laos. There were reports that General Nguyen Chi Thanh, a member of the North Vietnam Politburo, had taken command of the communist-led forces in the South. There also were fragmentary reports of increased tensions between southern and northern elements of the communist forces. Obviously, whatever political and military initiative and autonomy had remained in the hands of southern NLF leaders had decreased markedly.

With the expanded role of ethnic northern troops in the war, allied analysts came to distinguish between "the two wars": one marked by larger hostilities between the (northern) People's Army of Vietnam (PAVN) and mainly American units; and the other fought usually by the ARVN against smaller NLF forces, perhaps reinforced by PAVN elements. By late November, the largest of the big campaigns, Operation Attleboro, ended after six weeks of sporadic combat pitting 26,000 Americans and a few ARVN companies against NLF units in Zone C, but most of the larger operations had occurred in the highlands and other regions of central Vietnam.

In the "first war," particularly, it was usually impossible for the allied forces to clear and hold much territory after enemy units had been thrown back; these operations were designed largely to spoil NLF-PAVN preparations for large offensives and in this they were successful, preventing the enemy from initiating a single major campaign during the year. This achievement took on added significance in the light of an apparent Hanoi decision for a major effort to exploit the political turmoil in the cities of central Vietnam and win a victory sufficiently impressive to influence the outcome of the US November elections as well as to weaken GVN morale.

The NLF Main Force and PAVN battalions continued to fight well despite the mauling suffered by some units in the half dozen major operations mounted against them since the arrival of US combat troops in 1965. In the big battles, the ratio of NLF-PAVN killed ranged from three to six to one for the Americans. This, plus the increased initiative and mobility of the allied forces, was reported to have brought communist strategists to a decision to put more emphasis on a more rudimentary stage of guerrilla warfare and to reorganize some battalions into smaller operational units. (The validity of the allies' "body-count" system for tabulating enemy dead was still challenged. One reason was the difficulty of distinguishing between bodies of guerrillas and ordinary villagers, although this was less troublesome in the sparsely inhabited central highlands and NLF base areas such as Zones C and D.)

It was expected that US forces would continue to bear the brunt of the "first war" and that ARVN units increasingly would be drawn off for pacification duty in the villages, a role in which they had not often distinguished themselves thus far. However, observers agreed that though communist leaders were becoming convinced they could not inflict spectacular military defeat on the allied forces, they could continue the "second" or guerrilla war for a long time. And even if the allied effort remained resolute, prosecution of that war would require better methods and more active South Vietnamese support than had been found thus far.

An offer made by the allies at Manila on October 25 to withdraw US troops within six months after "the other side withdraws its forces to the North, ceases infiltration and the level of violence thus subsides" aroused jitters among US and GVN officials who believed that a formal PAVN withdrawal might mask continued support for a long guerrilla campaign in the South. Later, US officials stressed that the withdrawal of NLF as well as PAVN units would be demanded and this, plus the subsidence of violence requirement would be a surer guarantee against renewed insurgency in the event that Hanoi, initially hostile to the proposal, later showed some interest.

NFL-PAVN defections climbed sharply, reaching almost 18,000 by late November as compared with 11,000 for 1965. Most of them were attributed to the hardships of protracted war and the fearsome firepower of the allies rather than to political conversions. Many of the defectors were youth who had been subjected to an NLF recruiting process of abduction first and indoctrination later.

The usual treatment of defectors left much to be desired in the view of many US advisors. In numerous provincial *chieu hoi* ("open arms") centers, political reorientation classes were heavily propagandistic and much-needed vocational training was largely nonexistent. After 45 days, ordinary defectors were released, often with bleak prospects for the jobs or military service they desired, the Vietnamese officials' general distrust of defectors posing a serious barrier to their integration in the GVN system.

Attrition in NLF ranks was felt both in the lower echelon village civilian cadre and in the rank-and-file of military units. Pressures of the expanded war made village agents increasingly heavy-handed in tax collections and recruiting, particularly in the contested zones. This, plus the increasing war-weariness of peasants in areas exposed to punishing military operations, continued to reduce drastically the more spontaneous types of peasant support received by the NLF earlier. This war-weariness was characterized by a preoccupation with the survival of the immediate family and indifference and dread toward all outside forces, GVN as well as NLF.

The North Vietnam and NLF position on negotiations[3] changed little although there was a flurry of hope that an interview given

Australian newsman Wilfred Burchett by Nguyen Huu Tho, chairman of the NLF Central Committee, on August 28 and broadcast by Hanoi a month later represented something of a compromise. Tho had seemed to indicate that US troops might not necessarily have to be withdrawn before negotiations and that the NLF might not reserve to itself the role of exclusive spokesman for the southern Vietnamese people in such parleys. Subsequent northern and NLF statements squashed these hopes, however, and a week later Hanoi also condemned U Thant's proposal that both sides gradually scale down ground hostilities.

In the Mekong Delta IV Corps, ground fighting was on a smaller scale than elsewhere, partly because NLF forces there had sent contingents to the bigger campaigns further north. But it was partly due also to an "accommodation" in some areas between NLF and especially the GVN local forces whereby neither side aggressively sought engagement, though the three regular divisions there performed well and were perhaps the ARVN's finest.

However, observers anticipated heavier NLF attacks in the Delta and a consequent need for the introduction of US troops there. A first battalion was stationed in Long An Province and more American units were to follow. Official planners had weighed the reluctance of some ARVN field commanders there to share operational responsibility and also warnings that political complications might increase as the foreign presence was enlarged. These problems became somewhat less difficult with the removal of the IV Corps commander, General Quang, who had resisted the American entry there partly because it would disturb his own satrapy. One question that remained was the political impact to be produced by stepped-up combat involving massive American firepower in this most heavily populated region of the country.

There was telling evidence, too, that heightened US and other foreign allied military effort was meeting with declining effort and aggressiveness from the South Vietnamese military. Thus, while US casualty rates were rising, those of the South Vietnamese were running lower than in 1965. The city bourgeoisie usually understood little of the complexity of the war in the countryside and was reluctant to make sacrifices for the war effort or nation-building under prevalent conditions of uncertainty; and it was this bourgeoisie which continued to staff the officer corps which also furnished most of the province and district chiefs. One potentially significant reform was in view: officers' commissions, hitherto awarded only to holders of the second baccalaureate, truly a bourgeois elite group, were to be offered to a first group of able non-commissioned officers after additional training.

Rural Pacification—"Revolutionary Development"

At the Honolulu conference, President Johnson and Premier Ky gave a highly publicized endorsement to GVN-directed "social revolution" to steal political thunder from the NLF. It was to be particularly channeled through the rural hamlet pacification program, thereafter renamed "Revolutionary Development," in four priority areas.

Considerable hope was held that the RD program, which trains 59-man cadre teams for 13 weeks, would provide new skills, political motivation, and protective military capability for the men and women in this exposed assignment. A large training camp at Vung Tau had been set up earlier by the CIA but was to be taken over by AID. Vietnamese and US pacification experts, recalling the haste and superficiality of the "strategic hamlet" and other earlier programs, stressed the need for high quality in training and operations and to guard against unrealistic pressure for statistically impressive results.

The 1966 goal was set at 1,900 hamlets; in 1,000 of these, existing but shaky GVN control was to be consolidated and in the remaining 900, it was to be wrested from the NLF. The able director of the program, Brigadier General Nguyen Duc Thang, said he would be satisfied if 75 per cent of this quota were realized, as long as it represented genuine pacification, and he insisted that the cadre teams would remain in their target hamlets indefinitely if necessary to achieve real results.

In a minimum of two or three months in a hamlet, a team focused on "economic development" projects of the residents' choosing, such as the building of schoolrooms, dispensaries and roads; on "census-grievance" activities involving confidential, repeated interviews with all adult residents to probe local political responses to their own projects and the local administration and to obtain intelligence on the remaining NLF infrastructure; and on "civil affairs" preparation for election of a hamlet council.

Cadre training and motivation continued to pose problems reflecting the undeveloped state of South Vietnamese political consensus. A principal problem was one of reconciling demands for quantity and quality of cadres. Nine thousand new cadres and retrained older Civil Action cadres were turned out in the first two classes in the new series. Twenty-three thousand cadres, mostly training in earlier programs, were operating in the hamlets and the total was expected eventually to reach a possible total of 150,000. At mid-year it was revealed that the training program had been manipulated by the camp commandant to favor a Dai Viet Party faction over the government, which his political trainers described as inept and corrupt. In areas of central Vietnam, the cadre teams were dominated by the VNQDD party, arousing misgivings in GVN leaders having other political affiliations.

By late October, AID reports indicated that about 4,300 hamlets were rated as reasonably secure, an increase of some 840 in 1966. An additional 2–3 per cent or a total of about 57 per cent of the rural population thus was considered to be in GVN-controlled zones and the rest was believed to be fairly evenly divided between NLF and contested zone categories.

Unofficial sources continued to report, however, that the pacification effort had encountered serious problems in most areas except Binh Dinh Province, where it had enjoyed a combination of good leadership and strong protective screening by Korean, US and ARVN military forces. Other areas sometimes lacked these factors and were bedeviled by spotty cadre performance, and suspicion and misuse of the program by local officials. Another thorny problem was overall coordination, because the enterprise had grown to such huge proportions. (Perhaps three-fourths of all US "project aid"—that earmarked for specific projects and totaling $589 million in fiscal 1966—was being channeled into RD, and a sizable amount of US military aid money and effort were supporting it at least indirectly.) In November, top control was assigned more explicitly to program director Deputy Ambassador William Porter.

On the Vietnamese side, General Thang's Ministry of Revolutionary Development became a super-ministry, absorbing related organs. Thang was highly respected as dedicated and incorruptible but US officials were uneasy about expressing admiration for him too openly in the context of Vietnamese internal-political rivalries, particularly since the general did not have an influential personal following in the officer corps.

One encouraging part of this picture was some spontaneous village literacy training and social work being conducted by students in such groups as National Voluntary Service and the (Buddhist) Van Hanh University. Students originally had asked to be allowed to take over the post-military pacification of an entire province. Premier Ky instead encouraged them to direct their development efforts to Saigon's insecure, slum-ridden Eighth Ward, where they proceeded to do an outstanding job.

Meanwhile, the GVN moved slowly in examining ways of integrating land reform into the RD campaign. The GVN's conservative land reform had stalled after 1960 due to insecurity and lack of official enthusiasm. The government had begun again in September 1965 to issue new land ownership certificates to peasants and it ruled also that year

that village communal lands, formerly rented to the highest bidder, were
to be rented at fair rates to veterans and the poor. The "Komer Report"
of September 1966 said that the GVN was going ahead with the distribution of 1.2 million acres of expropriated and government land, and
that much of it would be given to refugees. All of these efforts, however,
remained sporadic.

An Giang Province was a special model in both the RD and land
reform programs. Because it already had been "pacified" by the zealously anti-NLF elements of the Hoa Hao sect, large-scale land redistribution was to be attempted soon. Aerial photography was being used
to speed up the preparatory cadastral survey.

The expanding war caught many peasants in the middle. No one
knew the total number of civilian noncombatants fallen casualty to the
fighting, for official records were not kept on such victims. One veteran
newsman estimated roughly in October that the monthly rate was running at somewhere around 1,000 killed per month and twice that number wounded.[4]

A certain amount of the damage to civilians and their property resulted from GVN/US operations against NLF resistance in and near
hamlets. In other cases, although Vietnamese government forces were
under orders not to use "harassing and interdiction" artillery fire against
any area not officially designated as NLF-controlled, they did not always
obey this directive. ("H and I" fire is laid down randomly without observation of results and hits noncombatants more frequently than observed fire.)

Air operations were stepped up until total tonnages of bombs
dropped on North and South Vietnam exceeded those loosed on Germany during peak months of World War II. Occasional strikes were
flawed by operational errors or initiated on the basis of erroneous intelligence. After the most grievous incident on August 9 in which US jets
attacted two Mekong Delta hamlets and killed and wounded about 150
noncombatants, General Westmoreland ordered a review of existing military procedures with a view toward minimizing such casualties. In cases
of acknowledged US responsibility for such a death, the US paid
an indemnity of about $35. (Over 6,000 claims were filed by August
for compensation for deaths and wounds resulting from allied military action.) Many peasants were hit also in NLF-instigated incidents of terrorism and sabotage as the NLF, under increasing military pressure and the attrition of protracted conflict, tended to become
less discriminating in its target selection and to rely on more random
violence for political intimidation.

The harshness of life in the countryside continued to drive throngs of refugees to GVN areas. The total of persons who had left their homes since the disastrous central Vietnam floods of 1964–65 now totaled over one million. In the year ending in September, over a quarter million had been resettled in new homes or returned to their own by the GVN; but the total housed in temporary facilities had increased to over half a million. GVN allowances to refugees frequently were held up by red tape and corruption, and many US advisors considered that the GVN was keeping these allowances too small. Originally, a refugee got seven cents a day for 30 days and then a lump sum of about US$35, and finally, after over a year, the allowance was raised to only ten cents.

Economic and Social Pressures

A billion-dollar military construction program poured additional men, material and money into the country. It taxed available labor and other resources seriously, but it also provided new and lucrative jobs for many thousands of Vietnamese including refugees from the hinterland, and provided hundreds of installations usable eventually for peacetime purposes. Among the projects were new docking facilities at Cam Ranh Bay, a new housing and storage center for the American top command at Long Binh and a nearby new port area (Newport) upriver from the overtaxed piers of Saigon.

Pressures on the Vietnamese economic system became intense. To check soaring inflation, the piaster was devalued in June from 73 to 118 to the dollar. Retail prices continued to rise an additional 25 per cent in the next two months, leveled off temporarily and then climbed again steeply. Retail rice prices rose over 42 per cent between June and mid-November, although the government set an artificially low price for a time to cushion the inflation for city dwellers, apparently without hurting rice farmers unduly. Even so, both the inflation and the devaluation hit the urban middle class hardest. Because some 400,000 tons of the rice crop would be lost during the year due to peasants' abandoning their fields, the US shipped in 450,000 tons.

The huge amounts of aid and military supplies rushed into the country brought reports of large-scale corruption and open blackmarket sales of such goods in the cities. Hard-pressed to break through red tape in 1965 to sustain their expanding programs and head off an inflationary crisis, AID and military planners had decided to expedite the shipments without elaborate, time-consuming distribution controls. But from September 1966 on, new controls were imposed. The problem was so huge, however, that portions of these supplies diverted to illegal purposes in some areas allegedly ran as high as 40 per cent but official estimates in November were 5–6 per cent.

The pressures of the new hordes of Americans and other foreigners and the economic opportunities available through higher-paying jobs and graft twisted the social fabric. Bar girls, cab drivers and profiteers flourished. Civil servants, squeezed to make ends meet, took their opportunities for supplementary income where they found them. US officials strove to prevent Saigon's being completely transformed into a garrison town and devised policies to transfer thousands of military personnel to housing outside the city and allow only one-quarter of off-duty men in a unit to visit the city at a time.

Thus in 1966 some aspects of the shooting war against the communist-led forces were relatively successful, particularly the campaigns fought by American troops. Their resources and enthusiasm channeled into civic action programs added another political dimension to their efforts, while the impact of their awesome destructive military capabilities in the countryside and the sheer size of the allied effort crammed into this small country added yet others. The original longer-range intention of erecting a security umbrella over South Vietnam long enough for indigenous leadership and nation-centered political motivation to strengthen seemed to be yielding meager results. Protracted political instability had long stimulated many in the middle and upper classes, including numerous ARVN leaders, to devote priority effort to the creation of a nest egg abroad to assure one's family's survival elsewhere if conditions at home became intolerable. Now many perceived the vastly increased influx of foreign military assistance and aid goods as additional resources to be exploited in this manner. An eventual leveling off of the rate of inflow, tighter official controls on its deposition and the prospects of greater political stability all would help to diminish the temptations and anxieties in this diversion of resources, but the habit by now was deeply enough ingrained to pose a continuing problem for a long time to come.

Thus, the still tenuous prospects for access to political power by a wider group of civilians had injected a certain note of challenge into politics which had not existed the previous year. But the possibilities for markedly more responsible and effective leadership still appeared to be remote.

Political, Military and Constitutional Arenas in Nation Building

During South Vietnam's 1967 presidential campaign numerous candidates including General Nguyen Van Thieu outlined steps for terminating hostilities.[5] Potentiality for peace initiatives loomed above other political issues. However, at the end of 1967 neither side was prepared to consider peace negotiations seriously. Both proclaimed "victory" policies. The NLF and Hanoi asserted they would win. Thieu would talk on his terms only. The United States' position articulated by Ambassador Ellsworth Bunker, General William Westmoreland, and Deputy Ambassador Robert Komer was that the war was being won.

Westmoreland spoke of four phases, a reverse adaptation of the Mao-Giap phases. Phase I was the period to mid-1966, a stage of saving an unviable nation, construction, and buildup. The third phase would occur in 1968 and involve an ARVN take-over, a local forces build-up, and Delta pacification, while the final phase would be victory with the ARVN in full charge and the opposition infrastructure destroyed. This optimistic time table assumed an American phase-out in two years. Westmoreland described Phase II, mid-1966 through 1967, as one of driving the enemy to sanctuaries (where PAVN regulars were increasingly centered), generally reducing the enemy's total potential, and building South Vietnam militarily and politically.

American estimates were based upon a revised intelligence system.[6] It is difficult to assess to what extent official 1967 statistics were a function of improved tabulation processes as opposed to military and pacification gains. Even a sophisticated system of intelligence operated in probabilities rather than charted fact. Yet, two and one-half years after the large mid-1965 buildup, real though extremely expensive gains were to be noted in official claims: (1) There was an NLF loss of control of from 4 to 2.5 million people during the entire period, and a population increase under GVN control to 67 per cent of South Vietnam's 17.1 million inhabitants—both estimates assume specific definitions for "loss" and "control" ("control" including hamlet types A, B, and C, being loosely defined for 4.3 million in type C); (2) PAVN infiltration decreased from 14,000 a month in mid-1966 to 5,000 to 7,000 during 1967; (3) officials noted a decrease of 40,000 in total opposition forces in 1967—Saigon estimated in November that NLF-PAVN forces totaled 223,000–248,000 (a considerable drop from the 297,000 claimed a year before, even accounting for new intelligence techniques), main line forces were 118,000, support and administrative were 35,000 to 40,000, local military units 70,000–90,000, local officials 75,000–85,000 and village self-defense and secret self-defense 30,000–50,000; (4) defections were double the 1966 totals, infiltrators' losses increased measurably (to 10–12 per cent), NLF recruitment dropped sharply and became less selective, many NLF main force groups consisted increasingly of PAVN forces (reportedly 50 per cent in numerous battalions) and approximately half the opposition battalions were so inadequately staffed as to be unfit for combat.

Combined with physical devastation in the DRVN resulting from intensified bombing, decreased production, poor harvests, halved export volumes since 1965, and increased dependency upon China, the Soviet Union and eastern Europe, the brutal statistics of war in the South were viewed as signs of victory by Washington. The picture appeared darker for the DRVN when southern manpower figures (unquestionably reflecting trends if not quantitative reliability) were added to manpower pressures in the North, which was estimated to have 55,000 in the South, 35,000 in the DMZ, 30,000–40,000 in Laos, 100,000 regulars in the North, a reserve twice the size of its regular force, 175,000 in air defense, and 500,000 in maintenance of the transport system. Yet, official estimates of significant morale problems among NLF-PAVN forces were not manifested in large-scale desertions even under the *chieu hoi* returnee program, nor did the opposition note a marked decline in leadership capacity, nor did the NLF ability to revert to Phase II guerrilla warfare and thereby its potential to continue the struggle indefinitely lessen appreciably. Soviet aid can increase greatly without undue strain, and it is unlikely the 15-ton daily supply infiltration rate can be effectively reduced.

In the final analysis, the most telling information was the number of administrative and local officials, many trained in the North but all capable of maintaining parallel hierarchies, struggle movements and the entire infrastructure (however amended) for an extended period (see Chapters 2 and 4). No amount of military personnel or material could dent the armor of that infrastructure. Instead this was a function of a viable administrative state. If the Second Republic actually governed the "67 per cent" of the population under its "control," optimizing the use of pacification structures while also providing services to and co-opting indigenous groups in the vastly diffracted South Vietnamese social system, the NLF infrastructure would find survival impossible. It was presumably a function of all the "democracy-building" steps throughout 1967, beginning with the activities of the Constituent Assembly, to move forward on an exchange of the GVN for the NLF infrastructure.

Constitutional Politics

The Constituent Assembly was able to force the Military Directorate to assume a stance of first among equals. This group was elected in a relatively open electoral process, representing on occasion the patronage of government and military leaders, but mostly representing party or regional interests (see the preceding section). There was no question of its being a bona fide competitor for power. Militant Buddhist and Catholic elements boycotted the 1966 election, but interests of the unrepresented were not ignored, as they retained power in other political arenas. A government bloc continually voiced sentiments a majority could not ignore. Occasions of blatant regime pressures were rare but significant. The government veto, which could be overruled by a two-thirds vote of the total membership, was a formality permitting continual unstated pressure. But Thieu assured Phan Khac Suu that it would not be used after its repeal was made an ultimatum by the Assembly. A covert threat by Premier Nguyen Cao Ky in the person of General Nguyen Ngoc Loan was a reminder of the nature of physical power in Saigon.

Yet, the Assembly heard criticisms previously not articulated in open, legitimate councils. The members represented constituencies, they could assume American support however tertiary, and the personalities assembled were important in national politics, e.g., Suu, Phan Quang Dan, and Dang Van Sung. Questions such as barring military men from politics, the appointment or election of local government chiefs, and the minimum age of the president (Tran Van Van proposed 40, which excluded Ky) were controversial, resulting typically in a compromise but never with a complete loss by the government. On March 9 the Assembly voted, 92:7, to remain in office as a National Assembly until the Second Republic took office, to write electoral laws, and to approve the election of the president, a violation of a government decree and in opposition to Thieu-Ky. It also agreed to "permit" the two directorate leaders to remain in office. On March 27 the Armed Forces Council approved the new Constitution, albeit hesitantly due to restrictions on executive power. The Constitution became effective April 1, although Catholics protested the deletion of reference to God Almighty (done at

Thich Tam Chau's insistence). Hassles continued as the Assembly decided to hold separate presidential and Senate elections despite government protests, relinquishing only at threat of a boycott by Le Phuoc Sang's Democratic Alliance.

The Constitution of the Republic of Vietnam contains the germ for a progressive, viable nation. It proclaims a republican form of government, explicitly opposes communism, and spells out in detail a set of citizen rights and duties, including procedural rights (e.g., bans torture, requires defense counsel), religious freedom, freedom for political parties, freedom of unionization, and the right to hold private property. It skirts land reform, advocating the raising of rural living standards and helping farmers obtain land. A bicameral National Assembly is provided. Members of the Lower House are elected by districts for four-year terms. Upper House members are elected nationwide for six years. The Assembly has powers to vote legislation, declare war, hold peace talks and "control the government in carrying out of national policy." Broad responsibility is allocated to the Lower House; bills must be submitted there and can be approved by a two-thirds majority even if disapproved by the Upper House. Budgetary proposals are approved by the Assembly, though expenditures approved above the executive budget must be accompanied by equivalent revenues. These powers are the most extensive of any elected body in Vietnam's history, particularly as neither the DRVN Assembly nor the one under Diem performed more than perfunctory ratifications of decisions.

The executive includes an elected president and vice president, and a prime minister and cabinet appointed by the president. Formally, the president is supreme commander of the armed forces, chairman of the National Security Council and presiding officer of the Council of Ministers. The president also "determines national policy." Under appropriate circumstances the vice president might serve primarily honorific functions. The Thieu-Ky compromise of June 1967, however, provides the new vice president with exceptional prerogatives for the period of the two executives' rapprochement. By law the vice president is chairman of the Cultural and Educational Council, the Economic and Social Council, and the Ethnic Minority Council (one-third appointed by the president and two-thirds elected by the ethnic minorities). These three councils, acting effectively, could provide a framework historically absent for liaison between the central regime and affected constituencies. For example, commitments to FULRO to avert tribal revolts could be consummated through an effective Ethnic Council.[7]

The Constitution recognized the principle of local separation of power, an important innovation if implemented, and recognized villages, provinces, cities, and the capital as legal entities. Each local government has an elected deliberative body (council) and elected heads of executive agencies (chiefs and mayors). Provinces did elect councils in 1965, but the president appoints province chiefs during his first term. This proviso, as well as omission of the important district level as a legal regional entity, were compromises. The result is to continue, regardless of promised administrative reforms, the important role of the national executive and presumably of the military in the administration of local affairs. An attempt at judicial reform and at checks-and-balances is also incorporated in the Constitution. A Supreme Court selected by the president and the Assembly from lists provided by associations of judges, prosecutors, and lawyers is empowered to interpret the Constitution and rule on the constitutionality of laws, decrees and administrative decisions. Further, a Special Court can remove members of the national executive from office in instances of high crimes and treason. Finally, and potentially quite significant, an Inspectorate is created to look into accounts, audit property of government officials and "inspect, control and investigate personnel of all public agencies directly or indirectly engaged in corruption, speculation, influence peddling or acts harmful to the national interest."

Nation Building and Political Viability

When Nguyen Van Loc, first prime minister of the Second Republic of Vietnam, announced the government's program in November, his position appeared anticlimactic. It was an inauspicious initiation by the Cochinchinese prime minister, culminating well over a year of intensive political activity beginning during the spring and summer of 1966. Loc's pronouncement was viewed by the universally cynical South Vietnamese elite as a continuation of discredited policies. Loc's cabinet of preelection ministers (technicians and generals) combined with Thieu's appointment of Nguyen Van Huong as secretary general to the presidency rivaling Loc, and with underlying threats of pro-Ky officials' resignations, hardly allayed this cynicism. Actually the new government's program was relatively progressive. Yet, any potential dent in the massive politico-socio-economic difficulties was contingent upon drastic steps aimed at complete revitalization of the body politic and a definitive co-optation of the disparate interest groups competing violently in the political arena. The nation-building, constitutional-electoral processes of 1966-67 were gauged to capture the imagination of these interest groups. Failure to achieve this goal hampered the viability of the Second Republic even prior to its formation.

Notably absent from Loc's program was reference to a possible peace initiative. Thieu's role as advocate of peace discussions was greatly predicated upon pressures in the Vietnamese political scene and upon contingencies arising from the campaign. Prior to the election, consideration of this possibility was viewed officially as prejudicial to the war effort and perhaps even traitorous. Restrictions placed upon candidatures for the various elective positions precluded not only communists but neutralists and those with certain improper leanings. Press censorship and closings of newspapers also reflected this policy. The writers of the Constitution managed assiduously to avoid overt acceptance of the concept of negotiations. However, the presidential campaign dramatically manifested the significance of civilian support for a termination of hostilities.

The NLF. In addition to the omission of a peace platform, the Loc program was modest in comparison to the new program promulgated by the NLF after the presidential election. The NLF statement, first since 1960, outbid the government on numerous counts. Modeled on the early Viet Minh platform of consolidation of all interests under a broad united front, protections for all groups except a few irreconcilable elements, and a generally social democratic, nationalistic, gradualist political philosophy, the NLF offered something for everyone. Included in the NLF platform were provisions for a social security system, ethnic and religious liberties, equal rights for women, land purchase for equitable distribution, property rights for religious institutions, low interest loans through a state bank, business protection through customs, import restrictions and foreign manufacturing prohibitions for indigenous industries, and a "democratic" national-union government. In fact, presumably the NLF would eliminate structures created during 1966–67 by the GVN and repeat the Constitution-writing and legislative and other electoral processes in its own version of a "democracy-building" process. Nothing is mentioned concerning negotiations, but rather a "victory" policy is proclaimed. Reunification of the two Vietnams is envisioned as a gradual, long-range goal.

In brief, the NLF program is to "unite the entire people, resolutely defeat the United States imperialists' war of aggression, overthrow their lackey puppet administration, establish a broad national, democratic, peaceful, neutral and prosperous South Vietnam, and proceed toward the peaceful reunification of the fatherland."[8] Timing of the program, agreed upon in August and officially presented by NLF Secretary General Huynh Tan Phat to an extraordinary Congress, was unquestionably tied to the establishment of the Second Republic.

The most difficult aspect of the NLF program to assess is the extent to which it is a southern manifesto. It mentions a nonsocialist South Vietnam, progressive and neutral, but a separate zone for the foreseeable future. Hanoi has officially acknowledged a similar goal. Yet Ho also spoke of the necessity for a socialist revolution to follow the liberation revolution, although agreeing upon the need for a broad front at each stage of struggle. Hanoi and the NLF also appear to have less than consistent policies concerning the nature of national liberation struggles. The NLF has indicated it perceives the Lin Piao rationale as correct, i.e., consolidation of united front forces in a revolutionary, guerrilla warfare strategy. But as part of North Vietnam's continued balancing act between its giant allies, Ho, Le Duan and Giap ended 1967 with lavish praise for the Soviet Union and praise for China. This could hardly offset Hanoi's summer condemnation of the cult of personality, i.e., Mao, and of the Chinese Cultural Revolution. Foremost, Giap's stand for use of large-scale forces and offensives, simultaneously with guerrilla warfare, appeared in opposition both to Lin Piao and the NLF.

By the end of 1967, Hanoi was definitely not in the camp of China, an event made more palatable to many by the death of Truong Chinh's ally, a Giap competitor and leader of PAVN forces in the South, General Nguyen Chi Thanh, as a result apparently of a bombing raid in Tay Ninh Province.[9] On the other hand, Hanoi was hardly a satellite of the Soviet Union. International politics prevented either Moscow or Peking from dominating Hanoi's strategy. This was a quite different story from the Hanoi-NLF relationship where the estimated 15-tons-daily infiltration of supplies and materials had an importance far outdistancing its volume and where increasingly PAVN were being used in NLF main forces operations, embracing the far south for the first time. Unquestionably elements in the NLF were attempting a balancing act themselves, but a letter from Nguyen Huu Tho to Ho declaring the latter as leader of the entire nation was perhaps more a sign of the shift in strength in the South rather than a tactical maneuver to please the NLF's ally.

Conclusion

The nation-building procedures of 1967, even when combined with definite military advances, did not permeate the underlying sources of

Saigon's difficulties. Corruption remained rampant, warlordism at corps and lower levels continued, disaffection among interests was only barely reduced, the NLF infrastructure was perpetuated as its principal source of strength, and external influences upset the political balance within both the GVN and the NLF.[10] Tremendous refugee problems, involving over 800,000 persons (two-thirds children), have led to what Gerald C. Hickey has spoken of as "a rootless urban proletariat." This, added to economic inflation and physical destruction, threatens the fabric of the nation's social structure. ARVN capabilities and motivations, with important exceptions, were often figments of American publicity.[11] Despite the weakened state of the NLF, it would remain a formidable competitor unless the Second Republic proved capable against fantastic odds of implementing the spirit and letter of both the new Constitution and Thieu's campaign pledges of administrative reform. Even after the electoral stages in "democracy building," the political-administrative system faced much more complicated problems of nation building and the creation of viable government, steps requisite to General Westmoreland's Phase III regardless of difficulties encountered by the DRVN and the NLF.[12]

The Politics of Peace

The politics of peace dominated 1968 in South Vietnam.[13] Peace as a thoroughly abstract concept was favored by all factions. The circumstances of peace, however, constituted another facet entirely. For peace could mean potentially a freedom of movement, a freedom from brutal physical annihilation, and national independence. But, depending upon numerous contingencies, it could mean many other things to specific groups constituting a large majority of the southern population. Fears ranged from loss of political power to the possibility of genocide. Tonkinese domination was vehemently opposed. Communist domination was unacceptable to the nationalists, the Catholics, the sects, the military, and to the host of Buddhist groups as well. National Liberation Front aspirations called for a certain type of peace, primarily one in which at the least its adherents would not face annihilation and at the most would involve participation in political power under conditions auspicious for fairly immediate full assumption of power.

Both the nationalists and the NLF felt their futures rested too much on a force beyond their control, namely, external support. Saigon feared an American betrayal, but perhaps no less than the NLF feared a betrayal by Hanoi. The nationalists had survived one withdrawal by a western power. Southern communist and other insurgent forces had experienced Tonkinese politics of expediency at their expense—in 1946 when Ho agreed to a French southern presence, after 1950 when the DRVN leadership effectively wrote off Cochinchina to a role limited to insurgents' survival in order to devote attention farther north, and in 1954 when the Viet Minh agreed to partition. While neither Saigon nor the NLF initiated peace moves, both were compelled to devote their energies to responding to the peace politics receiving increasing emphasis in Washington and Hanoi.

In the United States, public opinion, increasingly potent criticisms in the Senate, and a presidential election developed a phase of peace politics against which Saigon's varying attempts at sabotage were futile. President Johnson's March 31 announcement of a bombing halt north of the twentieth parallel (actually the nineteenth parallel) and his dramatic decision not to seek reelection in effect decided the issue. The politics of peace, not the politics of war, were to prevail. Agonizing as the politics of details would be, the agenda had been set. Hanoi's role in peace politics was evident before this point, but it too had to struggle through the agonies of the stages of this agenda. Foreign Minister Nguyen Duy Trinh in Hanoi and Mai Van Bo in Paris had changed the term "might" to "will" in describing events to follow a bombing halt. Ho's agreement to contacts following the Johnson announcement was a logical sequence in implementing the master strategy after the ill-famed 1968 Tet tactics. After various debates concerning the site for talks, Hanoi appointed Xuan Thuy, formerly foreign minister and head of the Lao Dong Central Committee Foreign Relations Department, to head its delegation in Paris. The appointment of W. Averell Harriman and Cyrus Vance on the U.S. side set the stage for the most important international exchange of the decade. Hanoi's decision to send the seventh-ranking member of the 12-member Politburo, Le Duc Tho, to Paris added to the seriousness of its intentions. As Tho had been charged with southern affairs for some time, his presence presented an increased air of reality to a situation contingent upon political processes elsewhere.

The US election suffered its own agonies as discontent increased and a principal candidate was assassinated. By November the Vietnam policy as it had developed no longer seemed to have supporters. Vice

President Humphrey and Secretary of Defense Clark Clifford spoke of ARVN potential to reduce the required US force level. Representative Melvin Laird, who was to become secretary of defense under the Nixon administration, spoke during the campaign of US reductions by cutting replacements. He also stated after the election that the war could end in 1969. And nearly all major US politicians criticized Saigon's independent position on expansion of the talks. McGeorge Bundy's provocative analysis of the requirement for altering the American presence appeared to subscribe to an inevitable necessity.

Hanoi remained in the delicate position of not offending either Moscow or Peking, although its criticisms of the latter were increasingly manifested. But the politics of both gargantuan communist powers operated against continued large-scale actions. When Le Duc Tho left Paris for Hanoi via Moscow and Peking in mid-October, it was to consummate further the outlines of the major strategy. President Johnson's formal cessation of all "air, naval and artillery bombardment" of the DRVN on October 31 and Hanoi's agreement to the participation of Saigon in the Paris talks completed this act of the scenario. Secretary Clifford's response to the lack of spontaneous support from Saigon for this phase was to assume that Hanoi and the US could readily determine a program to terminate hostilities, leaving the political settlement to negotiations between Saigon, Hanoi, and the NLF.

Peace Politics and the Southern Contingents

Neither of the southern contingents, i.e., Saigon or the NLF, exhibited clear enthusiasm for the role it was called upon to play in the major process of peace politics. Saigon fought a constant rearguard action against losing its identity in the process of peace politics and to preserve its role in the broader political picture. President Nguyen Van Thieu and Vice President Nguyen Cao Ky attempted to outdistance each other in opposing a policy short of military victory and in opposing a coalition and neutralism. Thieu's requisite position of reliance upon American assistance made him particularly susceptible to criticism of being a puppet, not an inconsiderable factor in his public criticism throughout the year of American "unilateral" peace moves. Repeatedly the National Assembly castigated US policy and demanded independence for the GVN. At the end of 1967 the Senate passed a resolution denouncing any possible dealings with the NLF. Once the question of a bombing cessation and a four-sided Paris conference became acute, each house criticized the US and protested against its betrayal of the interests of South Vietnam. Despite executive and legislative outcries, Saigon recognized early that it was inopportune to stand aloof from American peace moves. First Bui Diem, ambassador to Washington, and then former Foreign Minister Pham Dang Lam provided a GVN presence in Paris while the Harriman and Thuy teams held discussions. And once the possibility for expanded talks become apparent, Colonel Ho Van Loi was sent to Paris to establish radio links with Saigon and handle administrative details for establishing staff headquarters.

Meetings between Thieu and Ambassador Ellsworth Bunker, as well as between Thieu and the National Security Council, illustrated the intrinsic dilemma in US-Saigon relationships. Bunker, in line with Secretary Rusk's promises, consulted with the GVN on the American decision to cease bombing the DRVN. Thieu's reaction was to attempt to preserve his own integrity in consultations that involved giving his acquiescence to a decision already made while simultaneously protecting his own and his nation's position in a process beyond his control. Prime Minister Nguyen Van Huong and Thieu resorted to their previous position of nonrecognition of the NLF but agreed that direct discussions be held between the "principal parties," i.e., that Hanoi and Saigon each head a team. The GVN deputy leader in Paris, Colonel Nguyen Van An, even agreed that the NLF could be present during the Paris talks, but only as part of the DRVN delegation. In short, as Information Minister Ton That Thien stated, peace possibilities needed to be "de-Americanized." When Saigon did agree to four-sided talks, after recognizing the adamant nature not only of the Johnson but also the Nixon administration (whose chief advisor on national security, Henry Kissinger, favored a phased withdrawal and three forums of peace—Hanoi-US, Saigon-NLF, and international), appropriate steps were taken to insure that Paris actions would be an extension of the political process of South Vietnam. A double structure was agreed upon, an official one for negotiations headed by Pham Dang Lam and a second one including appropriate political forces headed by Ky. Some 200 members—a group soon changed to lessen Ky's influence—were involved, including representatives of diverse political factions, religious groups, and the National Assembly. Adapting to this phase of peace politics after a verbal battle with Secretary Clifford and after stating opposition to "red and white imperialism," Ky finally agreed to possible discussions with the NLF, preferably in Saigon, but recognizing the NLF as a reality, not an entity.

Exactly what role was taken by NLF leaders was as great a mystery as it had been since the beginning of insurgency in the 1950's. Ho Chi

Minh's comments during the 14th anniversary celebration of the Geneva accords, lauding the Alliance of National, Democratic, and Peace Forces first and only afterwards complimenting the NLF, could not have been received enthusiastically by those who had led the struggle in the South. Occasional statements by the NLF did not clarify any differences between the NLF and leaders in Hanoi. Pham Van Cung, the NLF press attaché in Prague, eliminated international supervision of elections as a topic for consideration. However, when the NLF established a Paris Information Bureau in September under Saigon area organizer and foreign affairs commission member Pham Van Bo and deputy director Ha Thanh Lam, it did counter the Saigon observer group and establish a presence for possible contingencies. The points issued by the NLF in November presented a position favorable to it rather than the Alliance: continuation of the struggle for a "unified, neutral, prosperous and democratic Vietnam," coalition and democratic elections with no "foreign interference," decision on the unity question by the North and South alone, and a neutralist foreign policy for the South.

Hanoi's decision for an expansion of the talks to four parties apparently occurred with consultation analogous to that of Thieu and Bunker but under conditions involving much greater pressures. Although contending that it did not recognize the government in Saigon, the NLF did approve an initial Paris delegation before a similar decision was made by its southern rival. The leader of this delegaton, Mme. Nguyen Thi Binh, an NLF Central Committee member who was also vice president of the Women's Liberation Union and the Committee for Solidarity with the American People, was, like Nguyen Huu Tho and Trinh Dinh Thao, a participant in the 1950 anti-American demonstration in Saigon. Her agreement that the NLF as the next government would provide diplomatic recognition to the US and accept US no-string economic and technical assistance appeared to be ample proof that the NLF was participating actively in the peace strategy. The arrival of NLF Foreign Minister Tran Buu Kiem in December to head the delegation, with Mme. Binh as his deputy, appeared to affirm NLF acceptance.

Government and Politics

Developments within the GVN were rapid, dramatic and significant, but few were unrelated to the peace issue. They were characterized by Thieu's improved position vis-à-vis Ky, by an increasing civilian role in administration, by widespread personnel changes throughout national and local administration, by the creation of new institutions for implementing provisions of the 1967 Constitution and for carrying out programs of the Thieu-Huong government. From the establishment of the Second Republic late in 1967 until Tet, governmental advances had been minimal. In fact, Major General Nguyen Duc Thang, supposedly charged with revising and reforming the army structure, especially as it applied to relationships between army officers in local government and the national ministries, felt that Thieu was stalling reforms and resigned. Thieu made certain provincial and division changes, but primarily as steps to replace Ky's men with his own and only very incidentally as reform moves. After Tet, however, he approved a significant army reorganization decree requiring the 44 province chiefs to report directly to Saigon rather than to Corps commanders and to be appointed by the Ministry of Interior. This move, matched with Corps commander changes, strengthened Thieu's control.

During May the new decree was pragmatically rendered more significant by a change in cabinets. After delicate negotiations by Thieu's brother, Nguyen Van Kieu, Tran Van Huong replaced Nguyen Van Loc as prime minister. This not only automatically weakened Ky's position but gave the regime a firmer nationalist base. Huong, the 65-year-old former prime minister, had impeccable credentials as a southern leader. An ancestor worshiper from Vinh Long in the Mekong Delta, he had been mayor of Saigon twice, a presidential candidate, a former Viet Minh, and foremost an independent personality throughout his career. Huong found it necessary initially to compromise on numerous points in order to obtain a balance among his goals, Thieu, and the military (whom Ky could not rally against the new government). His ambition for a set of three deputies (Dr. Nguyen Luu Vien, Tran Van Tuyen, and Ha Thuc Ky), which would have strengthened the nationalist posture of his government, went unrealized. Dai Viet leader Ha Thuc Ky, whose potential role was opposed by Hoa Hao leaders, refused participation because his party was denied the number of portfolios he demanded.

The new 16-member cabinet reflected Ky's loss of influence (7 of 17 in Loc's cabinet had been identified as pro-Ky), consisted of a Buddhist majority, lessened northern influence, and contained at least five former Can Lao members. It was more of a cabinet of technicians than Huong wanted, but it included such important political personalities and government critics as Ministers of State Mai Tho Truyen (lay leader of southern Buddhists) and Dr. Phan Quang Dan (whose reputation as an anti-Diemist had made him something of a national hero before

1963), and Information Minister Ton That Thien (*Guardian* editor who had suffered from press censorship, and vice dean at the Buddhist Van Hanh University). Also included, as minister of interior, was General Tran Thien Khiem, who had been one of the earlier post-Diem government leaders and was close to Thieu. Unfortunately Dr. Dan, during a visit to the US, was removed from the cabinet because he ostensibly favored negotiations with the NLF—actually, he had advocated an end to the war and elections in which anyone could compete.

Huong demanded increased appointive power, especially after Khiem named Colonel Do Kien Nhieu as Saigon mayor (an appointment much criticized by the House) and Major Tran Thien Phuong (Khiem's brother) as director of the Saigon port. Both appointees were alleged to exemplify qualities inconsistent with those called for in Huong's campaign against corruption in government. Thieu gave Huong his full support formally in the Council of Ministers. As a result, by the fall Huong had replaced nearly one-half of the province chiefs and approximately one-fifth of the nation's district chiefs. The prime minister created anticorruption committees and pushed to have officials declare their personal wealth. Courses in civil administration were begun for military officers, and Huong was pleased ironically with the fact there were fewer military volunteers for civil administrative positions. Important changes were made in police administration as well. This national force had already been increased by one-third in two years to 80,000, of whom one-fourth were in Saigon. Special committees to study previous arrests were created in all provinces, and orders were given to release prisoners unless they were in detention under specific charges.

Ky's ally, General Nguyen Ngoc Loan, after being wounded, was replaced as chief of the national police, numerous provincial police chiefs were replaced, inspection teams were formed, priority for leadership positons was given to career policemen (from each region) rather than to transferred army officers, and a training center was established. The heads of the Central Intelligence Office and the Military Security Department—both close to Ky—were replaced by two former Can Lao members closer to Thieu. Also, the Supreme Court required in the constitution was finally approved. This body was selected from a list presented by judges, public prosecutors, and the bar association. It has a separate budget, is independent of the Ministry of Justice, and has power to interpret the constitution, to hear appeals from all other courts, and to establish rules governing the judiciary. The Supreme Court's first important action, in December, involved a decision that the Senate and the House meet jointly to approve the GVN delegation to the Paris discussions—proving perhaps that no policy forum in Vietnam could long remain outside the processes of peace politics.

And this topic inevitably influenced every other action of the Huong government. The new prime minister wanted peace, as he had said repeatedly in the 1967 presidential campaign, but certainly not any peace. He wanted reform but could not begin to obtain it unless group interests were considered, and in 1968 this meant above all else maintaining GVN independence while offending as few groups as possible despite the evolving peace position of his nation's allies. A perfect example of the dilemma he faced was manifest in his and Thieu's attempts to liberalize the government's role vis-à-vis the press. Almost immediately after his cabinet assumed office, prior press censorship was formally lifted. A number of newspapers reopened, including pro-Diem ones. Tran Van Tuyen wrote openly in favor of recognizing the NLF as a reality. Yet papers were closed when they described an abortive coup attempt denied by Thieu. The president said that those spreading false rumors would be punished. This incident, followed by the temporary arrest of a number of persons who had been important Can Lao members, coincided with the return of the formal leader of the anti-Diem coup in 1963, General Duong Van Minh. The refusal of this former chief of state to serve as a presidential adviser, his being distinguished from the "puppets" in Saigon by Hanoi, and his being touted highly by the Buddhist newspaper *Chanh Dao* ("Right Path") made his presence politically volatile. "False rumors" would not be permitted if they fanned the fire of interest-group conflict relevant to the explosive peace issue. Later, while all Saigon papers supported Richard Nixon as the American most likely to opt for retention of GVN identity, even Thien closed newspapers which appeared not to criticize the American position adequately.

In the legislative branch, the National Assembly started slowly, divided into quite flexible blocs, generally acquiesced to the regime, displayed sympathy for a hard line on the peace issue, but, most important, showed more independence from the executive than had any parliamentary group in Vietnam's history. Its organization represented important interest groups. When, after Tet, Thieu asked to rule by decree in economic and financial matters, the House voted 85:10 against him. The House also cut the executive budget, including a cut in the amount requested for operating the vice president's office. Both houses demanded changes in Thieu's mobilization plan but voted overwhelmingly for full mobilization, a step believed politically impossible until this period. Individually and collectively, the Senate members were extremely critical of US policy considered favorable to a coalition. Catholic and Dai Viet leaders in the Senate were particularly severe in their criticisms. In June the House, led by Secretary General Pham Huu Giao, voted 72–2 that the NLF could have no role and that the US should clarify its peace policy. In August a House petition of 60 members headed by Tran Ngoc Chan anticipated later moves by calling for a Saigon-Hanoi discussion with other parties playing a minor role. On November 4 an Assembly resolution repeated that GVN-DRVN talks were acceptable, but not talks with the NLF; this resolution also condemned an American bombing halt in the absence of a DRVN response.

The House applied considerable pressure for the removal of Nguyen Van Loc as prime minister, and this was a significant factor in his replacement. In fact, the Assembly often proved critical of the government, and the House Anti-Corruption Committee under the chairmanship of Phan Huy Duc articulated accusations against the police and the Foreign Ministry. Bills were passed regulating and liberalizing party organization and the press. Parties were still required to register with the Ministry of Interior, but appeals to the Supreme Court were made possible. Parties were required to have 5,000 members from 19 provinces, or 10,000 members from five provinces, including ten members from the National Assembly. This did not preclude the proliferation of groups (over 60 registered and 30 illegal ones) calling themselves parties, but it was a step toward rationalization of party structures. The press code, passed in May, did nullify prior government censorship. However, the press boycotted the House because one segment of the code permitted life imprisonment for press comments favorable to neutralism or the NLF.

Interest Group Politics. In both the general peace politics and legislative politics the position of the Catholics especially presented a dilemma for the administration and even for Catholic leadership. It was difficult to reconcile the Vatican's unequivocal support of peace with the staunch anticommunism of Vietnamese Catholics and the fear and hatred of the large cohesive Tonkinese Catholic expatriate group. The Vietnamese Council of Bishops in January issued a statement—approved unanimously by its 17 members, including the most Reverend Nguyen Van Binh, the archbishop of Saigon—calling for a termination both of bombing of the DRVN and of PAVN infiltration, and for the beginning of serious negotiations. This statement also did not hesitate to criticize corruption within the GVN. The bishops constituted a force between the militants and the Trinh Bay group of priests of the left led by Father Nguyen Ngoc Lan. The dilemma was obvious shortly after the bishops' statement, when a group of some 300 northern Catholic refugees petitioned for rejection of any US-initiated peace actions. Similar sentiments were voiced by certain northern highland refugee and southern sect leaders. And after the May offensive against the cities, Catholics joined with Cao Dais in the Assembly to demand reprisals for rocket attacks on Saigon.

The revitalization of the Diemist Can Lao forces also was primarily a Catholic movement. The appointment of the two ex-Can Lao to important intelligence positions in September, while primarily an anti-Ky move, was part of a pattern. The surrender of Major General Lam Van Phat, a leader of previous so-called Catholic coup attempts who had been sentenced to death in absentia, increased speculation about the new Can Lao role. Social personalist gains in central Vietnam, supported by Monsignor Nguyen Van Thuan, were not unrelated to Thieu's attempts to improve his base of support through increased Catholic backing. Despite this, important Catholic elements lent their support to Ky once the question of Thieu's stand relative to the US-initiated bombing halt became a serious one. The Catholic paper *Xay Dung* ("To Construct") even hinted that an accidental US shelling, which killed a number of important Ky police and military aides and had a significantly adverse political effect upon the vice president's power, was less than accidental. Senator Nguyen Gia Hien's pro-Thieu comments after the halt were overtly contingent upon the president's maintaining a tough position in face of American pressures. It was thanks to this understanding that Thieu's appeal for calm prevailed and that the Catholic groups such as Father Hoang Quynh's Binh Thai parish, converging on Saigon, settled for a rally for self-aid and self-defense presided over by Ton That Thien and for a quiet anti-US demonstration by the Greater Unity Force on November 5 outside the American Embassy. This tactic also prevented a counter-demonstration by Thich Tri Quang's adherents, a situation that might have perilously renewed the internecine strike of 1964–65.

Buddhist activists actually were relatively quiet. Tri Quang was not cooperative when the NLF utilized An Quang Pagoda, which was in the area of heavy damage during the Tet offensive. Yet he was placed under "protective custody," as were his aides Thich Lieu Minh and publisher Thich Ho Giac, an action leading to "militant" Buddhist refusal to participate in the post-Tet unity groups. When he was released at the end of June it was partly because of Thieu's intensified unity drive and partly because Father Quynh, chairman of the Council of Religions, intervened. When other groups overtly opposed the bombing halt, An Quang supported it. And after the halt Tri Quang demanded an immediate ceasefire and spoke of potential demonstrations and of his readiness to return to prison for the sake of peace. This message was preached in pagodas of his persuasion but with the proviso that the Buddhists were in neither camp. The GVN's desire to pacify this group was manifested in December in the release, after two-and-a-half years, of Nguyen Van Man, former mayor of Da Nang and an important leader of the near-secession of central Vietnam in 1966, whom Ky had threatened to shoot at the time.

Student and intellectual groups, often Buddhist allies, opted for peace more vigorously than before. A six-page statement favoring the ending of hostilities, the unification of the GVN and the NLF, and elections, partly the product of Au Truong Thanh and Tran Van Tuyen, was issued on January 10 by a professors' group. And a petition by 65 professors, mostly from the University of Saigon, called for an extension of the proposed 36-hour Tet truce and for peace talks to begin. In June the Saigon University Student Union, together with Thich Tinh Khiet, called for Hanoi-Saigon negotiations. The call for ending the war was supported by the Catholic church and the "militant" and "moderate" Buddhist factions. In seminars at the Saigon Student Association and in an article in *Student Life,* it was stated that the NLF was unacceptable but must be recognized as a reality. Representative Ly Qui Chung (a young Huong supporter) and Reverend Nguyen Ngoc Lan (a liberal Da Lat and Hue University Catholic professor) attended the seminars, but the editor of *Student Life,* Nguyen Truong Con, was given a five-year prison sentence.

GVN Organization Building

Organization building was emphasized as an instrumentality for forging unity among the disparate nationalist interest groups and as a method for supporting the GVN in its political exchanges with the US and the DRVN-NLF combination. The four most important new post-Tet organizations were: the People's National Salvation Front, led by Senator Tran Van Don; the Free Democratic Front, created by Nguyen Van Huong, secretary general in the presidency, and financed by pharmacist Nguyen Cao Thang; the Humanist Socialist Revolutionary Party of Truong Cong Cuu, a conservative Catholic, quasi-Can Lao structure; and the People's Anti-Communist Front, including Father Quynh and numerous provincial and municipal organizations which led demonstrations in Hue and Da Nang. The first group, the People's National Salvation Front, was perhaps the most significant. Like the People's Anti-Communist Front, it appeared greatly to be a pro-Ky group, but its composition initially was broad. Although Ky's capable aide Dang Duc Khoi was its prime mover, it included sect and other group leaders, politicians, and former generals. At first Tran Van Tuyen served as chairman, Senator Tran Van Don was head of the standing committee, and Nguyen Xuan Oanh was secretary general. This liberal leadership was supplemented by the presence of Thich Minh (a militant Buddhist leader), Thich Tam Giac (a moderate Buddhist leader), Tran Quoc Buu (head of the Vietnamese Confederation of Labor), and three important political leaders and former presidential candidates—Phan Khac Sun, Tran Van Huong, and Ha Thuc Ky.

Despite the notable absence of pro-Thieu personalities (the primary reason for the creation of the Free Democratic Front), this was an impressive nationalist combination protesting the Tet tactics of the NLF. However, even temporary unity as usual was based upon opposition rather than support for any articulated policy. This surface unity was shattered almost immediately by "protective arrests" of certain union leaders, Diemists, VNQDD leader Vu Hong Khanh, Truong Dinh Dzu (who ran second in the 1967 presidential election and whose detention proved to be more than temporary after conviction for advocating relations with the NLF), and Tri Quang and two of his important aides. Buu, the militant Buddhists, Tran Van Tuyen, and numerous other nationalist leaders refused further association.

By mid-year, with the period of protective arrests ended and with Thieu attempting to consolidate the political gains he had made against Ky since Huong's appointment as prime minister, the president called a meeting of some 200 political and religious leaders, including militant Buddhists, Reverend Quynh and Senator Don, to encourage cooperation and unity among the diverse groups and to persuade the multiple parties to combine even if to oppose the government. Thieu extolled political parties as the "country's infrastructure, while the government, including both executive and legislature, is only its superstructure." The product of this unity meeting, in addition to Tri Quang's release from custody, was the creation of the National Social Revolutionary Front, including the People's National Salvation Front, the Free Democratic Front, and 26 other groups.

These organizations were in many ways replicas of numerous short-lived, nationalist compromise and unity structures; the pressures of the moment were certainly no more serious than those in 1954 when a Ngo Dinh Nhu-led group floundered on internal controversy before it was an active instrument. Numerous interests were present, questions of leadership and unity were unresolved, demands upon government were irreconcilable among the groups, and the objective environmental conditions of crisis were insufficient stimuli for the acceptance of common goals. The organizations were formed, met briefly, and succumbed quietly. Events proved again that South Vietnam has no parties except for combative interest groups. New parties, including the New People's Force formed by Phan Khac Suu, who had stressed UN peace supervision and possible confederation, and the Vietnam Force formed by Phan Ba Cam (a Hoa Hao leader whose slate barely missed election to the Senate) calling for an end of the war, South-North unity, and a socialist economy, hardly changed the patterns of Vietnamese party behavior.

Factions were recognizable in the Ky-Thieu split, in the military-civilian controversy, and in the perennial sectional competition. An overlay of varying religious interests also was present. There were few policy differences, although undoubtedly there was a range of opinion on the question of future NLF-Hanoi and Saigon relationships. Many members had been extremely critical of the GVN in the past, especially during the 1967 national elections. Questions of authoritarian behavior, corruption, inefficiency, militarism, and inability to cope with rural and urban problems had been raised previously by a high percentage of the organizations' membership. But governments create such intermediate structures to provide a facade of support, to present a united front, to issue public relations images for consumption abroad, and to quiet those whose voices might appear louder when alone than in a group. The difference in this respect between Hanoi and Saigon is that the former has always been adept at creating utilitarian structures of this kind.

DRVN–NLF Organizational Weapons

In fact, an integral part of the Hanoi-NLF contribution to peace politics was the formation of groups, national and local, to provide alternative lines of access to power and to provide a wider and tighter net encompassing large numbers of people from diverse strata. Nguyen Huu Tho, NLF president, had reemphasized the virtues of a coalition under the umbrella of a National Democratic Union and had invited ARVN into the PLA ranks as part of the Tet preparation. Committees to serve as branches of this coalition union were announced during Tet.

These branches proved to be neither instigators nor products of a general uprising. Hanoi presented claims of GVN administrative personnel, businessmen, intellectuals, and political figures joining spontaneously in a popular uprising, creating committees, and working for a coalition. For once the effort was less than successful. Leaders identified themselves too quickly, most of the presumably potential members among the nationalist personalities refused to be enmeshed in the overlapping structures because their faith in the Tonkinese and the NLF was even less than their faith in the GVN, and popular reaction was unmistakably hostile to the forced intrusion upon private lives that was the true impact of Tet.

Nonetheless, an organization considered of significant utility in the peace politics of Hanoi was created to provide an alternative for nationalist elements and a compromise for any future coalition. The Alliance of National Democratic and Peace Forces, supposedly consisting primarily of urban groups, was the principal structure to be prepared for a role following the first phase of peace politics. None of the major southern leaders yielded to the temptation of being cast in a favorable light for a future coalition role, although in Hue a number of persons who had been important in previous Buddhist crises were local members. The protective arrests by the GVN were not completely without foundation, although they were as much an offensive move against the opposition as a defensive one against possible kidnappings. Leaders of the Alliance were mostly persons who had been on the fringes of dissent and of Viet Minh politics for many years. As with many other groups, it was old home week for the 1950 protest group against US warships and the 1955 demonstrators under Nguyen Huu Tho against Diem. All ten members of the Alliance's Central Committee, most of whom were in hiding in the Delta, were sentenced to death in absentia by Saigon during July. The leaders, elected presumably in April near Saigon during a platform-adoption meeting, included: Trinh Dinh Thao, chairman, a former law partner of Nguyen Huu Tho and a member of the Japanese-installed cabinet of Tran Trong Kim in 1944; Ton That Duong Ky, secretary general, a former Saigon University history professor who had been deported to the North in 1965 in a grandiose act by the GVN; Dr. Duong Quynh Hoa, deputy secretary general, a lady who was ostensibly the only bona fide Communist within the formal leadership; Thich Don Hau, second vice chairman, a Hue dissident who broadcasted against the GVN during Tet but whom Tri Quang's aide Thich Thien Minh claimed was kidnapped by the NLF; Lam Van Tet, first vice chairman, an engineer and Cao Dai member in 1963 of the first post-

Diem national Council of Notables; Hoang Thanh Nghi, second deputy, and author; Le Hien Dang, third deputy, former Saigon Student Union secretary general; and permanent delegates Nguyen Van Kiet (once a professor at Saigon University), Huynh Dan Nghi, and Tran Trieu Luat (student leader).

While the Alliance was accepted by the NLF, its potential role as a substitute for the NLF and as an agent for Tonkinese control in the South did not appear to escape the NLF. On the eve of the beginning of the Paris talks the DRVN's Fatherland Front, Hanoi's primary instrumentality for southern operations, noted the virtue of the Alliance as a leader in a future broad coalition. This view that the Alliance—and not solely the NLF—was the proper group for coalition discussions was also voiced by Wilfred Burchett in a June interview with the *Far Eastern Economic Review*. Possible NLF reservations were given by Le Quang Chang, an NLF Central Committee member, who displayed an obvious lack of enthusiasm when he told a Paris group in July that the NLF was prepared to talk to the Alliance. He noted that the NLF held a senior position, and he lessened the potential base of a possible coalition by excluding both the Dai Viet and the VNQDD.

Viet Minh genius from its beginning was founded upon the ability to create intermediate structures to enmesh, indoctrinate, oversee, and control human activities of varied functional forms. The Alliance was much more than an additional organizational overlay of the sort seen in such structures as those for women, youth, etc. It was a vehicle for the programmed next stage. But of more immediate impact, the "organizational weapon," as Douglas Pike has termed it, became geared for quick inroads into the rural politic before any rapprochement could occur. This new emphasis was also an attempt at survival in response to the "Phoenix" attacks upon the vital NLF infrastructure. Phoenix (*Phung Hoang*), combined with the Accelerated Pacification Campaign (APC), represented the most significant potential threat to the NLF since the beginning of large-scale warfare. With a goal of putting 12,000 NLF infrastructure leaders out of commission during 1968, and for the first time with a program approaching its scheduled goals especially in the Delta, Phoenix was an immeasurably more dangerous threat to the NLF than was sheer opposition military force. The program called for special intelligence coordination centers in approximately 200 key districts, with district chiefs coordinating actions against local NLF leadership.

"Liberation committees" were the backbone of the new NLF strategy of quick inroads and counteracting Phoenix. By mid-November the

NLF had established some 1,800 liberation committees among the nation's 12,000 rural hamlets (most in the last quarter of 1968), 17 provincial committees, and 5 urban committees. A claim was even made at the end of the year that such committees controlled Quang Ngai Province. People's Revolutionary Party members, i.e., the southern communist party, were "elected" to these committees as was a small minority of elders. The NLF was preparing for the next phase of peace politics.

The War: An Instrument of Peace Politics

Organizational and other peace politics strategies were implemented in a milieu of war as a subsidiary tactic, as they had been since the early 1940s in the northeastern highlands of Tonkin. At the beginning of 1968, most objective appraisals of ARVN and allied military posture noted manifest general improvements compared to any time in the long war. ARVN desertions, while accounting for over 90 per cent of manpower losses, had dropped by about one-third during the previous year, an indication of professionalism not previously observable. Internal developments had added to this indication, e.g., an inspector general for the army, pay raises, promotions for enlisted personnel, and increased firepower with M-16 rifles distributed to the 1st Division. Declines in PAVN-PLA posture appeared to add to the improved allied one. PLA desertions had increased, recruiting problems in the Delta (the recruitment base) were serious, guerrilla totals had declined according to allied statistics, and, most important, the balance had shifted from a main force of southerners to one with a majority of northerners. The overall appraisal, while statistically objective, proved dangerously deceptive. It omitted reference to strategic decisions for Hanoi to supplement its forces and it did not refer to the basis of NLF strength, i.e., its infrastructure.

The NLF-PAVN winter-spring offensive of 1967–68 involved major struggles at Loc Ninh and Dak To and increased guerrilla actions and terrorism. Significant as these steps were, they could only be considered as failures by all precepts of traditional warfare. Their losses were considerable and no major battle was won. Yet allied casualties increased, not proportionate to those of the attacking forces but enough to create international publicity and augment the bitterness already clearly manifest in American public opinion. In addition, American force levels increased in areas creating difficult logistical problems, while urban defense, quite in accordance with General Westmoreland's plans, became an ARVN function. Under the circumstances the NLF's frequent claims in January of an end to the war after Tet and creation soon of a coalition appeared unwise as well as boastful. Increased action during this period around Saigon did not appear adequate to discredit allied claims that southern main forces had been pushed back to Cambodia. Indeed, 1968 pre-Tet military difficulties were centered along South Vietnam's borders.

When the Khe Sahn redoubt became compared internationally to the famous battle of Dien Bien Phu, it was at first only an extension of already significant action near the DMZ. PAVN preparations against Khe Sahn were referred to by Westmoreland as an "invasion," a unique stage for revolutionary warfare. The strength of the PAVN force, the use of tanks on one occasion, the heavy bombardment—in short, the siege—were reminiscent of Dien Bien Phu. But when the air had cleared and the tactical significance of the publicity and the straining of American might was analyzed, Khe Sahn was seen as but part of a much larger strategy. Perhaps it did not require clairvoyance to anticipate the Politburo's decision on the Tet strategy. Inspection of the frailty of the PAVN tunnels leading toward Khe Sahn after it had been abandoned led the skeptical to question the seriousness of the world's greatest tunnel digger's own analogy of Khe Sahn to Dien Bien Phu.

Tet and Götterdämmerung. For the DRVN and the NLF, the true significance of warfare as a tool in political strategy was exemplified in the Tet offensive, though the plentiful statistics on this historic event presented by the various concerned parties cannot be considered reliable. But the minus points are too clearly discernible—urban devastation, refugee totals of unbelievable dimensions, the touted Revolutionary Development program reduced from the form initially envisaged to an unrecognizable structure, civilian deaths by open warfare and assassination in numbers never before encountered even in this more than 20-year struggle, loss of the title of "safe" by any location in the nation, setback of all aspects of social and economic public policies that had at last shown improvement (health, welfare, education, agriculture, consumer purchasing power, etc.), and PAVN and NLF main-force and infrastructure losses on a scale requiring years of training for similar numbers of experienced replacements. While the destruction of Hue was most serious, it set the pattern for an almost nationwide lesser havoc.

Certain losses not subject to any systematic accounting had a long-range effect. For Tet had no winners. It determined the succeeding stages of peace politics for the losers: for the DRVN, who could not indefinitely sustain material losses of such a proportion; for the NLF, who could not count on spontaneous popular urban support but did have to rely even more heavily from this point upon DRVN assistance; for the US, whose foreign policy had to be revised to coincide with the realities of the Vietnam situation and of its own domestic situation; and for the GVN, which could be almost surprised at its survival capacity but could not ignore the increasing demands placed upon it by a combination of internal pressures and of peace politics instigated by allies and enemies. Tet was simultaneously the genius and the Achilles' heel of Hanoi's grand strategy for programming the politics of peace. It was a point of no return.

Post-Tet War Politics. After the Tet offensive, perhaps the most significant element of the military sphere was that an increasing number of the anti-Allied main forces were northerners. From Tet to May, presumably some 100,000 northerners were infiltrated south to reinforce depleted units and to prepare for an onslaught during May that was less strong than the Tet attacks but resulted in basically similar international publicity. The failure to obtain spontaneous urban support, the high casualty figures, and the devastating losses to NLF leadership cadres were offset by increasing burdens upon the Saigon administration (including an increase of approximately 80,000 refugees in Saigon), increases in allied resource losses and costs, and publicity for the ability of the communist forces to strike whenever they were prepared to pay the price as a prelude to the Paris talks.

Allied military posture, despite an 11-province April drive called "Complete Victory" involving 100,000 troops in III Corps, did undergo a shift in emphasis. General Creighton W. Abrams' replacement of Westmoreland as American commander, when the latter became Army chief of staff, was followed by a cut-down in search-and-destroy operations and an emphasis upon long reconnaissance, flexibility and smaller mobile units. Most important, Phoenix was emphasized although rural pacification was stalled. Abrams' tactics appeared as evidence that there was a stalemate for which there was no military solution. This was apparent when Washington decided on only 24,000 supplemental forces to add to the previously agreed 525,000 total to be present by July. The old military philosophy of a force level adequate to punish and simultaneously occupy could not survive the post-Tet era without a measurably greater increase.

Beginning with the summer, PAVN-NLF military activities were even more obviously than before primarily adjuncts of the politics of peace. Attacks, shellings and terrorism were tied to negotiating and post-negotiating position, as were even truce violations later during the Christmas holidays. There was no third wave of attacks as predicted, but rather a slowdown and even a pull-out of forces combined with greatly increased late-year desertions, although infiltration continued. But Saigon, Da Nang and Tay Ninh, for example, continued to be under considerable pressures from the exigencies of temporary tactical measures. PAVN and NLF main forces, as part of a preparation for the US bombing halt and expanded talks, rendered the summer and post-summer lulls very dramatic. PAVN Divisions 304, 308 and 320 left from north of Saigon. NLF Divisions 4, 5 and 7 pulled into Cambodia. The Dong Ngai regiment, already hard hit, remained northeast of Saigon. Delta NLF main force units were occupied in village political and administrative work. By mid-October it was acknowledged that perhaps as many as 60,000 had withdrawn to positions across South Vietnam's borders. Tactically, military action continued on all sides, but primarily as an aspect of the strategy of improved position relative to the politics of peace.

Politics with Peace

The "Indochina question" has been one of the most difficult international problems since the end of World War II. Each step, each cycle has been an element of a tragedy. Its impact upon France was immeasurable, manifesting itself in Algeria, in Paris, in the French military, and in the morale of the French nation. While the impact has been weaker on the United States, it has dominated the international and domestic policies of the world's greatest economic and military power to an unbelievable extent. It has hampered east-west relations, added to the political crisis within the communist world, and influenced greatly the positions and opinions of small nations throughout the world. But the true tragedy has always been within Indochina itself. Laos suffered the plight of the unfortunate man-in-the-middle. Cambodia survived with a series of temporary, unsatisfactory expedient steps permitting it to remain independent. In the two Vietnams, the entire fabric of existence suffered. The DRVN had made economic gains, despite serious handicaps, before the bombing began. Those advances have been eliminated. In the South, the holocaust of warfare has altered the society as a whole. Revolutionary warfare combined with more traditional warfare has struck down hamlet, village, and family mores.

South Vietnam is now an urban place, with over half the population residing in communities of over 25,000. Migration of this magnitude is unlikely to be reversed. Certainly there can never again be the type of village life so eloquently and profoundly described by Paul Mus. War has killed not only fantastic numbers but also the old life-style, the old elements of cohesion. In addition to the altercations of war there is a further, perhaps irreversible, strain, described in a speech by Ton That Thien: "The American values—rejection of authority, the equation of success with wealth, the insistence on ruthless efficiency—combined with American political dominance have produced an explosive threat on Vietnamese society and culture."

Corporate existence in the DRVN, finally implanted in the highlands as well as in the Delta, has produced a new society in the northern zone. But this new society has order, regimentation, and a certain efficiency despite the confused status of overlapping party and administrative jurisdictions. The South is without order. The NLF infrastructure provides order, but it has suffered vast losses despite the rapid campaign for liberation committees. Saigon's improvements would be impressive testimony to the GVN as an agent of governing, except that the GVN remains more of a holding firm than a government and except that small steps against corruption and administrative chaos are no substitute for an efficient administrative system. The southern interest groups have defied assimilation, much less coordination. These groups, including much of the complicated NLF matrix of organizations, are unprepared to acquiesce to a more general interest regardless of whether this interest is defined by an adapted form of the National Assembly or by a coalition regime.

South Vietnam's problems, even after completion of the stages of peace politics, are extremely severe. Hamlets and villages have been destroyed, communities are scattered and refugee numbers are immense, urban congestion and blight are foreboding, the economy is geared to external assistance, gigantic military projects have little utility for a peacetime role, large areas of forest are destroyed, and much utilizable land is fallow. In addition, problems of education, health, housing, etc., are geometrically greater than ever before. Foreign assistance is essential, not only for rebuilding but simply because budgetary deficits are large and percentages for education (5.1 per cent projected for the 1969 budget) and other nonmilitary items are inadequate to resolve the most pressing indigenous needs. The land reform question is paramount and certainly Thieu's willingness to accept the land-to-the-tillers philosophy, permitting those who have received land from the NLF to retain it with appropriate compensation to former owners, is at least a meager beginning. And the war has raised the level of expectations of many, including even the highlanders who undoubtedly will remain adamantly anti-Vietnamese regardless of any resolution of what to them is an outsider's war. Under such circumstances, any government will find tenure in power difficult. Perhaps such tenure will continue to be implausible in light of the perennial centrifugal forces that define the true power structure of Vietnam. For Indochina, unfortunately, things indeed do change but nonetheless remain the same.

Political Processes in the Two Vietnams

In recent years, numerous socio-economic-political developments have affected the political systems of the two Vietnams.[14] One element that will have an important impact on Vietnam south of the seventeenth parallel is that the decade of the 1960's inaugurated a decided shift toward the ascendancy of southerners. This trend was far from universal, and typically favored persons from the Center as opposed to the Mekong Delta, but it was an omen of vast significance for future political processes in South Vietnam.

Some 16 years after the Geneva Agreement, the Tonkinese-Annamese-Cochinchinese trichotomy had lessened, although old animosities had not been forgotten. What made the increased role of non-Tonkinese particularly relevant was that for one important interest group—the entire network of communist parallel hierarchies—the ascendancy of southerners was not the norm.

Thus the Viet Cong, the National Liberation Front (NLF), the People's Revolutionary Party, and the Provisional Revolutionary Government entered the new decade primarily as alien forces within what was for them by this time a truly foreign land.

In the communist structure, northerners were serving in nearly all roles. Militarily, the revolutionary forces had suffered extreme losses in personnel, in highly qualified and well-trained leadership cadres, in volume of supplies and materials. Most importantly, however, they had lost in two areas: (1) in the number of villagers compelled to offer allegiance and (2) in the number and general dispersal of military and commissariat cadres who were born in the South.

In the absence of a strong, expanding base of southern adherents, the Tonkinese maintained only the bare pretext of a southern civil war. More than a decade and a half after the formal termination of the First Indochina War, the nature of the Cambodia-Laos-Vietnam interrelationship in the total political-military struggle became evident. Actually, for the leadership and political elites of the four nations of Indochina there had never been any question of the struggle's regional aspects. For the four-nation complex, future inter-nation conflict was always simply a matter of timing. Neither Pnom Penh nor Vientiane were ever under any illusions as to the ambitions of any of the Vietnamese.

North Vietnam's incursions into Laos had been continual. Cambodian Prince Norodom Sihanouk had shrewdly opted for clandestine cooperation with Hanoi in an attempt to side with and to temporize with the group he correctly perceived as the strongest representative of twentieth-century Vietnamese imperialism. The result was a loss of power, the acceptance of a puppet role in a Tonkinese political-military front within his own nation, and reliance upon the Chinese, the force he feared most.

Not unexpectedly, the temporary restraints placed upon North Vietnam's colonialism during a period of setbacks were also to a certain extent offset in Cambodian eyes by a less than subtle inference from Saigon that Cambodia was now a part of South Vietnam's zone of influence. The ARVN expeditionary actions in Cambodia represented several changes in the previous balance of power. For South Vietnam, they were representative of her position in the future scheme of things. Her army behaved professionally; vis-à-vis the Cambodian military it was obviously a strong force in its own right even in the absence of the Americans; and it was manifestly an unquestioned force in Indochinese politics.

Luckily there was a quick halt to anti-Vietnamese actions taken by Cambodians under the pretext of eliminating Viet Cong influence. Some 400,000 Vietnamese had resided in Cambodia; of these, official counts tallied over 140,000 who evacuated because of massacres and general instability.[15]

The "Presence" of South Vietnam

The most significant political development in South Vietnam was the existence of a GVN presence throughout most of the country. This dramatic shift from the mid-1960's held considerable political significance. The decline of the Viet Cong allowed the Saigon government to move into many more villages than was previously possible. According to allied sources, in mid-1970 in excess of 92 per cent of the population of South Vietnam was living in areas not under NLF control and, following the allied military expedition into Cambodia and the evacuation of PAVN forces, there were no villages in III Corps under Viet Cong control. Official statistics also claimed that eight out of every ten persons lived in hamlets rated relatively safe as opposed to three out of ten in 1968 and that the NLF controlled only 6.5 per cent of the hamlets compared to its control of 40 per cent in 1968. (However, PAVN strength in the demilitarized zone region and its potential in I Corps continued to be considerable, particularly after Attopea and Saravan in Laos were taken by PAVN forces during April-June 1970.) Revolutionary development was relatively more effective. Areas of communal control, such as the areas where the Hoa Hao were dominant, had long since ended their rather formal agreements with the NLF and at least tolerated the GVN at a distance.

By 1970, most Vietnamese who opposed the NLF admittedly were surprised by the Saigon government's widespread presence and its control of village life. This surprise, however, was coupled with the continued disdain of most Vietnamese of all classes for the regime per se.

In general, the Vietnamese are unmoved by official pretenses. They are a population ruled but rarely governed. They put up with the French as a set of rulers, but did not regard them as representing an entity to which loyalty was required. They disdained the Diem regime, the only vestige of stability since World War II, largely because that regime rested upon an artificiality (certainly a generally recognized Asian artifact) in which a single family attempted the impossible feat of restoring the aura of the past court of Hue. They survived the utter chaos of the post-Diem years and the utter devastation of a seemingly never-ending war. Thus the Vietnamese could hardly be expected to be optimistic about the Thieu government.

There is a paradox in Nguyen Van Thieu's failure to become an accepted national leader. Despite his military background, he has displayed an excellent sense of what is and what is not politic. In a dangerously divisive political milieu, he has attained the closest approximation of executive control since the fall of Ngo Dinh Diem. This he has achieved in the face of an independent national power base behind Vice President Nguyen Cao Ky that can claim allegiances within Thieu's principal source of support, i.e., the military. In addition, the national legislature and the courts are much more independent than they were during the Diem period. And Thieu has been faced with a United States foreign policy increasingly at variance with his domestic politics. Yet he has consolidated his own position steadily, placing those considered more loyal to him (and incidentally generally more competent) in provincial and military leadership roles, coping one by one with religious, student and other interest groups by supporting rival organizations and by striking vigorously at the right moments against more militant elements of his opposition, and by utilizing the historic Vietnamese political tool of creating temporary support groups (without strength enough to become true rivals) for specific objectives.

Also, increased democratization has been a continued characteristic of the Thieu era. In spite of the continuation of certain government actions abhorrent by western standards of civil liberties, it is fair to state that since Thieu's rise to power the Saigon regime has gradually moved toward a society more open than ever before in Vietnam, certainly much more open than that of North Vietnam. To many, no doubt to most, Vietnamese, such reforms are too little and too late. None have been the object of an overall articulated policy, but rather have taken place because of pressures from the Americans, from legislative leaders, from the courts, and so forth.

Structural Differentiation

One source of pressure for reform is structural change. Today, villages are electing their own officials. During 1970 there were elections for 1,118 village council members and 4,462 hamlet chiefs and deputy chiefs. About 94 per cent of 2,151 villages had elected officials, and 96.8 per cent of 10,522 hamlets had elected officials. Civil servants continue to be appointed to perform provincial and district functions; following the French system, they are assigned from ministries or special offices. Still, provincial council elections have made this basically artificial tier a more visible government. Of 6,113,286 eligible voters in provincial and municipal council elections, 75.9 per cent voted in 1970 for 1,930 candidates for 554 provincial and six autonomous city level council positions. In Saigon, 350,000 voted, or 65 per cent of those registered. Such dry statistics naturally tend to be misleading. Yet these elections are important: (1) they bring the population into the political process, and (2) they place nonmilitary political personalities in positions of responsibility. Election of province chiefs would complete this phase of structural transformation.

The second pressure for reform has been the development of national government structures independent of the executive. While this constitutional change in the political system has hardly produced a pure separation of powers and checks and balances, it has brought about noticeable changes. The elected legislature is the most independent and most representative legislature in the history of Vietnam. The National Assembly of South Vietnam has given the population a new experience in democratic politics. Elections have provided forums for candidates to criticize not only each other but the government itself. Turnout has been high. Nongovernment candidates for the House and slates for the Senate have been elected. In fact, in 1970, an antigovernment militant An Quang Buddhist slate headed by a national hero who publicly broke with Diem at the height of the 1963 Buddhist crisis received the highest plurality in the election to the Senate.

Such elections have not been free of interference by officials. Nonetheless, fairly rigid electoral supervision by specific commissions and other bodies has kept these elections straightforward mechanisms for leadership selection by Southeast Asian standards. Political parties, institutions that have had an extremely checkered history in Vietnam, have had an opportunity to operate openly. Almost all major religious, ethnic and noncommunist interest groups have participated in electoral processes and have obtained representation in the National Assembly. In fact, the legislature manifests the divisions within Vietnamese society, a situation not without its problems.

To a great extent, the legislature operates through the process of shifting alignments; majorities are formed on the basis of issues and politics. Increasingly, legislators, and particularly House members, have become oriented to the role of serving as friends in court for their district constituents.

And both houses have displayed a considerable independence of the executive. For instance, government-sponsored legislation concerning anti-inflationary measures, increased executive decree powers, land reform, and budgets has met with serious criticism on the floor of each house, and certain propositions have been turned down. The legislature has also served a watchdog function, criticizing specific alleged government malfeasances and specific official personalities. Perhaps most important, the legislative institution has steadfastly demanded that its constitutional powers be respected and that it retain an autonomous position vis-à-vis the executive power.

During 1969–70, this question was dramatically brought to the foreground by Thieu's attempt to put the legislature in its place. He succeeded only in having one member arrested—for alleged procommunist activities. He was Tran Ngoc Chau, a man with a brilliant record as a province chief and as director of Revolutionary Development.[16]

The Chau case and a government-approved spontaneous demonstration against the House hardened the determination of many legislators to retain their independence and to protect the standard constitutional rights of legislatures against political harassment by the government.

It was in the Chau case, further, that the Supreme Court staked out a thoroughly non-Confucianist role as an independent judiciary. In declaring the military court trial of Chau to have been illegal, it simultaneously declared the independence of the legislative and judicial structures. It also declared Thieu's austerity tax unconstitutional, forcing him to try an equalization tax as a substitute anti-inflation measure, and ruled the special military field tribunals unconstitutional. The Supreme Court was not by any definition a serious block to executive misuse of power, nor did its members advance such pretenses. But this transplanted American-style institution provided an avenue of redress in the face of governmental transgressions against the Constitution. This was not a nicety of law for appearance's sake. Thieu was forced to devise alternative anti-inflationary measures. As Chau could testify, the subtleties of a Supreme Court declaration did not guarantee his release from prison, but his case resulted in the supremacy of the civil over the military judiciary.

Thus, while South Vietnam retains a unitary, strong executive, for the first time the executive is not absolutely supreme. Despite numerous qualifications, South Vietnam has become increasingly decentralized, and this decentralization has provided avenues of access to the total political system for a wide range of interest groups. This is potentially of vast significance for the political future of South Vietnam. While specific interest groups have been given less than a fair opportunity to move into positions of controlling administration in certain areas where they have considerable adherents vis-à-vis other groups—i.e., Buddhists, tribesmen, Khmers—because of prejudicial decisions by provincial and other GVN officials, the advances that have been made by the major interests in local government will be zealously guarded. Eventual popular election of province chiefs and an expanded role for provincial councils will provide a number of political parties with a solid base.

Political Parties

Despite their electoral experience to date and their roles in the national legislature and local councils, political parties are far from viable.[17] The old-line nationalist parties, especially the VNQDD and the Dai Viet, have gained electoral victories, but they continue to be divided into numerous factions. Parties primarily representing Catholic and Buddhist interests have had success at the polls. Splinter parties, like the Tan Dai Viet and the revitalized Diemist Can Lao party, have added to the vitality of the party system. But even the Can Lao has divided into central and southern factions.

In fact, government-sponsored parties or associations have added little in long-range terms. No generalization could possibly portray these groups as obvious leaders for the future. In a word, all of Vietnam, indeed all of Indochina, has seen only one truly successful political party, i.e., the communist party, under any of the names it has used in the twentieth century. It has never won a free election, except a quasi-open election before World War II in Cochinchina. It has relatively few members today even in the DRVN. A vanguard, not a mass structure, the key to its success lies in its ability to organize, coordinate, indoctrinate and control people through the creation of overlapping structures within a closely restrained hierarchy. It has also enjoyed a bit of luck and good timing.

The parties in the South today have had a long history of bad luck, terrible timing for their crucial moves, and an absence of real leadership (due largely to the physical annihilation of that leadership by the French, the communists and the Diemists). But their major problem has been organizational. Diem tried to create a nationwide party, although it was divided between his brothers, but he created a paper structure whose residual strength is only now beginning to be appreciated. The possibility that the state would create an all-encompassing party failed to materialize following the coup against Diem. For one thing, the military did not seek to create a viable competing structure, and the national leaders were blocked by their jealous and ever-suspicious military peers. This was an objective condition: a powerful institution whose support was requisite for any regime's survival was not prepared to acquiesce while any national leader or group created an alternative institution. To an extent, of course, Thieu did just this, indirectly, by accepting structural differentiation and directly, by personnel replacements. But this was not the substitution of an institution like the Lao Dong or Can Lao. Rather, it was a diffraction that created multiple centers of control, not cohesive, interconnected elements of a national institution.

The reasons for political party amorphousness in South Vietnam are subjective. In a real sense, South Vietnam is a complex matrix of interest groups; politics historically has been carried on through communalism, responsive to religious, ethnic and geographical interests. The instruments of a broader political system have been accepted as at best a disturbing alien intrusion in their affairs. Interest group leaders are finally gaining a stake in the system through councils and the legislature and through special arrangements like those for the tribesmen, but this experience has been of too recent a vintage to allow their constituents to accept the legislature as the sole initiator of national values, which must often be interpreted locally. Many other groups, primarily urban groups such as the university students and the squatters (veterans and refugees), but also groups such as the An Quang Buddhists, have continued to feel unrepresented—and to be oppressed by the regime—thus standing outside the regular political system.

Public Policy Issues

Even in the absence of viable political parties, there are several topics that are recognized as major public policy issues by practically all residents of South Vietnam.

The overriding question is the future role of the United States, not only because of military security but because of economic and other public policy questions. So-called Vietnamization has farreaching significance. From a high of 542,500 United States troops in Vietnam during February 1969, the number dropped to well below 400,000 by the end of 1970 and was scheduled to drop to 260,000 by the spring of 1971 under the Vietnamization program. Presumably United States withdrawal does not mean that overnight there will no longer be an American presence. Support groups, training contingents and supplies will probably continue in some form and in some magnitude. However, ironically, most Vietnamese are extremely uneasy about this process, despite their undoubted desire to have Vietnamese governing Vietnam without a force that has long since outlived whatever welcome it once enjoyed. What most Vietnamese fear is not the absence of Americans but the withdrawal of their economic input into the social system: jobs (nearly 150,000 persons were employed by American companies and agencies in 1970), construction, piaster support, import assistance, and so on. Despite the severe economic upheaval associated with United States investments in widespread activities related to the war effort, Vietnamese prosperity (as well as inflation) is tied to those investments.

In fact, the entire Vietnamese economic system, especially the increasingly important urban economies, depends on the United States to provide a continuing support level as the base for Vietnamese economics. Without that support, unemployment and inflation would be rampant, something neither the Thieu regime nor any conceivable nationalist government could survive. The war has made South Vietnam a nation of urban dwellers: over 60 per cent of the population now lives in genuine urban areas but even many "villages" today are urban areas by almost any standard definition. Such a population cannot survive on a subsistence economy but must rely upon a sophisticated economic system.

Inflation

Criticisms of Thieu already hinge on the topic of inflation. It is difficult to have a conversation with a Vietnamese without immediately hearing about the price of rice, of rent, of charcoal, of Hondas, including detailed comparisons of price rises and the fact that many Vietnamese must hold two jobs to make ends meet. There was an annual price rise of 30 per cent during 1967–69. Prices rose 50 per cent in the 12-month period before a change in rates from 118 to 275 piasters per dollar for American personnel, for luxury item importers, and for exporters in South Vietnam was approved in October 1970. The rate change was to counteract a thriving black market and to stabilize the economy. Increased prices on luxury items, increased interest rates—both encouraging savings—also served as anti-inflation measures. Presumably, an extremely unbalanced budget would also be brought more nearly into balance.

Corruption—the second topic for an unsolicited recitaton—is condemned but rationalized for junior level officials as an inevitable adjunct to their activities if they are to live normal lives under inflationary conditions. A late 1970 pay increase of 20 per cent for civil servants and soldiers, the groups hardest hit by inflation, was unlikely to resolve the corruption problem.

Other economic and social problems also plagued South Vietnam's government. Although the refugee problem had diminished greatly, well over three million persons had lost their homes since the intensification of the war in 1965. The nation had over 200,000 orphans. Many veterans were forced to live a substandard existence in urban ghettos. General urban problems were acute: slums, sanitation, welfare, education, fire fighting, traffic circulation, robbery and other crimes. Continued government failure to eradicate poor conditions aroused considerable criticism and intensified Saigon police efforts to crack down on "hippies" involved in minor criminal activities were not adequate to alleviate the core causes.

On the other hand, the Thieu government had taken steps to resolve socioeconomic problems in the rural areas. For example, rural banks were established and "miracle" rice production has been impressive. But by far the single most important public policy for assisting rural residents has been the "land to the tillers" program. In brief, land holdings beyond 15 hectares were expropriated under a compensation formula and procedures were established to distribute expropriated lands (basically 3 hectares in the South and 1 hectare in the Center) to present tillers (top priority) and to relatives of war dead, retired military men and civil servants, and others.[18] Administration of the program was made relatively simple and much of the decision making related to this administration was left to local village officials. This long overdue public policy undoubtedly reinforced the national government presence and strengthened local government.

Politics in North Vietnam

Although many of the public policy problems encountered by the GVN were not dissimilar from those faced by its northern counterpart, politically North Vietnam has maintained its traditional overall balance. The communist party dominates the branches of government and the structures for developing political support and for assisting in implementing public policies. The other primary political force, the military, has remained a source of support for party programs and for maintaining popular discipline. Unlike China, the DRVN has not retained military warlords, although a similar structure has existed in a much lesser way in the highlands. On occasion, military support has been vital, and no doubt incipient schisms have been stopped before reaching fruition.

Simplistically, the diametrically opposed ideologies of popular, continuing revolution and bourgeois-professionalization have both found periods of prominence. The controversy concerning communization or cooperative endeavors for rural areas has been the subject of heated disputes. In 1970, Le Duan and Pham Van Dong stressed the goal of increasing consumer supplies, in addition to increased food production and development of industry, communications and transportation.

North Vietnam has not enjoyed political processes in the usual sense. There have been elections, and chosen "opposition" members have been assigned victory in the uncontested referenda. Interest groups have been formed at all levels, but these are closely controlled instruments. Peasant unrest and intellectuals' criticisms have occurred but have been quickly repressed. Following ideological shifts or during periods of appeasing China or the Soviet Union, criticisms of policies and of leading personalities have been made—but in official organs. The major interest groups remain: the party, the bureaucrats and the military. The legislature ratifies; it does not initiate.

Undoubtedly, there is a Cabinet politics and a Politburo politics: all major policy shifts have been made following internal disputes at this level. But this is the politics of a closed political system, a system that survives due to the creation of a complex matrix .of overlapping structures, constant indoctrination and, when necessary, military backing. In short, the DRVN is a classic totalitarian state whose overall inclination toward ideological doctrinairism varies with the political fortunes of certain members of a small cabal.

Since the death of Ho Chi Minh, this totalitarian political system has had no national charismatic leader. Probably as President Ho had planned, Le Duan emerged as first among equals; Truong Chinh was in a decidedly secondary position for the moment; General Vo Nguyen Giap supported the war strategy shift and took at least a vocal part in advancing domestic policy shifts; Pham Van Dong remained the ever-present bureaucrat; President Ton Duc Thang continued as a respected elder; others in the cadre followed the lead of the top personalities. It was something of a Kosygin-Brezhnev (and perhaps Chou Enlai) posture: businesslike, relatively dull, with Le Duan and Dong, drawing on Giap's support, taking the lead.

In one sense, the DRVN had a more pro-Soviet regime after Ho, but economics, combined with the Chinese proximity and complicated by the revived Indochina war theater, led the Vietnamese to adopt their standard pragmatism. China's aid to the DRVN in 1969, which was only about half that of the USSR, was greatly increased, but the USSR also increased its aid because of the Indochina situation. Although the government was more pragmatic, it still thought it necessary to send Labor Youth League members to rural areas—they had served in urban areas already—to maintain discipline among a population considered susceptible to "counter-revolutionary" sentiments. In addition, local military task forces,. acting as labor units as well as army reserves, were assigned to stimulate production in the industrial sphere, particularly in the area of handicrafts. Because of economic difficulties (a product of war efforts and inclement weather), officials were known to have turned their backs on occasion to the existence of rice and other black markets; and "cowboys" and hippies also added a new dimension to urban life.[19]

In effect, the post-Ho DRVN was following ambivalent domestic policies—relaxing certain controls to offset economic problems and simultaneously moving cadres to reestablish or invigorate other controls. In the seventh decade of the twentieth century, public policy in the DRVN was in a state of flux. The turn it would take was contingent upon cabal politics, which depended in part on personalities, on Chinese and Soviet pressures and the level of their aid required for survival, on the status of army success in the Indochina war, and the effectiveness of the party control mechanism. Other factors were also important, particularly public (rural and urban) demands for more material benefits, intellectual and youth pressures for expanded freedoms, and highlander pressures for increased autonomy vis-à-vis the Vietnamese.

It appeared likely that the party, with continued military support, could handle these pressures as it had previously. What was less certain was the eventual outcome of cabal politics; the leaders were not young men and the balance established with Le Duan at first was precarious. During 1970, it appeared that he was indeed prepared to make a move to consolidate his position. In the February 14, 1970, issue of *Nhan Dan* he noted that a proletariat leadership was essential (although the Lao Dong party had given itself a special dispensation on this score years before). He condemned party members who were taking advantage of their positions, dishonesty on the part of certain responsible officials, and lack of initiative in the leadership. In March 1970 the Politburo passed a resolution condemning members of cooperatives who were engaging in private business. Press and radio attacks against lazy, dishonest officials began, and trials were held against those who committed violations (theft) against socialist property. A Party Secretariat was established by the Politburo. And a year-long drive to replace expelled party members with new recruits, the "Ho Chi Minh" class members, began in May.[20] All these developments overshadowed well-publicized international politics, except for Indochina.

The Two Vietnams

The political future of the two Vietnams is contingent on too many possible developments to warrant much speculation. To the North lies a totalitarian state with an experienced population-control mechanism, although it has a less totally controlled social system than its giant Chinese neighbor. To the South lies a state that must still be termed a dictatorship, despite its quasi-military and quasi-civilian regime and its increasingly decentralized political system. Future politics in each nation depends to a great extent upon developments in the war in Indochina. The DRVN will not cease its efforts to control the political system of the GVN. Hanoi is also unlikely to abandon its Indochina policy; at the very least, Vietnamese suzerainty over Laos and Cambodia has always been a Lao Dong objective. Developments at the Paris peace talks have always been dependent on Hanoi's interpretation of how an American proposal or how a Washington-Saigon acceptance of a Hanoi proposal related to politico-military conditions at a given moment in Indochina.

Despite the tremendous hardships of the past several years, North Vietnam remains the only nation in Indochina that has escaped the devastation of land warfare. However, the economy of the DRVN continues to be less prosperous than that of the GVN. It is possible that the economic equation will influence political changes in Hanoi. And the decisions of political leaders in Hanoi will affect political processes in Saigon. For the southern Vietnamese state, the major political questions are (1) the external political tactics of Hanoi, (2) the format of the decline of American economic support, and (3) the viability of the national government. Clearly, the most important question is the third. South Vietnam's persistent inability to formulate a political structure that obtains at least the acquiescence of her divergent groups remains her chief weakness. And the possibility that South Vietnam can overcome this weakness—or, contrarily, her failure to overcome it—will influence the cabal politics in Hanoi even more than domestic questions within the government of North Vietnam.

The Sequence of Vietnamese Political Warfare, 1966–73

Annual analyses of political and military events in South Vietnam in many ways, from hindsight, have a propensity to be subject to the well-known phenomenon of déjà vu. Often even the personalities as well as the events appear to be reliving sets of experiences for the umpteenth occasion. This is more true for purely political characters than for higher military leaders who, with notable exceptions such as Tran Van Don and Tran Thien Khiem, tend to lose out and remain both out of power and out of the country. But time has affected even this untrue generalization. Le Van Kim returned after a decade; Big Minh returned after a prolonged absence. Such personalities even when operating only on the fringes of politics continue to wait in the wings. The dream of the mandate or at minimum of a piece of the action never ceases to be there somewhere, perhaps tomorrow, perhaps next year, but never viewed as completely out of grasp. The sight of General Nguyen Chanh Thi—having fled from Diem following the 1960 abortive coup and left a second time upon failure to gain power in the mid-1960's—arriving at the Saigon airport in 1971 to be greeted by a prominent Buddhist delegation only to be kept on his commercial flight and to be flown again into at least temporary oblivion to await another day—this epitomized much of nationalist politics.

Partly a perpetual dream, partly a less-than-practical appreciation of power politics, partly a semi-clandestine thrust toward grasping for at least some portion of the mandate, and partly pure obstinacy in playing the game, the orientation of South Vietnam's political personalities has been to keep plodding along regardless of the odds against their eventual succession to power. And of course many have achieved a power base only to see it slip from their grasp. Ministerial positions, posts near the presidency or to the prime minister, military slots of importance, legislative and council spots, provincial jobs, etc., have had literally thousands of occupants since 1954. Tenure normally has been short, turnover of aides and often party adherents of persons in high positions has been extreme, and shifting from one position to another one has been common.

Still a few things have changed over the years. The sequence of elections at all levels since 1966 has had an effect on political processes. In some instances this effect has been fairly subtle, such as increased recognition of the importance of prominent civilian political personalities by military province chiefs who still retain much actual raw power. In other instances the effect has been more dramatic. The elections at the village level were important. Village chiefs and councils gained real power, particularly over finances and local security forces. As actual power did exist it inevitably was coveted, and competition for village posts increased. Political parties, religious groups, influential villagers and representatives of the national government itself recognized this change, and their attempts to influence local elections reflected this recognition.

National Assembly elections have also stimulated political party development. This has been more manifest in the Lower House elections (and in provincial council elections) where constituencies are less than nationwide. As noted in Chapter 3, many groups can claim pluralities in specific districts which they could never presume to obtain nationally. The result has been that the Lower House is actually fairly representative of the diverse interests within South Vietnam. A corollary is that there have been real politics among members of the National Assembly. Political parties certainly do not even pretend to maintain legislative discipline, but there has developed within the legislature a maturity few had anticipated. This has been a complex maturity. Legislators have been bribed and browbeaten (and worse) by the Thieu administration. Constructive alternatives to administration programs have been offered in the legislature, although it has hardly become renowned in this regard. Actual opposition to the government has been manifested over and over again, although with few exceptions the legislature has ultimately buckled under to administration pressures.

These may appear to be small advances. Perhaps they are. And perhaps in the long run they will be viewed as irrelevant quirks of Vietnamese history. But to many Vietnamese and certainly to the legislators themselves a unique experience has occurred. Despite so much which remained as it always has been in Vietnamese politics, the legislative process engendered at least a certain awareness of political responsibility to an electorate. And this same process at least somewhat encouraged formulation of policies based not only upon constituency needs but also upon articulated proposals resulting from study and dialogue.

During the 1965–73 period of intensive political activity and of broad political developments, the Second Indochina War continued to take its toll of lives, property, morale and morality. Politics did not become a substitute for bestiality on either side. Possible measures for bringing about an end to hostilities were voiced by different interest groups, by candidates in the 1967 presidential election and in most subsequent elections. Formulae written in Washington and in Hanoi to bring peace to Vietnam were debated in Paris and even in Saigon. Still the war continued, sometimes more modestly than at other times, sometimes escalating to proportions which seemed actually to threaten the civilization of both the South and the North. And the potential for peace remained enmeshed in the web of Vietnamese political processes.

Peace politics, which commenced in earnest in 1968, continued as the primary arena of international conflict from that point. Four years later the actions of the major actors were also related to the time agenda demanded by the Constitution of the United States. The 1972 American presidential election was the target date of more relevance than many others from the perspective of the DRVN. Neither the 1968 Tet offensive nor the 1972 invasion was carried out solely for the purpose of influencing the television viewing public in the United States. Yet milestones beget strategies. And in a war as politicized as the Indochina

War a major political event inevitably became an element of programming other events. Hanoi's method of attack invariably has had political goals as indirect targets. Washington's foreign policies without exception have also considered indigenous American politics as a prime mover. The Nixon "Vietnamization" program was geared toward a nearly complete withdrawal of American combat troops prior to the 1972 election. Saigon went along. Hanoi's program of steps for Indochina considered the embarrassment of the Vietnamization program as of primary importance for immediate reasons and because such a development would influence the 1972 election and the peace politics of an American president inaugurated in 1973. The NLF went along. The die had been cast for an all-Vietnamese showdown on the ground.

All of the subtle wrappings of the ill-fated Indochina conflict were shorn during early April of 1972. PAVN forces in strength and using a format of conventional warfare invaded the Republic of Vietnam. Tanks, heavy artillery and ground-to-air missiles accompanied the invading army. Diversionary actions were undertaken elsewhere by NLF units and by other PAVN formations, but the main foray concentrated on troop movements across the Demilitarized Zone and into South Vietnam from Laos. Unlike other prior actions when PAVN units infiltrated and formed for attacks utilizing always some measure of strategy based upon clandestine movements, the 1972 Easter offensive was a classic instance of one nation sending its regular, assembled military might in a straight-forward attempt to punish the armed forces of its neighbors. A European-style conflict had supplemented revolutionary warfare. This was no commando action, no guerrilla attack, no clandestine terrorist action by *revolutionnaires* clad in black pajamas. The PAVN 304th Division (and later all regular PAVN divisions), an experienced, well-trained and tough instrument, was challenging the territorial claims of the Saigon government and indeed was staking a claim to influence in all of Indochina. It threw down the gauntlet to the forces of ARVN I Corps, forcing set-piece encounters and forging offensives of full strength against defending armies.

The new strategy could have been followed at any point Hanoi decided to press according to a new set of rules. Prior withdrawal of American personnel unquestionably was not irrelevant to placement of PAVN regulars on an offensive within northern South Vietnam. But the presence of American defenders would not have caused drastic tactical changes for the PAVN planners. Targets of 130-mm artillery do not survive regardless of their uniform or insignia. Retaliation by air was contingent upon weather conditions and not upon whether those attacked on the ground were American or Vietnamese. An attempt to provide evidence to a worldwide audience that "Vietnamization" was a hollow concept built upon drifting and easily disappearing sand was also not an irrelevant rationale for the invasion. Nor was the potential for influencing the American electorate in a presidential election year irrelevant. Indeed, the American audience unquestionably was important.

However, Easter of 1972 was perfectly consistent with Tet 1968, and with every strategy of the Viet Minh at least since 1950. PAVN attacks were not primarily to show the Americans a thing or two. The foremost objective was to underscore the weakness of the political system of South Vietnam. Gains achieved by that political system in terms of political and economic development were the main targets. Weakening the local infrastructure to permit the NLF to move back into vacuums created in village power structures was a strategic goal. Preparing the ground for any contingent developments in international peace politics required both hurting the Saigon government and strengthening the NLF's posture in local political processes. In 1972 and 1973 the DRVN and the NLF displayed once again that to them the Second Indochina War was definitely a case of "Vietnamese" political processes plus a war.

The scenario those processes would follow would not be determined until all relevant Vietnamese actors could compete according to rules they themselves would acquiesce to following signing of the 1973 Paris accords. "Peace" politics subsequent to the cease fire in South Vietnam entered the most complicated and difficult stage. Now the true "leopard spot" framework, including not only NLF- versus GVN-controlled areas but also including specific geographical areas and specific constituencies influenced by diversified South Vietnamese interest groups, underlying all politics of war and of peace in Vietnam would determine whether there would or would not soon be a Third Indochina War.

6

The Tragedy of South Vietnam's Political Processes

THE years have not affected one aspect of a tragic story. Determination to be themselves has continued to be an identifying characteristic of the Vietnamese. This determination has assumed herculean proportions in the face of inconceivable odds. Nonrecognition of this conscious resolution has resulted in a large number of non-Vietnamese relegating Vietnamese political behavior to the realm of puppetry. According to this widely accepted hypothesis, a powerful force provides a stimulus, and all Vietnamese in a semi-automatic manner react. The hypothesis presumes a uniformity of reaction and indeed a Pavlovian-type response based upon a prior conditioning. Such an interpretation of events is naive psychology. It is also an insult to a group of people who have shaped individual and national destinies under circumstances much more traumatic than any encountered by other peoples or nations in contemporary history.

The determination of the Vietnamese to be themselves would be much less complex, much less of a tragedy when viewed in full scenario, and much less controversial if it were purely a function of a uniform response to specific externally induced stimuli. Indeed, if their determination were less complex and less controversial, it would be considerably less tragic. Complexity and controversy have occurred because of the continuing presence of vast, ingrained individual and group differences and because of the rich, extremely varied interpretations of what it means to be oneself. Rather than a malleable mass, manifesting strains of conformity, the responses of Vietnamese over the long haul of the long, long war have been a function of their interpretations of their own goals, values and societal roles. This is not sociological jargon but a recognition of what is important to a set of human beings living in a certain time in history in a certain geographical locale, a set of human beings who happen to be Vietnamese.

The individual and collective suffering undergone by this set of human beings is unimaginable. Few are those who have escaped the loss of one or more family members. None has escaped various personal hardships. A large percentage have lived under numerous overlords— the French, the Viet Minh, the Diemist representatives. Most have witnessed the presence of the foreigner on their soil: French, Japanese, American, Thai, Korean, Tonkinese, et al. Millions have been rendered homeless, typically residing temporarily in settlements established by the Republic of Vietnam (GVN) with American financial and other assistance. Large numbers, unquestionably a majority of the population of South Vietnam, have become dwellers in communities in excess of 25,000 persons. Among the newer urban inhabitants, most have lost all that preceded their migration. This loss has been much deeper than the abandonment of homes, of lands tilled for a generation or more, and of businesses. The loss has also included an entire life style, a host of traditions and a social system. Much of an entire society has been destroyed. Perceptions of appropriate patterns of interaction within the family, within a basically cohesive small or moderately-sized social group, and within a village (the previously perceived microcosm of the universe) have been changed, crushed and irremediably replaced.

Anthropologically, sociologically and psychologically nearly everything has been affected. An economic revolution has transpired. A technological shift is ubiquitous. Politically nothing is the same. With the exception of the Carthaginian eradication at the hands of the Romans, precedents for this massive impact upon an entire population are difficult to find. The Vietnamese have been the victims of too many proponents of too many seemingly grand philosophies: colonialism (and its corollary of "assimilation"), the Greater Co-Prosperity Sphere of World War II Japanese imperialism; communism and anticommunism; democracy; independence and nationalism; neocolonialism by whatever title; "personalism." Each philosophy had adherents among honorable men and women. Each philosophy had apologists with ready explanations and rationalizations for actions that were taken. Each philosophy even had advocates among the Vietnamese, including advocates specifically among South Vietnamese before and after the partition of 1954.

The tragedy could be so much simpler if the lines had always been tightly drawn between opposing political philosophies or even between an oriental versus an occidental set of political interests. But as Bernard Fall noted eloquently, there were more Vietnamese than French on the side of the defenders at Dien Bien Phu during that historic confrontation of 1954. There were 5,480 Vietnamese regulars and auxiliaries, including many Thai tribesmen, as opposed to 2,810 Frenchmen, in the total defense force of 15,105 according to Fall's data.[1] Obviously the active combatants, at least among the Vietnamese, have had a cause they perceived as just during the entire struggle of the Indochina Wars. With the exception of the desire for ultimate independence from "outside" forces, none of the goals associated with such causes can lay claim to anything approximating universality among the Vietnamese combatants and noncombatants alike.

Human beings fight, suffer and die for quite diverse reasons. Typically these reasons are fairly pragmatic ones, which philosophers reifying seekers after political power justify for some audience (or for writers of history) in terms of political philosophy. During the Indochina wars pragmatic rationales were supplemented more than in most wars by rationales that actually were attuned to personal political philosophies. Imperialism and colonialism were real and not simply rallying cries. The injustices wrought by those enemies of all Vietnamese were felt dramatically by elite and nonelite alike. Independence was a concept all could accept as just. Rabid adherence to communism and to anticommunism was a real factor in unknown but unquestionably large numbers of personal decisions to struggle regardless of apparent odds. Religious factors, tribal factors, ethnic factors and regional factors were also of vast impact upon personal decisions to enter into and continue in a long struggle. Personal experience—murder of a family member by the French, the Viet Minh, the GVN, the Americans, the Viet Cong—provided the impetus for personal decisions in countless instances. Personal fortune, including the fortuitous event of being born and reared in a region under the influence of one of the contending forces, in fact eliminated choice in many personal decisions.

Pragmatism, philosophy, chance—each has been relevant. But the grand philosophies have served as the stimuli for the leaders of all sides of the war-making apparatus. "Communism" and "democracy" as interpreted by those leaders may be without significant meaning as philosophies for living by the Vietnamese population as a whole. For those leaders, however, and for their interpretations the concepts are germane to the requirement that millions of human beings submit to the indignities of losing true personal choice, to the psychological and physical pain of terror and its effects, to the trauma and torture of being uprooted and witnessing the elimination of all that has made up their lives, and to the constant uncertainty of simply continuing to exist. This is a terrible price to require an entire population to pay for fulfilling the objectives of competing political philosophies.

During all of the Second Indochina War, residents of South Vietnam to a great extent, although much more forcefully, relived the physical and psychological agonies suffered by all Vietnamese during the 1946–54 war. For the most part the first war had been fought in the North. Prior to 1950 and after 1953 struggles between contending armies occurred in certain sections of what became South Vietnam. However, in most sections for most of the war period there were insurgency conditions at a much lower level in the South than the intensified revolutionary (and eventually conventional) warfare in the North. Conditions in the South represented a special kind of Hell, but the inferno flamed with somewhat less intensity than farther North. There were many reasons for the disparity in level of warfare, including logistical, political, demographic and philosophical reasons. The Viet Minh were much less successful in the South than in the North in coopting support from highlander tribes. The Cao Dai and Hoa Hao in the far South (Cochinchina) competed on a par with the Viet Minh. And the Viet Minh main strength was in Tonkin, a factor the Annamese and Cochinchinese of all political persuasions appreciated very well.

Lucien Bodard's explanation of post-1950 warfare in the far South is most instructive.

In the first place it was a Cochinchina without a Resistance. The whole of the Resistance had died with Nguyen Binh [the southern Viet Minh leader and lieutenant general who had been betrayed to a group of Cambodian soldiers by political commissars accompanying him on a trip to the north]. From now on there was nothing left in the south but a weak, purged Communist Party in which Le Duan [later to become First Secretary of the Communist Party of North Vietnam] was the mere agent of the Tongbo [Tonkin] Committee, Ho Chi Minh and Giap. Discipline within the Party must come first—that was the watchword for the future. And sometimes I wonder whether the Tongbo Committee, having made use of the Resistance when that served its purpose, had not preferred that it should be crushed rather than that it should be victorious—whether it did not bring about this defeat on purpose. It all happened as though Cochinchina, having played its part, had been sacrificed because of its impurity when the right moment came: for it collapsed just as the new war began a thousand miles away—the real, huge-scale Communist war fought by Giap in Tonkin with Mao Tse-tung's support. This was to be the decisive war: at least according to the Tongbo Committee it was to be decisive. For years on end Giap's battalions were to be engaged in incessant fighting, and during all this time the propaganda in the south amounted to no more than this—"Maintain the Party but do not stir. Just do your utmost to improve Communist thinking and wait until the people's armies from Tonkin reach you and liberate you."[2]

Although Bodard understates the extent of Viet Minh activity in the South, he does touch upon an infrequently noted variable of considerable significance in explaining post-Geneva-Convention developments within South Vietnam. At the termination of the First Indochina War, while the Viet Minh had experienced brilliant successes in the North outside of the major Catholic bishoprics, its posture in the South was much more precarious. The really big victories against the French had been Tonkinese victories (often supplemented with support by the Tho and certain other northern tribesmen).[3] The Viet Minh made successful drives into central Vietnam (Annam) and the northern portion of the southern highlands in conjunction with preparations for the Dien Bien Phu battle and it retained throughout a maquis reserve strength in both the far south and portions of the Cambodian border regions of Cochinchina.

When the Republic of Vietnam (i.e., contemporary South Vietnam) was formed its number of true adherents was quite limited, but so was the percentage of true believers supporting any given cause or any specific political philosophy. The Viet Minh had many southern supporters, but this unknown number had to have been a minority of the total population of the South. Several relatively cohesive local interest groups comprised at least a near majority of the population, including the Cao Dai; the Hoa Hao; the various highland tribal groups; the indigenous Catholics and the refugee Catholics from Tonkin; the Chinese; and the Khmers. Each were advocates of their own goals, philosophy and relative autonomy. Some supported the Saigon regime of Ngo Dinh Diem. Most of those in this interest group matrix supported neither the Viet Minh nor the Republic, although they were prepared to cooperate in varying degrees with the new regime as long as that regime either did not suppress their perceived interests or had the power to implement policies perceived as detrimental to those interests.

When the noncommitted, the pro-Bao Daists, the pro-Cochinchina separatists, and the anti-Viet Minh but otherwise noncommitted are combined with adherents of religious and other interest groups, there probably was a large majority in the South which did not favor the Viet Minh. The new government of South Vietnam also inherited a Vietnamese National Army of 270,000 members, while the sects and many other groups had their own "armies." Regardless of initial lack of enthusiam for any Saigon government, the total armed contingents representing directly or indirectly political philosophies at variance with those of the Viet Minh were hardly inconsiderable.

In 1954 and 1955 a melange of political propensities was present in South Vietnam. Each had adherents more or less committed to goals of specific groups. The Second Indochina War did not change this dimension of extreme diversity. This war made the South rather than the North the principal battlefield. The "spread of communism" and the "containment of communism" again were presumably vital issues fought over by an unknown number of military forces representing North Vietnam and the National Liberation Front, American forces numbering over one-half million at one point, prior to American adoption of the so-called "Vietnamization" policy, and by ultimately nearly one million regulars and two million militia (Peoples' Self-Defense Forces) representing South Vietnam. For the second time around, the machinery for making war has become much more sophisticated and generally technologically advanced and much more devastating within the smaller piece of geography over which the battles were fought.

Bland statistics presented in this work on the numbers of deaths and casualties in battle and by torture, on the numbers of homeless, on the numbers of orphans and widows and families which no longer have sons, on the numbers of acres or hectares destroyed temporarily and even permanently, on gross economic dislocation, etc., cannot begin to describe what indeed is indescribable. No graphic narration can produce a true, accurate photo of the terrible price the Vietnamese population (North and South) and also the Laotian and Cambodian populations have been forced to pay for the fulfillment of the long-range goals of competing political philosophies. Yet, despite the price that has been paid, despite the magnitude of destruction associated with the application of the most advanced machinery for making war, despite the expertness of the highly sophisticated and singleminded application of concepts of revolutionary warfare, and despite the instability, unrepresentativeness and inefficiency of a series of Saigon governments, the resiliency of the residents of South Vietnam and of the diverse groups to whom most belong continues.

Even in the midst of the holocaust, they continued to be themselves. The irony of ironies remains that their continued adherence to centrifugal forces has been their primary source of strength. Where centripetal pressures exist they serve to increase cohesiveness of the very groups that resist the tensions forced upon them by even the representatives of grand political philosophies. The central government has proved unable to construct vehicles advancing a nationalist orientation which could gain adherence of all those who cling to the groups which continually pull away from the center. Those groups in turn have thus far been unable to forge structures, such as political parties, that would pull together varied interests in support of something approaching an articulated set of national priorities and programs.

The region which is now South Vietnam remains what it was in 1954 and even before. It is *not* and has never been a Tonkinese province. It is *not* an experimental ground for the military-economic-political practices of any foreign nation. It *is* a state including a diverse maze of ethnic, religious and economic groups. Much of the constituency of those groups now inhabits urban places—a distinctly new element since 1954, and one which unquestionably will have a long-range impact upon the political and social systems of South Vietnam. It *is* an "underdeveloped" nation with all this signifies in terms of its economy and technological status. It *is* a country with an awkward civil bureaucracy, an aggressive military bureaucracy, and a host of competing political parties, formal (and less than formal) interest groups.

Inexperienced in the mechanics of representative government and familiar with civil-military-judicial bureaucracies which have adopted an orientation of bureaucratic discretion as opposed to an orientation favoring the "rule of law," the residents of South Vietnam have continued to opt for the certainty of group allegiance rather than allegiance to an abstract nation state. Occasional policies of the national government have exhibited a potential for making the nation state a more acceptable presence and for encouraging at least vestiges of integration among the nation's numerous centrifugal forces. The government of the Republic of Vietnam indeed has increasingly become an "administering" polity. Considering the milieu of war, chaos and quasi-chaos encountered by South Vietnam throughout the 1960's any advance whatsoever is no mean achievement. However, it would be absurd to assume that South Vietnam has reached some magical point on an economist's paradigm and is prepared for a "spin-off" stage.

If its administrative system had been as weak as commonly portrayed, South Vietnam's survival would have been highly improbable. Despite something of an international myth, South Vietnam has always maintained an administrative system, an extremely weak one, certainly, but one with a long history with Confucianist-French roots. In the absence of total warfare, and undoubtedly in the absence of revolutionary warfare, the administrative system quite likely would have fumbled along in an inefficient manner, somewhat dishonestly with an orientation that people were to serve the administration rather than vice versa—in short, it would have emulated nearly all administrative systems in the third world. But this type of system buckled when faced by revolutionary warfare. The Ngo Dinh Diem regime failed partially because administratively it could not adapt to the world in which it found itself. Subsequent governments may have adopted public policies more realistic to the strains they faced but did not significantly improve the requisite administrative base without which any public policy could never be more than mere rhetoric. For a period the totality of corruption appeared to be the ultimate blasphemy in addition to being an added factor in crushing the efficacy of the administrative system.

Still, Vietnamese again manifested the quality of being themselves even in the morass of administrative confusion. Faced with the intrusions of the military bureaucracy, the chaotic milieu of warfare, the service burdens of warfare and increased urbanization, the administrative system stumbled, faltered and became criminally inefficient. However, it did not collapse. There were periods when all was madness—the last summer of the Diem regime, immediate post-coup periods, apparent anarchy during militant Buddhist uprisings—when an outsider could not see the existence of any political system in South Vietnam. Yet the administration provided "government" to most of the nation even during the nihilistic era of Tet 1968. During those frequent epochs of the 1960's, in its own way the administrative system (supplemented by quasi-government by local leadership of the wide range of interest groups) was the "government." It survived while national political leaders played musical chairs with positions of political power. The irony of administrative organization opportunism holding out against such formidable odds is a tribute solely to man's one universal characteristic, his ability to strive for survival sometimes because he performs his acts by rote and perceives few alternatives and the manifested occasional actions which can only be described as truly heroic.

There is no wonder that the total picture of politics and government in South Vietnam often is a portrait depicting apparent insanity. What is omitted from the vision of the camera is that the people themselves do understand the situation, or at least they understand their own portion of the grand panorama. What they cannot understand is why their lives have been continually affected by external designs of outside powers. They fear war as do all human beings. Even more they fear the fact that they are often pawns in political-military strategies against which they have always been helpless.

A revolution has been fought on their soil. Some have joined the forces of revolution; others have fought against those forces. Governments have been formed in Saigon, in provinces, in districts, and in villages and hamlets: some have supported those governments; others have opposed them; and still others have remained highly ambivalent about them. Some have primary allegiances to religious or ethnic or other groups rather than to the government or to revolutionary structures. Elections have been held to select representatives and leaders: some have participated actively; some have attempted to sabotage them; some have been "persuaded" to participate in them; and some have cast ballots pro forma. Government services have been provided and some have accepted them and others have refused them. In short, the residents of South Vietnam are not terribly different from residents in most of the world concerning the small spectrum of choice available to them vis-à-vis government and politics.

Even among those who have fought against the revolutionary military forces, who have given at least tacit support to one or more levels of government, who have at least a certain allegiance to the nation state, who have participated in elections, and who have accepted certain governmental services, it is typical to be highly critical of the Saigon government. Criticism of civil and military personnel has always been standard. Cynicism as to the objectives of civil and military leaders has always been common. Complaints concerning socioeconomic policies, levels of performance, corruption, authoritarianism, and conduct of the war are nearly universal among residents of South Vietnam. They understand that their government and politics have deficiencies of gigantic proportions.

They also understand what the war has done to augment the profundity of those deficiencies as well as what it has done to affect so adversely their own lives. Their personal vision of the situation assumes that insanity permeates the milieu. But they can understand its framework, and the motives of native participants in the political-military quagmire destroying their soil. This understanding typically is the objective basis for their cynicism and hatred. What will never be understood by them is the persistent intrusion of outside forces onto their soil, ever deepening the quagmire. To the residents of South Vietnam this intrusion is the real insanity, one rendering the situation truly imcomprehensible to them.

Their strength resides in their proven ability to continue even when faced with the incomprehensible. They have built and rebuilt. They have often adapted to changed surroundings and have adapted those new surroundings to service their own life style. They have continued to work with the groups to whom they have given primary allegiances. Despite everything that has happened to them, the residents of South Vietnam remain themselves. They will remain so after the outside forces eventually abandon their soil. Their persistence to survive to follow their own beliefs and practices will carry them through until the tomorrow when the Mandate of Heaven will at last be bestowed upon its proper recipient. In a society as diverse as South Vietnam, there will be no agreement as to who the proper recipient should be. But at the auspicious time this fundamental determination must be one they themselves make.

Epilogue

A REVIEW of any nation's political history presumably should conclude with a highly speculative essay. A diagnosis and a simple prognosis should be included. While this may be a standard procedure, it can assume foolhardy proportions regardless of the observer's astuteness. In the case of Vietnam, speculative endeavors are all too often not only brash exercises, but also a special plea for an author's political prejudices. Few interpretations of the Indochina situation have escaped this inherent difficulty of analysis. I most certainly cannot lay claim to immunity.

I quite simply do not know what the future holds for either of the two Vietnams. So-called "scenarios" are not difficult to construct. Assuming A, B, and C then the likely ABCD format can be projected. But this is not necessarily a useful methodology. No monolithic explanations suffice. Too many actors, too many interest groups, too many aspects of domestic politics of concerned foreign nations are involved to separate the forces which inevitably will be paramount.

I most certainly would not have assumed that the GVN's revolutionary development program would have been as successful as it was from 1969 to 1971. Nor would I have assumed that Hanoi would have raised the stakes so high in its 1972 winter-spring offensive, jeopardizing the DRVN's considerable domestic development—including an industrialization program which Le Duan claimed was necessary to eliminate the "backwardness" of North Vietnam—during the same 1969–71 period and sacrificing such large numbers of its own men and material in the process. In fact, there were many indications as a result of Lao Dong Politburo politics and of NLF actions that a stage of prolonged revolutionary and guerrilla warfare was about to become the primary strategy. Retrospectively, both Saigon's limited success and Hanoi's offensive can be explained quite logically, in terms any concerned observer would immediately recognize. But they were not predictable. They were possible, yet each was far from inevitable.

In many ways most of the important events during the Second Indochina War have defied projections of objective analysis. I would not have predicted, for example, that the Buddhists would have been the prime mover in Diem's downfall, that the GVN could have regained even relative stability after the series of post-Diem upheavals including near-sectional civil war in 1966, that the NLF and PAVN would have made the type of concerted drive which occurred in 1968 without absolute assurance of success, that the electoral process of South Vietnam would have been as relatively successful as it was after 1967, or that the Thieu government could have survived in a turbulent domestic political milieu. It was easy to explain why each of these things happened. Indeed in each case a "scenario" could have been devised before the event, but this would have been only one of a host of potential paths the strands of political fate might have followed.

The Buddhist leaders, for instance, were never happy with Diem. They were not overly discriminated against but their actions were curtailed. In 1962 the GVN refused Buddhist lay leaders permission to attend an international congress abroad. This was not necessarily significant, but it did help to align and harden opposing forces. Still the Buddhists had been passive, public funds had been used for pagodas, during the First Indochina War Buddhist militancy had been minimal, the Sangha was no more or less infiltrated by the NLF than were many other institutions, its leadership had been coopted by the GVN at least on the surface. No, this was not the place to look for king-makers. The Buddhists had a potential for many things, including struggle against the regime. It had more organization and charisma than many competing interest groups, but it was not really a national organization (it is not today) and its leaders did not have a reputation for forging major movements or enterprises. When the days of Buddhist militancy began, as noted in Chapter 2, the movement was disorganized, its leaders were at odds and fighting among themselves as much as with the Diem government, and the numbers involved in its opposition activities were small and limited to a few urban centers. The reasons for its success are easy enough to describe now, although an argument can be made that it failed rather than succeeded in 1963. When the generals moved against Diem and Nhu, the Buddhist movement had been stalled for some time. However, the mood had been set and the movement's protagonists in the presidential palace were destroying their bases of support by their own actions. By this time most observers were predicting the downfall of the regime, but none can claim to have predicted the evolution of events a few months earlier.

In view of this caveat, very little further can be stated intelligently. The operative word is "if," and this qualifier is all-important. "If" the DRVN bides its time and "if" the Saigon government becomes increasingly unstable and "if" American politics prevents continuation of any form of US military assistance, the DRVN can conquer South Vietnam in a few years. Such conquest could occur by straightforward combat or it could occur "if" insurgents destroy the total framework of the southern government at least locally. Or it could occur "if" the NLF becomes part of the national administration of South Vietnam (by elections or by treaty), and "if" the NLF eventually assumes national power, and "if" it decides upon union with the North under circumstances where the South would be in a completely subordinate position.

On the other hand, "if" the GVN becomes stable, "if" decentralization produces local control and local group support, "if" the ARVN and self-defense forces can reform their leadership structure and become more de-Americanized and exploit vestiges of improved morale shown when it proved during 1972 that the PAVN was not invincible, and "if" international economic assistance helps to maintain a relatively viable southern economy, the DRVN might wait for a prolonged period before initiating a military venture for unification. Indeed, a two Vietnams era such as that of the two Germanys is conceivable especially "if" younger leaders assume power in the Lao Dong Politburo and insist upon long-range emphasis for building an advanced, industrialized and professionalized North Vietnam. This might be more or less plausible "if" the NLF were to become party to a constitutional southern political system, either as a partner or as the controlling influence, "if" the NLF personnel represented a truly southern set of interests.

Nothing in the 1973 Paris accords dictates the path either South or North Vietnam will follow during the remainder of the 1970's and later. Innumerable new "ifs" have been raised. Questions of war and peace, regardless whether warfare is defined in traditional or revolutionary terms, continue to be paramount. Questions of representation of all interest groups in national and local government as always provide the bases for resolving the war and peace questions. The subject of unification, under a unitary or federal or confederate formula, meshed as it is in the matrix of southern political processes and questions of group representation and war and peace is a subject likely to be on the Vietnamese and international political agenda for an extended period of time.

Many of the "ifs" are contingent upon procedures adopted for future electoral processes, and those procedures will be primarily a function of Vietnamese group politics although the foreign policies of the great powers will not be irrelevant. A federal system in South Vietnam permitting various interests to gain access to provincial and other local governments combined with a national legislature and central administration providing recognition to all interest groups would greatly enhance chances for prolonged peace and for some form of Vietnamese unification under a federal or confederate arrangement. In a dream world an Indochina monetary and financial sphere might then be possible, a sphere involved closely with a Southeast Asian association devoted to regional development. If this scenario were followed, a vast array of secondary "ifs" would first have to be resolved. The military, political, economic and administrative problems working against resolution of immediate serious practical difficulties in all of Indochina are enormous. And the array of tremendous human problems culminating from a generation of warfare must receive first priority not only because this is a moral imperative but also because it is a political and therefore pragmatic prerequisite to conflict resolution in political and economic spheres in both Vietnams and also in Laos and Cambodia.

The "ifs" of peace, unification under terms mutually acceptable to northern and southern group interests, equitable treatment of and representation for all major interests, and regional economic development may be the equivalent of swords into plowshares. The only hopeful aspect of such unrealistic possibilities is that I definitely do not predict they will occur.

Notes

Chapter 2

1. For a brief explanation of the Dai Viet, see p. 24.
2. VNQDD: Nationalist or Kuomintang Party (see p. 24).
3. Reprinted from *Journal of Southeast Asian History,* 8 (1967), pp. 83–98.
4. Ellen J. Hammer, *The Struggle for Indochina* (Stanford, Cal.: Stanford U. P., 1954), pp. 54–59. De Tham continued guerrilla resistance under the Nguyen banner until 1909. Joseph Buttinger, *The Smaller Dragon: A Political History of Vietnam* (New York: Praeger, 1958), pp. 383–84.
5. See the next section of ch. 2. Also: John T. Dorsey, "The Bureaucracy and Political Development in Vietman," in Joseph La Palombara, ed., *Bureaucracy and Political Development* (Princeton, N.J.: Princeton U. P., 1963), pp. 318–59.
6. I. Milton Sacks, "Marxism in Vietnam," in Frank N. Trager, ed., *Marxism in Southeast Asia* (Stanford, Cal.: Stanford U. P., 1960), pp. 102–70.
7. "And above all, while proclaiming themselves nationalists and patriots, these leaders seemed to lack a minimum of consensus as to common goals. Nationalism in Viet-Nam in the 1919–40 period was overwhelmingly a movement of personalities, highly elitist and generally lacking in popular participation." Phan Thien Chau, "Vietnamese Nationalism, 1919–40," a paper delivered April 6, 1966, at the 18th Annual Meeting of the Association for Asian Studies, New York.
8. Phan Boi Chau was betrayed to the French by Ho Chi Minh. P. J. Honey, ed., *North Vietnam Today* (New York: Praeger, 1962), p. 4.
9. An earlier attempt by Phan Chau Trinh to improve education for Vietnamese and to adopt closer relations with France led to this leader's brief imprisonment in Poulo Condore. Ho Chi Minh's father was a follower of Trinh. Denis Warner, *The Last Confucian* (New York: Macmillan, 1963), p. 23.
10. Jean Lacouture, *Cinq Hommes et la France* (Paris: Editions Du Seuil, 1961), Ch. 1; and Jean Chesneaux, *Le Viet-Nam* (Paris: Editions Sociales, 1955), Ch. 11.
11. There have been several Dai Viet parties, labeled as civil servants' parties, people's parties, and national socialist parties, as well as "Great Vietnam" parties.
12. Sacks, "Marxism in Vietnam."
13. Donald Lancaster, *The Emancipation of French Indo-China* (London: Oxford U. P., 1961), pp. 76–78.
14. Matusita, chief of Japanese intelligence, was the principal instigator of sect, Dai Viet, and other party attempts to prepare a Vietnamese nation cooperating in the "Greater Co-Prosperity Sphere." Philippe Devillers, *Histoire Du Viet-Nam* (Paris: Editions Du Seuil, 1952), p. 91. Tran Van An, a Restoration

League central committee member, was a leader of this attempt. In 1966, An was a leader of the Electoral Commission of the Ky government.

15. *Ibid.,* Ch. 9.

16. A National Congress to aid Bao Dai in 1948 met in separate sessions because delegates from the North, Center, and South refused to sit together. Bernard B. Fall, *The Two Viet-Nams* (New York: Praeger, 1963), p. 213.

17. Jean Chesneaux, "Stages of the Development of the Vietnam National Movement 1862–1940," *Past and Present,* No. 7 (April 1955), pp. 63–75.

18. Unquestionably the most comprehensive analysis of political party activity during the Diem era is to be found in John C. Donnell's "Politics in South Vietnam" (unpublished Ph.D. dissertation, University of California, Berkeley, 1964). Also see Donnell's "Personalism in Vietnam," in Wesley R. Fishel, ed., *Problems of Freedom* (New York: Free Press, 1961), and "National Renovation Campaigns in Vietnam," *Pacific Affairs,* 32 (March 1959), pp. 73–88.

19. Nguyen Thai, *Is South Vietnam Viable?* (Manila: Carmelo and Bauermann, 1962), Ch. 4.

20. Robert Scigliano, "Political Parties in South Vietnam under the Republic," *Pacific Affairs,* 33 (1960), pp. 327–46.

21. Robert Scigliano, *South Vietnam: Nation Under Stress* (Boston: Houghton Mifflin, 1963), pp. 75–80.

22. Robert Scigliano, "The Electoral Process in South Vietnam," *Midwest J. Pol. Sci.,* 4 (1960), pp. 138–61. Also: Nguyen Tuyet Mai, "Electioneering: Vietnamese Style," *Asian Survey,* 2 (1962), pp. 11–18.

23. For a description of the various groups of exiles in Paris during the Diem period see Helen B. Lamb's "The Paris Exiles," *The Nation* (August 10, 1963), pp. 65–68. During 1963 the Free Democratic Party of the exiled Dr. Pham Huy Co, in cooperation with General Nguyen Chanh Thi then in exile in Cambodia, was involved in a terrorist campaign in Saigon against the Diem government. Malcolm W. Browne, *The New Face of War* (Indianapolis: Bobbs-Merrill, 1965), pp. 206–7, 222.

Perhaps the most important "neutralist" party remaining in exile after 1963 was the Committee for Peace and Reconstruction in South Vietnam headed by former Premier Tran Van Huu. Jean Lacouture, *Vietnam: Between Two Truces* (New York: Random House, 1966), pp. 237–41.

24. Browne, *New Face of War,* pp. 119–20 and ch. 14.

25. The militant Phat Diem and Bui Chu bishoprics which moved south from Tonkin after the partition still retain militia strength. Father Hoang, once a militant leader in Phat Diem under Bishop Tu and an elected provincial council member in 1953, remains the most important leader of the several Catholic struggle parties. The Buddhist "Boy Scout" and youth groups have supported Tri Quang as have military elements, while Tam Chau maintains a formidable group of "Knights." The best continuing accounts of the religious group conflict since 1963 are found in contributions of Robert Shaplen to the *New Yorker* and of Denis Warner to the *Reporter.*

26. For statements on Truyen's program for a revitalized Buddhism see Kenneth W. Morgan's "The Buddhists: The Problem and the Promise," *Asia,* No. 4 (Winter 1966), pp. 72–84. Also see Marguerite Higgins, *Our Vietnam Nightmare* (New York: Harper & Row, 1965), pp. 272–73.

27. Dr. Nguyen Ton Hoan, a Dai Viet leader, was vice premier for pacifica-

tion. One of his lieutenants was minister of interior and formally in charge of provincial appointments. Luther A. Allen, "Pacification in Quang Tri," *The New Leader* (June 8, 1964), pp. 9–12.

28. *Vietnam Press,* August 29, 1964.

29. Diem did create anticommunist cells and bases without appreciable success, as well as work with the National Union Front. Robert Shaplen, *The Lost Revolution* (New York: Harper & Row, 1965).

30. See Bernard B. Fall's *Viet-Nam Witness* (New York: Praeger, 1966), ch. 4, for an account of the 1953 elections. Dr. Hoang Co Binh, who was elected mayor of Hanoi in 1953 despite the strong influence in Tonkin of Governor Nguyen Huu Tri's Dai Viet Party, was elected to the Saigon municipal council in 1965.

31. It was officially estimated that 5,091,843 voters would be registered for elections in September 1966, i.e., 72 per cent of the population in the government-controlled areas. *Vietnam* (News Bulletin: Embassy of the Republic of Vietnam), June 1, 1966. In the May 30, 1965, provincial and municipal elections 4.5 million voted, some 70 per cent of eligible voters. The percentage ran as high as 85 per cent in Chau Doc Province, a predominantly Hoa Hao province. *Washington Post,* April 24, 1966.

32. Lieutenant General Nguyen Huu Co, deputy prime minister, early in 1966 called for a two-party system in a statement announcing that a "Democracy Building Consultative Council" would be formed. *Vietnam* (News Bulletin: Embassy of the Republic of Vietnam), Feb. 15, 1966.

33. Roy Jumper and Nguyen Thi Hue, *Notes on the Political and Administrative History of Viet Nam: 1802–1962* (Saigon: MSUG, 1962), pp. 31–35, 82–85. The MSUG publications were products of research on South Vietnam concerning politics, administration, society and economics. Most were initially in English, French and Vietnamese. A selected number of revised studies was later published by USAID. References designate either original works published in Saigon or revised texts published in Washington.

34. Roy Jumper, "Sects and Communism in South Vietnam," *Orbis,* 3 (Spring 1959), pp. 85–96.

35. For a fuller discussion of both aspects see Chapter 2: "Organizing Bureaucrats," and "South Vietnam's Buddhist Crisis."

36. Early in 1964 the Cao Dai formed a United Cao Dai and Lien Minh (Alliance) Veterans Committee under the chairmanship of Nguyen Thanh Phuong. *Vietnam Press,* Jan. 29, 1964. In general, despite certain "neutralist" elements, the Cao Dai Party has supported the military tribunals.

37. In June of 1964 three companies of Social Democratic Party troops, which had been fighting the central government for several years under Pham Van Dom, rallied to the government. *Vietnam Press,* June 20, 1964. Later three splinter Hoa Hao parties, under Trinh Quoc Khanh, Phan Ba Cam, and Truong Kim Cu, united in a shaky coalition, the Vietnam Social Democrat Party. *Vietnam Press,* Oct. 17, 1964.

38. For excellent descriptions of the procedure followed by the Viet Minh see: Vo Nguyen Giap, *People's War, People's Army* (New York: Praeger, 1962); Truong Chinh, *Primer for Revolt* (New York: Praeger, 1963); and George K. Tanham, *Communist Revolutionary Warfare* (New York: Praeger, 1961).

39. The state-within-the-state program of the NLF is described by Wilfred

G. Burchett in *The Furtive War: The United States in Vietnam and Laos* (New York: International Publishers, 1963), ch. 5, and in *Vietnam: the Inside Story of the Guerrilla War* (New York: International Publishers, 1965), pp. 59–62, 223–26. Also see George A. Carver, "The Faceless Viet Cong," *Foreign Affairs,* 44 (1966), pp. 347–72.

40. David Marr, "Political Attitudes and Activities of Young Urban Intellectuals in Viet-Nam," *Asian Survey,* 6 (1966), pp. 249–63. The youth organizations often are bitter opponents. Catholic and Buddhist groups have been known to battle in the streets, and during the spring of 1966 the important Saigon Students Union supported the Ky regime against Thich Thien Minh's Buddhist youth group.

41. Charles A. Joiner, *Public Administration in the Saigon Metropolitan Area* (Washington: USAID, 1963), chs. 1, 6, 7.

42. "An Giang—A Blueprint for Development," *Saigon Post,* Oct. 17, 1965.

43. Pp. 37–50 reprinted, by permission, from *Asian Survey,* 2 (1963), 203–15. Dr. Roy Jumper, the co-author, is a Professor of Political Science at Indiana University. He was formerly a consultant to the National Institute of Administration in Saigon and the Public Affairs Representative for the Middle East and North Africa of the Ford Foundation.

44. John D. Montgomery, *The Politics of Foreign Aid* (New York: Praeger, 1962), pp. 20–24.

45. Ngo Dinh Nhu is president of the Cong Hoa Youth and Madame Nhu is "Chairman-Founder" of the Vietnamese Women's Solidarity Association.

46. "Personalism" is the official doctrine of the Diem regime. An ambiguous concept, it referred initially to individual self-realization through reliance upon spiritual factors rather than material ones; it also stressed the importance of the family and of the positive role of the national government.

47. The Federation of Vietnamese Laborers' Trade Unions did request that the Civil Servants' Union be given regular trade union status. *Dan Thanh,* Feb. 15, 1954.

48. Lancaster, *Emancipation of Indo-China,* pp. 117–18.

49. Nhu was an organizer of the Vietnamese Federation of Christian Workers and the Movement for National Union and Peace prior to his brother's rise to power.

50. Translation from *Tu Do,* June 25, 1955.

51. *Vietnam Presse,* June 30, 1955.

52. Ibid., July 7, 1955.

53. Joseph J. Zasloff and Nguyen Khac Nhan, *A Study of Administration in Binh Minh District* (Saigon: MSUG, 1961), p. 29.

54. Roy Jumper, "Mandarin Bureaucracy and Politics in South Vietnam," *Pacific Affairs,* 30 (1957), p. 57.

55. Certain specifics concerning the League's formal organization were obtained from a translation of the original bylaws in Vietnamese.

56. John D. Donoghue and Vo Hong Phuc, *My Thuan: The Study of a Delta Village in South Viet-Nam* (Saigon: MSUG, 1961), p. 35.

57. From the director general's address to the seventh annual League congress on March 16, 1962.

58. *Vietnam Press,* March 19, 1962.

59. Translation in United States embassy Vietnamese *Press Review,* March 28, 1962.

60. *The Times of Viet Nam,* March 17, 1962.

61. From a speech by Finance Secretary Nguyen Luong at the National Institute of Administration in Saigon-Cholon on March 22, 1962.

62. Other examples of League members hiring out "volunteer" work are given by Jason Finkle and Tran Van Dinh, *Provincial Government in Viet Nam: A Study of Vinh Long* (Saigon: MSUG, 1961), p. 7.

63. *The Times of Viet Nam,* March 17, 1962.

64. Charles A. Joiner, *Public Administration in the Saigon Metropolitan Area,* ch. 7.

65. Pp. 53–80 reprinted, by permission, from *Admin. Sci. Q.,* 8 (1964), pp. 443–81.

The co-author, Guy H. Fox, is a consultant of the Institute of Public Administration to the National Institute of Administration in Saigon. He has previously been a professor of political science and a public administration consultant in Japan, Okinawa, Iraq, Lebanon and Jordan.

66. Max Weber, *The Theory of Social and Economic Organization* (New York: Oxford U. P., 1947), p. 328. "Bureaucratization" as used here refers to an administrative system's transition toward meeting the criteria of the Weberian bureaucratic or legal model.

67. Fred W. Riggs, "Prismatic Society and Financial Administration," *Admin. Sci. Q.,* 5 (1960), p. 30.

68. Francis Carnell, "Political Ideas and Ideologies in South and South-East Asia," in Saul Rose, ed., *Politics in Southern Asia* (London: St. Martin's, 1963), p. 275.

69. S. N. Eisenstadt, "Bureaucracy, Bureaucratization, and Debureaucratization," *Admin. Sci. Q.,* 4 (1959), pp. 301–20.

70. S. N. Eisenstadt, *The Political Systems of Empires: The Rise and Fall of the Historical Bureaucratic Societies* (New York: Free Press, 1963), p. 252.

71. Fred W. Riggs, *The Ecology of Public Administration* (New Delhi: Asia Publ. House, 1961), p. 92. Also see Riggs, "Agraria and Industria—Toward a Typology of Comparative Administration," in William J. Siffin, ed., *Toward the Comparative Study of Public Administration* (Bloomington: Indiana University, 1957), p. 88.

72. Carnell, "Political Ideas and Ideologies," p. 267.

73. This phenomenon noted by Carnell as a pattern for Asian countries is simply the extreme instance of executive concentration of decision-making power. "In almost all contemporary political systems leadership has shifted to the executive with the legislature acting mainly as a forum for the airing of grievances"—introductory note to Part 3 in Roy C. Macridis and Bernard E. Brown, eds., *Comparative Politics* (Homewood, Ill.; Dorsey, 1961), p. 304. Poul Meyer, *Administrative Organization: A Comparative Study of the Organization of Public Administration* (London: Stevens, 1957), pp. 56–61, provides an analysis of the distinction between administrative concentration of decision making and administrative centralization of authority.

74. Robert V. Presthus, "Behavior and Bureaucracy in Many Cultures," *Publ. Admin. Rev.,* 19 (1959), p. 35.

75. In Class A there are 818 contract employees in addition to the 1,334 career (cadre) officials. The total number of public employees in Vietnam as of December 31, 1962, was 173,465. Besides the 31,846 career employees there were 1,668 contractuals, 35,872 daily workers without tenure or status, 44,079

floaters, and 60,000 paid a flat sum for specific services. Career employees are classified into A, B, and C; contractual into A and B1; daily workers into B1, B2, B3, C1, C2 and D1; and floaters into D2. For the only study in English of the Vietnamese personnel system, see Dale Rose, *The Vietnamese Civil Service System* (Saigon: MSUG, 1961).

In Vietnam, as in any dictatorial country where the atmosphere is charged with fear and suspicion, it is difficult to obtain a representative sample of public employees who are not afraid to speak frankly. It was our experience, however, that high-ranking Vietnamese officials, both in Saigon and in the field, if assured that their identity would not be revealed, were usually rather outspoken with American academicians.

76. The interviewees' expressions of disillusionment with the regime appear to substantiate the evidence gathered by Wesley R. Fishel during three visits to Vietnam in 1962. After talking at length with 118 prominent persons whom he had known in Vietnam between 1954 and 1958, Fishel concluded that "the morale of public servants, of 'the intelligentsia,' and of substantial segments of the population in general has slipped badly." He found during his 1962 visits that only three of the 118 supported the government "with discernible enthusiasm," whereas when he visited Vietnam in 1959 at least 70 of them had been among the president's strong adherents (unpublished MS, "Vietnam Reconsidered," p. 2).

77. There was unanimity among the interviewees that the Ngo family constitutes by far the most important power group in Vietnam. Ngo Dinh Nhu, one of the president's brothers, is "political advisor" of the president; his authority is probably second only to the president's. Mme. Nhu, his wife, is hostess for the bachelor president and is usually referred to as the "first lady of the Republic." Although she is a member of the National Assembly, her considerable influence in government affairs is chiefly extra-legal. Another brother, Ngo Dinh Can, does not hold public office but exercises tight control over the central lowlands and is influential in central decisions. Still another brother is Ngo Dinh Thuc, a Catholic archbishop, whose views are highly respected by the president and who also has an important role in shaping policies. Other relatives of President Diem and Mme. Nhu now hold, or have held, high government offices.

78. Among the numerous examples related by the interviewees was an incident which was also witnessed by a Michigan State University faculty member. At a rally of one of the two virtually unknown and woefully weak opposing candidates whom President Diem permitted to run against him in the spring of 1961, hundreds of civil servants arrived early at the meeting and pre-empted most of the seats, causing a large crowd arriving later but on time to be turned away because of lack of room. As soon as the rally commenced, the crowd heckled and booed the speaker; soon the "audience" filed out leaving an almost empty auditorium and proceeded to climb into a fleet of waiting government trucks to be driven away. The controlled press of the next day, making no mention of the packing of the auditorium, reported blandly that the speaker had so disgusted and bored his listeners that they had walked out.

79. The existence of Can Lao is openly acknowledged but its membership list is kept secret. No one knows the exact number. A *New York Times* correspondent reports that Nhu has claimed 70,000 members of Can Lao (May 22, 1960, p. 4). However, in a personal interview with Robert Scigliano, Nhu

set the membership at approximately 20,000. Vietnamese civil servants generally believe even the latter figure is exaggerated.

80. It may be significant that none of the interviewees mentioned the military among the principal groups used to preserve the regime's power. In 1963 Ngo Dinh Nhu used special forces rather than regular military to meet the "Buddhist crisis."

81. The interviewees confirmed John T. Dorsey's observation that "the knowledge that they may be under surveillance by unidentified members of such an organization may well induce caution in high-level administrators who are not members, and inhibit the flow of communication." "Stresses and Strains in a Developing Administrative System," in Wesley R. Fishel, ed., *Problems of Freedom: South Vietnam since Independence* (New York: Free Press, 1961), p. 150.

82. At least 12 interviewees expressed the belief that Can Lao members were receiving money through graft and two said they were certain of it; however, no tangible evidence was produced. There was general consensus that the Can Lao owns Phuoc My, a firm which supervises and contracts all work in loading and hauling at the port of Saigon.

83. See preceding section of Chapter 2. A few respondents said that the Republican Youth (Cong Hoa) controlled by Nhu was superseding the Civil Service League in importance.

84. However, one example of a contradiction of a presidential decision was given, and, if the incident is accurate, it attests to the strong will and authority of Mme. Nhu. According to a middle-manager respondent from the Directorate of Information, President Diem ordered the suppression of certain remarks made by Mme. Nhu while she was in France. This action incensed Mme. Nhu who, upon her return to Vietnam, asked the director general of information, without the knowledge and consent of the president, to release and publish what she had said in France. The director general complied with her request and it was the president's turn to become infuriated. But when the director general, summoned by the president for an explanation, explained that he had acted in accord with Mme. Nhu's request, the president passed the matter off with a shrug. When we later investigated the story, we were told by several high officials that it was essentially true. In addition, developments of the summer of 1963 indicate that the decision-making role of Ngo Dinh Nhu has increased considerably, perhaps at the expense of the president himself.

85. Interviews with President Diem are generally monologues. Once on what was supposed to be a 15-minute courtesy call on the president, one of the authors was kept for four and a half hours during which Diem, while chain-smoking more than a package of cigarettes, expounded his theories of government. Robert S. Elegant of *Newsweek* magazine once listened to a six-and-a-half-hour discourse from the president.

86. There are occasional differences and even friction among members of the family. For example, Nhu and Can have engaged in bitter disputes with one another, and the Nhus have openly criticized Diem in press interviews.

87. This characteristic of the Vietnamese bureaucracy was noted in 1954 by Walter R. Sharp, "Some Observations on Public Administration in Indochina," *Publ. Admin. Rev.,* 14 (1954), pp. 40–41.

88. A province chief, not among the officials interviewed, said that civil

servants, though not yet sharing the values and outlook of the population, are beginning to gain the confidence of the country. He cited as evidence that more people now than previously attend government-sponsored meetings where they voice opinions and ask questions whereas they were once silent. Dorsey says that government officials in Vietnam "tend to be distinguished from the rest of the population by their greater education, their origin in middle- and upper-class families, and the stronger influence upon their outlook and values of the urban industrial West" (Dorsey, "A Developing Administrative System," p. 143).

89. See below, pp. 69–70.

90. When the question of the personnel system was specifically discussed during the interview, 33 respondents said they would like to see a system of open, competitive examinations introduced in Vietnam. However, the interviewees were almost evenly divided as to whether or not the cadre system should be replaced by a position classification system; most of the support for the position classification system came from the top managers. For the weight of various factors which enable civil servants to reach the upper levels of the bureaucracy, see pp. 73–74.

91. As of September 30, 1962, 36 out of 41 province chiefs were military officers. The number of military district chiefs is kept secret but probably at least two-thirds of them (numbering 228 as of November 1, 1962) are military officers.

92. It is doubtful that the slighting of the good features can be attributed to modesty or oriental courtesy. The interviewees readily praised many aspects of Vietnamese culture outside the political and administrative realm, and some spoke with pride of their own agencies. For instance, the interviewees from the Budget Directorate said that until recently their agency was an exception to many of their general criticisms of the bureaucracy.

93. Based on his studies of national income in Vietnam, Frank C. Child, an economist, has expressed the view that Class A civil servants receive relatively high incomes and are among the economic elite of the country. *Economic Growth, Capital Formation, and Public Policy in Viet-Nam* (Saigon: MSUG, 1962).

94. Above, pp. 58–59. Also see below, pp. 73–74. Moreover, officials were in universal accord that there is no effective means of removing inefficient employees from the service. One top-level manager said, "I have never known of a case in which a Vietnamese civil servant was dismissed because of inefficiency."

95. For present warlike conditions in Vietnam, see Robert Scigliano, "Vietnam: A Country at War," *Asian Survey,* 3 (1963), pp. 48–54. For an analysis of Viet Cong tactics see Joseph J. Zasloff, "The Problem of South Vietnam," *Commentary,* 33 (1962), pp. 126–35. Also Wesley R. Fishel, "Communist Terror in South Viet Nam," *The New Leader,* 43 (1960), pp. 14–15.

96. Three battalions of Vietnamese paratroopers attempted a coup d'état on November 11, 1960, and were crushed only after two days of bitter fighting. On February 27, 1962, two Vietnamese Air Force pilots bombed and strafed the presidential palace in an unsuccessful attempt to kill the president and the Nhus. Many Vietnamese are convinced that the attack, if it had accomplished its mission, was intended to be the signal for a revolution; the numerous arrests following the raid lend credence to this view. Present unrest and tensions are reflected in an incredible number of political arrests—between five and eight

thousand each month during a year and a half period ending in mid-1962. The figures on arrests are from official records shown to us by a high-level police official. Frequently a political "arrest" entails only a few hours of detention for questioning. During 1963 the number of arrests increased considerably to stifle both Buddhist and student protests.

97. Civil servants from the North (Tonkin) are largely refugees who fled southward after the Geneva Agreement which placed the North in the hands of the communists. The Center (Annam), the long, narrow waist between the North and South, is now partly in the Republic of Vietnam and partly in the communist People's Republic of Vietnam. The South (Cochinchina) includes the high plateau and the Mekong delta regions. People from the three sections speak with different accents, vary somewhat in customs and manners, and are strongly conscious of their separate identities. During the French colonial period the South was a colony, whereas the North and Center were protectorates; the Vietnamese occupied more responsible civil service positions in the North and Center than they did in the South under French rule.

98. There is apparently more actual religious discrimination practiced in the central lowlands where Can and Thuc exert greater influence than in the remainder of the nation.

99. On at least one occasion an association failed to choose the government-designated leader (even after he had held a large reception to celebrate what appeared to be a foregone conclusion). This occurred in the election for president of the press association during the summer of 1962. The government, though miffed by the rejection of its candidate, accepted the association's choice, a well-known, conservative publisher with a record of loyalty to the regime.

100. Inculcation of a sense of civic responsibility beginning at the village level is one of the announced purposes of the primarily defense-oriented strategic hamlet program (*Viet Nam's Strategic Hamlets* [Saigon: Directorate General of Information, 1963], p. 4). Vietnamese academicians with whom we have discussed the subject of civic responsibility have said that only a nationwide educational program extending over many years can develop a spirit of enthusiastic, enlightened cooperation between civil servants and the public.

101. "Rural administration" was included in the question, because winning the allegiance and cooperation of the countryside is perhaps the most crucial problem faced by the Republic of Vietnam. Even ardent government supporters admit that the success of communist guerrillas is due in large part to the passive attitude or outright sympathy of peasants with the Viet Cong.

102. For progress of inservice training programs in Vietnam, see Final Report, covering activities of the Michigan State University Advisory Group for the period May 20, 1955–June 30, 1962 (Saigon, June 1962), pp. 30–35.

103. For example, the present secretary of state for health, after receiving his medical degree from a French university, took postgraduate work at Johns Hopkins University; his chief of cabinet, the number two man in the department, has a degree in dentistry from Northwestern University and specialized in public health at Yale University. Legally and theoretically, a distinction ought to be made between two kinds of officials, first, those who are frankly political, such as the directors general and chiefs of cabinet, and second, the permanent civil servants, such as the secretaries general, chiefs of services, and chiefs of bureaus. In practice the distinction has little or no meaning.

104. Our own opinion is that graft and corruption are not widespread. This

view is based on discussions with former French colonial officials and with Chinese and American traders who have dealt with Vietnamese civil servants for many years. Also, numerous interviews held with government officials and businessmen in every section of Vietnam over a four-year period frequently evoked scathing criticisms of the bureaucracy but only a few charges of extensive corruption. Several Saigon businessmen admitted privately to us that they had tried in vain to influence officials with pressure and money in order to obtain a government contract or to receive a high priority for a telephone. It is true, however, that two Vietnamese friends—one, a professor at the National Institute of Administration and the other, a former director general—who read and criticized the preliminary draft of this paper, said they believed the respondents had exaggerated civil servants' standards of incorruptibility.

105. For example, although a person in Vietnam cannot obtain a telephone through bribery, he may, provided he is entitled to one, reduce his waiting period by months by having someone take up his case directly with the director general of post office, telephone, and telegraph. We know of several cases in which Japanese and Hong Kong businessmen obtained entry visas to Vietnam quickly by having someone with influence intercede for them with the secretary of state of interior; ordinarily, they would have had to wait an indefinitely long period.

106. We believe the figures are fairly accurate. For example, National Institute of Administration officials, with whom one of the writers worked closely for over four years, were generally fair and impartial in selecting on the basis of qualifications 100 new students each year from the 800 to 1,200 candidates who sought admission. Despite determined efforts of numerous powerful individuals to influence selections, the Institute (though directed by a politically conscious former minister) yielded to pressure in only two or three cases out of a hundred. Also during our active participation for several years in a large construction program, we were, though dismayed by the slow, cumbersome procedures, impressed with the meticulous concern for fairness in deciding upon vendors and contractors and making inspections to ascertain compliance with specifications.

107. The regime equates loyalty to itself with loyalty to the nation. Thus before granting permission to publish a newspaper, the government makes sure the publisher will support the regime; or before allowing a student to study abroad, the government seeks assurance that the student will not criticize the regime while abroad and that he will return to Vietnam after his period of study. In such cases testimonials from important personages as to the applicant's loyalty are often decisive. Efforts of the regime to maintain control over various strata within the social system may result in considerable pressures applied to businessmen, professionals, and the like, but this is a practice distinct from the actions of individual corrupt bureaucrats who might pressure such persons for private gain.

108. This behavior pattern is the antithesis of that included in Morroe Berger's ideal western bureaucratic model. *Bureaucracy and Society in Modern Egypt* (Princeton, N.J.: Princeton U.P., 1957), especially pp. 49, 217–19.

109. Montgomery, *Politics of Foreign Aid*, pp. 71–72.

110. The traditionalistic orientation of the Vietnamese mandarinic class is of the familiar "guardian bureaucracy" type of the "Chinese scholastic bureau-

cracy." Fritz Morstein Marx describes this orientation in *The Administrative State: An Introduction to Bureaucracy* (Chicago: Univ. of Chicago Press, 1957), pp. 55–58.

111. For a description of another contemporary predominantly personalized administrative system see Edgar L. Shor, "The Thai Bureaucracy," *Admin. Sci. Q.*, 5 (1960), pp. 66–86.

112. John T. Dorsey, "The Bureaucracy and Political Development in Viet Nam," pp. 318–59. A similar instance of administrative concentration of decision-making authority in a nation in the Middle East is presented by Lynton K. Caldwell, "Turkish Administration and the Politics of Expediency," in Siffin, ed., *Comparative Study of Public Administration*, pp. 117–44.

113. Debureaucratization procedures in Vietnam, like a number of other techniques of control practiced by the Saigon regime, are quite similar to those followed in Hanoi and Peking. See for example A. Doak Barnett's discussion of Chinese communist secondary organizations which supposedly represent certain interests, including civil servants, but which serve as instruments of regime control and manipulation. *Communist China and Asia* (New York: Harper, 1960), pp. 17–19.

114. Riggs, *Ecology of Public Adminstration*, p. 143.

115. The potentiality of insurgency is a dimension which must be considered overtly or as a "silent dimension" by the political elite in all underdeveloped countries when making decisions concerning development administration or the bureaucratization of that administration. Note Albert O. Hirshman's analysis of this problem in his study of Chile, Colombia, and Brazil, *Journeys toward Progress: Studies of Economic Policy-Making in Latin America* (New York: Twentieth Century Fund, 1963), p. 279.

116. For an exposition on the interest activity concept, reference should be made to Arthur F. Bentley's classic *The Process of Government: A Study of Social Pressures* (Bloomington, Ind.: Principia, 1908). An elaboration of how the concept may be used as an analytic tool is given by Charles B. Hagan in his "The Group in a Political Science," in Roland Young, ed., *Approaches to the Study of Politics* (Evanston, Ill.: Northwestern U.P., 1958), pp. 38–51.

117. Presthus, "Behavior and Bureaucracy."

118. The following article is reprinted, by permission, from *Asian Survey*, 4 (1964), pp. 915–28.

Monsignor Thuc is an elder brother of the assassinated President Ngo Dinh Diem and Political Advisor Ngo Dinh Nhu. Thuc was attending the Ecumenical Council when his brothers, including Ngo Dinh Can who ruled in central Vietnam, were deposed. He has remained in Rome since the November 1, 1963 coup d'état.

119. Reports that Diem was outraged by the display of papal flags without simultaneous display of the national flag, and that he took steps to remedy the unconstitutional ceremony, cannot be proved or disproved at this juncture.

120. *Vietnam Press*, May 12, 1963.

121. Ibid, June 2, 1963.

122. Ibid, June 9, 1963.

123. Georges Lebrum, in "Beliefs and Religions in Vietnam," *Asia*, (1951), pp. 75–84, presents a description of the historic lack of organizational unity or religious agreement in Vietnam. Buddhism in Indochina was not an active

element of the new nationalism as it was in several other nations in Asia following World War II. Joseph M. Kitagawa, "Buddhism and Asian Politics," *Asian Survey,* 2 (1962), pp. 1–11.

124. *The Hindu Weekly Review,* July 15, 1963.

125. *Vietnam Press,* June 16, 1963.

126. Ibid.

127. Available evidence does not substantiate the regime's claim of communist leadership in the Buddhist crisis. The National Liberation Front has created its own Buddhist organization, and one of its vice presidents, Thich Thien Hao, is a Buddhist bonze. Burchett, *The Furtive War,* pp. 105–6. Superior Bonze Son-Vuong, of the Cambodian Buddhist minority, also was listed in 1962 as a member of the Central Committee of the National Liberation Front. Fall, *Two Viet-Nams,* pp. 356–57.

128. *Vietnam Press,* June 30, 1963. As shown in an earlier section of this chapter, Nhu relied heavily upon such organizations as the Cong Hoa Youth to control the population and implement his programs.

129. Lancaster, *Emancipation of Indo-China,* pp. 154–55.

130. Robert Shaplen, "Letter from Saigon," *The New Yorker* (Dec. 14, 1963), pp. 201+.

131. *New York Times,* Aug. 4, 1963.

132. Ibid., Aug. 7, 1963.

133. *Washington Post,* Aug. 22, 1963.

134. *Vietnam Press,* Aug. 25, 1963.

135. Ibid., Sept. 1, 1963.

136. Ibid., Sept. 22, 1963.

137. Robert Scigliano provides an account of the history of America's inability to persuade Diem of the need for program and personnel changes. *South Vietnam: Nation Under Stress,* pp. 206–16, and "Vietnam: Politics and Religion," *Asian Survey,* 4 (1964), pp. 666–73.

138. David Halberstam provided a comprehensive account of the stages leading to the coup against the Ngos. *New York Times,* Nov. 6, 1963.

139. General Nguyen Khanh assumed the position of prime minister himself following his "bloodless internal purge" of the first Military Revolutionary Council. Nguyen Ngoc Tho was retired to private life, while nonmilitary leadership in the government was to a great extent allocated to the old Dai Viet party.

140. Instances of Buddhist persecution of Catholics since the fall of the Ngo family have been criticized by the new regime. Attempts also have been made to maintain Catholic support. Nguyen Ton Hoan, leader of the Dai Viet party and a vice prime minister in charge of pacification in the Khanh government, is a Catholic. Perhaps even more important, the governments of both General Minh and General Khanh have made concerted attempts to obtain support from the Cao Dai and Hoa Hao sects by appointing sect members to posts as province and district chiefs.

141. *New York Times,* Dec. 27, 1963.

142. *Vietnam Press,* Jan. 5, 1964.

143. The Institute as planned was somewhat similar to the organizational arrangements of the Executive Council of the Sangha in Thailand, where there is a hierarchy paralleling that of the Thai government. David E. Pfanner and Jasper Ingersoll, "Theravada Buddhism and Village Economic Behavior: A Burmese and Thai Comparison," *Journal of Asian Studies,* 21 (1962), pp. 341–61.

144. Sangha influence in the rural areas historically has been quite limited. John D. Donoghue provides an excellent description of locally oriented Buddhism as perceived by Vietnamese peasants and fishermen. *Cam An: A Fishing Village in Central Vietnam* (Saigon: MSUG, 1962).

145. *Vietnam Press,* Jan. 19, 1964.

146. The general commissions are divided into working groups, for example, the Commission for Youth Affairs headed by Thich Thien Minh includes four groups: the Buddhist Family, the Buddhist University Students, the Buddhist School Children, and the Buddhist Boy Scouts. Ibid., Feb. 15, 1964.

147. Thich Tri Quang, formerly a lecturer at the Hanoi Buddhist Institute, was one of the most articulate of the younger militant leaders. He received sanctuary in the American embassy after Nhu's August crackdown. In addition to his organizational duties he has been appointed, as have several other Buddhist notables, to the faculty of the Advanced Buddhist Studies Institute. This faculty is responsible to the Institute for the Propagation of the Faith.

Chapter 3

1. Paul Mus, "Cultural Backgrounds of Present Problems," *Asia,* No. 4 (1966), p. 12; also "The Role of the Village in Vietnamese Politics," *Pacific Affairs,* 22 (1949), pp. 265–72.

2. Nghiem Dang, *Viet-Nam: Politics and Public Administration* (Honolulu: East-West Center, 1966), p. 31.

3. I. Milton Sacks, "Marxism in Viet Nam," in Frank N. Trager, ed., *Marxism in Southeast Asia* (Stanford, Cal.: Stanford U. P., 1960), p. 115.

4. Philippe Devillers, *Histoire du Viet-Nam* (Paris: Editions du Seuil, 1952), p. 69.

5. Dang, *Viet-Nam,* p. 59.

6. Ellen Hammer, *The Struggle for Indochina* (Stanford, Cal.: Stanford U. P., 1954), p. 143.

7. Joseph Buttinger, *Vietnam: A Dragon Embattled,* 2 (New York: Praeger, 1967), pp. 724–25.

8. Hammer, *Struggle for Indochina,* p. 290.

9. Bernard B. Fall, *Viet-Nam Witness* (New York: Praeger, 1966), p. 44.

10. Hammer, *Struggle for Indochina,* p. 290.

11. Frank N. Trager, *Why Viet Nam?* (New York: Praeger, 1966), p. 100.

12. B. S. N. Murti, *Vietnam Divided: The Unfinished Struggle* (New York: Asia Publ. House, 1964), p. 172.

13. Ibid., ch. 11.

14. Nguyen Thai, *Is South Vietnam Viable?* (Manila: Carmelo and Bauermann, 1962), p. 136.

15. Robert Scigliano, *South Vietnam: Nation Under Stress* (Boston: Houghton Mifflin, 1963), pp. 91–98.

16. Buttinger, *A Dragon Embattled,* p. 941. For another analysis of electoral processes and groups related to those processes during the Diem era see: John C. Donnell, "Politics in South Vietnam" (unpublished Ph.D. dissertation, University of California, Berkeley, 1964).

17. Bernard B. Fall, *The Two Viet-Nams* (London: Pall Mall Press, 1967), pp. 146–48.

18. Scigliano, *South Vietnam: Nation Under Stress,* pp. 99–100.

19. Denis Warner, "Vietnam Prepares for Elections," *Reporter* (Aug. 11, 1966), p. 12.

20. Robert Shaplen, *The Lost Revolution* (New York: Harper & Row, 1965), ch. 11.

21. See Chapter 2: "Struggle Politics"; also I. Milton Sacks, "Restructuring Government in South Vietnam," *Asian Survey*, 7 (1967), pp. 515–26.

22. *Washington Post*, April 21, 1967.

23. Ibid., May 13, 1967.

24. Ibid.

25. *Washington Post*, June 16, 1967.

26. *Saigon Post*, June 20, 1967.

27. *Washington Post*, June 25, 1967.

28. Charles A. Joiner, *Public Administration in the Saigon Metropolitan Area* (Washington: USAID, 1963), pp. 242–43.

29. *Washington Post*, June 23, 1967.

30. Ibid., June 26, 1967.

31. Ibid., June 27, 1967.

32. Ibid.

33. *Washington Post*, July 2, 1967.

34. Ibid., July 1, 1967.

35. *New York Times*, July 2, 1967.

36. *Washington Post*, July 4, 1967.

37. Ibid.

38. *Washington Post*, July 12, 1967.

39. Ibid.

40. *Washington Post*, July 19, 1967.

41. *Public Administration Bulletin, Vietnam*, No. 39 (Saigon: USAID, August 1, 1967), pp. 43–44.

42. *Washington Post*, July 28, 1967.

43. Ibid., Aug. 2, 1967.

44. *Saigon Post*, Aug. 4, 1967.

45. Ibid.

46. Ibid.

47. Ibid.

48. Ibid.

49. *Philadelphia Inquirer*, Aug. 6, 1967.

50. *Washington Post*, Aug. 7, 1967.

51. *Saigon Post*, Aug. 8, 1967.

52. Ibid.

53. *Saigon Post*, Aug. 12, 1967.

54. Ibid.

55. *Washington Post*, Aug. 7, 1967.

56. Ibid.

57. *New York Times*, Aug. 13, 1967.

58. *Washington Post*, Aug. 14, 1967.

59. *Saigon Post*, Aug. 15, 1967.

60. *New York Times*, Aug. 15, 1967.

61. Ibid.

62. *Washington Post*, Aug. 11, 1967.

63. Ibid.
64. *New York Times,* Aug. 17, 1967.
65. *Saigon Post,* Aug. 16, 1967.
66. Ibid.
67. *Saigon Post,* Aug. 15, 1967.
68. Ibid.
69. *Washington Post,* Aug. 12, 1967.
70. *Saigon Post,* Aug. 9, 1967.
71. *Washington Post,* Aug. 7, 1967.
72. Ibid., Aug. 12, 1967.
73. *New York Times,* Aug. 13, 1967.
74. Ibid., Aug. 17, 1967.
75. Ibid.
76. *Saigon Post,* Aug. 17, 1967.
77. Ibid., Aug. 19, 1967.
78. *Washington Post,* Aug. 15, 1967.
79. *Saigon Post,* Aug. 15, 1967.
80. *New York Times,* Aug. 19, 1967.
81. Ibid.
82. *New York Times,* Aug. 20, 1967.
83. Ibid.
84. *Saigon Post,* Aug. 20, 1967.
85. *New York Times,* Aug. 21, 1967.
86. *Washington Post,* Aug. 23, 1967.
87. *Saigon Post,* Aug. 22, 1967.
88. Ibid., Aug. 23, 1967.
89. *New York Times,* Aug. 24, 1967.
90. *Saigon Post,* Aug. 24, 1967.
91. *Washington Post,* Aug. 25, 1967.
92. *Saigon Post,* Aug. 25, 1967.
93. *New York Times,* Aug. 25, 1967.
94. *Saigon Post,* Aug. 25, 1967.
95. Ibid., Aug. 26, 1967.
96. Ibid.
97. *New York Times,* Aug. 27, 1967.
98. *Philadelphia Inquirer,* Aug. 27, 1967.
99. *Washington Post,* Aug. 27, 1967.
100. *Saigon Post,* Aug. 27, 1967.
101. *New York Times,* Aug. 28, 1967.
102. *Washington Post,* Aug. 28, 1967.
103. *New York Times,* Aug. 28, 1967.
104. Ibid.
105. *Washington Post,* Aug. 29, 1967.
106. *New York Times,* Aug. 30, 1967.
107. *Saigon Post,* Aug. 30, 1967.
108. *Washington Post,* Aug. 31, 1967.
109. *New York Times,* Sept. 1, 1967.
110. *Saigon Post,* Sept. 1, 1967.
111. Ibid.

112. Ibid.

113. *Washington Post,* Sept. 1, 1967.

114. Ibid., Sept. 2, 1967.

115. *New York Times,* Sept. 2, 1967.

116. *Washington Post,* Sept. 3, 1967.

117. *New York Times,* Aug. 25, 1967.

118. For rules on administration of the election, see: *Public Administration Bulletin, Vietnam* (Saigon: USAID), No. 37 (May 1967) and No. 39 (August 1967).

119. *New York Times,* Aug. 25, 1967.

120. Charles A. Joiner, "Politics in South Vietnam," *Current History,* 54 (1968), pp. 50–51. Also see: Dennis J. Duncanson, "Pacification and Democracy in Vietnam," *World Today,* 23 (1967), pp. 410–18.

121. *Saigon Post,* July 29, 1967.

122. Ibid., Sept. 2, 1967.

123. "The Presidential Election," *Vietnam Report,* 7 (Washington: Embassy of Vietnam, September 1967) provides detailed statistics for the presidential election.

124. *Saigon Post,* Sept. 11, 1967.

125. Ibid., Sept. 5, 1967.

126. *New York Times,* Sept. 6, 1967.

127. Ibid.

128. *New York Times,* Sept. 5, 1967.

129. Ibid.

130. *Saigon Post,* Sept. 11, 1967.

131. *Washington Post,* Sept. 14, 1967.

132. *Saigon Post,* Sept. 11, 1967.

133. Ibid., Sept. 12, 1967.

134. *Washington Post,* Sept. 14, 1967.

135. Ibid., Sept. 16, 1967.

136. *New York Times,* Sept. 25, 1967.

137. *Philadelphia Bulletin,* Sept. 28, 1967.

138. *Washington Post,* Sept. 29, 1967.

139. Ibid., Sept. 22, 1967.

140. Ibid., Sept. 23, 1967.

141. Joiner, "Politics in South Vietnam."

142. *New York Times,* Aug. 3, 1967.

143. *Saigon Post,* Aug. 2, 1967.

144. Ibid., Aug. 30, 1967.

145. Certain of the statistics concerning the Lower House are from an unpublished statistical analysis by Wesley Fishel.

Chapter 4

1. The first section of Chapter 4 is reprinted, by permission, from *Vietnam Perspectives,* 2 (1967), pp. 15–34. It was written as a critique of a book by Douglas Pike, *Viet Cong: The Organization and Techniques of the National Liberation Front of South Vietnam* (Cambridge, Mass.: MIT Press, 1966).

2. See, for example, Philippe Devillers, *Histoire du Viet-Nam* (Paris: Editions du Seuil, 1952); Ellen J. Hammer, *The Struggle for Indochina* (Stanford: Stanford U. P., 1954); and Donald Lancaster, *The Emancipation of French Indo-China* (London: Oxford U. P., 1961).

3. For the most comprehensive articulation of this philosophy, see Truong Chinh, *Primer for Revolt* (New York: Praeger, 1963), and Vo Nguyen Giap, *People's War, People's Army* (New York: Praeger, 1962). See also George K. Tanham, *Communist Revolutionary Warfare* (New York: Praeger, 1961).

4. Bernard B. Fall, *Street Without Joy* (Harrisburg, Pa.: Stackpole, 1964).

5. William J. Pomeroy, defending the Hukbalahap movement, notes that: "Wherever a national liberation movement has adopted the correct tactics and made use correctly of the forces at its disposal, it has triumphed and won freedom and independence for its people." *Guerrilla and Counter-Guerilla Warfare* (New York: International Publishers, 1964), p. 71.

6. Ralph H. White, "Misperception and the Vietnam War," *J. Social Issues*, 22 (1966), entire issue.

7. Throughout this essay, citations to Pike's work are included in the text in parentheses.

8. John D. Donoghue has pointed out that in the South, as compared to the Center, there has been a "relative absence of voluntary, spontaneous, territorial or occupational associations." *Cam An: A Fishing Village in Central Vietnam* (Washington: USAID, 1963), p. 2. James B. Hendry makes a similar observation in *The Small World of Khanh Hau* (Chicago: Aldine, 1964), pp. 260–62.

9. Organizations are here viewed as instrumentalities for providing inducements in exchange for contributions. Charles A. Joiner, *Organizational Analysis* (East Lansing: Institute for Community Development, Michigan State University, 1964), pp. 5–6, and *Dynamics of Administrative Situations* (Saigon: MSUG, 1962), pp. 85–95.

10. For the DRVN's attempt to implement this concept, see Hoang Van Chi, *From Colonialism to Communism: A Case History of North Vietnam* (New York: Praeger, 1964), ch. 10.

11. Hammond M. Rolph, "The Viet Cong: Politics at Gunpoint," *Communist Affairs*, 4 (1966). "Liberation associations serve to enmesh the villager in a strangling organizational web of persuasion, indoctrination, and intimidation." p. 7.

12. Tran Van Giau and Le Van Chat, *The South Viet Nam Liberation National Front* (Hanoi: Foreign Languages Publishing House, 1962), pp. 61–65.

13. Wilfred G. Burchett, *The Furtive War* (New York: International Publishers, 1963), ch. 5.

14. Tran Nam Trung, *Military Report of the National Front for the Liberation of South Vietnam* (Washington: JPRS, 23, 971, March 31, 1964).

15. Wilfred G. Burchett, "People's Government in South Vietnam," *New Times* (Moscow), June 30, 1965, pp. 5–7.

16. Bernard B. Fall, *Le Viet Minh: 1945–1960* (Paris: Armand Colin, 1960), pp. 76–79, provides an outline of the Viet Minh's concept of democratic centralization.

17. "Control of the masses through a tight organization, often through several parallel organizations is the master weapon of modern warfare." Roger Trinquier, *Modern Warfare: A French View of Counterinsurgency* (New York: Praeger,

1964), p. 30. For Bernard B. Fall's comments upon the importance of parallel hierarchies, see his *The Two Viet-Nams* (New York: Praeger, 1963), pp. 133–38. Arthur J. Dommen also describes the system of overlapping horizontal and vertical structures in Laos. *Conflict in Laos: The Politics of Neutralization* (New York: Praeger, 1964), pp. 87–93.

18. B. S. N. Murti, *Vietnam Divided: The Unfinished Struggle* (New York: Asia Publ. House, 1964). "The cult of Ho Chi Minh and the patriotic war, the glories of the Republic of Ca Mau and the People's Government of Lien Khu, could not be allowed to fade away in the people's memory but was left to smoulder in embers which would at any time be fanned into a flame." p. 82.

19. George A. Carver, Jr., "The Faceless Viet Cong," *Foreign Affairs*, 44 (1966), pp. 347–72.

20. John C. Donnell, "North Vietnam: A Qualified Pro-Chinese Position," in Robert A. Scalapino, ed., *The Communist Revolution in Asia: Its Tactics, Goals, and Achievements* (Englewood Cliffs: Prentice-Hall, 1965), pp. 140–72, provides an analysis of the evolution of structures in the DRVN dealing with South Vietnam.

21. A number of observers have commented upon the role of the sects in the insurgency. See, for example, Philippe Devillers, "The Struggle for the Unification of Vietnam," in P. J. Honey, ed., *North Vietnam Today* (New York: Praeger, 1962), pp. 25–46; David Hotham, "General Considerations of American Programs," in Richard W. Lindholm, ed., *Viet-Nam: The First Five Years* (East Lansing: Michigan State University, 1959), pp. 346–54; and Malcolm W. Browne, *The New Face of War* (Indianapolis: Bobbs-Merrill, 1965), p. 238.

22. For statements relating to the Hoa Hao "Allied Forces of Religious Sects Against the Americans and Diem," see John D. Donoghue, *My Thuan: A Mekong Delta Village in South Vietnam* (Washington: USAID, 1963), ch. 4. See also Troung Ngoc Giau and Lloyd W. Woodruff, *The Delta Village of My Thuan: Some Administrative and Financial Aspects* (Washington: Department of State, 1963), p. 44; and Joseph J. Zasloff, *Rural Resettlement in Vietnam: An Agroville in Development* (Washington: USAID, 1963), pp. 38–40.

23. See Chapter 5: "Struggle Politics and the Bigger War." See also *Prospects for the Viet Cong* (Saigon: US Mission in Vietnam, December, 1966).

24. Jean Lacouture, *Vietnam: Between Two Truces* (New York: Random House, 1966).

25. Wilfred G. Burchett, *Vietnam: Inside Story of the Guerilla War* (New York, International Publishers, 1965), p. 183.

26. Bernard B. Fall, "Viet Nam in the Balance," *Foreign Affairs*, 45 (1966), pp. 1–18.

27. Robert A. Scalapino, "Communism in Asia: Toward A Comparative Analysis," in Scalapino, ed., *The Communist Revolution in Asia:* "Indeed, it is crucial to recognize that in contemporary Asian communism, concern over organization often takes precedence over all other considerations, including those of program and policy" (p. 14).

28. Bernard B. Fall, *Viet-Nam Witness* (New York: Praeger, 1966), ch. 23.

29. John C. Donnell, "The War, the Gap and the Cadre," *Asia*, No. 4 (1966), p. 68.

30. Rural pacification "ultimately requires national political leadership, not

just bureaus of pacification experts and teams of field cadres. And that leadership must be Vietnamese." John C. Donnell, "The War, the Gap and the Cadre," p. 70.

31. The importance of elections in counterinsurgency is stressed by David Galula in *Counter-Insurgency Warfare: Theory and Practice* (New York: Praeger, 1964), ch. 7.

32. Administrative centralization has been a continuing Vietnamese operational problem (see Chapter 2: "Perceptions of the Vietnamese Public Administration System").

33. Sir Robert Thompson in particular has outlined in detail the thesis that the fundamental first principle in counterinsurgency is an effective administrative structure staffed by well-trained administrators. *Defeating Communist Insurgency: The Lessons of Malaya and Vietnam* (New York: Praeger, 1966).

34. The excellent work of Nghiem Dang provides the most comprehensive treatment in English of public administration in Vietnam. See his *Viet-Nam: Politics and Public Administration* (Honolulu: East-West Center Press, 1966). See also Charles A. Joiner, *Public Administration in the Saigon Metropolitan Area* (Washington: USAID, 1963).

35. See Chapter 2, "Patterns of Political Party Behavior in South Vietnam," and Robert Shaplen, *The Lost Revolution* (New York: Harper & Row, 1965), pp. 340–41.

36. Ellen Hammer, *Vietnam: Yesterday and Today* (New York: Holt, Rinehart and Winston, 1966), p. 268.

37. See Richard L. Clutterbuck, *The Long, Long War: Counterinsurgency in Malaya and Vietnam* (New York: Praeger, 1966), p. 66. See also Edward B. Glick, "Conflict, Civic Action and Counterinsurgency," *Orbis*, 10 (1966), pp. 899–910; and George K. Tanham, *War Without Guns: American Civilians in Rural Vietnam* (New York: Praeger, 1966).

38. Francis Carnell, "Political Ideas and Ideologies in South and Southeast Asia," in Saul Rose, ed., *Politics in Southern Asia* (New York: St. Martins Press, 1963), p. 294.

39. The following section is reprinted, by permission, from *Vietnam Perspectives*, 1 (1965), pp. 19–37.

40. Statistics on the highlands cited here are at best approximations. It is possible to count over a hundred tribes, and the inclusion of the Koho is always possibly misleading as they are frequently considered as part of numerous other tribes. The figures are quoted from *The Highland Refugees* (Saigon: Directorate General of Information, 1963) and appear to be fairly consistent with other more recent estimates. Comparison can be made with the figures used by Joseph Buttinger's *The Smaller Dragon: A Political History of Vietnam* (New York: Praeger, 1958), pp. 54–56, for other highland tribal groups.

41. *The Montagnard Tribes of South Vietnam* (Washington: JPRS, 13433, April 1962) and David A. Nuttle, *EDE* (Banmethuot: International Voluntary Services, n.d.) are useful statements concerning the social practices of the highlanders. For a comparison of the social practices described in these two works with Vietnamese social practices a valuable guide is Nguyen Van Thuan's *Rites of Passage* (Saigon: MSUG, 1962).

42. Gerald C. Hickey's excellent study, *Preliminary Research Report on the High Plateau* (Saigon: MSUG, 1957), is one of the most important and perceptive commentaries by an American on the highlands.

43. Joseph Buttinger, "The Ethnic Minorities in the Republic of Vietnam," in Wesley R. Fishel, ed., *Problems of Freedom* (New York: Free Press, 1961), p. 103.

44. Hickey, *Preliminary Research Report.*

45. Hammer, *The Struggle for Indochina,* p. 236.

46. Fall, *Street Without Joy,* p. 30.

47. Fall provides an extremely detailed and moving account of this period. Ibid., ch. 9.

48. Vo Nguyen Giap, *People's War, People's Army* (New York: Praeger, 1962), pp. 193–206.

49. Hickey, *Preliminary Research Report.*

50. Roy Jumper, "The Communist Challenge to South Vietnam," *Far Eastern Survey,* 25 (1956), p. 162.

51. Roy Jumper and Marjorie Weiner Normand, "Vietnam," in George McTurnan Kahin, ed., *Governments and Politics of Southeast Asia* (Ithaca, N.Y.: Cornell U. P.), 2nd ed., pp. 498–501.

52. The DRVN recognized that difficulties remained including apparently the attitudes of a number of Vietnamese cadres toward the highlanders. For the official DRVN position on the autonomous zones see the *Documentary Record of the Third National Congress of the Vietnam Lao Dong Party—North Vietnam* (Washington: JPRS, 7137, January 1961) especially, pp. 375–84, and *Implementation of the Policy on Zonal Autonomy with Regard to the Various Nationalities in the Viet Bac Zone* (Washington: JPRS, 20739, August 1963). P. J. Honey describes the difficulties of the Hanoi regime in persuading the highlanders to accept Vietnamese rule even under the autonomous zone scheme. *North Vietnam Today* (New York: Praeger, 1962), pp. 1–24.

53. Fall, *The Two Viet-Nams,* p. 167.

54. Hoang Van Chi, *From Colonialism to Communism,* pp. 148–52.

55. Gerald C. Hickey provides a brief summary of medical practices among the tribespeoples in his *Report of the Indigenous Health Practices of Some Highland Groups* (Saigon: MSUG, 1959).

56. See Wolf I. Ladejinsky's essay, "Agrarian Reform in the Republic of Vietnam," in Fishel, ed., *Problems of Freedom,* pp. 153–75. Other pertinent sources are Joseph J. Zasloff, "Rural Settlement of South Vietnam," *Pacific Affairs,* 35 (1962–63), pp. 327–40, and David Wurfel, "Agrarian Reform in the Republic of Vietnam," *Far Eastern Survey,* 26 (1957), pp. 81–92.

57. Frederic Wickert, "The Tribesmen," in Lindholm, ed., *Viet-Nam,* p. 135.

58. Wilfred G. Burchett, an Australian communist, has long been something of an official reporter for the Viet Minh. His "eyewitness report" on the highlands is found in *Vietnam,* ch. 9.

59. US Department of State, *A Threat to the Peace: North Viet-Nam's Effort to Conquer South Viet-Nam* (Washington: GPO, 1961).

60. Burchett, *The Furtive War,* ch. 5.

61. *The Highlands Refugees.*

62. Denis Warner's *The Last Confucian* (New York: Macmillan, 1963), ch. 10, provides an account of the early Special Forces activities in the highlands.

63. Dommen, *Conflict in Laos,* p. 294.

64. A very well-conceived document written in 1963 and published by the

Office of Rural Affairs pointed explicity to the problems of the strategic hamlet program as it was being administered at the time. The document provided a condemnation of harassment of highlanders as a result of the program. *Notes on Strategic Hamlets* (Saigon: USOM, 1963).

65. *Viet Nam's Strategic Hamlets* (Saigon: Directorate General of Information, 1963) lists a much greater number of hamlets as being completed and secure than apparently ever existed. Statistics published by the Office of Rural Affairs after the 1963 revolution showed the number of strategic hamlets as being far less than Nhu appears to have believed.

66. For an example of the types of warfare such infiltration permits according to the Viet Minh code see Truong Chinh, *Primer for Revolt* (New York: Praeger, 1963), pp. 113–17.

67. Bernard B. Fall, "North Viet-Nam: A Profile," *Problems of Communism*, 16 (1965), p. 23.

68. Bernard B. Fall, "Vietnam: The Agonizing Reappraisal," *Current History*, 48 (1965), pp. 97–98. Also see Browne's *The New Face of War*, pp. 141–44. For an account of the revolt and of the American Special Forces role in preventing a much wider attack against Banmethuot see Howard Sochurek's "American Special Forces In Action in Vietnam," *National Geographic*, 127 (1965), pp. 38–65.

69. Jerry A. Rose provides a very vivid description of attacks by the Viet Cong against Special Forces camps, "I'm Hit, I'm Hit," *Saturday Evening Post* (March 23, 1963), pp. 34–47.

70. Wesley R. Fishel, "The Eleventh Hour in Vietnam," *Asian Survey*, 5 (1965), pp. 104–6.

71. A map of the Viet Cong infiltration routes and secret bases is produced in the official government publication, *Communist Aggression Against the Republic of Vietnam* (Saigon: Republic of Vietnam, 1964).

72. Tanham, *Communist Revolutionary Warfare*, pp. 53–55. Roger Trinquier describes his Composite Intervention Group tactics in *Modern Warfare*, ch. 12.

73. As Wesley R. Fishel noted at the Wingspread meeting the use of political action through Civic Action teams was begun in Vietnam as early as 1954. These teams were very successful but were hamstrung by lack of government support. *Vietnam, a Report on the Wingspread Meeting* (Racine, Wis.: The Johnson Foundation, 1964). The refusal in 1956 to permit Civic Action to work in the villages is outlined by John D. Montgomery in *The Politics of Foreign Aid* (New York: Praeger, 1962), pp. 70–72. See also Amos A. Jordan, Jr., *Foreign Aid and the Defense of Southeast Asia* (New York: Praeger, 1962), pp. 138–41.

74. The importance to counterinsurgency of such public administration programs is stressed by John S. Pustay, *Counter-Insurgency Warfare* (New York: Free Press, 1965), pp. 147–50.

75. Peter Paret and John W. Sly suggest the importance of reforms as an appeal to social groups and as a tool in counterinsurgency. *Guerrillas in the 1960's* (New York: Praeger, 1962), p. 79.

76. The section that follows is reprinted, by permission, from *Asian Survey*, 7 (1967), pp. 540–54. The first two paragraphs deal with William A. Nighswonger, *Rural Pacification in Vietnam* (New York: Praeger, 1966).

77. Clutterbuck provides an excellent comparison of counterinsurgency in Malaya and Vietnam. *The Long, Long War.*

78. Davis B. Bobrow, "The Civil Role of the Military: Some Critical Hypotheses," in the book he edited, *Components of Defense Policy* (Chicago: Rand McNally, 1965), p. 283.

79. Edward W. Weidner, *Technical Assistance in Public Administration Overseas: The Case for Development Administration* (Chicago: Public Administration Service, 1964), p. 202. Clarity of goals is considered as a factor influencing the propensity of organization members to contribute their talents and energies in an optimum fashion to organizational activities. James G. March and Herbert A. Simon, *Organizations* (New York: Wiley, 1958), p. 185.

80. Dang, *Politics and Public Administration*, p. 323.

81. Thompson, *Defeating Communist Insurgency*, p. 161.

82. Edgar Snow, *Red Star Over China* (New York: Random House, 1938).

83. Fall, *Le Viet Minh*, pp. 75–85.

84. Roy Jumper and Nguyen Thi Hue, *Notes on the Political and Administrative History of Viet Nam: 1802–1962* (Saigon: MSUG, 1962).

85. Walter R. Sharp, "Some Observations on Public Administration in Indochina," *Pub. Admin. Rev.*, 14 (1954), pp. 40–51.

86. Paul Mus, "The Role of the Village in Vietnamese Politics," *Pacific Affairs*, 22 (1949), pp. 265–72.

87. Roy Jumper, "Mandarin Bureaucracy and Politics in South Vietnam," *Pacific Affairs*, 30 (1957), pp. 47–58.

88. Browne, *The New Face of War*, p. 216.

89. Nguyen Thai, *Is South Vietnam Viable?* (Manila: Carmelo and Bauermann, 1962), p. 46.

90. See Chapter 2: "Perceptions of the Vietnamese Public Administration System." Also John T. Dorsey, "The Bureaucracy and Political Development in Viet Nam," in Joseph La Palombara, ed., *Bureaucracy and Political Development* (Princeton, N.J.: Princeton U. P., 1963), pp. 318–59; and Roy Jumper, "Problems of Public Administration in South Vietnam," *Far Eastern Survey*, 26 (1957), pp. 183–90.

91. On these aspects: Charles A. Joiner, *Public Administration in the Saigon Metropolitan Area* (Washington: USAID, 1963), ch. 3; Dale L. Rose, *The Vietnamese Civil Service System* (Saigon: MSUG, 1961); and Dang, *Politics and Public Administration*, chs. 5, 6; Marvin Murphy, *Budgetary Administration in Vietnam* (Saigon: MSUG, 1956).

92. John C. Donnell, "The War, the Gap, and the Cadre"; also Robert Shaplen, "Letter from South Vietnam," *The New Yorker* (March 12, 1966). Major General Nguyen Duc Thang has listed RD program targets as being the following, from a press review quoted in *Viet-Nam Bulletin*, 1 (1967), p. 55:

"—Eradication of Communist terror and interference, by destroying their local infrastructure and making it possible for the rural population to escape communist tyranny and control and thus to restore peace and security;

—Establishment of administrative machinery to allow the rural population to govern themselves and develop their villages and hamlets;

—Building of popular self-defense capacity, with proper training systems to enable the rural population to resist Vietcong interference, and to prevent VC infiltration;

—Promotion of a new national spirit of solidarity, respect of freedom and human rights, moral integrity, self-respect. Also, a spirit of science and progress, a spirit of responsibility toward the national purpose.
Measures being carried out to bring a bright new life to the peasants included:
—Eradication of illiteracy, development of mass education;
—Land reform, rational redistribution of land as well as changes in land tenure;
—Development of agricultural and artisanal techniques, in order to improve production and reduce poverty;
—Development of means of communication and transportation.
—Elimination of corruption, nepotism and feudalism.
—Eradication of diseases."

93. Joiner, *Organizational Analysis,* ch. 4. A good discussion of organizational goals is found in Amitai Etzioni's *A Comparative Analysis of Complex Organizations* (New York: Free Press, 1961), ch. 4.

94. Joiner, *Dynamics of Administrative Situations,* pp. 132–37.

95. Charles A. Joiner, "Adaptations of Operating Structures of Government Administrative Organizations," *J. Acad. Management,* 4 (1961), pp. 189–97.

96. Marion J. Levy, Jr., *Modernization and the Structure of Societies* (Princeton, N.J.: Princeton U. P., 1966), p. 605. Also Edward B. Glick, *Peaceful Conflict: The Nonmilitary Use of the Military* (Harrisburg, Pa.: Stackpole Books, 1967).

97. Tanham, *Communist Revolutionary Warfare,* p. 140.

98. Jordan, *Foreign Aid,* pp. 184–88.

99. Trinquier, *Modern Warfare,* Part 2.

100. S. N. Eisenstadt, *The Political Systems of Empires* (New York: Free Press, 1963); Karl A. Witfogel, *Oriental Despotism* (New Haven, Conn. : Yale U. P., 1957).

101. Weidner, *Technical Assistance,* p. 216.

102. Charles A. Joiner, *Working Paper on Human Resource Needs in Vietnam and the Relationships of Those Needs to Participant Policies and Priorities* (Saigon: MSUG, 1962).

103. James Eliot Cross, *Conflict in the Shadows: The Nature and Politics of Guerrilla War* (Garden City, N.Y.: Doubleday, 1963), p. 111.

104. "The guerrilla's claim can only be beaten when the forces of government forcefully demonstrate their ability and determination to satisfy the legitimate aspirations of the governed, while at the same time exhibiting greater day-to-day concern for the popular welfare." Napoleon D. Valeriano and Charles T. R. Bohannon, *Counter-Guerrilla Operations: The Philippine Experience* (New York: Praeger, 1962), p. 28.

105. Fred W. Riggs, *Administration in Developing Nations: The Theory of Prismatic Society* (Boston, Mass.: Houghton Mifflin, 1964), pp. 228–34.

106. Pike, *Viet Cong,* ch. 5. Also *Prospects for the Viet Cong.*

107. Kenneth E. Boulding, *Conflict and Defense* (New York: Harper, 1962), p. 159.

108. See Chapter 2: "South Vietnam's Buddhist Crisis," and Chapter 4: "Administration and Political Warfare in the Highlands." See also Roy Jumper, "Sects and Communism in South Vietnam," *Orbis,* 3 (1959), pp. 85–96.

109. Lucian W. Pye, *Guerrilla Communism in Malaya: Its Social and Political Meaning* (Princeton, N.J.: Princeton U. P., 1956), p. 355.

110. Lucian W. Pye, *Politics, Personality, and Nation Building: Burma's*

Search for Identity (New Haven, Conn.: Yale U. P., 1962), p. 39. For an elaboration of the concept of adaptive, purposeful organizations, see Daniel Katz and Robert L. Kahn, *The Social Psychology of Organizations* (New York: Wiley, 1966), ch. 3.

111. Tanham, *War Without Guns,* p. 130.

112. Galula, *Counter-Insurgency Warfare,* p. 77. "The authority of the government, then, rests on its acceptance as legitimate and its support by the dominant groups of subjects, that is, by the majority of those who participate in political life and are concerned with public matters, not necessarily a majority of the total population." Peter M. Blau, *Exchange and Power in Social Life* (New York: Wiley, 1964), p. 213.

Chapter 5

1. The first section of Chapter 5 is reprinted, by permission, from *Asian Survey,* 7 (1967), pp. 53–71. Dr. John C. Donnell, the co-author, is professor of political science at Temple University. He was a war crimes field investigator for SCAP in Tokyo following World War II, has served the United States Information Service in Vietnam and Taiwan, and was public affairs officer for the United States government in Hanoi in the early 1950's. He has also worked for the Rand Corporation and is the author of numerous articles and works on Asia, especially on Vietnam.

2. Tran Van Van was assassinated in December after having been elected to the Constitutional Assembly.

3. The North Vietnamese four-point position announced by Premier Pham Van Dong in Hanoi on April 8 was supported by the NLF. It demanded a US withdrawal from the South and an end to air attacks on the North, a prohibition by both North and South Vietnam of foreign troops on their soil, a settling of South Vietnamese internal affairs by the South Vietnamese in accordance with the NLF program, and reunification without foreign interference.

4. Neil Sheehan, "Not a Dove, but No Longer a Hawk," *New York Times Magazine,* Oct. 9, 1966. Some other estimates ran even higher.

5. This section of Chapter 5 is reprinted, by permission, from *Asian Survey,* 8 (1968), pp. 58–71.

6. The statistics on the evolution of GVN, NLF, PAVN, and US military fortunes were publicly announced through numerous channels first unofficially and then officially beginning in October. However, Robert Komer presented slightly different figures in Saigon on December 1: 66.1 per cent, i.e., 11,237,900, in secure areas (including 3.5 million in urban areas); 16.2 per cent in contested areas; 17.2 per cent in NLF areas; 659,700 in "A" hamlets (most secure) and 2,804,000 in "V" hamlets (NLF controlled). *New York Times,* Dec. 2, 1967.

7. In August, Thieu promulgated a Declaration of Minority Rights permitting tribesmen to own land they till. *Saigon Post,* Aug. 30, 1967.

8. *New York Times,* Oct. 2, 1967.

9. General Nguyen Chi Thanh reportedly was replaced by Lieutenant General Hoang Van Thai, deputy chief of staff of PAVN. Thai's role, close to Giap, has reflected the Soviet vs. Chinese camps in Hanoi. His changing position, e.g., first favoring military "modernization" in opposition to Thanh and his later emphasis upon "manpower," is an example of the tenuous balance in the DRVN.

See John C. Donnell, "North Vietnam: A Qualified Pro-Chinese Position," in Robert A. Scalapino, ed., *Communist Revolution in Asia* (Englewood Cliffs, N.J.: Prentice Hall, 1965), p. 158; and, P. J. Honey, *Communism in North Vietnam* (Cambridge, Mass: MIT Press, 1963), p. 97.

10. A penetrating critique of the inability to stop corruption and curb warlordism is given by David Halberstam in his "Return to Vietnam," *Harper's* (Dec. 1967), pp. 47–58.

11. A defense of the ARVN as a military competitor to the NLF-PAVN forces is given in *Vietnam Report*, No. 8 (Washington: Embassy of Vietnam, 1967).

12. Dennis J. Duncanson presents a critique of democracy building as depicted in the new Constitution, a process he regards as unlikely to succeed in the absence of either a viable local administrative system or a rural police force. "Pacification and Democracy in Vietnam," *World Today*, 23 (1967), pp. 410–18.

13. The following section of Chapter 5 is reprinted, by permission, from *Asian Survey*, 9 (1969), pp. 138–54.

14. The following section of Chapter 5 is reprinted, by permission, from *Current History*, 59 (1970), pp. 356–361, 366–68.

15. *Viet-Nam Bulletin*, July 27, 1970.

16. For a provocative analysis see "The Chau Trial," I and II (March, 1970 and April/July, 1970) by Elizabeth Pond, published by the Alicia Patterson Fund (New York).

17. An excellent catalogue and critique of recent developments in South Vietnam's political party system is given by Allan Goodman in "South Vietnam: Neither War nor Peace," *Asian Survey*, 10 (1970), pp. 107–32.

18. *Public Administration Bulletin* (Saigon, July 1, 1970).

19. Arthur J. Dommen, "The Future of North Vietnam," *Current History*, 58 (1970), pp. 229–32, 245.

20. An extremely critical review of these developments in the DRVN is given by P. J. Honey in two issues of the *China News Analysis*, No. 804 (June 12, 1970) and No. 815 (Sept. 18, 1970).

Chapter 6

1. Bernard B. Fall, *Hell in a Very Small Place: The Siege of Dien Bien Phu* (Philadelphia: Lippincott, 1966), Appendix A.

2. Lucien Bodard, *The Quicksand War: Prelude to Vietnam* (Boston: Little, Brown, 1967), pp. 201–2.

3. A most penetrating analysis of tribal roles is presented by John T. McAlister in "Mountain Minorities and the Viet Minh: A Key to the Indochina War," in Peter Kunstadter, ed., *Southeast Asian Tribes: Minorities and Nations* (Princeton, N.J.: Princeton U. P., 1967), ch. 20.

Index